Psalms 45–100

"What an extraordinary study! Abraham Kuruvilla has applied himself with resolution and enthusiasm to all 150 psalms, and here he shares the results with us. He thus takes us through the entire Psalter with careful and suggestive outlines of the Psalms for preachers, and with judicious comments on their theological significance. It will be wonderful if pastors make them a resource for preaching. Indeed, any student of the Psalms will learn from them."

—**John Goldingay**, senior professor of Old Testament, Fuller Theological Seminary

"What a delightful surprise this series of commentaries on the Psalms is. Working with proper regard for the newest academic insights, Abraham Kuruvilla makes an innovative synthesis of the meaning of each psalm, building a bridge between its theological essence and practical application of the text in various situations. This series will be extremely useful for anyone who preaches, teaches, or studies the Bible seriously."

—**Philippus (Phil) J. Botha**, professor emeritus of ancient and modern languages and cultures, University of Pretoria, Pretoria, South Africa

"Whenever my friend and former colleague Abe Kuruvilla speaks about preaching, I'm all ears. If you've read his books on preaching or listened to his sermons, you understand why. His hermeneutical approach is carefully crafted, producing penetrating insights and proposals worthy of consideration. This commentary is wonderful and, crafted in the crucible of Abe's personal suffering, will be immensely helpful to those who love the Psalms and the God who inspired ancient authors to compose them."

—**Robert B. Chisholm Jr.**, chair and senior professor of Old Testament studies, Dallas Theological Seminary

"Why is it that we don't hear more excellent sermons on the Psalms that engage the text in deep and serious ways? Abe Kuruvilla has written a monumental three-volume work to help address this shortcoming. He recognizes that the Psalms, as captivating as they may be, are not necessarily easy to interpret and many of their contexts and occasions remain in the shadows. Nevertheless, through close attention to each psalm, Kuruvilla shows that their theology can result in preaching that engages both the heart and the mind."

—**Stanley E. Porter**, president, dean, and professor of New Testament, McMaster Divinity College

"Although preaching from the Psalter was a regular practice in the early church, nowadays Christians might sing and pray the Psalms, but rarely listen to a sermon on one of them. Abraham Kuruvilla's commentary skillfully reverses this trend. He takes seriously each psalm in its poetic Hebrew medium, then applies its theological message, however difficult, to Christian discipleship today. No minister now has an excuse for avoiding preaching from the book of Psalms."

—**Susan Gillingham**, professor emeritus of Hebrew Bible, University of Oxford

"This three-volume series on preaching the Psalms is a masterful work, combining exegesis, hermeneutics, biblical theology, and homiletics. Abraham Kuruvilla astutely guides the preacher through the most difficult step of sermon development in the Psalms. In my opinion, this is the best work on preaching the Psalms that is available today, and it should be on the shelf of all preachers who aspire to proclaim the wonderful message of the Psalms to their congregations."

—**J. Daniel Hays**, senior professor of Old Testament, Southwestern Baptist Theological Seminary

"Abraham Kuruvilla has provided the kind of theological exegesis preachers need to engage in sermon preparation. His thorough exploration draws on his own attention to the literary complexities of the text and his engagement with the best of scholarship. A literal translation, structural analysis, theological focus statement, discerning commentary, and sermon map for each psalm efficiently guide the preacher through the essential steps of sermon development. This will be my go-to commentary on the Psalms."

—**Timothy S. Warren**, senior professor emeritus of pastoral ministries, Dallas Theological Seminary

"In his commentary, Abe Kuruvilla approaches the Psalms with the eye and the heart of a preacher/pastor. He draws deeply from the scholarly literature, but he focuses on the needs of the expositor. His primary emphasis is upon how Christians are to align their lives to what God reveals in the various songs in the Psalter, and how the Psalms guide the people of God in their spiritual transformation toward Christlikeness. What he has written will both stretch the mind and warm the heart of the reader. I highly recommend it!"

—**Daniel Estes**, distinguished professor of Old Testament, Cedarville University

"Abraham Kuruvilla has produced another helpful commentary to guide faithful preaching of God's word. Although best known as a leading scholar in homiletics, he proves himself to be a competent Hebrew exegete as well. His Christiconic hermeneutic allows the Psalms to fully speak their multidimensional message for spiritual formation today."

—**John W. Hilber**, professor of Old Testament, McMaster Divinity College

"This is a valuable addition to Abraham Kuruvilla's existing work on Christian preaching of Scripture. He knows the issues, provides a fresh translation of the Hebrew text to ponder, and offers theologically robust content. Though it is oriented to those who would preach the Psalms, it also has value for those who pray them."

—**Walter Moberly**, professor emeritus of theology and biblical interpretation, Durham University

"Abraham Kuruvilla's commentary set on the Psalter is unique and helpful. He clearly explains the text of each Psalm, laying out its meaning as well as aspects of divine demand, calling its readers to Christlikeness. I thank him for his faithful ministry in helping students bring and use God's word to push believers toward Christlikeness."

—**Michael A. Grisanti**, distinguished research professor of Old Testament, The Master's Seminary

"With keen appreciation for literary and rhetorical features of each psalm, Kuruvilla keeps his finger on the text. He resists a 'homiletical hermeneutic' that is driven by what one wants to preach *out of the text* rather than what the psalmists tried to communicate *with the text*. Although he is an authority on preaching, Kuruvilla does not prescribe how to preach individual psalms, but teachers of Scripture will be inspired by his commentary and find the 'sermon maps' that conclude the commentary on each psalm helpful."

—**Daniel I. Block**, professor emeritus of Old Testament, Wheaton College

PSALMS 45–100

A Theological Commentary for Preachers

Abraham Kuruvilla

CASCADE *Books* • Eugene, Oregon

PSALMS 45–100
A Theological Commentary for Preachers

Copyright © 2024 Abraham Kuruvilla. All rights reserved. Except for brief quotations in critical publications or reviews, no part of this book may be reproduced in any manner without prior written permission from the publisher. Write: Permissions, Wipf and Stock Publishers, 199 W. 8th Ave., Suite 3, Eugene, OR 97401.

Cascade Books
An Imprint of Wipf and Stock Publishers
199 W. 8th Ave., Suite 3
Eugene, OR 97401

www.wipfandstock.com

PAPERBACK ISBN: 978-1-6667-5170-3
HARDCOVER ISBN: 978-1-6667-5171-0
EBOOK ISBN: 978-1-6667-5172-7

Cataloguing-in-Publication data:

Names: Kuruvilla, Abraham, author.
Title: Psalms 45–100 : a theological commentary for preachers / Abraham Kuruvilla.
Description: Eugene, OR: Cascade Books, 2024. | Includes bibliographical references and index.
Identifiers: ISBN 978-1-6667-5170-3 (paperback). | ISBN 978-1-6667-5171-0 (hardcover). | ISBN 978-1-6667-5172-7 (ebook).
Subjects: LCSH: Bible—Psalms XLV-C—Commentaries. | Prreaching.
Classification: BS1430.3 K87 2024 (print). | BS1430.3 (epub).

VERSION NUMBER 05/16/24

To
Jacob
who delights
in music-making
for the Lord

Contents

Abbreviations | ix

Psalm 45:1–17	*God-King and God's People-Queen*	1
Psalm 46:1–11	*Chaos to Cosmos*	10
Psalm 47:1–9	*One People of God*	17
Psalm 48:1–14	*City of God for the People of God*	22
Psalm 49:1–20	*Opulent Stupid and Upright Saints*	29
Psalm 50:1–23	*Sacrifice and Sin*	35
Psalm 51:1–19	*Reprieve and Re-Creation*	41
Psalm 52:1–9	*Lucre or Lovingkindness?*	49
Psalm 53:1–6	*Fools vs. Wise*	54
Psalm 54:1–7	*Emancipation and Exaltation*	59
Psalm 55:1–23	*Friend and Foe*	63
Psalm 56:1–13	*Promises of Protection Evoke Praise*	70
Psalm 57:1–11	*Exaltation for Liberation*	76
Psalm 58:1–11	*Wicked Judged*	81
Psalm 59:1–17	*God-King Defeats the Wicked, Defends the Righteous*	87
Psalm 60:1–12	*Faithfully Working with God*	94
Psalm 61:1–8	*Security under God's King*	99
Psalm 62:1–12	*Only Trusting in God Always*	103
Psalm 63:1–11	*Yearning for God and His Lovingkindness*	109
Psalm 64:1–10	*Rejoicing in the Refuge*	114
Psalm 65:1–13	*God's Blessings: Spiritual, Social, Physical*	120
Psalm 66:1–20	*Faithfulness of God; Faithfulness of His People*	126
Psalm 67:1–7	*Covenant Keeping and Global Praising*	132
Psalm 68:1–35	*God: Provider, Warrior, Ruler*	137
Psalm 69:1–36	*Devastation to Deliverance*	149
Psalm 70:1–5	*Help!*	159
Psalm 71:1–24	*God for the Entirety of Life*	164
Psalm 72:1–20	*God Bless the King!*	171
Psalm 73:1–28	*Peace and Prosperity of the Wicked*	179

CONTENTS

Psalm 74:1–23   *Lament in Chaos and Destruction* | 187
Psalm 75:1–10   *Praise to the Exalting Judge* | 195
Psalm 76:1–12   *Fearsome Deity Defeats Foes* | 200
Psalm 77:1–20   *Remembering the Shepherd* | 205
Psalm 78:1–72   *Perceiving the Past to Preclude Punishment* | 212
Psalm 79:1–13   *Confession amidst Calamity* | 224
Psalm 80:1–19   *Plea for Deity to Relent and Rescue* | 229
Psalm 81:1–16   *Plea of Deity That People Would Listen* | 235
Psalm 82:1–8   *Against Evil Heavenly Entities* | 240
Psalm 83:1–18   *Foes Turned into God-Fearers* | 246
Psalm 84:1–12   *Pilgrimage of Life Towards the Presence of God* | 252
Psalm 85:1–13   *Restoration to Divine Presence* | 258
Psalm 86:1–17   *Servants and Their Savior* | 264
Psalm 87:1–7   *New Citizens in the City of God* | 271
Psalm 88:1–18   *Darkness and Desperation* | 277
Psalm 89:1–52   *Faith in God's Faithfulness in Distressing Times* | 284
Psalm 90:1–17   *Lovingkindness and Lifespan* | 296
Psalm 91:1–16   *Devout Delivered from Catastrophe* | 303
Psalm 92:1–15   *Righteous Flourish; Wicked Wither* | 309
Psalm 93:1–5   *The God-King's Reign of Stability* | 315
Psalm 94:1–23   *God's Care for the Assaulted Weak* | 320
Psalm 95:1–11   *Worship and Submission* | 327
Psalm 96:1–13   *Community, Converts, and Creation Worship the God-King* | 334
Psalm 97:1–12   *Joy in the God-King* | 340
Psalm 98:1–9   *Joy of Creation in the Justice of the Creator* | 346
Psalm 99:1–9   *Exalting a Great, Just, Merciful God-King* | 351
Psalm 100:1–5   *Serving the Shepherd with Praise and Submission* | 356

Bibliography | 361
Index of Authors | 367
Index of Scripture and Apocrypha | 369

Abbreviations

ANET	*Ancient Near Eastern Texts Relating to the Old Testament*, edited by James B. Pritchard
b. Sanh.	*Babylonian Talmud, Sanhedrin*
Jub.	Jubilees
LXX	Septuagint
MT	Masoretic Text
NPNF[2]	*Nicene and Post-Nicene Fathers, Series 2*, edited by Philip Schaff and Henry Wace
NT	New Testament
OT	Old Testament

PSALM 45:1–17

Psalm of Reorientation

God-King and God's People-Queen

PSALM 45 HAS TRANSLATIONAL and interpretive difficulties galore, not to mention a somewhat opaque structure and absence of parallels with the rest of the Psalter, making a precise reading elusive. The main issue is the identity of its protagonists, especially the "king" and the "daughter"/"queen." While the poetic work, apparently a wedding psalm, is addressed to the former (45:1b) with the intention of causing his "name" to be remembered for ever (45:17a), it is remarkable that the "king" is never named in the psalm.[1] That in itself suggests the circle of identity for this ruler is wider than appears on the surface.

Identity of the Protagonists

The king is mentioned in 45:1, but there is a nuanced oscillation of identity attribution between this individual and God himself: the vocative "God" links deity with the king in 45:6a;[2] the eternality of this king's reign "forever and always" (45:6a);[3] God's blessing of the king "forever" (45:2c); and the king's deserving of thanksgiving "forever and always" (45:17b). The attributes of this ruler, "splendor" and "majesty" (45:3b), are together elsewhere in the Psalter applied only to God (96:6; 104:1; 111:3; 145:5); his promotion of "truth" and "righteousness" (45:4b, 7a) is also a divine characteristic (11:7; 33:5; 48:10; 99:4), as also is his "uprightness" (45:6b; of God, in 67:4; 99:4). And in the previous psalm, God was noted to be both "king" and "lord" (44:4a, 23a), epithets applied to the regent in Psalm 45 ("king": 45:1b, 5c, 11a, 14a, 15b;[4] "lord": 45:11b), not to mention that God in 45:6 is said

---

1. "This deviation demands critical attention. The employment of kings' names and titularies was essential for the ideological justification of royal houses throughout the ancient Near East" (Starbuck, *Court Oracles*, 68). Indeed, none of the royal psalms provide the specific identity of this individual. All translations of Scripture in this work are my own.

2. While אֱלֹהִים, *ʾelohim*, "God," in 45:6a does not have the definite article, as is usually the case for vocatives, neither does גִּבּוֹר, *gibbor*, "warrior," in 45:3a. Indeed, Isa 9:6 combines both these epithets to refer to God: אֵל גִּבּוֹר, *ʾel gibbor* ("Mighty God"), a phrase also used of Yahweh in 10:21. Note that the Targum on Ps 45:2a has "Your beauty, King Messiah [מלכא משיחא, *mlkʾ mshychʾ*], surpasses that of humans."

3. And Heb 1:8–9 makes christological use of Ps 45:6–7.

4. "Kings" in 45:9a refer to the regal status of the queen's noblewomen; "king" in 45:13a refers to the parent of the queen, the bride, indicating her own royal lineage (see below).

to possess a "throne," a "scepter" (×2), and a "Kingdom." The military victory of the king is described in 45:3–5; yet the futility of human war-making was clearly noted in 44:3, 6; and will be discountenanced again in 46:10. Psalm 44:8 has "and to Your name forever we will give thanks"; 45:17 has "your name . . . give you thanks forever."[5] Also, of the thirty-six uses of שִׁמְךָ, *shimka*, "your name," in the Psalter, thirty-five unambiguously refer to God's name; no doubt the term in 45:17a refers to deity, too.

Yet, this king appears to be simultaneously a human distinct from God (45:2a, 2c, 7b). The sudden shift from predication of kingship to deity in 45:6 to a distinction between king and deity in 45:7 generates an element of mystery regarding the former's identity.[6] In any case, this mingling of deity and humanity in historic Israel was rendered conceivable by the consideration of the Davidic king as occupying both a *divine* throne that was eternal (1 Chr 29:23; 2 Chr 9:8; akin to Ps 45:6; also see 9:7; 10:16; 93:2; 145:13), as well as a *Davidic* throne that was established forever (2 Sam 7:12–13, 16; 1 Kgs 2:45; 9:5; 1 Chr 17:12, 14; 22:10; Pss 89:4, 29, 36–37; 132:11–12; etc.).

It is best, then, to see "king" (Ps 45:1b, 5c, 11a, 14a, 15b) and "lord" (45:11b) as referring to deity, hence my denotation of this personage in the commentary as "God-King" (and, in translation, the use of capital letters for this individual's titles and for pronouns referring to him). Such a reading also fits well with the universality and eschatological overtones of the God-King's reign in the vicinity of Psalm 45 (see especially 46:10; 47:2, 6, 8; 48:2, 8).

Then there are the women in 45:8–17. The first female to show up in the singular in Psalm 45 is the "queen," in relation to the King's right hand and adorned in gold (45:9b). The simplest solution to the identity of this woman is to see her as the King's bride in this wedding psalm: thus, this "queen," the singular "daughter" addressed in 45:10–11, and the singular "*daughter of the king*" in 45:13–15, refer to the same individual.[7] The plural "*daughters of kings*" in 45:9a are, as explained in that verse, the "noblewomen" in the court, perhaps the same ones as the "virgins, her attendants" (45:14b). The "daughter of Tyre" in 45:12a represents the peoples of that foreign nationality,[8] indicating in parallelism "the richest of the people" (45:12b)—attendees at the wedding who seek the bride's favor with lavish gifts.[9]

The identification of the "bride," then, is best made with the people of God; hence my occasional designation of this person-people as "God's people-queen." Interestingly, only two verses in the OT describe an entry into another's presence with "joyous jubilation" (43:4) or "joy and jubilation" (45:15). In the former, it is the psalmist, representing God's people, who

---

5. In 45:17b, ידה, *ydh*, in the *hiphil* ("will give thanks"; the verb in 44:8 is also in the *hiphil*) has the king at the receiving end of this activity. Cheung, "'Forget Your People,'" 328n20, notes that of the 97 instances of the *hiphil* form of ידה in the OT, 93 explicitly take deity as their object, suggesting that this is likely to be the case in 45:17, too. Interestingly enough, in one of the exceptions, Gen 49:8, its context indicates messianism in a manner similar to that in Psalm 45: praise and bowing down (Gen 49:8; Ps 45:11, 17); defeat of enemies (Gen 49:8; Ps 45:5); use of a scepter (Gen 49:10; Ps 45:6); reverence of people (Gen 49:10; Ps 45:17); riding on a mount (Gen 49:11; Ps 45:4); and superior appearance (Gen 49:12; Ps 45:2) (see Postell, "Literary, Compositional, and Intertextual Analysis," 161–62).

6. Harman, "Syntax and Interpretation," 345. He likens it to the oscillation between deity and other-than-deity in the OT portrayals of the "angel of Yahweh." Other messianic prophecies also demonstrate an equally abrupt shift in representation, for example, Isa 9:5–7; Dan 7:13–14; Mal 3:1–6.

7. They are attired identically with gold, 45:9b, 13b, though different words for "gold" are employed.

8. "Daughter" for an entire group of people is also used in Ps 9:14; Isa 22:4; 62:11; Jer 4:11; 46:24; Lam 2:2; 4:21; Zech 9:9.

9. The term "your favor" (or "your face," פָּנַיִךְ, *panayik*; 45:12b) has a second-person feminine suffix, indicating the bride's visage. Also note that "to you" in 45:14b translates a similar suffix attached to a preposition.

"goes" (בוא, *bw'*) into the presence of God with "joyous jubilation" (שִׂמְחַת גִּילִי, *simchat gili*); in the latter, it is the "bride" (also representing God's people) who "goes" (בוא) into the presence of the God-King "with joy and jubilation" (וְגִיל בִּשְׂמָחֹת, *wagil bismachot*).[10]

In sum, given all this evidence, I see the "King" as a personage with the qualities of both deity and humanity ("God-King"), and the bride as the nation of Israel—but also encompassing the people of God of all time ("God's people-queen").[11]

After the laments of Psalms 42–44, Psalm 45 thus forms a transitional hinge to the celebratory poems of Psalms 46–49. For instance, the problem of God not helping his people (44:26) is reversed in 46:1, 4–5, and the rejection of his people (44:9), in 46:7, 11—all leading to occasions for praising deity: 47:1, 6–9; 48:1–14.[12] In fact, Psalm 45 itself points to these reversals: from rejection (44:9) to reception (45:14); from being plundered by the "adversary" (צָר, *tsar*; 44:10) to being gifted by the "daughter of Tyre" (בַּת־צֹר, *bat-tsor*; 45:12a); from being reproached (44:13) to being beautified (45:11a); from being covered with the death-shadow (44:19) to being royally gowned (45:13–14); from reproach and disgrace before "peoples" (44:14–16), to submission of "peoples," including their seeking the favor of God's people-queen, and giving thanks to the God-King (45:5a, 12a, 17b). There is an obvious trans-psalmic movement from humiliation and affliction (44:24) to joy and gladness culminating in a celebration in the "palace of the king" (45:15).[13] Such a stark reversal between the circumstances of Psalms 42–44 and those of Psalms 46–49 can only be explained by the reading of Psalm 45 as the hinge of that *volte-face*, as espoused here.[14] In short, while the origins of Psalm 45 may be the celebrations of a marriage of a king and a queen, it is "much more than just a pure profane epithalamium (a wedding song) composed for the occasion of the marriage of a particular royal couple."[15]

---

10. Postell, "Literary, Compositional, and Intertextual Analysis," 153. Of course, a number of prophetic texts talk about the relationship of God and his people with a marital motif: wedding (Jer 2:1–2; 31:32; Isa 54:5); adultery (Jer 3:1–2, 6; Ezek 16:15–34; Hos 1:2; 2:2); divorce (Isa 50:1; Jer 3:8); and remarriage (Isa 54:6–7; Hos 2:16–20). Also note the similarities between God's bride in Ezekiel 16 and the King's bride in Psalm 45: both are attired in "embroidered" cloth (Ezek 16:10, 13; Ps 45:14a); both are adorned with "gold" (Ezek 16:13; Ps 45:13b); and both display beauty (Ezek 16:13–15, 25; Ps 45:11a). Interestingly enough, the perfection of the bride's beauty was the result of God's "splendor [הָדָר, *hadar*]" bestowed on her (Ezek 16:14); in Ps 45:3b, we have the King exalted for his "splendor [הוֹד, *hod*]." See Postell, "Literary, Compositional, and Intertextual Analysis," 154.

11. Of course, with subsequent revelation, this divine-human union was manifested in the Lord Jesus Christ, God's Messianic King and the Second Person of the Trinitarian Godhead. That being said, Psalm 45 is not christocentric in its thrust: as will be developed, it talks primarily of the *union* of God (in the person of this God-King) with his peoples (in the person of God's people-queen). That God had to take on humanity to accomplish this union is, no doubt, an entailment of the psalm applicable to Christ, but that is not the thrust, force, or import of the Spirit-inspired poem considered as a whole pericope.

12. See Postell, "Literary, Compositional, and Intertextual Analysis," 156–59.

13. See Attard, "Bride and Her Companions," 467.

14. ("Espoused" was deliberately used!) Therefore, I characterize this psalm as one of reorientation.

15. Ausloos, "Psalm 45," 239.

Translation

45:1   My heart is stirred up with a good word;
       I utter my [poetic] works for the King;
       my tongue is the pen of a skilled writer.

45:2   You are the most beautiful of humans;
       grace is poured upon Your lips;
       therefore God has blessed You forever.

45:3   Gird Your sword on the thigh, warrior,
       [in] Your splendor and Your majesty.

45:4   And let Your majesty be victorious;
       ride [on] for the cause of truth and humility [and] righteousness;
       and may Your right hand teach You awesome things.

45:5   Your arrows are sharpened;
       peoples—beneath You they fall;
       [the arrows are] in the heart of the King's enemies.

45:6   Your throne, God, [is] forever and always;
       a scepter of uprightness [is] the scepter of Your Kingdom.

45:7   You have loved righteousness and hated wickedness;
       therefore God, Your God, has anointed You
       with the oil of joy above Your companions.

45:8   All Your garments are myrrh and aloes [and] cassia;
       out of palaces of ivory, stringed instruments have made You joyful.

45:9   Daughters of kings are among Your noblewomen;
       the queen stands at Your right hand [adorned] in gold from Ophir.

45:10 Listen, daughter, see and incline your ear:
       and forget your people and your father's house.

45:11 Then the King will desire your beauty;
       because He is your Lord, bow down to Him.

45:12 The daughter of Tyre [will come] with a gift;
       your favor they will court—the richest of the people.

45:13 All glorious within is the daughter of the king;
       trimmed with gold thread is her clothing.

45:14 In embroidered robes she is led to the King;
       the virgins, her attendants following her,
       are brought to you.

45:15 They are led forth with joy and jubilation;
       they go into the palace of the King.

45:16 In place of your fathers will be your sons;
       you shall set them as princes in all the earth.

45:17 I will cause Your name to be remembered in all generations;
       therefore the peoples will give You thanks forever and always.

Structure

The psalm's structure may be delineated as follows:[16]

> **Introduction (45:1–2)**
> 45:1: Perpetuation of king's reputation
> 45:2: Prelude to psalm
>> first-person authorial self-reference (45:1)
>> direct address to King; בְּנֵי אָדָם, *bne 'adam*, "humans" (45:2)
>
> **The King (45:3–9)**
> 45:3–5: Military prowess
> 45:6–7: Reign
> 45:8–9: Attire, accompaniment, attendants
>> King defeating enemies (45:3–5); submission to King (45:5b)
>> "God" ×3 (45:6a, 7b [×2]); "Your right hand" (45:4c)
>> "*palaces* of ivory" (45:8b); "joyful" (45:8b)
>> Last verse (45:9) links to next section: mention of the "queen"
>
> **The Queen (45:10–15)**
> 45:10–12: Leaving old alliances
> 45:13–15: Joining new alliance
>> King marrying spouse (45:10–12); submission to King (45:11b)
>> No mention of "God"; "Your right hand" (45:9b)
>> "*palace* of the King" (45:15b); "joy" (45:15a)
>> Last verse (45:15) links to next section: mention of the "King"
>
> **Conclusion (45:16–17)**
> 45:16: Postlude to psalm
> 45:17: Perpetuation of king's reputation
>> direct address to King; בֵּן, *ben*, "sons" (45:16)
>> first-person authorial self-reference (45:17)

It is also significant for the line of interpretation adopted here that, as noted above, while "God" is mentioned thrice in 45:3–9 (*The King* section), he is not labeled as such in 45:10–15 (*The Queen* section; though pronouns referring to this God-King are used). As well, the element of submission in *both* sections is to the King (by defeated enemies, 45:5b; and by married spouse, 45:11b). Moreover, the imperatives with the King as the subject—"gird" and "ride [on]" (45:3a, 4b)—are to be exercised on behalf of his people, whereas the imperatives with the queen as the subject—"listen," "see," "incline your ear," and "forget" (45:10)—concern her relationship to her consort. There is an asymmetry here, reflecting the relationship between the God-King and God's people-queen, that is hard to miss.

---

16. Modified from Ausloos, "Psalm 45," 241–42.

Theological Focus

The intimate relationship of a resplendent, gracious, mighty, and righteous God-King with his people who remain committed exclusively to him—and whose enemies are utterly defeated by him—results in their reflecting his beauty and glory, experiencing joy and gladness, and sharing in his eternal reign over all the earth, joined by all humanity's praise of this great God.

Commentary

Introduction (45:1–2)

The poet, the psalmist, introduces his poem—his "good word," a piece of skillful writing from his "tongue"/"pen"—with a first-person authorial self-reference. He uses his "heart" (45:1a), his "tongue" (45:1c), and his whole being, the "I" (45:1b) in this endeavor. The composition is in honor of the King, in order to perpetuate the King's reputation. And with typical courtly nimiety, he labels this God-King the most beautiful of humans, one with gracious lips, one whom God had blessed forever (45:2). With the conjoining of humanity and deity in the personage of this ruler, such praise and such eternal blessing is hardly an exaggeration or excess.[17]

The King (45:3–9)

Strikingly, in *The King* section, there are seventeen instances of the masculine singular suffix ךְ-, -*ka* (with nouns and verbs) indicating this ruler,[18] but none representing the King in the next section, *The Queen*. Here, the King's military prowess (45:3–5: defeat of foreigners and their submission to him), his reign (45:6–7: eternal and just), and his wedding attire, music accompaniment, and attendants (45:8–9) are noted. With 45:9 and its mention of the bride ("queen") this section begins a transition to the next.[19]

The God-King is a military commander-in-chief, a "warrior" (45:3a). But his martial proficiency is not merely battle prowess: it is for the "cause of truth and humility [and] righteousness" (45:4b), against foes who ostensibly favor untruth and pride and unrighteousness: this regent "loves righteousness" and "hates wickedness" (45:7a). His exploits in the battlefield are legendary, his "right hand" teaching him—and displaying to one and all—"awesome" deeds of valor and victory (45:4c). Perhaps as a consequence of these magnificent triumphs accomplished by his "right hand" on behalf of his citizenry, God's people-queen would soon be at his "right hand," too (45:9b).

---

17. For divine beauty, see Isa 33:17 (employing יְפִי, *yaphi*, derived from the same root, יפה, *yph*, as is the verb "you are . . . beautiful" in 45:2a); and 1 Chr 29:11, 13 that ascribes "beauty" (תִּפְאָרָה, *tiph'arah*, related to יפה) both to Yahweh and his name. After all, "God is . . . the foundation and fountain of all being and all beauty" (Edwards, *Dissertation II: The Nature of True Virtue*, 551).

18. In 45:3a, 3b (×2), 4a, 4c (×2), 5a, 5b, 6a, 6b, 7b (×2), 7c, 8a, 8b, 9a, 9b.

19. In terms of the poetic speech, this section is made up of direct address to the king (45:3–5, 7–9), with an intervening address to God (45:6). Similarly, the next section, *The Queen*, is taken with direct address to the bride (45:10–12, 14c), but likewise with an intervening narration (45:13–14b).

In any case, not only are these characteristics of deity—the establishment of order and the defeat of chaos—45:6 also conflates the King with "God," as the permanence of the ruler's "throne" and "scepter" are asserted (see above). The anointing by God (45:7bc) stands as a divine verdict of acceptance of the work of this King, but in the context of marriage, the act is also likely to have been part of the ceremony for that union. So also are garments redolent of aromatics, music from palaces decorated with ivory, and the accompanying "noblewomen" (45:8–9). The pleasure of God resting upon this ruler is evident in the parallel between 45:2c and 45:7b, equating divine blessing with divine anointing:[20]

	Why?	What?	How?
45:2c	"therefore	God has blessed you	forever"
45:7bc	"therefore	God … has anointed you	with the oil of joy"

The exultation with which the God-King is anointed is because of his cleaving to righteousness and cleaving from wickedness—a reward for his loyalty to God. And, no doubt, that reward culminates in the union of this God-King with his bride, God's people-queen. And before the next section commences in 45:10, 45:9 primes us with details of daughters of kings being among the king's noblewomen, and of his bride, the queen, stationed at the King's right hand clad in gold (45:9[21]).

The Queen (45:10–16)

As was noted, "God" is not mentioned in *The Queen* section dealing with God's people-queen, but the God-King is not forgotten here. Whereas that regent was defeating his foes in 45:3–5, here he is marrying his queen (45:11). Whereas earlier it was those defeated "peoples" who were submitting to him (45:5b), here it is the bride, leaving her "peoples," who is (45:10b, 11b). Perhaps she is of foreign origin, yet her ancestry is not insignificant: she, too, is a royal daughter (45:13a), a person of standing and prestige to whom even other nations bring lavish gifts to court her favor (45:12).[22] Whereas it was the king's "right hand" that showed its dexterity in working wonders in battle (45:4c), here it is his bride who is positioned at his "right hand" (45:9b).

Also linking the two sections is the presence of "make … joyful" (שמח, *smch*, predicated of the king proceeding to the wedding with his bride; 45:8b) and "joy" (שִׂמְחָה, *simchah*, that of the bride and her entourage; 45:15a[23]). In *The King* section, we had "*palaces* of ivory" whence came music (45:8b); in *The Queen* section, it is the "*palace* of the King" into which the wedding procession enters (45:15b).

---

20. "Oil of joy" occurs elsewhere only in Isa 61:3, also in a context of marriage. See 1 Sam 10:1; 2 Sam 12:7; Ps 89:20 for the anointing of the Davidide.

21. The location of Ophir (45:9b) is uncertain, though the gold from that land is mentioned several times in the OT to indicate the choicest form of the metal (1 Kgs 9:28; Job 22:24; 28:16; Isa 13:12; etc.).

22. The royal antecedents of God's people-queen are not surprising; after all humanity was created in the image of the God-King, and besides, God's people, chosen and redeemed by him, and anointed by his Holy Spirit, are children of royalty: Exod 19:6; Isa 62:3; Rom 8:17; 1 Pet 2:9; Rev 1:6; 5:10; etc.

23. This group, queen + attendants, is further unified in the parallel use of verbs: "led" and "bring"/"go" are both applied to each party, in 45:14 and in 45:15.

The "daughter," i.e., God's people-queen, is bidden to "listen," "see," "incline your ear," all pointing to the fourth and most important exhortation: "forget your people and your father's house" (45:10), i.e., to turn her back upon every other loyalty that might dilute her commitment to the God-King. "Forgetting is an act of dissociation. The bride's rise in power is in the first place predicated on her willingness to forsake her native culture and her ethnic origin."[24] That becomes a call for the people of God. Indeed, it is only with such commitment that "the [God-]King will desire your beauty" (45:11a).

Remarkable are the affinities between bride and King: both are beautiful (יפי in 45:2a and יפִי in 45:11a); both are attired grandly (45:8a and 45:13–14a); both parties are joyful (45:8b and 45:15a); both have attendants (45:7c and 45:14bc); both are related to palaces (45:8b and 45:15b); both are supreme over others (45:3–5 and 45:12); and both have imperatives applied to them (45:3a, 4b and 45:10). It is also notable that while both King and queen are said to be beautiful (45:2a, 11a), it is the attribute of the former that receives a superlative epithet (45:2a: "most beautiful of humans") that continues with an extrapolation (45:2b: "grace . . . upon your lips," extending the description of his appearance; this is not a statement of oratorical handiness, but of facial handsomeness); the pulchritude of God's people-queen, on the other hand, is noted to be "glorious" and desirable to the God-King (45:11a, 13a).[25]

Just as the last verse of *The King* section linked to *The Queen* section (45:9), so also the last verse in *The Queen* section is a transition to the *Conclusion*, with the mention of the King's palace (45:15b).

Conclusion (45:16–17)

The psalm had begun with a first-person authorial self-reference (45:1); now it ends with another (45:17). In both, the perpetuation of the King's reputation is the goal of the composition. Divine blessing "forever" is mentioned in 45:2c, and in response, the whole world ("peoples," 45:17) will give thanks to the God-King "forever and always"—appropriate for a sovereign whose throne is "forever and always" (45:6a). In the prelude, the ruler's appearance was prominent (45:2); in the postlude, it is his (their) descendants that get emphasized (45:16).[26]

Perhaps it is appropriate that *The Queen* section that ended with a move towards the King's palace (45:15) is now followed by glimpse of their joint progeny (45:16). These descendants of God's people[27] are appointed as rulers "*in all* the earth" (45:16b)—taking over the whole world!—and thus the God-King's name is remembered "*in all* generations" (45:17a) as the peoples give thanks "forever and always" (45:17b). In other words, both in space and in

---

24. Cheung, "'Forget Your People,'" 336.

25. No doubt, with regard to the symbolic union of deity and humanity (i.e., the people of God), it is God who makes his people beautiful (יפִי in Ezek 16:14; Zech 9:16–17). Also see Isa 60:9; 61:10, but employing פאר, *p'r*, "to make beautiful." Indeed, in Ps 50:2, Zion (God's people?) is said to be "beautiful" (יפִי), out of which, and through which, God's own beauty "radiates" (יפע, *yp'*). No doubt God's refulgent beauty is the cause, and the beauty of his people is the effect—the beauty of God manifest in the beauty of his people. The root יפה and its derivatives in the Psalter are found in 45:2, 11; 48:2; 50:2a; there is also יפע in 50:2b; 80:1; 94:1.

26. Both 45:2a and 45:16a mention בן, "sons" ("humans" in the former is literally "*sons* of men")—including both genders, of course.

27. The second-person pronoun, "your," is plural in 45:16a (referring to God's people-queen) and singular in 45:17a ("Your," referring to the God-King; so also "You" in 45:17b).

time, the dominion of the God-King (and of his chosen, personified in God's people-queen) is established for eternity, and he, the sovereign of the whole cosmos, is exalted!

Notice the progression of thought in the mention of "people(s)" through Psalm 45: The king subdues the "peoples" (45:5b); then, in a shift of loyalties, the queen leaves her apparently foreign "people" to cleave to the king (45:10b); the "peoples" subsequently court her favor, recognizing her intimate relationship and standing with the God-King (45:12b), and acknowledging his reflected "glory" in God's people-queen (45:13a). Finally, the "peoples" will give the God-King thanks for all eternity (45:17b), just as the psalmist, representing the people of God, does (45:17a). And thus the work of God in relationship to his people is portrayed in its entirety, all the way to eternity!

Sermon Map

I. Identity of "King" and "Queen"
   Reasons for labels: "king-God" and "queen-God's people"
   Move-to-relevance: The king-God's choice of his queen-God's people
II. King-God
   Character (45:2, 6, 7, 8)
   Campaign (45:3–5)
   Move-to-relevance: God's might, glory, grace, and righteousness for us
III. Bride-God's People
   Character: reflected beauty, glory (45:9, 12, 13–15)
   Commitment: loyalty (45;10–11)
   Consequence: co-reign, praise (45;16–17)
   Move-to-relevance: Need for remaining intimate with God
IV. *Leave and Cleave!*
   Specifics on commitment of the queen-God's people to the king-God

PSALM 46:1–11

Psalm of Orientation

Chaos to Cosmos

LABELING IT A PSALM of orientation indicates that Psalm 46 sings of how things are/should be: despite trouble and turmoil, God is the one who can be trusted, and whose presence therefore precludes all fear. So this composition does not have a thanksgiving or testimony, a lament or complaint. It is, essentially, a psalm of confidence in the might of Yahweh, thus a psalm of orientation.[1]

Translation

46:1	God [is] to us a refuge and strength,	
	a help in distress, He is present always.	
46:2	Therefore we will not fear when the earth quakes	
	and when the mountains totter into the heart of the seas,	
46:3	when its waters roar [and] roil,	
	when the mountains shake at its surging.	
46:4	A river—its streams make the city of God joyful,	
	the holy abodes of the Most High.	
46:5	God [is] in her midst, she will not totter;	
	God will help her at the turning of dawn.	
46:6	The nations made a[n up]roar, the kingdoms tottered;	
	He gave His voice, the earth melts.	
46:7	Yahweh of Armies [is] with us;	
	a stronghold to us [is] the God of Jacob.	
46:8	Come, behold the deeds of Yahweh,	
	who has wrought desolations in the earth.	

---

1. Along with Psalms 48; 76; 84; 87; and 122, this psalm is considered one of the Songs of Zion, with a reference to the "city of God" (46:4).

46:9   He terminates wars unto the end of the earth:
        the bow He breaks and He snaps the spear;
        shields He burns with fire.
46:10 "Stop and know that I am God;
        I will be exalted among the nations, I will be exalted in the earth."
46:11 Yahweh of Armies [is] with us;
        a stronghold to us [is] the God of Jacob.

Structure

Psalm 46 describes God as refuge in natural chaos (46:1–3), in national/political chaos (46:4–7), and closes with a reaffirmation of the divine refuge (46:7–11):[2]

A	"God"; "to us"; "refuge" **(46:1)**	*God as Refuge:*
B	"earth"; "totter"; "roar" **(46:2–3)**	*Chaos Natural* **(46:1–3)**
C	"will not totter" **(46:4–5)**	*God as Refuge:*
B′	"[up]roar"; "tottered"; "earth" **(46:6)**	*Chaos National* **(46:4–7)**
A′	"stronghold"; "to us"; "God" **(46:7)**	
D	"come," "behold"; "in the earth" nature/nations subdued **(46:8–9)**	*God as Refuge:*
D′	"stop," "know"; "in the earth" nature/nations exalt **(46:10)**	*Cosmos Universal* **(46:7–11)**
A″	"stronghold"; "to us"; "God" **(46:11)**	

The hinge verse, 46:7 (*A′*), is shareable between the sections 46:4–7 and 46:7–11: it forms the end of the chiasm of 46:1–7 (*A, B, C, B′, A′*) and the beginning of the chiasm of 46:7–11 (*A′, D, D′, A″*; hence the ill-defined gradation of shading at that verse in the figure above[3]). Craigie asserts that the thrust of the psalm concerns divine protection (46:1, 7, 11) on the "earth" (46:2a, 6b, 8b, 9a, 10b), "when chaos attempts to reassert its primacy over order, both in the natural world and in the world of nations and human affairs."[4]

---

2. See Jacobson, Rolf A., "Psalm 46," 313.
3. In the third section of the psalm, by "cosmos," I mean the antithesis of "chaos," divine order that subjugates doomed disorder; and by "universal" I intend to show the extent of God's order.
4. Craigie, *Psalms 1–50*, 343, 344. "Earth" is the last word in those lines in the Hebrew.

Theological Focus

Despite the chaos of nature and of nations, the people of God, ensconced in a divine space with God their stronghold in their midst, remain safe, fearless and joyful, for God subdues the chaos of both nature and nations, transforming it into cosmos, rendering nature and nations as orderly entities that exalt him, as all the earth becomes the city of God!

Commentary

God as Refuge: Chaos Natural; Chaos National (46:1–7)

The first section of the psalm is carefully structured:[5]

46:1a	"God [is] to us a refuge"	
46:2a	"the earth"	
46:2b	"totter"	
46:3a		"roar"
46:5a		"not totter"
46:6aα		"[up]roar"
46:6aβ	"tottered"	
46:6b	"the earth"	
46:7b	"stronghold to us [is] the God of Jacob"	

There is also rhyme and alliteration: בְּמוֹט הָרִים בְּלֵב יַמִּים, *bmot harim blev yammim* ("when the mountains totter into the heart of the seas," 46:2b), as well as a chiasm in 46:2b–3 with collapsing earthly eminences serving as crumbling bookends:

"mountains totter" (46:2bα)
"seas" (46:2bβ)
"waters" (46:3a)
"mountains shake" (46:3b)

Indeed, 46:1a and 46:7b (within the parallel elements A and A', respectively; see the psalm structure above, and see below) are even more intricately matched.[6]

---

5. See Auffret, "La Ville de Dieu," 328, 331.
6. Tsumura, "Literary Structure," 44.

Initials			
אֱ, '	"God [אֱלֹהִים, *'elohim*]		
לָ, l	[is] to us [לָנוּ, *lanu*]		46:1a
מַ, m	a refuge and strength [מַחֲסֶה וָעֹז, *machaseh wa'oz*]."		
מִ	"A stronghold [מִשְׂגָּב, *misgav*]		
לָ	to us [is] [לָ-, *–lanu*]		46:7b
אֱ	the God of Jacob [אֱלֹהֵי יַעֲקֹב, *'elohe ya'aqov*]."		

The sequence of the first letters of each of the elements is: אֱ, לָ, מַ (46:1a) and מִ, לָ, אֱ (46:7b), a masterful piece of chiastic alliteration. The centering upon God as refuge, strength, and stronghold tells it all!

The psalm commences by describing God with two single words, "refuge" and "strength" (46:1a), and then with two double words in Hebrew, "help in-distress" (עֶזְרָה בְצָרוֹת, *'ezrah btsarot*) and "He-is-present always" (נִמְצָא מְאֹד, *nimtsa' m'od*) (46:1b)—thus accentuating aid from deity. The earth and its major constituent parts, the mountains and the seas, may undergo turbulence, but another location, the "city of God" (46:4), remains unshaken, a source of joy to the people of God, its inhabitants. Indeed, God himself has his "holy abodes" there—he is in its midst (46:4b–5a).[7]

In light of the central placement of the "untottering" city of God (C; 46:4–5; see psalm structure above), in between the quaking, tottering, roaring, roiling chaos of nature (B; 46:2-3) and of nations (B'; 46:6)—both marked as being on "earth" (46:2a, 6b)—it is very likely that the refuge and strength is the "city of God" itself.[8] Of course, behind this bastion is God himself, bookending 46:1–7 (A and A'; 46:1, 7). Thus the "contrast presented in the psalm is not simply between Yahweh and chaos but more specifically between the city of God and the surrounding tumult" on the rest of the planet.[9] There is also the pointed opposition between the chaotic waters of the earth ("seas"; 46:2b–3a) and the joyous waters of the city of God ("river," "streams," 46:4a).[10] The chaotic waters may "roar" (המה, *hmh*; 46:3b[11]) and the unruly nations may create an "[up]roar" (also המה; 46:6a),[12] but God's abode only rejoices (46:4a). And, while "totter" describes both the mountains in 46:2b and the kingdoms in 46:6a, the city of God—it does *not* "totter" (46:5a), because of the very presence of God "in her midst"—she constitutes the "holy abodes of the Most High" (46:4b)!

> While other celebrated cities owe their significance, power, and splendor preeminently to natural conditions for example, to their commanding situation on streams or seas, to their position in the midst of the paths of commerce, or to the fruitfulness and productivity of the surrounding country, Jerusalem, the most significant and celebrated of all the cities in the world, is distinguished precisely

---

7. The plural "holy abodes" likely indicates the majesty of the location wherein dwells deity.

8. The repeat of "help" (noun in 46:1b anticipating the verb in 46:5b) also indicates that divine help is directed to the city, rendering it unshakable.

9. Kelly, "Psalm 46," 308.

10. The rivers and streams of the city of God are reminiscent of the waters of Eden (Gen 2:10–14).

11. The "its" in 46:3a could be read as "his," i.e., "God's," thus placing the waters completely under divine control.

12. The phrase יֶהֱמוּ יֶחְמְרוּ, *yehemu yechmru* (46:3a, "roar [and] roil") even sounds like a ruckus out of control.

by the absence of these natural advantages. Standing lonely in the wilderness, built upon hard and rocky soil, with no rich pastures, with hardly a field, without a river, indeed with hardly a spring, far from the great paths of commerce, she owes her unique significance and fame to quite other causes than those of the other great cities of the world. She is what she is without a peer, only through the divine world-conquering revelation of which she was the scene, and which, proceeding from her, has penetrated the whole world. She plays no manner of rôle in any other direction whatever. He who has no eye for these facts will be very much disappointed in a journey to Jerusalem.[13]

The preeminence of God's city is simply because it was the dwelling of the divine revealer—and it will be so again, one day!

This notion of God overcoming chaos is, of course, grounded in prior language of creation (Gen 1:1–2).[14] But the moment of divine intervention in this psalm, "at the turning of dawn" (לִפְנוֹת בֹּקֶר, *lipnot boqer*; Ps 46:5b), is also when God interjected himself into the fracas to finish off the Egyptians at the exodus (Exod 14:27; also employing לִפְנוֹת בֹּקֶר, the only other occurrence of the phrase in the OT)—another subduing of chaotic waters. Thus, in the sequence of Psalm 46, a turn from the chaos of nature (46:1–3) to the chaos of nations (46:4–7) is deftly accomplished. Now it is these human organizations that pose a threat to the wellbeing of God's people, but they are no match for God: he raises his voice and all opposition melts away (46:6b). How can it not, when it is the "Yahweh of Armies" who is with his people and in his city (46:7a)?

God as Refuge: Cosmos Universal (46:7–11)

With the *inclusio* of the refrain in 46:7, 11 (A' and A"; see structure of psalm above), the final section of the psalm reaffirms God as refuge and strength, with chaos finally neutralized and "cosmos" (order) universally established.

Centering upon the divine "stronghold," 46:7 is itself cleverly created:[15]

"Yahweh	Personal noun
of Armies [is]	
with us;	Prepositional phrase
a stronghold	
to us	Prepositional phrase
[is] the God	
of Jacob."	Personal noun

Both "Yahweh" and "of Jacob" emphasize the personal nature of deity and his intimacy with his people—they are blessed by his protective presence.

---

13. Ninck, *Auf biblischen Pfaden*, 90–91 (translated by McFayden, "Messages of the Psalms," 101).

14. God's conquest of the chaos of the sea is not only protological, pertaining to creation (Job 38:8–11; Pss 33:6; 65:7; 104:5–9; Prov 8:22–31; Jer 5:22), but also eschatological, pertaining to consummation (Pss 18:16–18; 93:3; 77:17; Isa 17:12–14; 59:15–20; Hab 3:8; Nah 1:4).

15. From Auffret, "La Ville de Dieu," 327.

"Come" and "behold," bids the psalmist, what God has done (46:8a): blustering nature ("earth") has been rebuked with desolation (46:8b), and cantankerous nations have been rebuffed with a decisive termination of their wars (46:9). The very instruments of battle are destroyed (46:9bc), attesting to God's sovereignty over history and his dominion over every human power. Notice the echoing of "earth" in 46:8–10 describing the work of God in this final section of the psalm:[16]

46:8b	Desolation "in the *earth*"
46:9aα	"terminates wars"
46:9aβ	"unto the end of the *earth*"
46:9bc	"bow," "spear," "shields" destroyed
46:10b	Exaltation "in the *earth*"

Despite the rambunctious rioting of the "earth" (46:2a), God gives voice and the "earth" melts (46:6b) as he wreaks desolations in the "earth" (46:8b) and as wars are terminated unto the end of the "earth" (46:9a). Instead of the explosive ferment of nature and nations on "earth," it is the exaltation of God by the faithful that will encompass all the "earth" (46:10b). What is remarkable is that the peace and stability of the city of God appears to be spreading to the entirety of the globe: God who is in the midst of the former (46:5a) will soon be exalted all over the latter (46:10b). What was characteristic of the city of God is becoming the norm in the earth of God. And so, the planet, like God's city, will never totter again (46:5a), and the chaotic waters of the earth will acquire the characteristics of the joyful waters of the city of God (46:5b)—perhaps as these fluids flow out into the rest of creation.

> In a word, the cosmos has come into being according to the microcosmic model of the city of God. Likewise, as the proleptic model of peace, the city is the substantive source from which political peace flows, at which and through which political peace takes place, a point signified particularly by the destruction of the weapons of war . . . [46:9]. The city is the mythico-geographical creative center or navel of the universe: here is the vertical point of contact where the Most High God overcomes the chaotic deep; horizontally, this is the point where the nations of the earth are overcome and peace is established to "the end of the earth."[17]

In sum, creation has transitioned "from chaos to cosmos," as a result of divine activity.[18] All of the "earth" has become the "city of God"!

Following the psalmist's dual invitation to "come" and "behold" (46:8), out of nowhere and unannounced, Yahweh speaks, himself endorsing another pair of imperatives: "stop" and "know" (46:10a). He is likely addressing his own people, perhaps stricken with fear at the chaos of 46:1–3. There is no need for panic, avers deity. He is in control.[19] The community of God can stop fretting and know with confidence that the God of the hosts of the universe ("Yahweh of Armies") is with them, a stronghold to his people (46:11). Amen!

---

16. Auffret, "La Ville de Dieu," 329. In 46:9c, עֲגָלוֹת, *'analot* ("wagons/carts") is revocalized as עֲגִלוֹת, *'anilot* ("shields").

17. Kelly, "Psalm 46," 309.

18. Kelly, "Psalm 46," 309.

19. And so Craigie, *Psalms 1–50*, 342, translates 46:10a "relax, and know that I am God."

Sermon Map

I. Chaos against God
   The turbulence of nature and of nations (46:1–3, 6a)
   Move-to-relevance: Chaos in our world today

II. City of God
   The joyous safe-space for the people of God (46:4–5)
   Move-to-relevance: God as a refuge

III. Campaign of God
   Subduing of nature and nations (46:8–9)

IV. *Come, See, Stop, Know!*
   Trusting God amidst the turmoil of nature and nations

PSALM 47:1–9

Psalm of Reorientation

One People of God

PSALM 47 IS THE only enthronement psalm that occurs outside of Book IV (Psalms 90–106). It invites God's people to praise him (worship), proceeds to give a reason to do so (kingship) and the consequence of divine regency for humanity (relationship), concluding with deity's exaltation over all (lordship).

Translation

47:1 All peoples, clap hands;
    shout to God with the sound of a joyful exclamation.
47:2 For Yahweh Most High is to be feared,
    a great King over all the earth.
47:3 He subjugated peoples under us,
    and populations under our feet.
47:4 He chose for us our inheritance,
    the pride of Jacob whom He loves.
47:5 God has ascended with a shout of joy,
    Yahweh, with the sound of a horn.
47:6 Make music to God, make music;
    make music to our King, make music.
47:7 For King of all the earth is God;
    make music with understanding.
47:8 He reigns—God—over the nations;
    God, He sat on His holy throne.
47:9 The nobles of the peoples have assembled themselves
    [with] the people of the God of Abraham,
    for to God [are] the shields of the earth;
    He is greatly exalted.

Structure

This "storying" in the psalm is performed in duplicate—in two parallel rounds: 47:1–5 and 47:6–9, the difference being the primary groups of "people" addressed:[1]

	Round 1	Round 2	
	Worship		
47:1	"all peoples"	God's people	47:6
	Kingship		
47:2	כִּי (*ki*) clause "King" "all the earth"	כִּי clause "King" "all the earth"	47:7
	Relationship		
47:3–4	"peoples" "populations" "Jacob"	"nations" "people(s)" (×2) "Abraham"	47:8–9c
	Lordship		
47:5	"ascended" (עָלָה, *'lh*)	"exalted" (עָלָה)	47:9d

Theological Focus

> The union of humankind as one people of God—adumbrated in God's subjugating of, and his people's victory over, unbelieving nations, as he reigns as King—will be consummated in his exaltation as Lord of all, giving all humanity reason to praise God.

Commentary

Round 1: Worship, Kingship, Relationship, Lordship (47:1–5)

"All peoples" are bidden to worship with sound—clapping[2] and shouting, noises made by hands and by mouths (47:1; *Worship*). The reason is clear: "Yahweh Most High" is the "great King over all the earth" (47:2b; *Kingship*). Almost like a heading, 47:1 addresses "all peoples," recommending what they do/should do after God's subjugating of them and after the establishment of divine reign over the entire earth (47:2–5): "*all* peoples" praise because God is to be feared as King over "*all* the earth" (47:2b). This King "over" all the earth has subjugated peoples "under" the divine community and placed populations "under" their feet (47:3).[3]

---

1. See Goldingay, *Psalms*, 2:75; and Beuken, "Psalm XLVII," 41–42. Such a duplication of movement is not unusual: see also Psalms 96 and 100.
2. Literally, "clap a hand" (47:1a).
3. "Subjugate" in 47:3a translates a homonym of the verb דָּבַר, *davar*.

The "inheritance" and "pride of Jacob" (47:4) are parallel expressions likely referring to the promised land and the defeated nations subsequently within Israel's control.[4] In other words, 47:3–4 reflects something that has already happened in the past, the conquering activity of God on behalf of the people he loves (47:4b; *Relationship*). And, in a celebratory tone, deity ascends with a joyful shout and a trumpet sound (47:5; *Lordship*). Indeed, in light of the Kingship of God—a theme echoing throughout this psalm—and the explicit notation of God seated on his throne to reign (47:8), the ascent may indicate his enthronement.[5] In any case, a clever *inclusio* linking the Kingship and Lordship of God binds this section, 47:1–5:[6]

47:1b	"shout"; "*sound* of a joyful shout"	
47:2a	"Yahweh Most High [עֶלְיוֹן, *'elyon*]"	
47:5aα	"God has ascended [עָלָה, *'alah*]"	
47:5aβ–b	"shout"; "*sound* of a horn"	

Reason enough to praise God!

Round 2: Worship, Kingship, Relationship, Lordship (47:6–9)

Once again there is a bidding to praise ("make music" ×5 in 47:6, 7b; *Worship*), but this time it is not "all peoples" who are invited to celebrate (as in 47:1), but those who call God "*our King*"—the community of God (47:6b). And here, too, a reason is given that is similar to that in 47:2: the rulership of God over "all the earth" (47:7a; *Kingship*). But unlike in 47:2, the fearfulness of Yahweh is left out in 47:7. While the fear of God is certainly an appropriate attitude of reverence for all humanity, in the light of their subduing and conquest (47:3–4), it is especially appropriate for the "peoples" of the nations (47:2–3).[7] But here in *Round 2*, God's people are instead called to praise "with understanding" (47:7b). But what is the "understanding" that their praise is founded upon?

The answer is in the *Relationship* section of this half of the psalm (47:8–9c), subtly but significantly different from the corresponding section in the first half (47:3–4). In the latter, the relationships were distinct: there were the "peoples" (47:1a, 3b), and there were those who belonged to God ("our," "Jacob," "whom He loves"; 47:4). Here, however, these two groups seem to merge, as God reigns, not only over his people, but also "over the nations"—even over the ones he has conquered (47:8), emphasized by the central placement of these once-non-godly folk in that verse (below).

---

4. Craigie, *Psalms 1–50*, 349. See for "inheritance": Deut 32:8–9; Exod 15:17; 1 Sam 26:19; 2 Sam 14:16; 20:19; 21:3; Pss 79:1; 105:11; and for "pride of Jacob": Amos 6:8; Nah 2:2.

5. The sounds of horns frequently accompanied a proclamation of kingship (2 Sam 15:10; 1 Kgs 1:39; 2 Kgs 9:13). The Israelite conquest was, for its deity, an act of taking dominion: Exod 15:17–18; Ps 114:1–2.

6. Auffret, "'Il est Monté, Dieu,'" 63. Cohen, "Psalm 47," 259, notes that 47:5 is the middle verse of the psalm and "Yahweh" in 47:5b its middle word, with 36 words before and after it.

7. As in Josh 9:24; 10:2; etc.

> "He reigns—
> God—
> **over the nations;**
> God,
> He sat on His holy throne."

In other words, the ultimate and final sovereignty of God is being manifested—a protological and originary Kingship (47:2) extending into an eschatological and consummative Kingship (47:8). Yet the certainty of this dominion renders the recital of deity's rulership in the past tense (47:8–9c).

At any event, the distinction between deity's *Relationship* with his people on one hand, and with the rest on the other, appears to be blurring. In fact, in 47:9ab, the higher echelons of the "peoples"[8] assemble together *with/as* the "people" of the God of Abraham![9] "Because the foreign princes gather around God's throne and in this way accept his sovereignty, they end up being part of [or in association with] the people of Abraham's God ... Israel acclaiming God's reign over the earth has now reached the point where it opens its frontiers in order to let the world enter so that it may truly become itself [or be in fellowship with] the people of Abraham (Gen 17:4)."[10] The "peoples" who were subdued by God under the "people" of God are now joining the latter, in either identity or company, to praise the God who subdued them! "The logic of the entire poem from the beginning leads directly to this amazing statement, that the princes of the peoples are gathered as [or with] the people of the God of Abraham."[11] Just as the psalm began with these "peoples" bidden to render praise "to God" (לֵאלֹהִים, *le'lohim*; Ps 47:1a), so it also ends with their "nobles" and "shields" being subject "to God" (again לֵאלֹהִים, 47:9c; *Lordship*). And, as was noted, "Abraham" shows up in the corresponding verse and in the place (47:9c) where "Jacob" was mentioned (47:4b). "They are most appropriately used each in its actual location. Jacob comes forth where the antagonism between Israel and the nations is at play, Abraham where the nations gather as the people of God."[12] Once Jacob indicated God's particular people; one day, Abraham will indicate the "multitude of nations" that he has fathered (Gen 17:4–5; also see 18:18; 22:18; etc.). One unified people! One day! No wonder God is "greatly exalted" (Ps 47:9d; employing the same root עלה, as also for "ascended," 47:5a). What a marvelous era that will be!

---

8. Perhaps these "nobles" are also being indicated by "shields" (47:9c); see 84:9.

9. "With" is provided in the translation, reflecting the LXX's μετά, *meta*. It is conceivable how the original עַם עַם, *'im 'am* ("with the people") may have dropped the first word of the pair, the preposition עַם (rendering the phrase "as the people"). Then again, those foreign peoples may have *become* the people of Abraham—they worship *as* the latter! In either case, this is a very remarkable occurrence, indeed!

10. Beuken, "Psalm XLVII," 46.

11. Muilenburg, "Psalm 47," 243.

12. Beuken, "Psalm XLVII," 49.

PSALM 47:1–9

Sermon Map

I. Peoples vs. People
   God's subduing of peoples on behalf of his people (47:2–5)
   Move-to-relevance: Our victory in our microcosms

II. Peoples *and* People
   The union of one people under God (47:8–9c)
   Move-to-relevance: What we can look forward to, one day

III. *Praise and Praise!*
   The exaltation of God (47:1, 6, 7, 9c)
   Specifics on prudent praise

PSALM 48:1–14

Psalm of Orientation

City of God for the People of God

In Psalm 48, the Kingship of God is closely tied to the city of God, Zion. As Yahweh's royal residence (see Pss 46:4; 48:8; 76:2), "Zion is a symbol of this security against chaos," a mighty haven of refuge, just as God himself is.

Translation

48:1 Great [is] Yahweh, and much praised
    in the city of our God, His holy mountain.
48:2 Beautiful in elevation, the gladness of the whole earth—
    Mount Zion, the peaks of Zaphon, town of the great King.
48:3 God, in her citadels,
    makes Himself known as a stronghold.
48:4 For, behold, the kings, they assembled,
    they passed over together.
48:5 They—they saw, then they were stunned;
    they were terrified, they fled.
48:6 Trembling seized them there,
    writhing, like a birthing woman.
48:7 With the East wind
    You break up the ships of far-off lands.
48:8 As we have heard, so we have seen
    in the city of Yahweh of Armies,
in the city of our God;
    God will establish her unto forever.
48:9 We have contemplated, God, Your lovingkindness,
    in the midst of Your temple.

48:10 As is Your name, God,
          so is Your praise to the ends of the earth;
          Your right hand is full of righteousness.
48:11 May Mount Zion be joyful,
          may the daughters of Judah jubilate
          because of Your judgments.
48:12 Walk about Zion and go around her;
          count her towers.
48:13 Set your heart on her rampart[s];
          go through her citadels,
          that you may recount to a later generation:
48:14 For this is God,
          our God forever and always;
          He—He will guide us until death.

Structure

The structure of the psalm points to a central verse, 48:8, that in turn has elements referring to the verses before and after:[1]

A	*Celebration* (**48:1–3**) גָּדוֹל, *gadol* (48:1a); "our God" (48:1b) "in the city of our God" (48:1b); "citadels" (48:3a)		North
	B	*Confrontation* (**48:4–7**) (כֵּן, *ken*, "then," 48:5a)	East
		C *Consolidation* (**48:8**) (כֵּן, "so," 48:8a) "our God" (48:8c); "in the city of our God" (48:8c); "forever" (48:8d)	
	B'	*Contemplation* (**48:9–11**) (כֵּן, "so," 48:10b)	South
A'	*Confession* (**48:12–14**) מִגְדָּל, *migdal* (48:12b); "citadels" (48:13b); "our God" (48:14b); "forever" (48:14b)		West

It is likely that each of the four sections, A, B, B', and A', suggest a point on the compass: צָפוֹן, *tsaphon* ("Zaphon"; 48:2b) also means North (see 107:3; Ezek 48:10, 16, 17; etc); there is "East" in Ps 48:7a; יָמִין, *yamin* ("right hand"; 48:10c) also means South (Josh 17:7; 1 Sam 23:19, 24; etc.); and אַחֲרוֹן, *'acharon* ("later"; Ps 48:13c) also means West (Deut 11:24; Job 18:20; Joel 2:20;

---

1. See Smith, "God and Zion," 67.

etc.). This "theological geography" reminds the one praying Psalm 48 about God's location in his city as the focal point of all cardinal directions and of every place in between.²

Theological Focus

The divine space, protective and unassailable, symbolizing a powerful God, is the stronghold for his people, for its foes are utterly routed and its inhabitants absolutely joyful, rendering the city and its God worthy of praise for all generations and in all the world.

Commentary

Celebration, Confrontation (48:1–7)

God and his city are equally celebrated in 48:1–3, almost linking the two entities in equivalent fashion: Yahweh is "great" and "much praised," but his mountain is "holy" and "beautiful," the "gladness of the whole earth" (48:1–2). The reason for the celebration of the city is simple: it is the "town of the great King" (48:2b).³ Ultimately, even though the city is exalted, it is God who deserves the praise for it is his presence in it that makes the city what it is. "The invocation indicates that the central theme of the psalm is the praise of God's greatness; the particular expression which the praise takes is that of God's greatness as reflected in the symbolism of Mount Zion."⁴

Yet, as has been noted elsewhere, both the city, Jerusalem, and its hill, Zion, are rather insignificant entities. Zion is no comparison with Zaphon (48:2), Tabor, Hermon (89:12), or even the nearby Mount of Olives. Zaphon, in particular, the highest peak of the North of Syro-Palestine, was considered to be Baal's mountain. Indeed, Baal claims this locus as "my mount Godly Zaphon"; elsewhere he is called "Baal of Zaphon" and "Baal of the Summit of Zaphon."⁵ The use of this peak is clearly polemical.

> The psalm knows that Yhwh, not Baal, is the real sovereign power in heaven and on earth. The mountain where Yhwh lives is therefore a much more important place than the mountain where Baal lives and is the real impressive mountain, the real thing of which Mount Zaphon is a shadow.... To identify Zion as Zaphon was thus not an empty conceit but a theological assertion. Mount Zion is Zaphon because it is the Great King's town.... Perhaps it is also theologically significant that Yhwh chooses to live on a small and unimpressive mountain, not a tall and impressive mountain.⁶

---

2. Palmer, "Cardinal Points," 357.
3. "Great" in 48:1a is גָּדוֹל; "great" in 48:2b is רַב, *rav*.
4. Craigie, *Psalms 1–50*, 352–53.
5. "Poems about Baal and Anath," V AB C 28–29 (*ANET* 136); I AB vi.12 (*ANET* 141); V AB E 83; I AB i.11 (*ANET* 137, 138).
6. Goldingay, *Psalms*, 2:86–87.

The preeminence of Zion is thus symbolic, and assertions about it are theological rather than geographical, reflective of its status as the locus of the divine temple and the dwelling of God himself. References to topography or to elements of the city resound in the psalm, fourteen times in fourteen verses: "city" (48:1b, 8b, 8c), "mountain" (48:1b), "Mount Zion" (48:2b, 11a), "Zaphon" (48:2b), "town" (48:2b), "citadels" (48:3a, 13b), "temple" (48:9b), "Zion" (48:12a), "towers" (48:12b), and "ramparts" (48:13a). An amazing collocation of captions for God's place. For the purposes of God's people located far away from biblical Zion in time and space, the motif of the city of God bespeaks a new kingdom, a new world apparent in microcosm now, but to be manifest as a macrocosm in the eschaton.

At any rate, Mount Zion is described in a careful structure with seven epithets in 48:1b–2:

"city of our God"	*Deity*
"His holy mountain"	*Sacrality*
"beautiful in elevation"	*Locality*
"gladness of the whole earth"	*Internationality*
"Mount Zion"	*Locality*
"peaks of Zaphon"	*Sacrality*
"town of the great King"	*Deity*

And with that comparison (equation?) of Mount Zion with Zaphon, a confrontation brews and boils: God in his citadels prepares for battle, "making Himself known [נוֹדָע, *noda'*]" as a stronghold (48:3b) as kings "assemble [נוֹעֲדוּ, *no'adu*]" (48:4a). The wordplay suggests that the rallying of foes is a response to deity's announcement of his status as a stronghold for his people. Apparently adversaries disagree with this divine assertion and, in response, mount a strike against the holy city, i.e., its people. Effectively it is a battle between the "great King" (48:2b) and sundry petty "kings" (48:4a) all acting in concert against deity "together" (48:4b). But there will be no battle at all: these puny despots "pass over," they "see," they are "stunned," they are "terrified," and they "flee," "trembling" and "writhing" (48:4–6). The defeat of the enemy rulers is absolute and unambiguous![7] "Like and unlike Caesar, they came, they saw—and they fled."[8] And, no doubt, what they saw was the impregnability of the citadels of the divine city that had none other than God as its stronghold, bastion, and bulwark (48:3).

Consolidation (48:8)

The victory wrought by God consolidates and establishes the status of the city of God and the people in her refuge—after all, it is the city of "Yahweh of Armies" (48:8b). And it will be a forever city (48:8d). This central verse in the psalm's structure recollects the defeat of foes in previous verses with that appellation of a martial deity and references to the "city of

---

7. Including the destruction of foreign seaborne vessels (48:7). This seeming side note is also likely to be polemical—Baal, he of Zaphon fame, was also known as a watercraft demolisher: "May . . . Baal-saphon [Zaphon] raise an evil wind against your ships, to undo their moorings, tear out their mooring pole, may a strong wave sink them in the sea" ("Treaty of Esarhaddon with Baal of Tyre" iv; *ANET* 534). The word תַּרְשִׁישׁ, *tarshish* (translated "of far-off lands," 48:7b) is likely to refer to the open sea and, by extension, craft from places distant (see Gordon, "Wine-Dark Sea," 51–52).

8. Goldingay, *Psalms*, 2:88.

our God" (48:8c; from 48:1b). As well, 48:8 foreshadows the solidity and longevity of the city mentioned in the following verses with the description of her establishment "forever" (48:8d; because the deity of the people of God is himself "forever"; 48:14b).[9] Notice the precise parallels between 48:1a, 3a and 48:8bcd:[10]

48:1a	**"Yahweh"**	
48:1b		"in the city of our God"
48:3a		"God"
48:8b	**"Yahweh"**	
48:8c		"in the city of our God"
48:8d		"God"

Clearly, while the psalm is about the city of God, it actually showcases the God of the city!

Again the verb "see" shows up in 48:8a, but this time it is the people of God who "see" in faith, not the kings who "see" in fear (as in 48:5). Ironically, the optic apparatuses of both sets of actants are seeing the same thing, but their respective occipital cortexes give different interpretations to what their retinas image: the people of God see God, their security and protection and peace, symbolized by the city of God!

Contemplation, Confession (48:9–14)

The people of God address him directly in 48:9–11, contemplating God's wondrous "lovingkindness" (48:9a), "righteousness" (48:10c), and "judgments" (48:11c), unlike the enemies who had only apprehension concerning this threatening and dangerous deity who was jealous for his people. Truly, this God is worthy of the praise of his people to the ends of the earth (48:10ab). What was heard and seen in the city of God is now broadcast and acknowledged everywhere. Notice the parallels between 48:8 and 48:10:

48:8a	"as [כַּאֲשֶׁר, *ka'asher*] we have heard"
48:8b	"so [כֵּן, *ken*] we have seen"
48:8b, 8c	"in the city"
48:10a	"as [כְּאֲשֶׁר] is Your name, God"
48:10bα	"so [כֵּן] is Your praise"
48:10bβ	"to the ends of the earth"

This God of the city is worthy of praise!

Despite the global implications of the praise in 48:10, the subsequent verses are more parochial and personal—they concern the people of God: "Mount Zion" and "the daughters

---

9. And as was depicted in the psalm's structure, כֵּן, "so"/"then," occurs in 48:8a, and in the surrounding sections in 48:5a, 10b.

10. See Auffret, "Dans la Ville de notre Dieu," 311. Another structural element linking 48:8 with the verses following is shown below.

of Judah" (48:11ab), both metonyms for the inhabitants of those locales.[11] God's community is then called to admire the city of God ("count," ספר, sphr; 48:12b) and advance God's praise ("recount," also ספר; 48:13c) to future generations.

The emphasis on the rejoicing of the inhabitants of the city of God is not to be ignored (48:11ab; employing different verbs: "be joyful" and "jubilate"); it is hoped, of course, that this will turn out to be "the gladness of the whole earth" (48:2a), with God's praise being widespread, indeed global (48:10b). That this wonderment at the magnificence of the city of God is actually worship of God himself is hinted at in the wordplay of גָּדוֹל ("great") used of Yahweh in 48:1a and מִגְדָּל ("tower") used of the city in 48:12b—both from the same root. "'This is God' [48:14a]: that is to say, this mountain is in a sense God . . . God's presence and protection were as eternal and real as the rocks and structures of Mount Zion and its city. The symbolic procession [48:12-13] was a means by which the sensory perceptions could feed and strengthen faith in that greater, but intangible, reality, namely God."[12] The people of God "set their heart" upon the city, i.e., its God—"this is God" (48:13a, 14a). Not only does God establish Zion "unto forever" (עַד־עוֹלָם, 'ad-'olam; 48:8d), God himself is God "forever *and always*" (עוֹלָם וָעֶד, 'olam wa'ed; 48:14b), again identifying deity with his city. "It is not that the battlements demonstrate the strength of the city but that the battlements demonstrate the strength of the God who kept them intact. This is the message that needs to be conveyed to future generations as they face attack."[13] And this God, the one who transcends space and time, will be with his people, even unto death.[14]

---

11. "Daughters of Judah" could indicate the villages of that tribe as the parallelism with Mount Zion suggests (that equation is also seen in 97:8).

12. Craigie, *Psalms 1–50*, 355. He continues: "In much of Western Christendom, and especially in the Protestant tradition, worship has largely been reduced to words and thoughts, with only the added dimension of music. Psalm 48, and many like it, functions as a reminder of the added dimension which ritual, symbol and activity may contribute to the act of worship." Perhaps that might be a notion introduced into the application for a sermon on Psalm 48. Indeed, what God's people are called to do in 48:12, "walk about" (סבב, svv) and "go around" (נקף, nqph), was exactly what had been commanded of them when they were established by God in Canaan (Josh 6:3, 11 use both verbs together, too) (see Goldingay, *Psalms*, 2:91). Thus the origin as well as the eternal establishment of God's people in his city, in proximity to deity, are now linked. Also notice that in yet another wordplay the contrast between the terror of the enemy kings and the transport of God's people is made poignantly: "writhing" in 48:6b is חִיל, chil; "rampart" in 48:13a is חֵיל, chel. One might say that turmoil of one is the thrill of the other!

13. Goldingay, *Psalms*, 2:92.

14. See deClaissé-Walford et al., *Book of Psalms*, 438.

Sermon Map

I. City of God
   The divine space (48:1–3)
   Move-to-relevance: God's space in our lives, a microcosm

II. Challengers of God
   The enemies of God overthrown (48:4–7)
   Move-to-relevance: How God protects his people

III. Celebration of God
   The praise of the people of God (48:8–9, 11–14)
   The praise of all peoples (48:2, 10)
   Move-to-relevance: God's space on earth, a macrocosm

IV. *Make a Microcosm!*
   Specifics on participating in a divine space now

PSALM 49:1–20

Psalm of Orientation

Opulent Stupid and Upright Saints

Psalm 49 is commonly considered a wisdom psalm, more a didactic piece of advice cultivated by experience, rather than a song of prayer or a hymn of praise. The issue being dealt with here is that of the finality of death and the impermanence of human wealth and power.[1]

Translation

49:1	Hear this, all peoples;
	give ear, all inhabitants of the world,
49:2	even the children of mankind, even the children of humanity,
	rich and poor together.
49:3	My mouth will speak wisdom,
	and the meditation of my heart, understanding.
49:4	I will incline my ear to a proverb;
	I will disclose my riddle on the lyre.
49:5	Why should I fear in days of evil
	when the iniquity of my deceivers surrounds me—
49:6	those who trust in their wealth,
	and [who] in the abundance of their riches praise?
49:7	Certainly, no person can redeem a brother
	or give to God a ransom for him—
49:8	for the redemption of their soul is costly,
	and he ceases forever—
49:9	that he should continue to live perpetually,
	that he should not see the grave.

---

1. See Craigie, *Psalms 1–50*, 358.

49:10 For one sees wise men die;
>> together the stupid and the senseless—they perish
>> and leave their wealth to those following.
49:11 Their tombs [are] their houses forever,
>> their abodes from generation to generation.
> They called their lands after their [own] names,
49:12 but mankind in [its] pomp will not remain;
>> he is like beasts that perish.
49:13 This is the path of those who are stupid,
>> and of those following [them]
>> who are pleased with [the words of] their mouth.
49:14 As sheep they are appointed for Sheol—
>> death their shepherd;
> and the upright shall rule over them in the morning,
>> and their form [is] for Sheol to consume—
>> no exalted residence for them.
49:15 Yet God—He will redeem my soul from the hand of Sheol,
>> for He will take me.
49:16 Do not fear when a person becomes rich,
>> when the glory of his house abounds.
49:17 For in death he will not take away anything;
>> his glory will not go down following him.
49:18 While he blesses his soul in his life,
>> and they laud you when you do well for yourself,
49:19 he shall enter into the generation of his fathers;
>> unto perpetuity they will not see light.
49:20 Mankind in [its] pomp, yet without understanding—
>> he is like beasts that perish.

Structure

The structure of Psalm 49 is best considered as two stanzas plus refrains—the stanzas dealing with specific issues in a chiastic fashion. The whole composition is introduced by a prelude:[2]

Prelude (49:1–4)

STANZA 1 (49:5–11)

A   **49:5–6**: *Fearlessness 1*
"fear" (49:5a); "abundance" (49:6b); "riches" (49:6b)

B   **49:7–9**: *Future 1: Certainty of no redemption for wealthy oppressors*
"God" (49:7b); "redeem/redemption" (49:7a, 8a)
"soul" (49:8a); "grave" (49:9b); emphasis: "certainly" (49:7a)

C   **49:10–11**: *Fate 1: Doom of oppressors*
"die" (49:10a); "stupid" (49:10b); "following" (49:10c)
"graves" (49:11a); "houses" (49:11a) / "abodes" (49:11b)

Refrain 1 (49:12)

STANZA 2 (49:13–19)

C'   **49:13–14**: *Fate 2: Doom of oppressors and rulership of righteous*
"death" (49:14b); "stupid" (49:13a); "following" (49:13b)
"Sheol" (49:14a, 14d); "exalted residence" (49:14e)

B'   **49:15**: *Future 2: Certainty of redemption for righteous oppressed*
"God"; "redeem" (49:15a)
"soul"; "Sheol" (49:15a); emphasis: "yet" (49:15a)

A'   **49:16–19**: *Fearlessness 2*
"fear" (49:16a); "abounds" (49:16b); "rich" (49:16a)

Refrain 2 (49:20)

Theological Focus

> Because the end of righteous sufferers is redemption by God, reception into the presence of God, and rulership with God, they remain without fear, despite the oppression of the wealthy wicked, whose life is mere pomp, whose death is irredeemable, and whose eternal fate is endless darkness.

---

2. From Raabe, *Psalm Structures*, 84–86; and Girard, *Les Psaumes: Analyse Structurelle et Interprétation (1–50)*, 395–96.

Commentary

Prelude (49:1–4)

The prelude is bracketed by "ear" in 49:1b and 49:4a; it summons all to hear—all humans everywhere (49:1–2)—for the teacher was going to utter "wisdom" and "understanding," a "proverb" and a "riddle" (49:3–4).[3] That the pedagogue, the psalmist, was himself inclining his ear to teaching (49:4) suggests the source of the wisdom as being from elsewhere, likely from God himself. In any case, he had inclined his ear; therefore, so must all people.

The first mention of "rich" (an adjective; 49:2b) raises the issue of wealth. Incidentally there are seven instances of nouns indicating riches in the psalm: "wealth" (49:6a, 10c); "riches" (49:6b); "pomp" (49:12a, 20a); and "glory" (49:16b, 17b). And in parallel there are seven occurrences of nouns relating to the grave/death: "grave" (49:9b); "tombs" (49:11a); "death" (49:14b); "Sheol" (49:14a, 14d, 15a); "generation of . . . fathers" (49:19a). This sevenfold distribution and equipoise points to the two related issues that this psalm primarily deals with.

Stanza 1: Fearlessness 1, Future 1, Fate 1, and Refrain 1 (49:5–12)

Immediately, we see the psalmist and his cohort address the topic of fear. Apparently, iniquitous deceivers, who were also wealthy, were oppressing the people of God, creating for them "days of evil" (49:5a).[4] It seems these aggressors were employing their wealth to assail God's people, perhaps with bribes or other devious financial stratagems, confident that their money would talk and that they could buy off anyone for any reason to suit a multitude of their maleficent ends. Thus they "trust" and "praise" their riches (49:6), not God the provider of all things. In fact, their imprudent faith in wealth gives them a false assurance of a long and comfortable life: with lucre, they plan to cheat even death. To which the psalmist responds with 49:7–11: Impossible! *All* die![5] By pointing out that the "redemption" (i.e., its price) is "costly" (49:8a), the psalmist points out that a reprieve from death is priceless—no amount of riches will avail. "Money can no more buy you life than it can buy you love."[6] And such doomed-to-fail enterprises to obtain something that "is costly" (יָקָר, *yqr*; 49:8a) is nothing more than the "pomp" (יְקָר, *yqar*; 49:12a) of mankind that is, in the end, utter beastliness (49:12b).

Ultimately, these wealthy depredators will cease "forever" (49:8b) and their tombs will be their dwellings "forever" (49:11a). In their conceit, they think they will not "see" the grave (49:9b), but anyone can "see" that all people, even the wise, die (49:10a). Thus, even smartness (or the lack thereof—because the fate of death afflicts even the "stupid and the senseless" [49:10b]) cannot guarantee immortality. In the final calculus, the opulence of these pompous opposers and sophisticated operators will, after their day, be appropriated by others. They might leave mansions behind and property bearing their names, but it is their

---

3. The "riddle" in this case is the "profound and puzzling life question" that this psalm seeks to elucidate (Goldingay, *Psalms*, 2:100). The employment of a harp in the transaction (49:4b) is the only reference to teaching aided by music in the Psalter.

4. It is preferable to read עֲקֵבַי, *'aqevay* ("my heels") in 49:5b as עֲקְבַי, *'aqubay* ("my deceivers").

5. That this is the dire lot of all humanity is also hinted at in the wordplay: "world" in 49:1b is חֶלֶד, *cheled*; and "cease," i.e., die, in 49:8b is חדל, *chdl*, an anagram of the former.

6. Goldingay, *Psalms*, 2:101.

graves that will end up being their abodes (49:11).[7] The "children of *mankind* [אָדָם, *'adam*]" (49:2a) need to remember that nothing can be carried away from the earth upon death, not even "lands" (אֲדָמוֹת, *'adamot*; 49:11c). Thus the refrain of 49:12 follows: the ostentations of humanity ("mankind," אָדָם) are transient, and those who maintain these delusions of grandeur are no better than "beasts that perish."

Stanza 2: Fate 2, Future 2, Fearlessness 2, and Refrain 2 (49:13–20)

This stanza continues the theme of the previous one, but with a critical difference. It begins by (re)asserting the fate of humanity, exactly what the wealthy oppressors were ignorant of: *all* die. Therefore, the flaunting of wealth is "stupid" (49:13a), for even the "stupid" perish (49:10b). And these senseless ones are followed by their sycophants who hang on to every word of their "mouth" (49:13c)[8]—in contrast, of course, to the "mouth" of the psalmist uttering wisdom (49:3a). Collectively, these gullible ones are like "sheep shipped to Sheol" with death as their shipping agent ("shepherd," 49:14ab); their bodies are devoured by Sheol where they will make their home (49:14de).[9]

But the fate of the oppressed righteous is significantly divergent. One day, these upright ones will be the rulers of the foolish "in the morning" (49:14c), when the former are vindicated.[10] These, in another remarkable paronomasia, are the יְשָׁרִים, *ysharim*, "upright" (49:14c), who counter the philosophy of the "rich" (עָשִׁיר, *'ashir*; 49:2b) who only attempt to "become rich[er]" (עשׁר, *'shr*; 49:16a) and who trust only in, and praise, their "riches" (עָשְׁרָם, *'ashram*; 49:6b). The contrasting experiences of these two parties, wicked and righteous, are declared with finality: the former with a negated infinitive absolute, לֹא־פָדֹה יִפְדֶּה אִישׁ, *lo'-phadoh yiphdeh 'ish*, "certainly, no person can redeem" (49:7a); and the latter with an imperfect plus emphatic subject (with an adverb), אַךְ־אֱלֹהִים יִפְדֶּה, *'ak-'elohim yiphdeh*, "yet God—He will redeem" (49:15a). "God" cannot be given a ransom or bribe for the "redemption" of another's "soul" from the "grave" (49:7–9), but it will be "God" himself who will "redeem" the "soul" of the righteous from "Sheol" (49:15a). Yes, the upright will trump the rich, redeemed as they are by God.

This reversal might be referring to an event that happens to the righteous this side of death, as God delivers them from the days of evil that are marked by fear and oppression (49:5). In such a view, 49:14c might be visualizing the victory and vindication of the righteous who then take the place of the defeated and perishing foolish and wicked. But with the verb לקח, *lqch* ("take," 49:15b), for the psalmist's being taken by God, there is a hint of an afterlife for the righteous, particularly with the mention of the wicked not "taking away"

---

7. I read קִרְבָּם, *qirbam* ("inner part") as קְבָרִים, *qvarim* ("tombs") in 49:11a, following the LXX: οἱ τάφοι, *hoi taphoi*, "tombs."

8. The property of the stupid and senseless are left to "those following" upon their death (49:10c); but even "those following" (49:13b), who apparently acquiesce with the acquisitive philosophies of those who preceded them (49:13c), will die.

9. Craigie, *Psalms 1–50*, 360. Notice the parallel elements in C (49:10–11) and C' (49:13–14), in the structure of the psalm above.

10. "Morning" is בֹּקֶר, *boqer*, in 49:14c; and בִּיקָר, *biqar*, is the vain "pomp" of the stupid who perish like beasts (49:12a, 20a). Incidentally, one of those perishing beasts, "cattle," is also בָּקָר, *baqar* (no doubt this allusion is intentional). See 30:5; 90:14 for morning as a time of redemption.

(also לקח, 49:17a) anything into Sheol: the same verb was used of Yahweh "taking" Enoch and Elijah (Gen 5:24; 2 Kgs 2:3, 5, 9, 10).[11]

The final verses of the psalm return to the rhetorical question initially posed: "Why should I fear?" (Ps 49:5a). Here it is reaffirmed as an imperative: "Do not fear!" (49:16a). The reason to be fearless is, of course, provided in the preceding verses: righteous sufferers are vindicated, redeemed, and received by God (C' and B': 49:13–15; see structure of psalm). Here in 49:16–20 it is the doom of the wicked wealthy that is reiterated in order to reaffirm the rationale for fearlessness. Whereas the glory of the "house" of the wealthy wicked increases (49:16a), in reality it will be the grave that will become their "house" (49:11a). The "glory" of these monied malfeasants may abound (49:16b), but that "glory" will not be carted off anywhere, least of all to Sheol (49:17b). The foolish ones will "go down" (יֵרֵד, yered; 49:17b) without their riches, but the upright, it was noted earlier, would "rule" (יִרְדּוּ, yirdu; 49:14c) over them. The evil ones wanted to "continue . . . perpetually" (עוֹד לָנֶצַח, 'od lanetsach; 49:9a), but they end up darkened "unto perpetuity" (עַד־נֵצַח, 'ad-netsach; 49:19b).[12]

Through the psalmist, God speaks "understanding" (49:3b), but unfortunately, pompous mankind remains without "understanding" and perishes like beasts (49:20).[13] But of course! It had not listened to the "proverb," מָשָׁל, mashal (49:4a), so mankind "is like" (נִמְשָׁל, nimshal; 49:12b, 20b) animals meeting their doom. "In failing to understand fully the dimensions of death it is inevitable that they also fail to understand fully the dimensions of life."[14] As for the righteous, redeemed by God they are taken by him to be with him forever!

Sermon Map

I. Fate of the Wealthy Wicked

Pomposity, irredeemability, endless darkness (49:5–14b, 14d, 16–20)

Move-to-relevance: The true worth of wealth

II. Fate of the Righteous Sufferers

Redeemability, reception, rulership (49:14c, 15)

True wisdom, from God (49:1–4)

Move-to-relevance: The true worth of wisdom

III. *Be Worthy and Wise, not Wealthy and Wicked!*

Specifics on manifesting uprightness and understanding

---

11. But the verb is also used of the rescue accomplished by God in this life (18:16) from the clutches of Sheol (16:10; 18:5; 30:3), and in those psalms the focus is more clearly on the here and now.

12. They will fail to "see" light perpetually (49:19b): earlier they had desired not to "see" the pit (49:9b), but anyone could "see" that all humanity would end up dying (49:10a).

13. The only difference between the refrain of *Stanza 2* (49:20) and that of *Stanza 1* (49:12) is a curious wordplay: vain mankind "will not remain" (בַּל־יָלִין, bal-yalin; 49:12a); and vain mankind would be "without understanding" (לֹא יָבִין, lo' yavin; 49:20a): again the paronomasia is likely to have been intentional.

14. Craigie, *Psalms 1–50*, 360.

PSALM 50:1–23

Psalm of Orientation

Sacrifice and Sin

For most of Psalm 50, it is God addressing people, unlike most of the other compositions in the Psalter where it is his people who address him. Almost seventeen of this song's twenty-three verses are direct speech of deity (50:5, 7–15, 16b–23).[1] The mentions of "covenant" in 50:5b, 16c, render this composition an accusation of its breach. So in its essence, this is a courtroom scene, though only the divine judge speaks.

Translation

50:1 El, God, Yahweh—He speaks,
 and summons the earth from the rising of the sun unto its going [down].
50:2 Out of Zion, the perfection of beauty,
 God shines forth.
50:3 Our God comes and is not silent;
 fire consumes before Him,
 and all around Him it is very tempestuous.
50:4 He summons the heavens above,
 and the earth, to judge His people:
50:5 "Gather to Me My devout ones,
 those who have made My covenant over sacrifice."
50:6 And the heavens declare His righteousness,
 for God, He is judge.
50:7 "Hear, My people, and I will speak;
 Israel—and I will testify against you;
 I am God, your God.

---

1. This is the first psalm of Asaph in the Psalter; the others are Psalms 73–83 (superscriptions are untranslated in this work).

50:8 Not for your sacrifices will I reprove you,
>or [for] your whole-offerings continually before Me.

50:9 I shall not take out of your house a young bull,
>[or] out of your folds a he-goat.

50:10 For Mine is every beast in the forest,
>the cattle on a thousand hills.

50:11 I know every bird of the hills,
>and the moving creature in the field is Mine.

50:12 If I were hungry I would not tell you,
>for Mine is the world, and all it contains.

50:13 Do I eat the flesh of bulls,
>or the blood of he-goats drink?

50:14 Sacrifice to God a thank-offering
>and pay to the Most High your vows.

50:15 Call upon Me in the day of distress;
>I shall save you, and you will glorify Me."

50:16 But to the wicked God says,
>"What [right] have you to recount My statutes
>and to take up My covenant in your mouth?

50:17 For you—you hate instruction,
>and you throw away My words behind you.

50:18 If you see a thief, you are pleased with him,
>and with adulterers you associate.

50:19 You let go your mouth for evil
>and your tongue joins together deceit.

50:20 You sit and against your sibling you speak;
>your mother's child you vilify.

50:21 These you did and I was silent;
>you imagined I was exactly like you;
>I will reprove you and formulate [the charge] before your eyes.

50:22 Do understand this, you [people] who forget God,
>lest I tear [you] apart, and [there will be] none who can rescue.

50:23 The one who sacrifices a thank-offering glorifies Me;
>and the one who sets [rightly his] path—
>I shall show him the deliverance of God."

Structure

The psalm may be structured as follows:

50:1–6	*Introduction:* theophany; summons to courtroom
50:7–15	*God's judgment re: sacrifices* (inappropriate attitude) "will I reprove you" (50:8a) "call upon Me … I shall *save* you" (50:15) Anthropomorphism of God derided (50:12–13)
50:16–22	*God's judgment re: sin* (inappropriate action and articulation) "I will reprove you" (50:21c) "none who can *rescue*" (50:22b) Anthropomorphism of God derided (50:21ab)
50:23	*Conclusion:* recommendation to the righteous and the wicked

Theological Focus

The deliverance of the supreme and numinous God from the distresses of life is contingent upon loyalty to him manifest in right attitude in worship—marked by gratefulness—and right words and actions on the part of the worshiper—marked by obedience in life, the absence of which results in abandonment by God.

Commentary

Introduction (50:1–6)

Both the earth and heavens, as well as God's people, are summoned for a hearing (50:1b, 4a, 4b, 5) amidst a theophanic description of deity that is markedly solemn and momentous with him being addressed as "El, God, Yahweh" (50:1a).[2] "'El' designates God as the great creator, sovereign among the heavenly beings.... It is a title that links Israelite faith with the faith of other peoples around. 'God' designates God as deity over against humanity. 'Yhwh' designates God by the name revealed to Israel as the one especially active in Israel's story."[3] This sovereign, personal God "speaks," "summons" (×2), "shines forth," "comes," and "is not silent" (50:1a, 1b, 2b, 3a, 4a), with fire and tempest his aura and luster (50:3bc). The inanimate witnesses, particularly the "heavens," declare divine righteousness (50:4a, 6a), serving as a spotless backdrop to the accusations leveled against the defendants: in effect, the heavens and the earth are participating in divine judgment (50:4). The "rising" and "going down" of the sun (50:1b) could represent both the spatial scope (from east to west) and temporal extent (from day to night) of the divine trial. Once, God was "silent" (50:21a), but now the time for

---

2. The only other instance of this trio of divine appellations is in Josh 22:22. There some of the tribes appealed to "El, God, Yahweh" to vindicate them from false accusations. Here, however, "El, God, Yahweh" is the plaintiff, bringing true accusations against his people.

3. Goldingay, *Psalms*, 2:111.

reckoning has come: and he is "*not* silent" (50:3a), and he speaks (50:5 and on). The seriousness of it all is amplified in the theophanic description of God's coming: consuming fire before him, and all around him stormy disturbances (50:3bc)—"there is no safety zone."[4]

The defendants are "His people" and "My devout ones" (50:4b, 5a), further described as "those who have made My covenant [i.e., covenant with God] over sacrifice" (50:5b). These are no outsiders who are being judged, but those in a personal relationship with deity who should have been loyal to him (50:7c has God labeling himself "your God").

God's Judgment of the Righteous re: Sacrifices (50:7–15)

There is obvious disparagement in the divine speech of 50:7–15, especially in the negated actions of God: "I [do not] reprove" (50:8a); "I shall not take" (50:9a); "I would not tell" (50:12a); and the implied negative answer to the rhetorical question in 50:13: "Do I eat . . . ?" This section is therefore all about the peoples' inadequacy: "your God" (50:7c); "your sacrifices," "your whole-offerings" (50:8); "your house," "your folds" (50:9); "your vows" (50:14b). Yet it is actually all about God: "Mine" (50:10a, 12b [לִי, *li*], and 50:11b [עִמָּדִי, *'immadi*]); "before Me" (50:8b); "I know" (50:11a); "Do I eat . . . drink?" (50:13); "sacrifice to God," and "pay to the Most High your vows" (50:14); "call upon Me," "I shall save," and "glorify Me" (50:15).

In 50:7–13, it is all about God disclaiming any desire for provisioning—as if the commanded sacrifices had to do with God needing to be fed—he, the owner of "every beast" and "cattle" and "every bird" and "moving creature" on earth. His was "the world and all it contains" (50:10–12; "for Mine," כִּי־לִי, *ki-li*, is repeated in 50:10a, 12b)! And so, that anthropomorphism of deity—creating a hungry God in the image of humanity—is derided (50:12–13). The rebuke of sacrifices is clearly made in the chiastic structure of 50:8–14:[5]

A "sacrifices" (50:8a)		Mere sacrifices are
B "young bull [פַּר, *phar*]"; "he-goat" (50:9)		unsatisfactory to God.
C "for Mine" (50:10aα)		
D "beast in the forest" (50:10aβ)		
E "hills" (50:10b)		Every sacrificial animal
E' "hills" (50:11a)		belongs to God anyway.
D' "moving creature in the field" (50:11b)		
C' "for Mine" (50:12b)		
B' "bulls [אַבִּיר, *'abbir*]"; "he-goats" (50:13)		Mere sacrifices are
A' "sacrifice" (50:14a)		unsatisfactory to God.

The last two verses of this section, 50:14–15, actually clarify what God *does* desire: not just the physicality of the sacrifices, but also the appropriate attitude behind those offerings, one of gratitude to God for all of his provisions, especially for deliverance from distresses (107:21–22; Jonah 2:9). This explains Ps 50:15: if God's people were to call upon him in

---

4. Goldingay, *Psalms*, 2:112. Other incendiary and searing theophanies are found in Exod 13:21–22; 19:18–19; Deut 33:2; the divine "shining forth" is also noted in Pss 80:1; 94:1. God's intrinsic "beauty" (יֹפִי, *yophi*; 50:2a) and its perfections are what result in his "shining forth" (יָפַע, *yph'*; 50:2b), as the wordplay implies.

5. Girard, *Les Psaumes: Analyse Structurelle et Interprétation (1–50)*, 406.

their days of distress, he would save, and they would/should be glorifying him gratefully with those sacrifices of thanksgiving. Absent that attitude of gratefulness (and its manifestation in those thank-offerings), such actions would become mere rituals deserving only divine reproof; 50:8 implies that this rebuke was the consequence of *not* offering sacrifices of thanksgiving (50:14). If God's people do not respond to his "summoning" (קרא, *qr'*; 50:1b, 4a) to change their attitudes in sacrifices, they could expect a failure of divine deliverance when they "called" (also קרא; 50:15a) upon God in times of trouble.

God's Judgment of the Wicked re: Sin (50:16–22)

While the prior section dealt with an accusation of God's community ("My people," 50:7a) regarding their attitudes, this section explicitly labels the guilty as "the wicked" (50:16[6]) with regard to their actions. No doubt, they are also within the community of God,[7] but have carried their malpractices to a greater degree of evil—not just their thoughts, but even their deeds were wicked. Thus the prior section dealt with sacrifices (inappropriate attitude thereof), and this one deals with sin (inappropriate articulations [words] and actions thereof). The rebuke is therefore escalated. In sum, these accused wicked were engaging in sin and associating with vile sinners (50:18–20) while continuing to pay lip-service to God's words (50:16–17), perhaps in a setting of the cult; that would link the two major parts of the psalm as focusing upon proper vs. improper worship of God.[8] Again there is an anthropomorphism of deity that is ridiculed: they thought God was just like them, that he did not care for righteousness and would therefore keep mum about any violation thereof (50:21ab). No, that would not be the case: God would "reprove" them, and their hypocrisy would be judged (50:21c), just as those performing inappropriate sacrifices were "reproved" (50:8a).

Much of the accusation is against the speech of the wicked: they cavalierly "recount My statutes," take up matters of the covenant "in your mouth" (50:16bc), "let go your mouth for evil" with their "tongue joining together deceit" (50:19), and "against your sibling you speak,"[9] and that one "you vilify" (50:20). As noted, this recounting of statutes and utterances of covenant are likely to have been worship-related activities. But God, once "silent" (50:21a) would now be "not silent" (50:3a): he would "reprove" and "formulate" charges against these trespassers (50:21c). The lawbreaking seems to have involved the commandments of the Decalogue against adultery, stealing, and giving false testimony (50:18–20; see Exod 20:14–16; Deut 5:18–20). Besides, Ps 50:16–17 has "My statutes," "My covenant," "instruction," and "My words." All that to say, these evildoers had the effrontery to reject God's word.

With the shift to a plural imperative in 50:22—"do understand"—these wicked who "forget God" are threatened with the absence of anyone to rescue them from their distress. God was not going to intervene on behalf of those who had rejected him (again corresponding to 50:15 at the end of the previous section, though God was more amenable to accomplishing a rescue for those addressed therein).

---

6. The noun is singular but clearly encompasses a whole gang of offenders.

7. Notice the reference in 50:5 to God's "devout" who have made "*My covenant over* sacrifice" (בְּרִיתִי עֲלֵי־זָבַח, *briti 'ale-zavach*; 50:5b). A similar Hebrew phrase is employed of these wicked in 50:16b, where they are said to have taken up "*My covenant in* your mouth" (בְּרִיתִי עֲלֵי־פִיךָ, *briti 'ale-phika*; 50:16c).

8. This is probably the best tack to take in a sermon on this psalm.

9. This was particularly nefarious, for they "spoke" evil (דבר, *dbr*; 50:20a), while rejecting God's "words" (דָּבָר, *davar*; 50:17b).

Conclusion (50:23)

This last verse of the psalm ties both the preceding sections into a finale. "Sacrifice" (50:8a, 14a), "thank-offering" (50:14a), and "glorify Me" (50:15b) are all repeated in 50:23a: those who correct their attitudes in sacrificing (50:7–15) are sure to see divine "deliverance" (50:23c). And "the one who sets [rightly his] path" (50:23b), i.e., all those sinners who have learned their lesson (50:16–22)—they, too, will enjoy God's deliverance.

Sermon Map

I. Sacrifices of the Worshiper
    Attitude of ungratefulness in worship (50:7–14)
    Move-to-relevance: Our own wrong attitudes to God's provision

II. Sins of the Worshiper
    Words and deeds in disobedience to Scripture (50:16–21)
    True wisdom, from God (50:1–4)
    Move-to-relevance: Our disloyal actions to God

III. Sequel
    Judgment at the hands of an awesome God (50:1–6)
    Deliverance or abandonment (50:15, 22–23)

IV. *Act with an Attitude!*
    Specifics on right attitudes and actions of worshipers

PSALM 51:1–19

Psalm of Reorientation

Reprieve and Re-Creation

PSALM 51 IS ONE of the seven traditional penitential psalms (the others are Psalms 6; 32; 38; 102; 130; and 143).[1]

Translation

51:1 Be gracious to me, God, according to Your lovingkindness;
    according to the abundance of Your compassions
    wipe away my rebellions.
51:2 Thoroughly wash me from my iniquity
    and from my sin cleanse me.
51:3 For I—I know my rebellions,
    and my sin is before me continually.
51:4 Against You—against You only, have I sinned
    and what is evil in Your sight I have done,
    so that You are justified when You speak,
    [and] blameless when You judge.

---

1. The superscription of Psalm 51 (untranslated in this work) reads: "David's. When Nathan the prophet came to him, as he had gone in to Bathsheba." While there are, no doubt, assonances between Psalm 51 and 2 Samuel 11–12, there are also a number of dissonances: David's death is averted, yet the psalmist pleads for deliverance from death; despite the king's immediate forgiveness, there is a constant plea for pardon in the psalm—David's only plea in the narrative, at least as far as we know, was for the life of his son, not for forgiveness; one has to wonder if David's sin was "against You—against You only" (Ps 51:4a); David never asked, in the account in 2 Samuel, for a clean heart or a spirit of steadfastness (Ps 51:10); the king is a "much diminished person" after his sin, though one would expect that after the psalm, the confessor would have found relief (Middleton, "Psalm Against David?," 40). All this to say, it is best to consider the superscription as a scribal aid to reading, not necessarily an inspired reference to a historical account. Nonetheless, the fact that "iniquity" and "sin" in this psalm are in the singular (51:2), though "rebellions" is in the plural (51:1c), hints that a particular sin might have been the key issue here.

51:5 Behold, in iniquity I was brought forth,
    and in sin my mother conceived me.
51:6 Behold, truth You desire in the inner person,
    and in the hidden being You make me know wisdom.
51:7 Remove my sin [by sprinkling] with hyssop, and I shall be clean;
    wash my guilt, and I shall be whiter than snow.
51:8 Make me hear gladness and joy,
    let the bones You have crushed jubilate.
51:9 Hide Your presence from my sins,
    and all my iniquities wipe away.
51:10 A clean heart create in me, God,
    and a spirit of steadfastness renew inside me.
51:11 Do not dismiss me away from Your presence
    and the spirit of Your holiness do not take from me.
51:12 Return to me the joy of Your deliverance
    and [with] a spirit of willingness sustain me.
51:13 I will teach rebels Your paths,
    and sinners will return to You.
51:14 Rescue me from [the guilt of] blood[shed], God, the God of my deliverance;
    my tongue will shout joyfully of Your righteousness.
51:15 Lord, open my lips,
    and my mouth will praise You.
51:16 For You do not delight in sacrifice, or I would give [it];
    with whole-offering You are not pleased.
51:17 The sacrifices of God are a broken spirit;
    a broken and crushed heart, God, You will not despise.
51:18 By Your pleasure do good to Zion;
    build the walls of Jerusalem.
51:19 Then You will delight in sacrifices of righteousness,
    whole-offering and whole [burnt-offering];
    then young bulls will be taken up on Your altar.

Structure

Thematically, it may be structured thus:[2]

STANZA 1: Reprieve (51:1–9)	**A**	Plea for mercy (**51:1–2**)
	B	Personal confession (**51:3–6**)
	C	Prayer for reprieve of sin (**51:7–9**) "joy" (51:8a); "Your presence" (51:9a)
STANZA 2: Re-creation (51:10–17)	**C'**	Prayer for re-creation of self (**51:10–12**) "joy" (51:12a); "Your presence" (51:11a)
	B'	Personal commitment (**51:13–17**)
Conclusion (51:18–19)	**A'**	Plea for blessing (**51:18–19**)

Theological Focus

Intensely convicted of one's sins and equally convinced of one's depravity, the child of God, on the basis of divine grace, seeks reprieve from God for past sin (positional holiness) and re-creation by God for future purity (practical holiness), resulting in the joy of divine presence and motivating the reprieved and re-created sinner (and the particular community of the forgiven sinner) to praise and to share the good news of divine deliverance from sin.

Commentary

Stanza 1: Reprieve (51:1–9)

The number of expressions of anti-God deviances in the psalm is considerable and striking: "sin" and its cognates ("sin," 51:2b, 3b, 5b, 7a, 9a; "sinned," 51:4a; "sinners," 51:13b); "rebellion/rebel" (51:1c, 3a, 13a); "iniquity" (51:2a, 5a, 9b); "evil" (51:4b); and "[the guilt of] blood[shed]" (51:14a).[3] "Because of the nature of the psalm, the psalmist is deeply concerned with self—with guilt and stain, with self-recrimination and self-reproach, with the fervent wish for life and renewal, cleansing and recreation. But all such concern finally turns him not further inward but outward, not to self but to God," upon whom each of the two stanzas are centered (for *Stanza 1*, below: 51:4c; for *Stanza 2*, see further below: 51:14a).[4]

---

2. Modified from Wendland, *Studies in the Psalms—Supplement*, 528.
3. "Blood[shed]" is literally "bloods."
4. Gaiser, "David of Psalm 51," 385–86.

```
A    "wipe away" (51:1c)
 B    "wash" (51:2a)
  C    "cleanse" (טהר, thr; 51:2b)
   D    "I know" (51:3a)
    E    "sinned" (51:4a)
     F    "You are justified" (51:4c)
    E'   "sin" (51:5b)
   D'   "make me know" (51:6b)
  C'   "clean" (טָהֵר, taher; 51:7a)
 B'   "wash" (51:7b)
A'   "wipe away" (51:9b)
```

Each of the first two verses of the psalm is chiastic, emphasizing the intensity of the plea: the first is centered on divine mercy, the second on human failure; both are surrounded by pleas for forgiveness.[5]

51:1	51:2

"Be gracious to me, God
    according to Your lovingkindness
    according to … Your compassions
wipe away my rebellions."
	"Thoroughly wash me
	    from my iniquity
	and from my sin
	cleanse me."

There are three trios in these two verses, again underscoring the depth of the psalmist's feelings, the desperation of sin, and the utter dependence on God to be forgiven:[6]

Objects of forgiveness	"my rebellions" (51:1c); "my iniquity," "my sin" (51:2)
Grounds for forgiveness	God's "gracious[ness]," "lovingkindness," "compassions" (51:1)
Actions of forgiveness	"wipe away" (51:1c); "wash," "cleanse" (51:2)

Only the "abundance" (רֹב, rov; 51:1b) of divine compassion could "thoroughly" (רָבָה, ravah; 51:2a) remove sin's residue. Continuing the emphasis, the next four verses (51:3–6: personal confession) are exemplars of synonymous parallelism, with each of the five pairs of lines being similar in theme and construction. Those sins are "before me" and they are "against You" (51:3b, 4a)—humanity is the offender, and God is the ultimate "offendee." And therefore, first and second persons (the "I" and the "You") predominate in this section.

Further, we see "behold" in 51:5a, 6a. In the first instance, it points to the depth of the sinner's depravity—guilty from conception;[7] in the second, to the height of God's demand—

---

5. So also 51:9, similar to 51:2: "Hide Your presence / from my sins, // and all my iniquities / wipe away."
6. See Goldingay, *Psalms*, 2:126.
7. This guilt from conception is not pointing to the sexual act as being sinful and sin as being hereditary. Rather, it points to the pervasiveness of sinfulness, extending from the very moment of conception, and extending to all of humanity (as also in Pss 130:3; 143:2). Perhaps Gen 8:21 is analogous, where God asserts

truth in every aspect of one's life. Though every part of every person is so affected from conception, God still requires truth in the "inner person" and in the "hidden being" (51:6), i.e., even in those facets of persons that are invisible. The sinner does "know" his rebellions and sins (51:3a), but God would "make me *know*" divine truth and wisdom (51:6b), accomplishing recognition of sin even in the deeper parts of one's being, leading to subsequent confession and repentance.

The prayer for the removal of sin (51:7–9[8]) has a description of crushed bones that suggests that sin had left some physical residue upon the sinner, either directly, or indirectly by way of God's punitive action ("*You* have crushed," 51:8b). So much so, the psalmist begs that the divine presence (literally, "face") be turned away, so that sin may not provoke further animus from a holy God (51:9a). The defilement of sin was so great, and the potential for further divine discipline so high, God's gaze needed to be averted. Instead of such chastisement, the sinner pleads for "gladness and joy," the consequence of divine forgiveness (51:8a).

Stanza 2: Re-creation (51:10–17); Conclusion (51:18–19)

The pattern of *Stanza 2*, as with *Stanza 1*, is centered upon God, as was noted (D, 51:14).

    A   "clean *heart* …, *God*" (51:10a)
        B   "spirit" (×2; 51:10b, 11b, 12b)
            C   Utterance: "I will teach" (51:13a)
                D   **"God, the God of my deliverance" (51:14a)**
            C'   Utterance of "tongue"; "lips"; "mouth" (51:14b–15)
        B'   "spirit" (51:17a)
    A'   "broken and crushed *heart*, *God*" (51:17b)

Stanza 2 opens with three verses (51:10–12; prayer for the re-creation of self), the second line of each of which begins with וְרוּחַ, *wruach* ("and . . . spirit") + qualifier of the spirit + imperative verb of appeal with a first-person suffix (51:10b, 11b, 12b). Whereas in *Stanza 1* sin was more a stain or an impurity that needed wiping or cleansing (51:1–2, 7), in *Stanza 2* it is more a transit on a wrong track that needs to be detoured to "Your paths" (51:13a). In that regard, notice the verbs of spatiality in 51:10–12: "dismiss . . . away," "take [from]" (51:11); "return [to]," "sustain" (or "support," "hold up," 51:12); as well as a number of spatial prepositions with first-person suffixes: "in me," "inside me" (51:10); "from me" (51:11); "to me" (51:12a; and "from Your presence," 51:11a). All this demarcates this *Stanza 2* as one in which restoration is sought, into the "presence" (literally, "face," 51:11a) of God, i.e., restoration to proximity with God.[9]

---

that "a person's heart is evil from his youth."

8. The exact species of the hyssop plant mentioned in 51:7 is uncertain, but it served as a convenient tool for sprinkling liquids: Exod 12:22; Lev 14:51; Num 19:18.

9. The *hiphil* of שׁלך, *shlk*, "dismiss," with God as subject and taking the preposition מִן or מֵעַל (*min* or *me'al*) and the direct object "presence" (i.e., face), as in 51:11a, is always used in the OT with a fixed syntax: God's people "dismissed" by him "away from" his "face/presence" (2 Kgs 13:23; 17:20; 24:20; Jer 7:15; 52:3; see van Wolde, "Prayer for Purification," 347). Thus Ps 51:11a essentially pleads, "Do not cast me away from you," and 51:11b beseeches, "Do not take yourself away from me" (Goldingay, *Psalms*, 2:134).

For this to happen "a clean heart" would need to be "created [ברא, br']" by God in the sinner (51:10a)—"nothing less than a miracle could effect his reformation."[10] Also rendered necessary was the renewal of a "spirit of steadfastness" (51:10b), one that would no longer be susceptible to the vagaries of sinful impulses, but would be "firm and reliable, determined and committed, prepared and set to go God's way."[11] "Heart" and "spirit" in 51:10, particularly in light of the same pair of words in 51:17, is a merism indicating the totality of the person.[12]

The question of what רוּחַ קָדְשְׁךָ, *ruach qadshka*, in 51:11b indicates is a thorny one. While "Your Holy Spirit" is a possible reading, in light of the fact that רוּחַ in 51:10b, 12b, 17a clearly indicates the human spirit, "spirit of Your holiness" is a better option for 51:11b.[13] Thus it indicates "the psalmist's inner desire for God's holiness," a human spirit yearning for God's holiness, one that is focused and centered upon God in personal spirituality.[14] No doubt, such a human "spirit of Your holiness" (51:11b) is sustained by the divine Holy Spirit. After *Stanza 1* that sought reprieve for sin (a look to the past), in *Stanza 2* the psalmist seeks a spiritual re-creation and a revitalization (a look to the future):

> [He] wants to return to a lifestyle of holiness, inwardly and as a result outwardly, which will please God, and enhance communion with God . . . David, having asked earlier to be forgiven and thus positionally holy before God, is now [in 51:11], as in [51:10 and 12], asking God to strengthen him spiritually so that he might become more practically holy and then be able to enjoy God's presence.[15]

Likewise, in 51:12, what is requested is for God "to transform him so completely that he freely and willingly lives for him" with a "spirit of willingness."[16] "The willing spirit is to be understood as the supplicant's desired frame of mind, which comprises of a total adjustment of the volitional centre onto the divine will."[17] This is nothing but a congruence or alignment of one's life with divine demand.

In sum, what is requested in the first several verses of *Stanza 2* goes beyond the seeking of a reprieve for sin (as it was in *Stanza 1*, to attain positional holiness); the sinner wants the divine (re-)creative work to produce a new dynamism of life that evermore remains pure and restores communion with God (to attain practical holiness). And such restoration brings joy (51:12; anticipated in 51:8a).

---

10. Calvin, *Commentary on the Book of Psalms*, 2:298 (on Ps 51:10). That "cleanse/be clean" is employed in 51:2b, 7a (טהר, *thr*) and in 51:10a (טָהוֹר, *tahor*) suggests that the actions/states called for in these verses are related.

11. Goldingay, *Psalms*, 2:134. This "spirit of steadfastness" is thus "not a temporal state of mind, but an enduring spirit or force that can uphold him against future attacks of impurities or sins" (van Wolde, "Prayer for Purification," 356).

12. Likely also the referent of the "inner person" and "hidden being" of 51:6.

13. In Isa 63:10, 11, the only other instances of the phrase, it is more certain that רוּחַ קָדְשׁוֹ, *ruach qadsho*, means "His Holy Spirit"; note רוּחַ יְהוָה, *ruach yhwh*, "Spirit of Yahweh," in 63:14.

14. VanGemeren, *Psalms*, 438.

15. Marlowe, "'Spirit of Your Holiness,'" 41. There are likely echoes between 51:10–12 (and 51:17) and Ezek 36:26: both texts have "heart" and "spirit," and both have the placement of these "within/inside" a person of God (קֶרֶב, *qerev*, in both Ps 51:10b and Ezek 36:26). The notion of cleansing, טהר, is also shared between Ps 51:2b, 7a and Ezek 36:25.

16. Estes, "Spirit and the Psalmist," 132.

17. Klein, "From the 'Right Spirit,'" 173.

Along with the restoration, including the "rescue ... from [the guilt of] bloodshed" (51:14a),[18] comes personal commitment to the rest of the community of God's people (51:13–15): the restored sinner promises to teach other sinners "Your paths" (51:13a)[19] and publicly declare "Your righteousness" (51:14b) via "tongue," "lips," and "mouth" (51:14b–15). The "return" of the joy of God's deliverance unto the repentant sinner (51:12a), in turn, leads to the action of this individual to cause other sinners to "return" to God (51:13b). These latter ones are labeled "rebels" (פֹּשְׁעִים, phoshʻim; 51:13a); it was not long ago that the psalmist had described himself to be in a state of "rebellion" (פֶּשַׁע, peshaʻ; 51:1b, 3a).

Stanza 2 then takes a cultic turn regarding forgiveness in 51:16. The assertion here is more of the nature of "not this [i.e., sacrifices] without that [i.e., appropriate spirit]" rather than of "not this at all, but only that," i.e., relativizing the values of each—sacrifices and spirit—rather than an absolute blacklisting of one over the other.[20] In other words, sacrifices are not being rejected *in toto*; but sacrifices without the brokenness of spirit and heart (51:17) are unacceptable to God.[21] After all, while 51:16 asserted that "You do not delight [חפץ, chphts] in sacrifice," the psalm concludes by declaring that "You will delight [חפץ] in sacrifices of righteousness" and proceeds to list them (51:19[22]), those that are preceded by contrition for sin and sinfulness: "the sacrifices of God are a broken spirit" (51:17a).[23] Such enervated and devitalized spirits and hearts will not be rejected by God; rather he will re-create and renew them, as 51:10 anticipates. Thus while deity is "*not* pleased [רצה, rtsh]" with sacrifices that come from an *un*broken spirit (51:16), corrected attitudes result in God undertaking restorative work in his "pleasure [רָצוֹן, ratson]," as he rebuilds the destroyed walls of Jerusalem that will protect it (51:18). This reconstruction is thus symbolic of the restoration of the fallen sinner, that will protect from future impurities. Notice the sequence:

"You do not delight in sacrifice" (51:16a)
"You are not pleased" (51:16b)
Sacrifices that "You will not despise" (51:17b)
"Your pleasure" (51:18a)
"You will delight in sacrifices" (51:19a)

Divine displeasure with improper sacrifices (when performed with *un*broken spirits/hearts) are transformed into divine pleasure with proper sacrifices (when performed with broken spirits/hearts). "Thus everything falls into place: the metaphor in which the effect of sin

---

18. Perhaps this indicates absolution from the guilt of not instructing others about the divine deliverance the psalmist has just experienced; Ezek 3:17–19; 33:7–9 might be analogous—these verses, too, have "rescue" and "blood[shed]," as does Ps 51:14a.

19. This is particularly reminiscent of Exod 33:13, where Moses asks God to "make me know Your paths," the paths of mercy. Besides, divine "graciousness," "lovingkindness," and "compassion" are reflected in Exod 34:6 (as also in Ps 51:1), as also are the categories of disobedience—"rebellions," "iniquity," and "sin"—in Exod 34:7 (as also in Ps 51:1–3).

20. Goldingay, *Psalms*, 2:138.

21. See 1 Sam 15:22; Prov 21:3.

22. Such "sacrifices of *righteousness*" are in accord with divine "righteousness" (51:14b; also see 51:4c for the employment of the same root, צדק, tsdq, translated "justified"). Also note God's "desire" for truth (also חפץ, 51:6a).

23. Also see 34:18 for divine acceptance of the "brokenhearted" and of "those crushed in spirit."

is described in terms of states of destruction and brokenness and the metaphor in which forgiveness is described in terms of reconstruction and rebuilding build into one coherent metaphorical pattern."[24]

So, finally, we have traveled from "Be gracious to me, God" (51:1a) to "Then You will delight" (51:19a). Yet even at the end, there is no explicit affirmation that God has actually heard and forgiven; neither is there any praise subsequent to the (expected) deliverance and rescue of God. But there is, throughout the psalm, a confident anticipation of reprieve and restoration and trust that God *has* heard and that therefore God *will* act, in his grace, because of his lovingkindness, according to the bounty of his compassion (51:1). And on those verities, the sinner rests!

Sermon Map

I. Reprieve
   Sinners' acknowledgment of sin (51:1–9)
   Move-to-relevance: Our sensitivity to sin in the past

II. Re-Creation
   God's re-creation of self (51:10–12, 16–19)
   Move-to-relevance: Our separation from sin in the future

III. Recounting
   Joy, praise, teaching others (51:13–15)

IV. *Experience and Exhort!*
   Specifics on experiencing God's forgiveness
   Specifics on exhorting others about God's forgiveness

---

24. van Wolde, "Prayer for Purification," 359. If the psalmist was also the leader of the community, this pivot to Zion, Jerusalem, and their walls also makes sense. The sinner's re-creation and that of Zion may not be entirely disparate: sin does have an effect of the community at large (and thus on society and the city itself). Thus the restoration of the sinner leads to the reparation of the community.

PSALM 52:1–9

Psalm of Orientation

Lucre or Lovingkindness?

IN PSALM 51, THE psalmist had promised God that he would "teach rebels Your paths" so that "sinners will return to You" (51:13). In Psalm 52, he keeps his promise. Picturing a stark contrast between the lives and fates of the wicked and righteous, the poet "leads the audience to see that indeed there is only one way to live"—God's way, "trusting in the lovingkindness of God forever and always" (52:8).[1]

Translation

52:1   Why do you boast in evil, warrior?
         The lovingkindness of God [is for] every day.
52:2   Destruction you devise with your tongue
         like a sharpened razor, worker of deceit.
52:3   You love evil more than good,
         falsehood more than speaking righteousness.
52:4   You love all words that consume,
         deceitful tongue.
52:5   But God will demolish you for perpetuity;
         He will snatch you up and tear you out from [your] tent,
         and uproot you from the land of the living.
52:6   And the righteous will see and fear,
         and will laugh at him:
52:7   "Behold, the man who would not make God his stronghold,
         but trusted in the abundance of his riches,
         strong in his [evil] desire."

---

1. deClaissé-Walford et al., *Book of Psalms*, 459.

52:8 But I [am] like a flourishing olive tree in the house of God;
 I trust in the lovingkindness of God forever and always.
52:9 I will give You thanks forever,
 because You acted,
 and I will hope in Your name—for [it is] good—
 before Your devout ones.

Structure

The structure of the psalm is straightforward:

    The wicked (**52:1–4**)
A   "lovingkindness of God" (52:1b); "every day" (52:1b)
    "worker" (עשׂה, *'sh*; 52:2b); "good" (52:3a)
    B   *Response of God* to the wicked (**52:5**)
    B' *Reaction of the righteous* to God's response to the wicked (**52:6–7**)
    The righteous (**52:8–9**)
A' "lovingkindness of God" (52:8b); "forever and always" (52:8b)
    "acted" (עשׂה; 52:9b); "good" (52:9c)

Theological Focus

The powerful wicked, exulting in evil and uttering deceit, not loving good or speaking righteousness, and trusting in their riches, are punished severely by God, while the righteous flourish in the presence of deity, trusting forever in the constancy of God's lovingkindness, and praising God for his deliverance.

Commentary

The Wicked; Response of God to the Wicked (52:1–5)

Rather than commencing with an address to God, Psalm 52 begins by questioning a "warrior" who exults in evil (52:1a); in fact, he "loves" evil (52:3a).[2] Apparently, this person of renown, a hero, a big shot, has succumbed to the temptation to employ his power for the cause of evil, matching his actions and speech with his delusions of omnipotence. But he is sadly mistaken and sorely misguided: divine lovingkindness is all that counts and should be all that one wants and seeks. Not only is it extravagant, coming from God himself, it is for "every day," i.e., ample

---

2. "Warrior," גִּבּוֹר, *gibbor*, describes a seasoned fighter: one who is mighty and virile.

in supply and abundant for every need (52:1b). In other words, there is no need to indulge in evil to sustain oneself, to extend oneself, to secure oneself, or to inflate oneself in this life. God's lovingkindness is sufficient for all things, for all time. But unfortunately, the mighty "warrior" seems to have disregarded divine beneficence, opting to go his own wicked way for self-centered advantage and gain—an attempt to bless himself. To this end, rather than trusting God, this strong one trusts the plenitude of his wealth (52:7ab; see below).

While there can be no doubt that this one who "loved evil more than good" and was "strong in his [evil] desire" (52:3a, 7c) engaged in wicked deeds, for the most part the focus here is on this malefactor's utterances: his "boast" in evil (52:1a); the workings of his "tongue" (52:2a, 4b); his love of falsehood rather than "speaking [דבר, *dbr*] righteousness" (52:3b); and the discharge of "words [דָּבָר, *dabar*] that consume" (52:4a). So much so, while this character is a "worker of *deceit*," (רְמִיָּה, *rmiyyah*; 52:2b), it is his tongue that is actually labeled "deceitful" (מִרְמָה, *mirmah*; 52:4b). The parallel constructions of 52:3 and 52:4 attest to such a focus on speech:

| 52:3 | "You *love* evil more than good, | falsehood more than *speaking* righteousness." |
| 52:4 | "You *love* all words that consume, | deceitful *tongue*." |

All that to say, the workings of this warlord were mostly verbal and his weapons mostly words, at least as indicated in the psalm.

> The profile which emerges of the wicked person is thus that of a wealthy individual who, because of his sound financial power-base, arrogantly thinks that he can say what he likes and use his power to dominate or intimidate other people. It is also implied that the wealth of this person has been gained through the misuse of speech. This person's speaking is not only limited to the hurting of and lying to other human beings, but it also constitutes rebellion against God.[3]

The lovingkindness of God which is for "every [כֹּל, *kol*] day" (52:1b) is cavalierly rejected in favor of "all [כֹּל] words," emitted by a deceitful tongue, that "consume"—ostensibly the devouring of the innocent righteous intimidated by this *mafioso*'s words (52:4). Such an affinity for evil would have its consequences and evoke a response from deity. And it does.

God's response is scathing and scary: He would "demolish" them perpetually; this terrifying action is explained as his tearing them out of their dwellings and ripping them out of their grounding in life (52:5). Yes, there may be "natural" consequences to evil deeds, but here those insalubrious outworkings of wickedness are eradicated by God's active execution of punishment. They who loved evil "more than" good, and falsehood "more than" righteous speech (מִן, *min*, ×2; 52:3) are now expelled "from" their dwellings and ejected "from" life itself (מִן, ×2; 52:5bc): comeuppance that fits the crime!

---

3. Potgieter, "Profile of the Rich Antagonist," 2.

And notice what happens to the label of the wicked person:

> "warrior" (גִּבּוֹר; 52:1a)
>   "tongue ... worker of deceit" (52:2)
>   "you love" (52:3aα)
>   "evil more than good" (52:3aβ)
>   "falsehood more than speaking righteousness" (52:3b)
>   "you love" (52:4a)
>   "deceitful tongue" (52:4b)
> "man" (גֶּבֶר, *gever*; 52:7a)

The composition began by calling the evil one a "warrior" (52:1a); it ends his denunciation by marking him as a mere "man" (52:7a); that those words in Hebrew are related adds to the sense of doom, downfall, and derision!

Reaction of the Righteous to the Response of God to the Wicked; the Righteous (52:6–9)

And derision is indeed the response of the righteous to God's response to the wicked: They "see [וְיִרְאוּ, *wyir'u*]" and "fear [וְיִירָאוּ, *wyira'u*]," and they guffaw (52:6). The fear of the righteous is appropriate in the face of the divine justice executed on evildoers. God is not to be trifled with, they learn, but they laugh at the same time at the ruination of the evildoers! The wicked may have hated "righteousness" (52:3b), but now it is the turn of the "righteous" to see their oppressor(s) defeated (52:6a).[4]

Striking is the contrast between the "trust" of the wicked—in wealth's abundance (52:7b)—and the "trust" of the righteous—in divine lovingkindness (52:8b). The former trust in evanescent mirages; the latter in eternal mercies—"forever and always" (52:8b). The trust of the righteous keeps them from engaging and exulting in evil to gain advantages and comforts in life, for God always provides all things all the time for his people—and what he gives is always good, plentiful, and sufficient. Though "the warrior is a man of faith" ("trust," 52:7b), too, his faith is in the wrong object. Likewise, "he is a man of love" ("love," 52:3a, 4a), but again his affections are warped.[5]

And so the righteous offer a funeral oration for the destroyed wicked in 52:7: "Wherever we see to-day [*sic*] a man great in sin and substance, we shall do well to anticipate his end, and view this verse as the divine *in memoriam*."[6] This late lamented person is the one who would *not* make God his "stronghold [מָעוֹז, *ma'oz*]" (52:7a); instead he was "strong [עֹז, *'zz*]" in his wicked impulses (52:7c). And that spells doom: "destruction [הַוָּה, *hawwah*]" was the first word of 52:2–4; "[evil] desire [הַוָּה]" is the last word of 52:5–7.

Then comes the contrast between the fate of the wicked and that of the righteous: the former, we saw, was "uprooted ... from the land of the living" (52:5c), while the latter becomes "a flourishing olive tree in the house of God" (52:8). The wicked one would be destroyed "for

---

4. The individual "warrior"/"man" (52:1a, 7a) is likely to represent a whole horde of malefactors.
5. Goldingay, *Psalms*, 2:427.
6. Spurgeon, *Treasury of David*, 2:480 (italics original).

perpetuity" (52:5a), while the righteous trusts in God's lovingkindness "forever and always" (52:8).[7] Thus, for eternity, God's people will dwell in the presence of their deity!

So there is cause for thanksgiving "forever" (52:9a)—because God has "acted" (עשׂה; 52:9b) against the "worker" of evil (also from עשׂה; 52:2). And whereas the wicked hated "good" (52:3a), the righteous will wait on God's "good" name, the goodness of his being (52:9c). These righteous are the ones who recognize God's "lovingkindness" as being for every day (חֶסֶד, *chesed*; 52:1b) and who trust in that "lovingkindness" (חֶסֶד; 52:8b) as being forever: no wonder they are called the "devout" of God (חָסִיד, *chasid*; 52:9d). May all of God's people be so devoted to his lovingkindness!

Sermon Map

I. Wicked and Their Fate

    Evildoing and evil-speaking (52:1–4)

    Trust in riches, not in God (52:7)

    Fate of the wicked (52:5–6)

    Move-to-relevance: Our seeking evil means to get ahead

II. Righteous and Their Fate

    Fearing God, waiting on God's good name (52:6a, 9cd)

    Trust in God and his lovingkindness (52:8b)

    Fate of the righteous (52:8a, 9ab)

    Move-to-relevance: Our failure to trust in God to provide

III. *Flourish or Demolish?*

    Specifics on trusting God to provide

---

7. That same "lovingkindness of God," we were told earlier, "[is for] every day" (52:1b).

PSALM 53:1-6

Psalm of Orientation

Fools vs. Wise

PSALM 53 APPEARS TO be a variant of Psalm 14, but "the presence of both versions in the Psalter invites us to treat them independently."[1] In Psalm 52 the wicked were confronted and threatened, and the righteous were comforted and thrived; in Psalm 53 the wicked are still confronted, but it appears these are evildoers who did not believe the threats of the previous psalm—none of them does any good.[2]

Translation

53:1 The fool has said in his heart,
    "[There is] no God."
They act ruinously and behave abominably in injustice;
    [there is] not [one] who does good.
53:2 God, from the heavens—He looks down upon humans
    to see if there is anyone who understands,
    who seeks God.

---

1. Goldingay, *Psalms*, 2:150. The major difference is in 53:5-6 (addressed to the righteous; the corresponding verses, 14:5-7, are addressed to the wicked), creating a new psalm. There is also the substitution of "God" in Psalm 53 instead of "Yahweh" in Psalm 14 (53:2a and 14:2a; 53:4c and 14:4b; and 53:6b and 14:7b). In addition, "Yahweh" in 14:6 lacks a counterpart in Psalm 53. "The persona of Psalm 14 might be characterized, imaginatively, as that of a little brother telling his older brother (read: tormentor), 'You're gonna get it when Mom gets home.' The persona of Psalm 53 is of an older sister reassuring her little brother, 'Don't worry, Mom will get home soon'" (Jacobson, Karl N., "Dualing," 295-96). While there are elements in this psalm that suggest the disorientation of God's people (53:1c, 4b, 5c, 6ab), I chose to label this a psalm of orientation simply because of its overwhelming focus on how things are/will be in the righteous economy of God (in his ideal world) with regard to the evildoing "fool."

2. Goldingay, *Psalms*, 2:150.

53:3   Everyone of them has deviated;
             together they have become corrupt;
        [there is] not [one] who does good,
             not even one.
53:4   Have the practitioners of harm not known—
             who eat up my people [as] they eat bread
             [and] do not call upon God?
53:5   There they greatly dread [where] there was no dread;
             For God—He scattered the bones of the one who besieged you;
             you shamed [them], for God—He rejected them.
53:6   Who will give deliverance to Israel from Zion?
        When God restores the restoration of His people
             Jacob will jubilate, Israel will rejoice.

Structure

The structure of the psalm is based on the centering of each half of the composition, 53:1–3 and 53:4–6, upon the response of "God" (×2 in both 53:2 and 53:5)—*Divine Investigation* and *Divine Intervention*:

Divine Investigation (53:1–3)
Bookends: "there is no one who does good" (53:1d, 3c)
"'no God'" (53:1b); "injustice" (עָוֶל, *'awel*; 53:1c)
Response of God (central verse, 53:2): divine investigation; "God" ×2
Location of God: "heavens" (שָׁמַיִם, *shamayim*; 53:2a)
           "from the heavens" (53:2a); אֵין, *'en*, "no"/"not," ×4 (53:1b, 1d, 3c, 3d)

Divine Intervention (53:4–6)
Bookends: "my people" (53:4b) and "His people" (53:6b); questions: 53:4, 6a
"do not call upon God" (53:4c); "harm" (אָוֶן, *'awen*; 53:4a)
Response of God (central verse, 53:5): divine intervention; "God" ×2
Location of God: earth: "there" (שָׁם, *sham*; 53:5a)
           "from Zion" (53:6a); לֹא, *lo'*, "not" ×2 (53:4)

Theological Focus

The foolish—the overwhelming majority of humans—denying God's involvement in life and doing acts of utter evil, including oppressing God's people, will be destroyed by God who sees and reacts to these wicked ones, and delivers and restores the righteous, giving them cause for joyful praise.

Commentary

Divine Investigation (53:1–3)

The negative particle אֵין occurs four times in 53:1–3; in each case the existence of someone is denied: "no God" (53:1a); "not [one] who does good" (53:1c, 3c); "not even one" (53:3d)—it is thus a "particle of nonexistence."[3]

The first half of the psalm seems to be all about the God-denying fool: his anti-God declaration (53:1b) that leads to his evil actions (53:1cd)—foolish words and foolish deeds. The declaration "[There is] no God" is unlikely to be one of metaphysical atheism as practiced by modern-day secularists. Rather the assertion is that God does not involve himself in the activities of mankind: deity is either ignorant of such matters or could not care less. And therefore, these fools engage in evil, with none of them performing any good (53:1cd).[4]

These arrogant ones are fools also because of what the central verse of the section asserts (53:2): God looks, God sees (and, implied, God acts). But the foolish are ignorant of such divine investigations, whereby God attempts to determine if anyone seeks him, and if anyone has insight into these matters of import. Unfortunately, no one does—that makes them fools all the more. Every one of them had become warped and "together [יַחְדָּו, *yachdaw*]" (53:3b) they had been corrupted, so much so there was none doing good, not even "one [אֶחָד, *'echad*]" (53:3c). And with that, 53:3 becomes the only verse in the psalm not bearing the word "God"—"a silent testimony to the fact [of] the total corruption of humanity."[5]

Divine Intervention (53:4–6)

The *Divine Investigation* was already a warning that deity would not stand by idly, permitting his name to be sullied and his people to be bullied. And so his intervention in 53:4–6 (especially in the central verse of this section, 53:5) comes as no surprise.

The ignorance of the fools/evildoers is abysmal: "Have [they] . . . not known?" is not a question, but an exclamation of surprise (53:4). Denying God's involvement in life, they have disregarded him, and have also sought to devour his people with their malevolent oppression. Their fiendish consumption of the divine community is probably what the ruinous acts and loathsome doings of injustice were pointing to in 53:1c. Thus the "fool" (53:1a) is one who does not "understand" (53:2b) and one who does not "know" (53:4a). "Real wisdom or knowledge, then, involves acknowledgment of God. Knowledge that leaves God out of account is not real knowledge. But in addition, knowledge that stops short of acknowledgment ['calling upon God,' 53:4c] is not the real thing."[6] Benighted, they are in particular ignorant about *Divine Intervention* (that is sure to follow *Divine Investigation*).

The consequence of God's intervention is fear: the word "dread" (פחד, *pchd*) occurs as a verb and a noun *three* times in 53:5, signifying the intensity of the fright of the wicked when God does act against them.[7] Thus those who "eat" God's people as though "they were eating"

---

3. deClaissé-Walford et al., *Book of Psalms*, 466.

4. That these individuals are well and truly evil is connoted by the word "corrupt" (53:3b), derived from שָׁחַת, *shachat*, that had been used of the vile inhabitants of the world of Noah's day (Gen 6:11, 12).

5. Botha, "Psalm 53," 590.

6. Goldingay, *Psalms*, 2:153.

7. "Greatly dread" (53:5aα) is literally "dread [with] dread."

bread (53:4) become those who are in "great dread," when there was no "dread" (53:5a). The repeats of "eat" and of "dread" poetically depict the aggression and the apprehension, respectively, of these nefarious operators.

As for the persecuted people of God, they will be "restored" by God with the "restoration" (שְׁבוּת ... שׁוּב, shuv ... shvut; 53:6b). With a careful scrutiny of the twenty-seven occurrences of שׁוּב שְׁבוּת, "restore the restoration," in the OT, Bracke shows that the phrase "is associated with promises which indicate Yahweh's reversal of his judgment, and the restoration of a condition of well-being. Additionally, the vision of restoration . . . often includes Yahweh's correction of that which led to his judgment."[8] Essentially, it is a removal of God's wrath and a return of God's favor upon his people (also see 14:7; 85:1; 126:1, 4). This may be a hint, albeit subtle, that some guilt of God's people had a role in God's delay in delivering them. Nevertheless, the repetition of the verb root (as with the other repetitions noted) intensifies the action described, in this case signifying the marvel of the turnaround, the pivot of this dramatic *Divine Intervention*. "My people" (53:4b) were enslaved by the evildoers, but God would emancipate "His people" (53:6b).[9] Needless to say, the wish for deliverance of one kind or another, from one kind of oppression or another, has been universally voiced by the people of God of all times.

As a consequence of *Divine Intervention* and their restoration, the community of God would "shame" the one(s) who was/were tyrannizing them (53:5c).[10] Rhetorically, the fronted positions of "for God" before the respective verbs in 53:5b and 53:5c emphasize the divine actions against evildoers—it is deity performing them, none other! And both the actions of these oppressors and the reactions of God's people are represented by single words at the center of the structure of 53:5bc:

"For God, He scattered the bones of the one who besieged you;	*Fronted placement:* כִּי־אֱלֹהִים, ki-'elohim
	Single word for evildoers' action: חֹנָךְ, chonan
you shamed [them],	*Single word for righteous' action:* הֱבִשֹׁתָה, hevishotah
for God, He rejected them."	*Fronted placement:* כִּי־אֱלֹהִים

In light of God's location pointedly noted in 53:2a, "heavens [שָׁמַיִם, shamayim]," "there [שָׁם, sham]" (53:5a) is likely to indicate his location again—but this time he is with his people on earth. Notice also that "*from* the heavens" (53:2a) has become, in the second half of the psalm, "*from* Zion" (53:6a), the source of deliverance attesting once again to God's presence with his people on *terra firma*, at the front end of the battle arena.

And so the psalm arrives to its close, the rhetorical question of 53:6a essentially becoming a wish for the deliverance of Israel, God's people, by their divine champion—the fulfillment of which is anticipated with a joyous sense of certainty (53:6bc). "The psalmist knows

---

8. Bracke, "*šûb šebût*: Reappraisal," 243.

9. This "restoration," though primarily indicating restoration from the Israelite captivity, can also refer to situations of tyranny other than the historical exile of that people: see Job 42:10; Ezek 16:53.

10. The singular adversary of 53:5b, "the one who . . ." (and elsewhere in this psalm), becomes the plural "them" in 53:5c. Likewise, the singular afflicted person, "you" (53:5b, 5c), becomes the community with "Israel," "His people," and "Jacob" (53:6). Such an oscillation is not uncommon in the Psalter: the single individual frequently stands for a whole group of people. Also note that "you shamed" in 53:5c does not have a specified object and could refer to either "him" or "them" (I have chosen the latter in the translation).

the fact that God is not acting is no indication that God will not act. Indeed, God's act is so certain it can be spoken of as if it had already happened."[11]

The composition then concludes with Israel/Jacob "shouting for joy" and "rejoicing" (53:6c). "Israel" (×2), "Zion," and "Jacob" in 53:6—"the three names ... not only make this psalm a national one, but also serve as the final contrast to the fool who does not know God, for these are the names for my people ... [53:4b]—the ones who know their God" and, perhaps more importantly, are known by him and never neglected by him.[12] Thus the song that began with fools ridiculing (53:1) ends with the wise (the divine community) rejoicing!

Sermon Map

I. Divine Investigation and Discovery
   The foolish (53:1, 3)
   God's research (53:2)
   Move-to-relevance: God's active involvement with his world
II. Divine Intervention and Deliverance
   Fate of the foolish, God's reaction (53:4–5)
   Fate of God's people (53:6)
   Move-to-relevance: Waiting for God's interventions
III. *Be Wise, not Foolish!*
   Specifics on being aware of God's involvement in life

---

11. Goldingay, *Psalms*, 2:156.
12. deClaissé-Walford et al., *Book of Psalms*, 467 (italics removed).

PSALM 54:1–7

Psalm of Disorientation

Emancipation and Exaltation

THIS COMPOSITION, CONSIDERED A "classic prayer psalm,"[1] invokes God, seeks his aid, addresses the community with full confidence regarding deity's imminent help, and closes by returning to speak to God with a promise to exalt him post-deliverance with sacrifice and praise.

Translation

54:1 God, by Your name deliver me,
    and by Your power execute justice for me.

54:2 God, hear my prayer;
    give ear to the utterances of my mouth.

54:3 For strangers have risen against me
    and violent ones have sought my soul;
    they have not set God before them.

54:4 Behold, God is a helper to me;
    the Lord is the very sustainer of my soul.

54:5 May evil be returned to my spying foes;
    in Your faithfulness annihilate them.

54:6 With a freewill offering I will sacrifice to You;
    I will give thanks to Your name, Yahweh, for it is good.

54:7 For from all distress it has rescued me,
    and upon my watching enemies my eye has looked [triumphantly].

---

1. Goldingay, *Psalms*, 2:158.

Structure

The structure is, thus, quite straightforward:[2]

54:1–3	Entreaty to God ("name," 54:1a)
54:4–5a	Exhortation for community
34:5b–7	Exaltation of God ("name," 54:6b)

Each of the verses of the psalm includes parallelisms in their two respective lines. Besides, in Hebrew, each of the two lines of the first verse and each of the two lines of the last verse end with a first-person suffixed verb or noun, נִי-, *-ni* (הוֹשִׁיעֵנִי, *hoshi'eni*, "deliver me," and תְדִינֵנִי, *tdineni*, "execute justice for me," 54:1; הִצִּילָנִי, *hitstsilani*, "rescued me," and עֵינִי, *'eni*, "my eye," 54:7). In addition, the "name" of Yahweh links the opening and closing sections (54:1a, 6b).

> The major stress in the psalm is clearly on the powerful and effective Name of Yahweh. Yahweh may seem absent from the world, but those who invoke his Name with faith and courage will discover the reality of his awesome presence. Those who forget his Name and seek to disregard his will may experience the terrible recoil of their own wickedness, a recoil which is sustained by divine power. The message of the psalm is clear enough: the Name of Yahweh will not fail the suppliant in a time of crisis. The enemies will not prevail. Yahweh will make a necessary connection between act and consequence, and the power of ruthless foes will be turned back against themselves.[3]

Thus the psalm that commenced with an entreaty to God's *name* for deliverance (54:1a) concludes with an exaltation of God's *name* for rescue (54:6b–7a).

Theological Focus

> Righteous sufferers, in dire distress under violent oppression and facing threats to life, look to God for refuge and praise him for his deliverance, for he is their helper and the sustainer of their life, he whose name is good, who is antithetical to all the evil unleashed by foes, and who therefore, in faithfulness to his people, will destroy the wicked.

Commentary

Entreaty to God (54:1–3)

Rather than begin with the situation of distress, the psalm opens directly into its plea for deliverance and justice (54:1). The parallelism between "by Your name" and "by Your power"

---

2. From Botha, "Psalm 54," 509.
3. Tate, *Psalms 51–100*, 49.

(54:1a, 1b) indicates that the "name" of God points to his divine personhood, all his actions and all his attributes (Exod 34:5–7; Isa 9:6).[4]

Only after the first two verses, each of which begins with "God" (Ps 54:1a, 2a), and pleads for deliverance and for deity to listen, respectively, does the psalmist get to the reason for his supplication (54:3). So "we might have expected the verses to come in the order 3, 2, 1 [*I'm in trouble* (54:3). *Hear me* (54:2). *Deliver me* (54:1).]. The actual order expresses urgency rather than logic."[5] Besides, such a sequencing also juxtaposes in stark contrast the action of God (54:4) with the action of the violent (54:3). Who the "strangers" in 54:3a are is unclear. Perhaps they are foreigners,[6] but in any case, they and the "violent ones" are alienated from God (54:3ab); indeed they seem to disregard him totally (54:3c). And now these ungodly ones wreak havoc on the lives of God's people. That the supplicant is in dire straits is evident: not only is he under attack from strangers, these wicked are out to kill him ("violent ones have sought my soul," 54:3b). And so, in a fourfold plea, God's aid is beseeched: "deliver me," "execute justice for me" (54:1), "hear my prayer," and "give ear to the utterances of my mouth" (54:2).

Exhortation for Community (54:4–5a)

The psalmist then turns from God to address his own community, with a word of exhortation and confidence. He describes God with two participles: "helper" and "sustainer" (54:4). The latter, however, is a masculine *plural* carrying the preposition בְּ, *b*. It literally it reads: "the Lord is among [בְּ] the sustainers of my soul." This is likely to be idiomatic and indicating an intensive statement: "the Lord is the *very* sustainer of my soul."[7] Notice the contrast that is created, each party affecting the psalmist's "soul": violent ones seek the psalmist's "soul" (54:3b), but God is the very sustainer of his "soul" (54:4b).

And to this divine supporter of life, the fearful psalmist implores that the evil being dealt to him by the wicked would be returned upon them—those "spying foes" out to ambush him as they seek his soul (54:5a).[8] "The implicit assumption is that once evil . . . is let loose, it either must or can find a resting place somewhere. The suppliant expects or prays that it may find this resting place in the perpetrators of the evil, the watchful foes, rather than in the person for whom they undeservedly intended it. It is either them or me."[9]

---

4. Ross, *Psalms*, 2:237.
5. Goldingay, *Psalms*, 2:159.
6. Two of the four instances of "strange," זָר, *zar*, in the Psalter describe foreign deities (44:20; 81:9).

7. This labeling of a singular individual with a plural participle prefixed with בְּ is also found in Jdg 11:35; God himself is described thus in Ps 118:7. In all these cases, intensification of the attribute/predicate in question is what is intended.

8. The *ketiv* (what is written) has a *qal* imperfect: יָשׁוֹב, *yashov*, reads "it [evil] will return." Considering the imperative in 54:5b, the *qere* (what is read) that has the *hiphil* imperfect as a jussive, יָשֵׁב, *yashiv*, "may it [evil] return," makes better sense.

9. Goldingay, *Psalms*, 2:160–61.

Exaltation of God (54:5b–7)

Switching in the middle of 54:5 to address God, the supplicant pleads that deity would finish off the oppressors (54:5b). The confidence of the psalmist that God will hear his prayer is so high, he anticipates exalting this delivering God with sacrifices and thanks (54:6).[10] So, just as the psalm began with an appeal to "Your name" (54:1a), it ends with thanks to "Your name" (54:6b). And the psalmist makes another contrast: what the wicked were meting out to the righteous was "evil" (54:5a), but the name of Yahweh, deity's person, is "good" (54:6b). And that name, the good name of a good God, will most certainly rescue the psalmist from all his distresses (54:7a), for this deity is faithful to his people (54:5b).[11] So much so, enemies, who are "watching" the ones they oppress, will in turn be looked upon one day by the delivered sufferer(s) in triumph (54:7b). Saved at last!

Sermon Map

I. Oppression and Character of Oppressors
    Dangerous violence (54:3)
    Ungodly evildoers (54:3c, 5a)
    Move-to-relevance: Oppression in our lives

II. Salvation and Character of Savior
    God's name, his power, help, faithfulness (54:1–2, 4, 5b)
    Divine rescue of the righteous, destruction of the wicked (54:5, 7)
    Move-to-relevance: Salvation in our lives

III. *Expect and Exalt!*
    Specifics on confident praise

---

10. Psalm 54:6 "combines worship in symbol ['sacrifice'] with worship in word ['thanks'], two complementary expressions of a personal gratefulness for Yhwh's act of deliverance" (Goldingay, *Psalms*, 2:161).

11. Taking the psalm at face value, such a deliverance seems to have occurred between 54:5b and 54:6a. Prior to 54:6, rescue was only expected and sacrifice only promised. But subsequently, especially considering the perfect verbs of 54:7, salvation from enemy oppression seems to have become an accomplished fact. This idiosyncrasy is best explained by considering the perfect forms of the verbs translated "rescue" and "look" as indicating an absolutely certain *future* outcome.

PSALM 55:1–23

Psalm of Disorientation

Friend and Foe

PSALM 55 IS COMMONLY considered one of the imprecatory psalms.[1] It is unusual in its rapid and abrupt redirections of thought that give it an "uneven, disjointed, and complex structure" placing the reader on "the emotional roller coaster that is suffering."[2]

Translation

55:1 Give ear, God, to my prayer;
      and do not hide Yourself from my supplication [for grace].
55:2 Pay heed to me and answer me;
      I am restless in my complaint and I am agitated
55:3 from the voice of the enemy,
      from the face of pressure of the wicked;
      for they push upon me harm,
      and in anger they bear animosity towards me.
55:4 My heart, it quakes within me,
      and the terrors of death, they have fallen upon me.
55:5 Fear and trembling, it comes on me,
      and horror has covered me.
55:6 I said, "Who will give to me wings—
      like a dove I would fly away and I would rest.
55:7 Behold, I would flee to be at a distance;
      I would lodge in the wilderness.

---

1. They others are Psalms 59; 69; 79; 109; and 137. See the Introduction for more on imprecations in the Psalter.

2. deClaissé-Walford et al., *Book of Psalms*, 473. The text is also difficult to decipher, with several Hebrew words and syntactical idiosyncrasies that are rather opaque.

55:8 I would hasten to a place of refuge for me,
    from the rushing wind, from the tempest."
55:9 Confuse, Lord, divide their tongues,
    for I have seen violence and strife in the city.
55:10 Day and night they go around her upon her walls,
    and harm and trouble are within her.
55:11 Destruction is within her;
    oppression and deceit do not leave from her streets.
55:12 For it is not an enemy who reproaches me—
    I could bear [that];
it is not one who hates me who exalts himself over me—
    I could hide from him.
55:13 But you—a man my equal,
    my companion and one known by me;
55:14 [with] whom together [I] had sweet fellowship:
    in the house of God we walked with the throng.
55:15 May death deceitfully come upon them;
    may they go down to Sheol alive,
    for evil is in their dwelling, within them.
55:16 I—upon God I will call
    and Yahweh, He will deliver me.
55:17 Evening and morning and midday,
    I complain and I am agitated, and He hears my voice.
55:18 He will redeem my soul in peace from my battle,
    for they are many against me.
55:19 He will hear and thwart them—God,
    even the One who sits [enthroned] of old—
[those] who do not change
    and for whom there is no fear of God.
55:20 He put forth his hands against those at peace with him;
    he violated his covenant.
55:21 Smooth [as] butter, his mouth,
    but his heart [was] battle;
softer his words than oil,
    but they [were] drawn swords.
55:22 Cast upon Yahweh your burden and He—He will sustain you;
    He will not forever allow the righteous to be shaken.
55:23 But You, God—You will bring them down to the hole of destruction;
    people of bloodshed and deceit will not [live out] half their days,
    but I—I will trust in You.

Structure

Pain links the whole "ride," so to speak with relapses, though it is the remission of pain that concludes the psalm.[3]

> **Petition and Pain: Foes (55:1–8)**
> *Petition* (**55:1–2a**)
> *Pain of suffering:* Terrors of foes (**55:2b–8**)
>   Vocative: "God" (55:1a); "push" (מוֹט, *mot;* 55:3c); "wicked" (55:3b)
>
> **Petition and Pain: Friend (55:9–15)**
> *Petition* (**55:9–11**)
> *Pain of suffering:* Treachery (**55:12–15**)
>
> **Peace, but *Relapse* of Pain: Friend (55:16–21)**
> *Peace:* Expression of trust (**55:16–19**)
> *Pain of suffering:* Treachery (**55:20–21**)
>
> **Peace and *Remission* of Pain: Foes (55:22–23)**
> *Preservation:* Exhortation to trust (**55:22**)
> *Pain of suffering:* Termination of foes (**55:23**)
>   Vocative: "God" (55:23ba); "shaken" (מוֹט; 55:22b); "righteous" (55:22b)

Besides, there is also the oscillation between a singular oppressor (55:3ab, 12–14, 20–21) and a plurality of them (55:3cd, 9–10, 15, 18b, 23ab).

Theological Focus

> When assaulted by foes and betrayed by friends—all mired in evil—generating the torment of terror and the peril of perishing, the people of God continue to trust their deity despite all odds, confident in the power of the divine King to defeat their enemies and to deliver his community.

Commentary

Petition and Pain: Foes (55:1–8)

The pathos of Psalm 55 is evident in its first five verses: four verbs deal with the appeal of the supplicant (A; 55:1–2a; below), and four more express the terror of the supplicant, a further motivation for God to respond (A'; 55:4–5). There are also two verbs describing the despair of the supplicant (B; 55:2b) and two more verbs denoting the persecution of the supplicant (B'; 55:3cd). In the center are two clauses, each introduced by the preposition מִן, *min*, "from" (55:3a, 3b), that name the foes, "the enemy" and "the wicked," the root of all the problems (C; 55:3ab).

---

3. Also see deClaissé-Walford et al., *Book of Psalms*, 473; Kselman and Barré, "Psalm 55," 442–43.

> **A**   **Four verbs**: *appeal of supplicant* (55:1–2a)
>   "give ear," "do not hide" (55:1); "pay heed," "answer" (55:2a)
> > **B**   **Two verbs**: *despair of supplicant* (55:2b)
> >   "I am restless," "I am agitated"
> > > **C**   **Two prepositional clauses**: *naming of foes* (55:3ab)
> > >   "from the voice of the enemy," "from the face of pressure of the wicked"
> > **B'**   **Two verbs**: *persecution of supplicant* (55:3cd)
> >   "they push upon me harm," "they bear animosity towards me"
> **A'**   **Four verbs**: *terror of supplicant* (53:4–5)
>   "quakes," "have fallen" (55:4); "comes," "has covered" (55:5)

The psalmist is in deep trouble. No wonder he wishes to flee to a "distance," "in the wilderness" (55:7), to "a place of refuge" far from the frenzy and ferment of wind and wave (55:8), to find "rest" (55:6).

Another chiastic structure in 55:3cd brings the issue to a head:

> **A**   "they push"   *yiqtol* verb
> > **B**   "upon me"   prepositional phrase
> > > **C**   "harm"
> > **B'**   "in anger"   prepositional phrase
> **A'**   "they bear animosity"   *yiqtol* verb

In the final analysis, "harm" (metaphorically described as "rushing wind" and "tempest," 55:8b) is what is causing the psalmist's pain, and that agony propels the entire composition.[4]

Petition and Pain: Friend (55:9–15)

Petition and pain continue in the second section, but with greater specificity. The plea (55:9) is that God would confuse and divide the speech of the evildoers to destroy their opposition—likely an allusion to what happened at Babel.[5] And like that evil city of yore, this one, wherein dwell the wicked, is equally vile: it is marked by "violence," "strife" (55:9b), "harm," "trouble" (55:10b), "destruction," "oppression," and "deceit" (55:11)—and all this happens "day and night" (55:10a)! The evildoers are apparently patrolling the city's walls (55:10a[6])—fortifications intended for protection but that have now become a base-station for ill and impiety. These malevolents were pushing "harm" upon the psalmist (55:3c), and probably not just against him, for "harm" was within this city incessantly (55:10b). Again, it is not surprising that the psalmist wanted to escape this infernal realm (55:6–8).

Then comes the twist: here the enemy is not a collection of foes but a friend—an unbearable situation indeed (55:12). One who was the psalmist's peer, comrade, and friend

---

4. "Fear and trembling" in 55:5a is a hendiadys, thus it takes a singular verb, יָבֹא, *yavo'*, "it comes."
5. The reason for this petition is given in the subsequent verses (55:9b–11, introduced with "for").
6. "They go around" (55:10a) likely refers to the perpetrators of harm circumambulating their town seeking out trouble.

(55:13[7]), with whom he had worshiped God with other devotees (55:14)—that was the very person now betraying the poet, "exalting himself over me" (55:12c). The plaint switches back to plural with an imprecation, as the psalmist wishes "death" to them (55:15) who had, in the first place, put him through the throes of the terrors of "death" (55:4b). This lethality would be a tit-for-tat reimbursement.

Notice the chain of events: The psalmist's heart was quaking "within me" (55:4a), because harm and trouble and destruction were "within her," the city (55:10b, 11a), for evil was "within them," in these malefactors who made their home in evil (55:15c). They deserved divine punishment.

Peace, but Relapse of Pain: Friend (55:16–21)

After two rounds of petition prompted by pain, dealing with the assaults from both foe and friend, the psalm takes a more confident turn. There is no explicit petition in this section—though the intent to call upon God and to lament is noted (55:16a, 17). Instead, there is the confidence of soon-coming "peace" (55:18a), for the psalmist is assured of God's deliverance. The "answer" (from ענה, ʿnh; 55:2a) that the psalmist was hoping for, he is sure will be forthcoming, for God will "thwart" (also ענה; 55:19a) all those executives of evil. Indeed, the psalmist had "complained" and he had been "agitated" from the "voice" of those enemies (55:2b–3a); he still "complains" and is still "agitated" (55:17b), but there is now a certainty that *his* "voice" (not the "voice" of the enemy; 55:3a) will be heard and acted on by God (55:17b):

55:2a	"answer" (ענה) from God
	"… in my complaint"
55:2b–3a	"I am agitated"
	"the *voice* of the enemy"
	"I complain"
55:17b	"I am agitated"
	"He hears my *voice*"
55:19a	"thwarting" (ענה) by God

Both lines of 55:16 have fronted subjects, "I" and "Yahweh," emphasizing the intensity of the psalmist's desperate call to God, and Yahweh as the exclusive source of deliverance, respectively. God, the poet is sure, will "hear" (55:17b, 19a); indeed, פָּדָה, *padah*, is in the perfect (*qatal*), the perfect of certainty, so to speak: "he *will* redeem" (55:18a). And thus the psalmist, who was in "fear" (55:5a), will see the defeat of foes for whom there is no "fear" of God (55:19d).[8] All this because God is King, "the One who sits [enthroned] of old" (55:19b), and this heavenly ruler of the cosmos, Yahweh, is faithful to his people and redeems them (55:18–19a).

But then, a note of uncertainty creeps in, the relapse of pain, as it were, as the psalmist switches back to a singular and familiar foe in 55:20–21—the so-called friend of 55:12–14. This one is described further as a violent betrayer of those who were at "peace" with him

---

7. This verse is verbless, except for a closing participle acting as a noun—the psalmist is literally stunned!
8. These non-God-fearers and those who do not change or learn wisdom and desist from evil (55:19cd) are, no doubt, the psalmist's opponents.

(55:20a)—perhaps it was the mention of divine redemption from battle into "peace" (55:18a) that reminded the psalmist of this treachery. That double-crossing, false-hearted "friend" was a violator of "covenant" (55:20b—likely a personal and implicit alliance of some sort, "a metaphor for a relationship that involved mutual commitment," rather than a formal compact[9]). Still hemorrhaging from this stab in the back, the pain of which has now recurred, the psalmist continues his description of the perfidious one in 55:21, with a series of words and phrases that are verbless.[10] The psalmist's "heart" was quaking with the onslaught of foes (55:4a), but Benedict Arnold's "heart" was only battle-craving (55:21b), his "mouth" producing drawn swords camouflaged in soft, smooth, and unctuous words (55:21a, 21cd). That is enough to create a horrible relapse of agony for anyone!

Peace and Remission of Pain: Foes (55:22–23)

But the psalmist's trust in God wins out and consolidates the peace that was first glimpsed in the previous section. So much so, from his own experience, he can now exhort his community to place their burdens confidently upon their sustainer, Yahweh (55:22a). Whereas the wicked had "pushed" harm upon the psalmist (מוֹט; 55:3bc), now the latter is safe in God's hands, for this deity will never permit the righteous to be "shaken" ever (also מוֹט; 55:22b). The psalmist had earlier wistfully asked who would "give" him wings to escape his torment (נתן, ntn; 55:6). Here it looks as though he has got his wish, for God "will not forever *allow* [also נתן]" him to be dislodged into instability (55:22b).

But the psalmist has to return one last time to his foes: in an emphatic utterance with the redundant second-person pronoun and אֱלֹהִים, 'elohim—"But You, God"—he proclaims the doom of the evildoers: they "will not [live out] half their *days* [יוֹם, *yom*]" (55:23ab), these malefactors who "*day* [יוֹם] and night" had been causing harm and trouble (55:10).[11] In 55:15b it appeared that they were "going down [ירד, *yrd*]" to Sheol as the natural consequence of their own wickedness; but here in 55:23a, it is made clear that God has a role, perhaps even a primary one: He "brings . . . down [ירד]" these nefarious ones into the "hole of destruction."

The components of 55:12–15 and 55:20–23 are precisely parallel:[12]

55:12–14	False friend
55:15bα	"may they [foes] go down to Sheol"
55:15bβ	"alive"
55:20–21	False friend
55:23a	"You will bring them [foes] down to the hole"
55:23b	"not [live out] half their days"

---

9. Goldingay, *Psalms*, 2:176.

10. As also in 55:13. The verbs "was" and "were" in 55:21 were added in translation.

11. That the singular foe (the masquerading "friend") is being equated to the plural foes is clear in the employment of the same term for each: אֱנוֹשׁ, *'enosh*, "man," for the former (55:13a), and אַנְשֵׁי, *'anshe*, "men/people," for the latter (55:23b).

12. From Kselman and Barré, "Psalm 55," 444.

In all likelihood, this indicates that the psalmist's pain is still present, though considerably ameliorated by his confidence in God; in other words, deliverance, though nigh, is yet to be accomplished. But no worries for the psalmist: "I—I will trust in You" (55:23c).[13]

> This psalm eloquently reflects the emotional roller coaster of one in pain. The twists and turns allow the audience to enter into that emotional territory. Its feeling of besiegement from within and without is one everyone has unfortunately experienced. Yet within the midst of being surrounded on all sides, the oasis is not found in that wished-for wilderness lodge, but in the confidence and security that the one suffering has God to deliver and to save. In that sense, it is both a prayer for help and a psalm of trust.... Thousands of years later, we can still relate to the roller-coaster emotions of betrayal and fear and know, as this prayer claims, that we too can call upon *God, the one enthroned from old*, to come to our aid.[14]

He will!

Sermon Map

I. Pain: Foes and "Friend"
    Attacks (55:3, 9–14, 19c–21)
    Effect on the victim (55:1–8)
    Move-to-relevance: Battles and betrayals in our lives

II. Peace
    Deliverance (55:16–18)
    Defeat of foes and "friend" (55:15, 19bcd; 23ab)
    Move-to-relevance: God's work on our behalf

III. *Terror, but Trust!*
    Attitude of trust (55:22, 23c)
    Specifics on confidence casting of burdens upon God

---

13. The emphatic first-person pronoun fronting the line is similar to that in 55:16a.
14. deClaissé-Walford et al., *Book of Psalms*, 479 (italics original).

PSALM 56:1–13

Psalm of Disorientation

Promises of Protection Evoke Praise

PSALM 56, LIKE ITS preceding psalm, is also one of prayer, addressing God throughout.

Translation

56:1 Be gracious to me, God, for a mortal has hounded me;
       all day the one who fights has oppressed me.

56:2 My watchful foes have hounded me all day,
       for they are many who fight against me on high.

56:3 [On the] day when I am afraid,
       I—in You I will trust.

56:4 In God—I praise His word—
       in God I have trusted;
  I shall not be afraid:
       what can flesh do to me?

56:5 All day they find fault with my words;
       against me all their intentions are for evil.

56:6 They stalk, they lurk,
       they—my heels they watch,
       as they hope for my soul.

56:7 Because of [their] harmfulness, there is no salvation for them.
       In anger bring down the peoples, God.

56:8 My wanderings You—You have recorded.
       Put my tear[s] in Your flask—
       are [they] not in Your record?

56:9 Then my enemies will turn back [from me] in the day I call;
       this I know, that God is for me.

56:10 In God—I praise [His] word;
        in Yahweh—I praise [His] word.
56:11 In God I have trusted,
        I shall not be afraid:
        what can a human do to me?
56:12 Upon me, God, [are] Your vows;
        I will fulfill [my] thank offerings to You.
56:13 For You have rescued my soul from death.
        Haven't [You kept] my feet from stumbling
    [so as] to keep [me] walking before the face of God
        in the light of the living?

Structure

The poem has two parallel stanzas, 56:1–4 and 56:5–11, each with a plaint and a plea (but not in the same sequence), and an almost identical statement of praise and trust in God (56:3–4 and 56:10–11). A final stanza concludes the psalm with a strong word of confidence in the deliverance anticipated (56:12–13).

> STANZA 1 (56:1–4)
>   *Plea* (**56:1a**): "God" (vocative, 56:1a)
>   *Plaint* (**56:1b–2**): "all day" (56:1b, 2a)
>   *Praise* (**56:3–4**)
>
> STANZA 2 (56:5–11)
>   *Plaint* (**56:5–6**): "all day" (56:5a)
>   *Plea* (**56:7–8**): "God" (vocative, 56:7b)
>   *Praise* (**56:9–11**)
>
> STANZA 3 (56:12–13)
>   *Promise* (**56:12**)
>   *Praise* (**56:13**)

The alternation between plea, plaint, and praise in *Stanza 1* and *Stanza 2* reflects the realistic nature of life that is filled with inimical elements that cause humanity to plead to God, to complain about its foes, and then to praise God for his deliverance.

There is a clear movement as one traverses the psalm. In *Stanza 1*, 56:1–4, the plea and plaint are quite intense, and the threat to the psalmist immediate and fearsome. In *Stanza 2*, 56:5–11, there is considerably less angst and far more assurance, with the plea almost turning into praise. In *Stanza 3*, 56:12–13, there is only unalloyed confidence and trust (no plea or plaint). Indeed, this faith in God's deliverance tacitly undergirds the psalm as suggested by the four rhetorical questions the psalmist poses (and their implied answers; below):

	Question	Answer
56:4d	"What can flesh do to me?" מַה־יַּעֲשֶׂה בָשָׂר לִי; *mah-yaʿaseh basar li*	*Nothing!*
56:8bc	"My tear[s] ... —are [they] not [הֲלֹא, *halo'*] in your record?"	*Of course!*
56:11c	"What can a human do to me?" מַה־יַּעֲשֶׂה אָדָם לִי; *mah-yaʿaseh 'adam li*	*Nothing!*
56:13bcd	"Haven't [הֲלֹא] [you kept] my feet from stumbling ...?"	*Of course!*

Theological Focus

Despite the incessant violence that the many wicked unleash upon the righteous, filling them with dread, the latter trust in God's promise of their protection, his remembrance of their woes, and his defeat of their enemies—mere mortals—as God keeps them in his presence, thus evoking their grateful praise.

Commentary

Stanza 1: Plea, Plaint, Praise (56:1–4)

The plea takes only one line in *Stanza 1*, 56:1a; the rest is balanced between plaint (56:1b–2) and praise (56:3–4). Clearly, as in previous psalms of this nature, the psalmist is in major trouble: he is "hounded" (56:1a, 2a) and "oppressed" (56:1b) and is being "fought" against (56:1b, 2b)—"all day" (56:1b, 2a, and later 56:5a), an unceasing "day" of fear (56:3a)—and that not only by "watchful foes" located "on high" (56:2),[1] but also by "a mortal" (אֱנוֹשׁ, *'enosh*; 56:1a). That latter appellation reminds readers of "the fundamental nature of enemies, who belong to the human realm of things and who will not prevail against God. They are 'man' and not God," only "flesh," only "human," and no match for deity (56:1a, 4d, 11c).[2]

One can see a structure in 56:1–4 that centers upon the psalmist's confident praise of God's word (below).[3]

---

1. "On high" refers to the self-exaltation of these foes; thus they are proud, conceited, and arrogant (see the parallelism in Ps 75:5 that links "on high" with a symbol of insolent pride; also see 73:8).
2. Tate, *Psalms 51–100*, 69.
3. See Auffret, *Voyez de vos yeux*, 36.

```
A    "a mortal ..., many ... against me [לִי, lî]" (56:1a, 2b)
  B    "when I am afraid" (56:3a)
    C    "I will trust" (56:3b)
      D    "in God" (56:4aα)
        E    "I praise His word" (56:4aβ)
      D'   "in God" (56:4bα)
    C'   "I have trusted" (56:4bβ)
  B'   "I shall not be afraid" (56:4c)
A'   "flesh ... to me [לִי]" (56:4d)
```

That "word" of God (56:4a, 10a, 10b) is likely a reference to one or more divine promises previously made, either directly or indirectly through the psalmist himself, as in the previous psalm (55:22 is a promise there that the psalmist vouchsafes).[4] "The one praying trusts that God is as good as the promises God makes . . . To praise God's word is to praise the very attribute that the one praying is depending on for his deliverance"—indeed, it is to praise God himself!⁵

Yet, there is no doubt that the psalmist's fear does coexist with his expressed trust: fear and trust are juxtaposed thrice in the psalm (56:3ab, 4bc, 11ab), almost to the point of contradiction: "When I am afraid [because of humans, 56:3a] . . . I shall not be afraid [because of God, 56:4c]."[6] The fact is that "trust does not bring an end to fear, but it makes it possible to live with fear."[7] So much so, 56:4 is essentially repeated in 56:10–11, almost serving as the "praise chorus" of the psalm.

Stanza 2: Plaint, Plea, Praise (56:5–11)

As was also the case with Psalm 55, this psalm cycles through pain once again, even after an expression of faith in God and an assertion of fearlessness (56:3–4): real life writ large and true. Indeed, in *Stanza 2*, the plaint comes first (56:5–6), followed by the plea (56:7–8), before returning to the solidity of trusting praise (56:9–11).[8]

Once again, the psalmist describes the opposition as being incessant, "all day" (56:5a; as in 56:1b, 2a). Besides, "all" of those days are filled with "*all* their intentions . . . for evil" directed against him (56:5b), dedicated as these predators are to "harmfulness" (56:7a). They are Machiavellian: intending only "evil" (56:5b), they "stalk," they "lurk," they "watch," and they "hope" to get rid of the righteous (56:6). Earlier the psalmist had emphatically asserted his faith with a fronted first-person pronoun, "I—in You I will trust" (56:3b); here he is equally emphatic about the rapacity of his adversaries, this time with a fronted third-person

---

4. All of Scripture and its promises would serve as the divine "word" in the current age, of course.

5. deClaissé-Walford et al., *Book of Psalms*, 484 (italics removed). This is the only psalm that explicitly praises God's word.

6. "The human beings are, after all, only flesh . . . Their real though limited capacity to do harm has set against it God's unlimited capacity to restrain them. All that is needed is for God actually to be gracious [56:1a]" and take action (Goldingay, *Psalms*, 2:185).

7. Goldingay, *Psalms*, 2:185.

8. Similarities between the plaint and pleas of the first two stanzas of the psalm were noted in the structure above.

pronoun: "They—my heels they watch," as they "hope" for his soul," i.e., for his life, nay, for his death (56:6bc)!

Notice the wordplay: the psalmist's foes find fault with his "words" (56:5), but that suffering one only praises God's "word" (56:4a); perhaps it is his human words of praise of the divine word that the enemies object to. In any case, the evil and harmfulness of these malefactors will only bear fruit lethal: "there is no salvation for them" (56:7a[9]), i.e., God's destruction of them is going to happen, in his wrath he is going to "bring [them] down" (56:7b). What had begun with "a mortal" and "the one who fights"—a single individual (56:1)—had grown into a group of "foes" who are "many" (56:2). But now in 56:7b, they are whole "peoples"—organized institutions of evildoing, afflicting the righteous, the community of God.

The grounds for asking for terminal punishment for evildoers (56:7) is stated in 56:8: divine remembrance of the harm done to the righteous sufferer. The confidence in divine compassion is evident in the parallelism and paronomasia of that verse:

> "my *wanderings*" (נֹד, *nod*)
> "You ... *recorded*" (סָפַר, *sphr*)
> "my tear[s] in Your *flask*" (נֹאד, *no'd*)
> "Your *record*" (סִפְרָה, *siphrah*)

The answer to the psalmist's rhetorical question, "Does God not remember?" is "Of course, he does." "God is the great rememberer who treasures pain so that the psalmist is free to move beyond that pain."[10] And so the supplicant continues in praise: Because God *does* remember, the enemies' fate is sealed—they will be routed (56:9a). At the beginning of the psalm, the "day" was one of fear (56:3a); now it has become one of faith, for on the "day" the psalmist calls, God defeats his foes (56:9a).[11] So he confesses that "God is for me" (56:9b), a personal, compassionate, powerful deity, working on behalf of his people on the day of their need. Because God is "for me" (לִי; 56:9b), the foes—those who were "against me" (again לִי; 56:2b)—are only humans who can do nothing "to me" (also לִי; 56:11c).

With that we arrive at the chiastically arranged praise of *Stanza 2* (54:9–11) that includes the refrain; as with the structure of 56:1–4 (see above), this, too, is focused upon praise for the divine word (see below).[12]

---

9. As the text stands, it reads, "because of harmfulness, salvation for them." It is quite likely that the negative particle אֵין, *'yn* ("there is no"), resembling the next word אָוֶן, *'wn* ("harmfulness"), was left out by a copyist. The translation restores it.

10. Brueggemann and Bellinger, *Psalms*, 254.

11. Thus far all the "days" mentioned in Psalm 56 were periods of terror (56:1b, 2a, 3a, 5a), but now in 56:9a, the "day" of the psalmist's calling upon God is one of rejoicing!

12. The two verses, 56:10–11, are identical to 56:4, the first "refrain," except for the addition of 56:10b, and the change from "flesh" in 56:4d to "human" in 56:11c.

> **A** "enemies will turn back" (56:9aα)
>> **B** "in the day I call" (56:9β)
>>> **C** "I know" (56:9bα)
>>>> **D** "God is for me" (56:9bβ)
>>>>> **E** **"I praise [His] word"** (×2; 56:10a, 10b)
>>>> **D'** "in God" (56:11aα)
>>> **C'** "I have trusted" (56:11aβ)
>> **B'** "I shall not be afraid" (56:11b)
> **A'** "what can a human do to me" (56:11c)

Stanza 3: Promise, Praise (56:12–13)

And after this chorus of praise, the psalm ends, with fear dispelled, enemies dispatched, and pleas disburdened—begone plaint! It is all thankful promise and exuberant praise now. The psalmist anticipates fulfilling his vows, ostensibly made in response to the divine "word" of promise (56:4a, 10a, 10b)—human promise of thanksgiving for the divine promise of safekeeping.[13] That this vow is in the future indicates that God's deliverance also is still to be accomplished, despite the perfect verb, "You have rescued" (56:13a)—the perfect of certainty, no doubt.

Once enemies were "stalking," "lurking," "watching" the "heels" of their prey, and "hoping" for his demise (56:6), causing him to "wander" (56:8a)—several of the verbs related to ambulation—but here, by the grace of God, the "feet" of the righteous are kept from "stumbling," enabling them to "walk" before the "face" and presence of God (56:13bc). Foes used to wait, hoping for the extermination of the supplicant's "soul" (56:6c), but God would rescue his "soul" (56:13a). These enemies, therefore, have "no salvation" (56:7a), but God's people see his "face" (56:13c), rescued as they are from "death" (56:13a) and brought into the "light of the living" (56:13d). Indeed, the psalm concludes by issuing a rhetorical question (56:13bcd) that implies a confident response: "Of course, God *has* kept his people safe and delivered them into the fullness of life!"

Sermon Map

I. Assault of Foes

　　Violence of oppression; fear of the oppression (56:1b–3a, 5–7a)

　　Move-to-relevance: Fear of oppression

II. Affirmation of Faith

　　God's promise and the righteous' praise (56:3b–4, 8–11)

　　Righteous' gratitude and praise for God's deliverance (56:12–13)

　　Move-to-relevance: God's work on our behalf

III. *Trust and Thank!*

　　Specifics on confidence and thanksgiving amidst the fear of oppression

---

13. For similar offerings as tokens of gratitude for deliverance, see Pss 7:17; 22:25; 50:14; 54:6–7; 61:8; 66:13–15; 69:30–31; 107:22; 116:14–18.

PSALM 57:1–11

Psalm of Disorientation

Exaltation for Liberation

LIKE PSALM 56, THIS one, too, is set in the context of lethal persecution from foes. The two psalms even share vocabulary: their opening lines have "be gracious to me, God, [. . .] for . . ." (56:1a and 57:1ab); the employment of the unusual verb "hound" (56:1a, 2a and 57:3b); and the pattern of a repeated refrain (56:4, 10–11 and 57:5, 11). But Psalm 57 is far more triumphant in tone than the one preceding, with a confident declaration of trust in deity's deliverance. In eleven verses of this psalm, God is referred to twenty-one times, by noun, pronoun, or pronominal suffix; and the domain wherefrom he operates, "heavens," is noted four times (57:3a, 5a, 10a, 11a). All of that underscores divine power and the resources available for the righteous, as well as the substantiality of their hope in divine deliverance.

Translation

57:1   Be gracious to me, God, be gracious to me,
           for in You my soul takes refuge;
        and in the shadow of Your wings I will take refuge
           until destruction passes by.
57:2   I cry to God Most High,
           to God who requites [the enemy] for me.
57:3   He will send from the heavens and deliver me;
           He confuses the one who hounds me.
        God will send His lovingkindness and His truth.
57:4   My soul is in the midst of lions;
           I will lie down [among] those humans who devour—
        their teeth a spear and arrows,
           and their tongue a sharp sword.
57:5   Be exalted above the heavens, God;
           above all the earth, Your glory.

57:6   A net they set for my steps;
             my soul was bowed down.
         They dug for my face a pit;
             they fell into the midst of it.
57:7   My heart is set, God, my heart is set.
             I will sing, I will make music.
57:8   Awake, my inner being; awake, harp and lyre;
             I will awaken the dawn.
57:9   I will give You thanks among the peoples, Lord;
             I will make music to You among the populace.
57:10 For great unto the heavens is Your lovingkindness,
             and unto the clouds, Your truth.
57:11 Be exalted above the heavens, God;
             above all the earth, Your glory.

Structure

Psalm 57 can be divided into two stanzas (57:1–5, 6–11), each with slightly different ordering of motifs, but ending with an identical refrain (57:5, 11):

STANZA 1 (57:1–5)
57:1–3	Petition to God; Protection by God
57:4	Persecution of foes; Protection from foes
57:5	Praise to God (refrain)

STANZA 2 (57:6–11)
57:6	Persecution of foes; Perishing of foes
57:7–10	Proclamation of God
57:11	Praise to God (refrain)

The psalm describes the past and present "destruction" by the wicked (57:1d), as well as the future and anticipated "deliverance" by God (57:3a).

> The certainty of God's act means a kind of collapse of chronology. Events that are literally future cease to be purely future because they are actual in the life of God. And because they are actual in the life of God, they are actual in the life of the suppliant. They mean that the suppliant's heart can be ready even now to glorify God before the people of God, the world, and the attackers.[1]

In other words, the future is as certain as the past!

---

1. Goldingay, *Psalms*, 2:200.

Theological Focus

The lovingkindness and truth of God, the manifestation of his graciousness and commitment, provide refuge for his oppressed people and establish their hearts in the midst of lethal danger, while also requiting their foes, thus prompting enthusiastic proclamation of him by the community of God to all people as he is exalted globally and cosmically.

Commentary

Stanza 1 (57:1–5)

The predation by the wicked of God's people, "destruction," is personified in 57:1d as a rampant and devastating pestilence or tempest that sweeps by (see 91:3). The righteous psalmist therefore requests God to be "gracious to me" (×2; 57:1a), that he might "take refuge" (57:1b, 1c) in God.[2] The first instance of the latter verb is in the perfect, perhaps the start of the sufferer's finding a sanctuary; the second is in the imperfect, perhaps indicating a continuance of this asylum until the disaster abates. At any rate, "instead of running from the arms of the enemy as many prayers of help express, here the one praying is running toward God . . . , where this one will be and remain safe."[3]

Though 57:2–3 seems to be talking about deity in the third person, it is still likely to be addressing God who is intended to overhear these words as a confident plea for protection. This God Most High, the psalmist is sure, will "send" deliverance from heaven, the ultimate source of all redemption (57:3a); and he will also "send" his "lovingkindness" and "truth" (57:3c)[4]—the manifestation of his graciousness (57:1a) and commitment to his own.

The verbs in the first three verses (57:1–3: petition to God; protection by God) sequentially show the direction of the actions taken by the protagonists (or appealed for by them): the psalmist's petition to God to act towards him (God → Psalmist; 57:1a, 3: being gracious, sending and delivering, confusing the oppressors, sending grace and truth) bounding, within, the assertion of action by the psalmist himself towards God (Psalmist → God; 57:1b, 2:[5] taking refuge, crying to God the enemy requiter). At the center is the supplicant's sustenance in that state of calm, taking refuge until the chaos blows over (57:1cd). Thus is the psalmist ensconced in safety, his haven in God whose graciousness and deliverance literally surround him:[6]

---

2. Refuge in the wings of God is a frequent metaphor in the psalms (Pss 17:8; 36:7; 57:1; 61:4; 63:7; 91:4), no doubt originating with the redemption during the exodus (Exod 19:4; Deut 32:11). It could also refer to the sanctuary, near the altar, the locus of the wings of the cherubim (Exod 25:20; 37:9; 1 Kgs 6:23–28; 8:6–7), where refuge was sought in the presence of God (Pss 80:1; 99:1; and elsewhere: 1 Sam 4:4; 2 Sam 6:2; 2 Kgs 19:15; Isa 37:16).

3. deClaissé-Walford et al., *Book of Psalms*, 488.

4. This pair of divine attributes, lovingkindness and truth, will be encountered again in 57:10. In the OT, they are most frequently seen together in the Psalter: 25:10; 26:3; 40:10, 11; 57:3, 10; 61:7; 69:13; 85:10; 86:15; 89:14; 108:4; 115:1; 117:2; 138:2.

5. The requital of enemies is expressed as a participle that serves as a description of the "God Most High"; thus it still fits the direction Psalmist → God, the enemy requiter.

6. See Auffret, "Note sur la structure," 69.

57:1a	God → Psalmist
57:1b	Psalmist → God
57:1cd	**Refuge in God**
57:2	Psalmist → God
57:3	God → Psalmist

Of the five instances of the verb שׁכב, *shkv*, "lie down," in the Psalms, only three are in the first person; of the three, 3:5 and 4:8 indicate a state of comfort, safety, and peace in the presence of God. It is therefore likely that this third occurrence of שׁכב in the first person (here in 57:4b) also denotes the rest of one taking refuge in God, particularly considering the momentum of Psalm 57. So while the threat of chaos has not diminished in 57:4—in fact, it sounds more personal and ferocious now, with devouring beasts whose teeth and tongues are weapons of liquidation (57:4cd)—the psalmist is able to relax, for God and God's lovingkindness and truth are with him. Indeed, though enemies are armed with the "sword" (חֶרֶב, *cherev*; 57:4d), God will accomplish their defeat by "confusing" (חֵרֵף, *chereph*; 57:3b) them. The petitioner's "soul" may be in the midst of lions and devouring humans (57:4ab), but in God his "soul" finds refuge (57:1b, 1c). Therefore the besieged one who has now become the becalmed one can praise God in the refrain of 57:5: "Be exalted . . ."[7]

Stanza 2 (57:6–11)

Persecution is not over, but *Stanza 2* moves rapidly to a confident close.[8] The psalmist's "soul" is said to have been "bowed down," as foes attempted to trap him (57:6ab). But in a remarkable coup, orchestrated by God, no doubt,[9] these wicked adversaries fell into the pit they had dug for the righteous sufferer (57:6cd).[10] Indeed, the supplicant was "in the midst" of lions once (57:4a); but now it is these malefactors who have fallen "into the midst" of the pothole they had created for their prey (57:6d).[11] No longer is the righteous "bowed down" (57:6b); instead, it is the wicked who have "fallen" (57:6d). The latter may have "set" nets for the former's steps (57:6a), but it will be the heart of the righteous that will be "set" (×2; 57:7a), steadfast and unshakable. And all because of God; so he deserves the praise.

And the psalmist gets ready to do just that. He decides to sing and make music (57:7b) and, in preparation, he awakes his inner being[12] and his musical instruments. Even the sun

---

7. The call to God to be "exalted" frequently accompanies the anticipated defeat of enemies (or of chaos) in the Psalms (18:46–47; 21:12–13; 30:1; 34:3–4; 46:9–10; 61:2–3; 89:13; 108:5–6; 118:15–16; 138:4–6). Therefore 57:5 might well be a request that God exalt himself by defeating enemies/chaos.

8. Psalm 57:7–11 is similar to 108:1–5, with only minor differences.

9. Perhaps signified in the wordplay: "bowed down" is כָּפַף, *kphph*, a rare verb used only five times in the OT, three of which are in the Psalms; and the "wings" of God in which refuge is found is כָּנָף, *knph* (57:1c). Divine pinions prevent the prostration of the petitioner by persecution!

10. The "pit" for the psalmist's "face" (57:6c) must have been intended for him to fall *face* down into it. Of course, that a reprisal for enemies would occur at God's hands was already anticipated in 57:2b.

11. The imperfects of *Stanza 1* are now replaced by perfects in 57:6: they are either perfects of certainty, future events so guaranteed to happen that they are described in the past, or "instantaneous qatals [perfects], describing something that is in the midst of happening" (Goldingay, *Psalms*, 2:197).

12. "Inner being" is literally "my liver" (amending the text's כְּבוֹדִי, *kvodi*, to כְּבֵדִי, *kvedi*, as in Pss 16:9; 30:12).

is summoned to the festivities—"I will awaken the dawn!" (57:8[13]). That "awake" shows up three times in 57:8 indicates the eagerness and enthusiasm of the psalmist to engage in praise. The celebratory party appears to include the "peoples" and the "populace" (57:9); whether these folks without the community of God have been persuaded to join in worship or are being taunted by the thanksgiving of those they were preying on is unclear. That it might be the latter is suggested by another wordplay: "lions" in 57:4a is לְבָאִם, lva'im; "among the populace" in 57:9ba is a similar sounding phrase, בַּל־אֻמִּים, bal-'ummim. Perhaps the lions were, indeed, constituted by that populace.

In any case, God is being proclaimed globally. The reason is straightforward: magnificent across the breadth of the heavens is his "lovingkindness," and his "truth" to height of the clouds (57:10). And so the psalm arrives at its end with the very words that it began: God was beseeched to send his "lovingkindness" and his "truth" from the "heavens" (57:3a, 3c). He has done so (or soon will). Therefore, God is to be—he *must be*—exalted everywhere, even above the "heavens" (57:11).[14] And he is!

Sermon Map

I. Foes and Faithful
    The predators: aggressive (57:1d, 3bβ, 4a, 4cd, 6a, 6c)
    The persecuted: alarmed (57:1a, 2a, 6bc)
    Move-to-relevance: Oppression in our lives

II. Fates of Foes and Faithful
    Foes: defeated (2b, 3bα, 6d)
    Faithful: delivered and devoted (57:1bc, 3a, 3c, 4b; and 57:5, 7–11)
    Move-to-relevance: God's work on our behalf

III. *Proclaim the Protector!*
    Specifics on confident proclamation

---

13. Another wordplay: "I will sing" is אָשִׁירָה, '*ashirah*, in 57:7b; "I will awaken" is אָעִירָה, *a'irah*, in 57:8b.

14. The last verse, 57:11, is identical to 57:5, except that "heavens" is inarticular in the former (even though the translation of that verse has the article).

PSALM 58:1–11

Psalm of Disorientation

Wicked Judged

PSALM 58 ADDRESSES NOT the issue of the wicked assaulting the righteous, but of the corrupt not judging in their favor. These latter thus become the evil operators in this psalm.

Translation

58:1   Do you, rulers, really speak righteousness?
          Do you equitably judge humans?
58:2   No. In the heart you do injustice;
          on earth you deal out the violence of your hands.
58:3   The wicked are estranged from the womb;
          they go astray from birth who speak lies.
58:4   There is venom to them in the form of the venom of a serpent,
          like [that of] a deaf cobra, stopping up its ear,
58:5   which does not hear the voice of charmers
          [or] the expert conjurer of spells.
58:6   God, break their tooth in their mouth;
          the jaws of the young lions smash, Yahweh.
58:7   Let them vanish like water that flows away on its own—
          he aims his arrows—like [ones that] wither;
58:8   like a snail that melts away as it goes,
          [like] the miscarriage of a woman that never beholds the sun.
58:9   Before they sense the thorns, He will strike them [with] a bramble
          when alive, when burning anger sweeps him away.
58:10 The righteous will rejoice when he beholds the requital;
          his feet he will wash in the blood of the wicked.
58:11 And mankind will say, "Indeed, there is fruit for the righteous;
          indeed, there is a God who judges on earth."

Structure

The composition is carefully structured, centering upon a cry to God to destroy these powerful but pernicious rulers. The psalm ends, not unexpectedly, with a celebration by the righteous of their God, the true Judge.

A	58:1–2	**Condemnation** אֵלִם, *'elim*; "righteousness"; "speak" (58:1a) בְּנֵי אָדָם, *bne 'adam*, "humans"; "judge" (58:1b) "on earth"; "hands" (58:2b)
B	58:3–5	**Corrupt**: their features Birth-related image (58:3a); "like" (כְּמוֹ, *kmo*; 58:4b)
C	58:6	**Cry** (God in the second person)
B'	58:7–9	**Corrupt**: their fate Birth-related image (58:8b); "like" (כְּמוֹ, 58:7a, 7b, 8a)
A'	58:10–11	**Celebration** אֱלֹהִים, *'elohim* (58:11b); "righteous" (58:10a, 11a); "say" (58:11a) אָדָם, "mankind" (58:11a); "judges" (58:11b) "on earth" (58:11b); "feet" (58:10b)

Theological Focus

The unrighteous and unjust dealings of those in power results in uncontrollable wickedness, falsehood, and violence heaped upon the righteous, who therefore seek refuge in God in prayer, confident in his power to comprehensively overthrow such evildoers and reward his people, for their God is the true judge on earth.

Commentary

Condemnation; Corrupt (58:1–5)

At the outset, rulers are directly condemned for *not* speaking in "righteousness" and *not* judging humans "equitably" (58:1).[1] Instead, they commit "injustice" and deal in "violence" against humanity (58:2).[2] The assonance is palpable in 58:1–2: "you speak" is תְּדַבֵּרוּן, *tidabberun* (58:1a); "you do" is תִּפְעָלוּן, *tiph'alun* (58:2a); and "you deal out" is תְּפַלֵּסוּן, *tphallesun* (58:2b), compounding the intensity of these assaults. "In the heart" and "on earth," i.e., both in their

---

1. In my translation, the MT's אֵלֶם, *'elem* ("silence") is emended to אֵלִם, *'elim* ("rulers," a form of the plene אֵילִים, *'elim*).
2. The theme of the failure of the powerful to execute justice for the weak is a frequent one in prophetic literature: see Isa 1:23–24; 5:23; 10:1–4; Mic 3:11; Jer 5:26–29. Seneca the Younger, in *Trojan Women*, II, 291, has Agamemnon say: "He who does not forbid wrongdoing, when he has the power, commands it" (*Tragedies*, 166–67). These are as culpable as the ones who perpetrate evil.

inner thoughts and deliberations, and in their outer expressions and actions, they were characterized by unrighteousness, inequity, injustice, and violence (58:2).

There appears to be a transition in 58:3, switching from the direct address to the "rulers" in the second person in 58:1–2, to a third-person description of the corrupt wicked in 58:3–5. That it is those same rulers and judges who are now referred to as the "wicked" in 58:3–5 is obvious. Besides, the verb דבר, *dvr* ("speak") is used of both the rulers and the wicked (58:1a, 3b).[3] So, after addressing these profane potentates directly in 58:1–2, their characteristics are delineated in 58:3–5. With a rhetorical flourish, the psalmist accuses these people in places of power of going astray even *in utero* (58:3).[4] They are even likened to venomous cobras (58:4).[5] The lethality of these reptiles is multiplied by their deafness and the inability of their keepers to keep them in check (58:5). All that to say, their evil was inimical and uncontrollable. A number of repetitions of words and notions further emphasize the danger those wicked rulers posed to the rest of the populace: "venom" (×2; 58:4a); "serpent" and "cobra" (58:4a, 4b); "deaf," "stopping up its ear," and "does not hear the voice" (58:4b, 5a); and "charmers," "expert," and "conjurer" (58:5a, 5b). When those in positions of dominance fail to discharge their duties righteously, everyone is in deep trouble.

Cry; Corrupt (58:6–9)

The suffering righteous—and these are the ones who are subjugated under whims of the unjust powerful—can do nothing but seek refuge in their God. So they beseech deity to act (58:6), but their pleas appear to be concentrating on the demolition of the teeth, mouth, and jaws of their oppressors (58:7). No doubt, these (body) parts stand for the whole, especially in light of the wicked being equated to lions, powerful in canine and mandible. But the notation of the rulers "speaking" in 58:1a and 58:3b is surely pertinent here. It is likely that the injustices perpetrated by these wicked were altogether in the verbal arena, in decrees enacted, in accusations leveled, in judgments delivered. But after God has operated on their mouthparts, these vile ones will speak no more! Those serpentine evildoers, to whom everything else seemed silent, deaf as they were (58:4–5), will now themselves be rendered silent in an act of chastisement and discipline from God (see below). The plea in 58:6 is carefully structured (centered on organs of speech), beginning and ending with a call to God in the vocative.

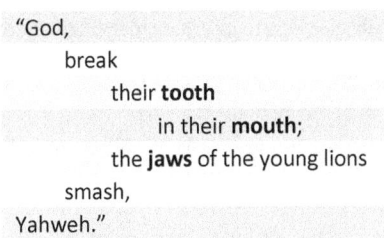

"God,
> break
>> their **tooth**
>>> in their **mouth**;
>>> the **jaws** of the young lions
>> smash,
> Yahweh."

---

3. See below for the possibility that the injustice and unrighteousness of these wicked and powerful entities have to do with speech.

4. Another birth-related image shows up in the corresponding section of the chiasm in 58:8b.

5. And also to lions, in 58:6. Neither is an inappropriate simile for these violent activists.

They who dealt in violence (58:2b) were now going to face some punitive counterviolence themselves. Such a call to God to act, the righteous hope and anticipate, will result in a divinely orchestrated overthrow of those corrupt, as outlined in 58:7-9 in a series of similes.[6] They will be like vanishing water, withering arrows, melting snails,[7] and an aborted conceptus[8]—all paint a picture of enervation, neutralization, devitalization, and destruction.[9] While there is no doubt that God is involved in this debacle of the wicked (58:7-9; especially in light of 58:6 that precedes it), there is a sense in which they bring perdition upon themselves, as the structure of 58:7 implies, with its center on "on its own" (the four verbs "vanish," "flows," "aims," and "wither" are all imperfect):[10]

> "Let them vanish
> like
> water
> that flows away
> **on its own—**
> he aims
> his arrows—
> like
> [ones that] wither."

Divine discipline is, therefore, not absent in their ruination: God would take direct action himself, flaying them with thorns and sweeping them away in his anger, ostensibly into death (58:9).[11] These powerful wicked would get their just deserts!

---

6. I see 58:7-9 as distinct from 58:6: as opposed to the imperatives in the latter, there are jussives in former, and God is talked about in the third person in 58:9 (but in the second person in 58:6).

7. Perhaps it is the slimy trail left by these terrestrial gastropod mollusks that generated the image of melting in the poet's mind.

8. This is another birth-related image, following the one in 58:3.

9. The surfeit of images in the text are emphasized by the particle "like/when" (כְּמוֹ) occurring in 58:7a, 7b, 8a, 9b (×2), in addition to 58:4b. Needless to say, these maledictions are not anything the psalmist or his cohort intend to act upon; the outcome is left entirely in the hands of God. See Introduction for more on imprecations. Note the wordplays: "vanish" in 58:7a is מאס, *m's*; and "melt away" in 58:8a is מסס, *mss*; also, "flows away" in 58:7a and "goes" in 58:8a are both הלך, *hlk*.

10. See Auffret, "Certes il y un Diue Jugeant sur la Terre!," 7. Indeed, what was "to them" (or "theirs," לָמוֹ, *lamo*; 58:4a)—i.e., their venom—has now become "on its own" (also לָמוֹ; 58:7a)—i.e., their self-induced downfall.

11. Psalm 58:9 is very opaque; no translation is satisfactory, and all propose emendations of the MT. Althann reads סִירֹתֵיכֶם, *sirotekem*, as סִירֹת יַכֵּם, *sirot yakkem*: the first word being the feminine plural of סִיר, *sir*, "thorn," and the second the third-person masculine singular *hiphil* imperfect of נכה, *nkh*, "to strike," with a third-person masculine plural suffix. Thus 58:9a: "Before they sense the thorns, He will strike them [with] a bramble." Althann's suggestion that מוֹ, *mo*, in 58:9b is a form of the Eblaite *ma-wu*, "water," thus rendering כְּמוֹ in 58:9b as "like water" is less plausible, for then there would be no reason for the psalmist to have employed כְּמוֹ־מַיִם, *kmo-mayim*, in 58:7a with the same meaning. See Althann, "Psalm 58,10," 122-24. Rather, it is best to understand the two instances of כְּמוֹ in 58:9b as "when" (as also in Gen 19:15; Ps 141:7). In any case, the denseness of the idiom resists any further clarity, but the import of the text is obvious.

Celebration (58:10–11)

At the action of God against the unrighteous despots, the righteous rejoice (58:10). The transition is abrupt, from imprecation to exultation, underscoring the oppression they had once suffered and the freedom they were now enjoying. Though the image in 58:10 is brutal, it is not uncommon either to Scripture or to ancient near Eastern literature.[12] There is a certain poesy about the statement: whereas once those rulers dealt out violence with their "hands" (58:2b), now it is the righteous who wash their "feet" in the blood of those wicked ones (58:10b). Note also that "in the blood" is בְּדָם, *bdam*, in 58:10a, and "mankind" is אָדָם, *'adam*, in 58:11a. These wordplays add to the sense that the descriptions are images, not necessarily to be taken literally: "The point is that there are harsh judgments on earth which set things right; let the wicked beware."[13] Whereas once the "wicked" were described as deviant and perverse even from conception (58:3), now the "wicked" are paying for their sinful aberrations with their lives (58:10b). The imprecatory wish was that these evil ones would never "behold" the sun, as aborted fetuses also do not (58:8b); now it is the turn of the righteous to "behold"—they spy the payback of those malefactors (58:10a). Once it was these "humans" (בְּנֵי אָדָם) who were being discriminated against and inequitably "judged" by the "rulers" (אֵלִם) as they disregarded "righteousness" "on earth" (58:1–2); now "mankind" (אָדָם)[14] rejoices that there is a "God" (אֱלֹהִים) who "judges," bringing a reward for the "righteous" "on earth" (58:11). Not only is the paronomasia palpable, the terms are arranged in chiastic order:

58:1a	"rulers"	(אֵלִם)
58:1b	"humans"	(בְּנֵי אָדָם)
58:11a	"mankind"	(אָדָם)
58:11b	"God"	(אֱלֹהִים)

The repetition of "indeed" in 58:11 entrenches the conclusion that all is now well for the people of God, for their God, he judges!

---

12. See Ps 68:23; Isa 63:3–6; Rev 14:20. In the "Ugaritic Baal Cycle" of myths, Anath the goddess is described thus: "She plunges knee-deep in knights' blood, Hip-deep in the gore of heroes" (V AB B 27–29 [*ANET* 136]). "It reflects the reality of human systems that are so polluted that there is nowhere to turn for justice. The pain is so real that the least of the society wishes for the destruction and violent deaths of their oppressors" (deClaissé-Walford et al., *Book of Psalms*, 496). In any case, the focus in the psalm is not human vengeance, but divine justice as Ps 58:1–2 asserts.

13. Tate, *Psalms 51–100*, 87.

14. Presumably, these are the righteous and everyone previously oppressed by the wicked.

Sermon Map

I. Lords of Unrighteousness Judge
   The wicked and the woes they unleash (58:1–5)
   Move-to-relevance: Dangerous injustice in our lives
II. The Lord of Righteousness Judges
   Divine action (58:6–10)
   Move-to-relevance: God's justice in our lives
III. *Refuge in the Referee!*
   Specifics on trusting God in times of injustice

PSALM 59:1–17

Psalm of Disorientation

God-King Defeats the Wicked, Defends the Righteous

PSALM 59 MAY BE considered a sustained petition in two parallel stanzas. Though the psalm has a personal touch throughout—after all, it begins with a petition to "rescue *me* from *my* enemies, *my* God; from those who rise up against *me* secure *me*" (five first-person singular suffixes)—it also has corporate elements referring to the divine community and their global foes (59:5, 8, 11, 13).

Translation

59:1 Rescue me from my enemies, my God;
  from those who rise up against me secure me on high.
59:2 Rescue me from those who do harm
  and from people of bloodshed deliver me.
59:3 For, behold, they laid an ambush for my life;
  strong ones attack me,
  not for my rebellion, and not for my sin, Yahweh.
59:4 For no iniquity [of mine], they run and set themselves [against me].
  Arouse Yourself to help me, and see.
59:5 Even You, Yahweh, God of Armies, God of Israel,
  awake to punish all the nations;
  do not be gracious to any [who are] treacherous in harm.
59:6 They return at evening, they howl like a dog,
  and they march around the city.
59:7 Behold, they belch forth with their mouth—
  swords in their lips:
  [they say,] "For who hears?"

59:8 But You, Yahweh, You laugh at them;
    You scoff at all the nations.
59:9 My strength, I will watch for You,
    for God is my stronghold.
59:10 The God of my lovingkindness will reach me;
    God, He will let me look [triumphantly] upon my watchful foes.
59:11 Do not slay them, lest my people forget;
    shake them up in Your power,
    and bring them down, Lord, our shield.
59:12 The sin of their mouth, the words of their lips—
    so let them be caught in their arrogance
    and through the curse and through the lie they utter.
59:13 Consume [them] in wrath, consume [them] so they are no more;
    and that they may know that God rules in Jacob,
    to the ends of the earth.
59:14 And they return at evening, they howl like a dog,
    and they march around the city.
59:15 They roam around for food
    if they are not satisfied, and they spend the night.
59:16 But I—I will sing of Your strength;
    and proclaim Your lovingkindness in shouts of joy in the morning,
    for You have been to me a stronghold,
    and a place of refuge in the day of my distress.
59:17 My strength, to You I will make music;
    for God is my stronghold,
    the God of my lovingkindness.

Structure

Each of the two stanzas of the psalm has a petition to rescue the appealer (59:1–2) or ravage the aggressor (59:11) and another petition to requite the antagonists (59:4b–5 and 59:12b–13). These two petitions, in each stanza, surround a central lament (59:3–4 and 59:12a). And also in each stanza, this initial trio of petition-lament-petition (59:1–5 and 59:11–13) is followed by a refrain (another lament; 59:6–7 and 59:14–15). Each stanza then concludes with a section of praise (59:8–10 and 59:16–17). This parallel setting of the two stanzas creates a sort of "seconding"—where one section shares lines and motifs with another, but is sufficiently different from the other. Together, they collaborate to yield a singular thrust for the composition, each part contributing unique elements to make the whole.[1]

---

1. See deClaissé-Walford et al., *Book of Psalms*, 498, 498n1. The structure is modified from Tate, *Psalms 51–100*, 96.

STANZA 1 (59:1–10)		STANZA 2 (59:11–17)	
59:1–5	**Petition, Lament, Petition**	**59:11–13**	**Petition, Lament, Petition**
59:1–2	*Petition to rescue*	59:11	*Petition to ravage*
59:3–4a	*Lament* "sin" (59:3c)	59:12a	*Lament* "sin" (59:12a)
59:4b–5	*Petition to requite* "Israel" (59:5a)	59:12b–13	*Petition to requite* "Jacob" (59:13b)
59:6–7	**Refrain**	**59:14–15**	**Refrain**
59:8–10	**Praise** "strength" (59:9a) "stronghold" (59:9b) "lovingkindness" (59:10a)	59:16–17	**Praise** "strength" (59:16a, 17a) "stronghold" (59:16c, 17b) "lovingkindness" (59:16b, 17c)

Theological Focus

In the face of life-threatening attacks from hubristic and iniquitous opponents who are anti-God in word and in deed, the people of God maintain their trust in him, their stronghold, and in his lovingkindness towards them, which faith is expressed in public praise as they anticipate this cosmic ruler triumphantly decimating wicked foes and protecting his righteous ones.

Commentary

Stanza 1 (59:1–10)

Clearly the danger to the psalmist and his cohort is great: their foes are a plurality ("enemies," 59:1a), they are "strong ones" (59:3b), they "rise up" against the supplicant (59:1b), they "do harm" (59:2a) and are "treacherous" in doing so (59:5c), they shed blood (59:2b), they ambush to kill (59:3a), and they attack (59:3b). Indeed, they hasten to perform all these fiendish deeds—"running"—and that in an organized fashion, "setting themselves [against me]" (59:4a).

Obviously, the psalmist needs help, so his petition, "rescue me," is repeated (59:1a, 2a), in addition to a request to be "secured" (59:1b[2]) and to be "delivered" (59:2b). The chiasm of 59:1 hedges the evil foes in the middle, with "rescue me" and "secure me" on the outside, literarily, and hopefully, literally. God in the center of it all is the one being appealed to.[3]

---

2. The security requested is located "on high" (59:1b), in a place inaccessible to enemies, but in a locus close to God.

3. The next verse, 59:2, is also chiastic in its structure: "rescue me / from those who do harm // and from people of bloodshed / deliver me."

> "Rescue me
>> from my enemies,
>>> **my God;**
>> from those who rise up against me
> secure me on high."

In the lament that follows the petition (59:3–4a), the psalmist is careful to disavow any wrongdoing on his part: all three major OT terms for offences against God are denied—"rebellion," "sin," and "iniquity." Appropriately, the petition that comes afterwards (59:4b–5) is to a deity also described with three titles: "Yahweh," "God of Armies," and "God of Israel"—deploying almost all the covenantal terms available for the deity-humanity relationship (59:5a). The supplicant bids God to requite the foes in parallel phrases: "arouse Yourself to help me" (59:4b[4]), and "awake to punish all the nations" (59:5b). To emphasize his petition, the psalmist employs a fronted second-person pronoun, "Even *You*, Yahweh" (59:5a). Recrimination is requested for all the wicked behavior of the foes: the psalmist recommends that God should punish them by withholding grace (59:5bc). The subjects of these imprecations are "all" the nations (כֹּל, *kol*; 59:5b)—expanding the scope of the wicked to a more global stage—and "any" treacherous one (also כֹּל; 59:5c).

> There is little that is moderate or balanced about the psalm. It describes the enemies in immoderate ways, and its petitions are immoderate. Christians are usually hesitant to address God with the freedom the psalms use. Christians behave as if God is more like a judge or headmaster than a father; the OT assumes we are rather like children in relation to parents in our freedom to address God and can speak as freely as children do to parents.[5]

The petition to requite is now followed by another lament in the refrain of 59:6–7, no doubt signifying the anguish of the sufferer. Here the opponents are contemptuously likened to "dogs" (59:6), baying (for blood?) and besieging the city. With the description of words erupting from their mouths and utterances slashing from their lips, the arrogance of the wicked attackers who think God does not hear is decried (59:7c). It parallels those earlier lines of lament in 59:3–4: both contain "behold" (59:3a, 7a)—"God, *look* at what they are doing/saying to me!"

The psalmist closes *Stanza 1* with a praise, an expression of confidence in God (59:8–10). The wicked may think God does not hear, "but *You*, Yahweh" (employing another emphatic second-person pronoun; 59:8a[6]): "You laugh" and "You scoff" at those "nations" and their evil coconspirators (59:8). Yes, God hears, alright!

The supplicant had begun the poem with a request to be made "secure" (שׂגב, *sgv*; 59:1b); of that security he is now sure, for "God is my *stronghold*" (מִשְׂגָּב, *misgav*; 59:9b). "Strong ones" (from עֹז, *ʿoz*; 59:3b) may have attacked God's people, but God is "my strength"

---

4. The Hebrew literally has "arouse Yourself to *meet* me" (59:4b). This, too, is part of the requital, for when Yahweh comes to "help/meet," he "sees," and then he acts against aggressors.

5. Goldingay, *Psalms*, 2:223.

6. Both uses of וְאַתָּה יְהוָה, *wʾattah yhwh*, "even/but You" (59:5a, 8a) appeal to God to respond to enemy threats.

(also עֻזּוֹ; 59:9a[7]), capable of overcoming any earthly potentate. Therefore "I will watch for You" (59:9a), for God's lovingkindness would be made available to his people who would ultimately be victorious over spying and ambushing foes (59:10). God who had been bidden to "see" (ראה, *r'h*; 59:4b) would, in the end, enable his people to "look" (also ראה; 59:10b) with triumph upon their enemies.

Stanza 2 (59:11–17)

This stanza resembles *Stanza 1*, but it does not begin with a petition for rescue; rather the theme of requital of enemies by God is continued from the end of the previous stanza (59:4b–5), extending it into a petition for the ravaging of those aggressors by God (59:11). So that the wicked may themselves be an object lesson to the people of God, the psalmist does not want these wicked ones slain, but for them to shaken up and brought down (59:11).

The lament of 59:12a mentions "sin" (of the foes), while the corresponding lament in the first stanza mentioned the absence of "sin" (on the part of the psalmist). But like the lament in the refrain (59:7), 59:11 also deals with the speech of the wicked; both have "mouth" (59:7a, 12a) and "lips" (59:7b, 12a). Their utterances had been described in the earlier text, but here the psalmist is so struck by the sinfulness of their words that he cannot even make a full sentence (59:12a is verbless).[8] In any case, the structures of 59:12ab and 59:12c are parallel to that of 59:7 (see below)—all referring to the same speech acts of those high-handed enemies. Apparently the "belchings" of their mouths and the "swords" of their lips (59:7ab) were producing "curses" and "lies" (59:12c):

59:7
- **A** "mouth" (59:7a)
  - **B** "lips" (59:7b)
    - **C** "'Who hears?'" (59:7c)

59:12
- **A'** "mouth" (59:12aα)
  - **B'** "lips" (59:12aβ)
    - **C'** "their arrogance" (59:12b)
- **A"** "curse" (59:12cα)
  - **B"** "lie" (59:12cβ)
    - **C"** "they utter" (59:12cγ)

Undoubtedly, the "arrogance" of the foes (59:12b) is their audacity in assuming that God does not hear (59:7c). But these overbearing ones will no longer exhibit such hotheadedness and express such hubris, for the psalmist is confident in his petition for requital (59:12b–13), that God will "consume" (×2; 59:13a) them in his wrath until they are destroyed. This is perhaps symbolic and not intended literally, for the poet follows up with a wish that they may thereby come to recognize God's rulership in relation to his chosen and in relation to the entirety of his

---

7. The MT has "*his* strength," but my emendation makes it conform to 59:17a.
8. Indeed, it was not *his* "sin" that was the cause of all this chaos (59:3b), but *their* "sin" (59:12a).

creation (59:13bc[9]). The symbolic nature of the destruction and consumption called for is also apparent in that the psalmist had earlier expressly asked that they not be slain (59:11a). There it was for the education of God's people; now it is for the information of the rest of the world: by the requital of these oppressors, it would be evident to one and all, that God rules not only his people, but all the peoples of the earth (59:13bc)!

The refrain of 59:14–15 is similar to that of the first stanza (59:6–7).[10] But here, these canines, "howling" and "marching" (59:14), do not seem to be giving voice to their arrogance as they were earlier (59:7). Rather, they seem to be starving, and that all night (59:15). A wordplay substantiates this conclusion: the psalmist had asked that the enemies be "shaken up" by God (נוּעַ, *nwʿ*; 59:11b); the consequence was that now they "roam around" famished (also נוּעַ; 59:15a). Unfortunately for these food-insecure foes, their prey had been taken from them: under the protection of God, the people of God have been sequestered securely from the rapacity of these ravenous beasts.

The psalm concludes with another confident assertion of praise (59:16–17) that corresponds to that of the *Stanza 1* (59:8–10[11]). It is notable that after the emphasis throughout on the anti-God vocalizations of the wicked, the psalm ends with pro-God exclamations of the righteous, underscored by the emphatic and fronted first-person pronoun in 59:16a: "But I—I . . ." The psalmist "sings" (59:16a), "proclaims" and raises "shouts of joy" (59:16b), and "makes music" (59:17a) to the God of his deliverance. He announces divine "lovingkindness" (59:16b) because this deity is "the God of my *lovingkindness*" (59:17c). The expectation of God "reaching" the supplicant and securing victory for him (as in 59:10aβ–b) is missing in 59:17: victory accomplished no longer need be anticipated![12]

And whereas the praise in *Stanza 1* (59:8–10) had a mention of foes and the psalmist's triumph over them, in the praise in *Stanza 2* (59:16–17) gone are the enemies forever; now there is only songs, shouts of joy, and music! Also, "watching" for God in the middle of the psalm is replaced with music-making for God at the end: "My strength, I will *watch* for You" (59:9a) has been transformed to "My strength, to You I will *make music*" (59:17a). The "evening" of howling (59:6a, 14a) has passed; the "morning" of celebration (59:16b) has come![13] And, quite appropriately, the last word of the psalm is "lovingkindness." "The final word on the matter then is not retribution to the enemies but the *hesed* [חֶסֶד, *chesed*] that preserved the life of the one praying."[14] Yes, God is our stronghold and a place of refuge![15]

---

9. "Jacob" stands for God's people, Israel in the OT, and in the current age includes Gentiles as well. Thus both petitions to requite, in 59:4b–5 and 59:12b–13, contain references to the divine community.

10. Both are laments; indeed 59:6 is identical to 59:14, except for the conjunction וְ, *w*, at the beginning of the latter.

11. The verbal repetitions were noted in the structure above. And except for slight alterations of 59:17a, this verse is identical to its counterpart, 59:9–10aα.

12. However, it is uncertain if deliverance has been accomplished at the end of the psalm. It is possible that that is still in the future, but the certainty of it happening is so high that the psalmist can praise God as though it were already achieved.

13. The phrases are parallel: "at [לְ, *l*] evening," 59:6a, 14a; and "in [לְ] the morning," 59:16b.

14. deClaissé-Walford et al., *Book of Psalms*, 503.

15. After all, he is "Yahweh, God of Armies, God of Israel" (59:5a)!

Sermon Map

I. Wicked: Deeds and Words
   Deeds of the wicked (59:1bβ, 2aβ, 2bα, 3, 4a, 5cβ–6, 14–15)
   Words of the wicked (59:7, 12a)
   Move-to-relevance: Conduct and conceit of oppressors

II. Righteous: Dependence and Words
   Dependence of the righteous (59:1a, 1bα, 2bβ, 4b–5cα, 9–11, 12b–13)
   Words of the righteous (59:16–17)
   Move-to-relevance: Dependence on the rule of God

III. *Depend and Declare!*
   Specifics on trusting God and proclaiming his praise

PSALM 60:1–12

Psalm of Disorientation

Faithfully Working with God

THIS PSALM OF DISORIENTATION moves in a direction at variance with those of preceding psalms: even though enemies are present and active (60:4b, 11a; and implied in all the pleas for deliverance and even in God's martial words), the distress is primarily caused by a seeming rejection of his people by deity. Essentially, then the psalm is a protest, and a congregational one at that—the psalmist is speaking on behalf of "Your people" (60:3a), "those who fear You" (60:4a), and "Your beloved" (60:5a). Uniquely, the psalm also has a quote of God at its center (60:6–9), and it is this utterance of deity that directs us towards the "story" of the psalm and its application.

Translation

60:1 God, You have rejected us, You have broken us,
       You have been angry: restore us.
60:2 You have made the land quake, You have split it open;
       heal its fractures, for it totters.
60:3 You have made Your people see hardship;
       You have passed us wine to drink making us reel.
60:4 You have given to those who fear You a banner,
       to rally round the banner from before the bow[s of archers].
60:5 So that Your beloved may be saved
       deliver with Your right hand and answer us.
60:6 God, He has spoken in His holiness:
       "I will exult, I will portion out Shechem,
       and the valley of Succoth I will measure off.
60:7 Mine is Gilead, and mine is Manasseh;
       and Ephraim is the stronghold of My head;
       Judah, My scepter.

60:8   Moab [is] My washing bowl;
      over Edom I will throw My sandal;
      over Philistia I will shout triumphantly.
60:9   Who will bring Me to the fortified city?
      Who has led Me unto Edom?"
60:10 Have You not Yourself, God, rejected us—
      and God, You do not go forth with our armies?
60:11 Grant to us help against the adversary,
      for worthless is deliverance [from] a human.
60:12 Through God we shall do powerfully,
      and He—He will trample our adversaries.

Structure

Structurally, Psalm 60 can be divided into three parts; the first and last sections are the words of *God's People to God* (constructed with parallel elements: rejection and reliance), the second central section are the words of *God to God's People*:[1]

> **God's People to God 1 (60:1–5)**
> *Rejection* (60:1–3)
> *Reliance* (60:4–5)
>   "You have rejected us" (60:1a)
>   Vocative: "God" (60:1a); "deliver" (60:5b)
>   Demand for an answer (60:5b) leads to answer from God …
>
> **God to God's People (60:6–9)**
> *Reassurance* (60:6–9)
>   Questions from God (60:9) lead to questions from people …
>
> **God's People to God 2 (60:10–12)**
> *Rejection* (60:10)
> *Reliance* (60:11–12)
>   "Have you … rejected us?" (60:10a)
>   Vocative: "God" (60:10a, 10b); "deliverance" (60:11b)

---

1. Modified from Anderson, "Politics of Psalmody," 317–18. Psalm 60:5–12 reappears in a variant form as 108:7–13.

Theological Focus

> Lack of success in God-ordained ventures does not necessarily indicate rejection and abandonment by God, but may point to moral failure on part of his people: their lack of faith in the availability of God's help—which alone yields success—and their reluctance to undertake bold action with divine aid.

Commentary

God's People to God 1 (60:1–5)

The theme of divine "rejection" begins both the first and the third sections of this psalm (60:1a, 10a). The grounds for God's displeasure and anger (60:1b) is unclear from this first section, *God's People to God 1*, but will become manifest in the central portion of the psalm, the utterance of *God to God's People*. In any case, they have been "rejected" and "broken" (60:1a); the land has been "quaked" and "split open" and "fractured," so much so, it is "tottering" (60:2). The community of God has been driven into "hardship" and they "reel" from its effects (60:3). The exact nature of these devastations is unclear; perhaps it is an invasion by a foreign army that has put the corporate body into consternation, as the military language of 60:6–9 seems to imply. As a result, the people make a request of their God: "restore us" (60:1b) and "heal [the] fractures" of the land (60:2b).

Despite the rejection, there is some sense of hope still remaining that leads God's people to rely on him: those who fear him have been given a "banner" (נֵס, *nes*; 60:4a) and they "rally round the banner" (נסס, *nss*; 60:4b) seeking refuge from the onslaught of enemies. Whatever the standard raised and rallied around stands for—and the banner might well be God himself as in Exod 17:15—it raises the expectation of God's people of being "saved" and "delivered" (Ps 60:5). Unfortunately, that rescue has not yet transpired. So the first section of the psalm, the words of *God's People to God 1*, ends with another plea: "answer us!" (60:5b). Which leads God to reply . . .

God to God's People (60:6–9)

At the center of the psalm God is quoted—his response to his people's demand, "answer us!" (60:5b): "God, He has spoken . . ." (60:6a). In what seems to be a *non sequitur*, deity reclaims his dominion over the land. "The section declares that both southern Israel (*Judah*) and northern (*Gilead*, *Manasseh*, and *Ephraim*) and the Transjordan (*Shechem* and *Succoth*) belong to God."[2] The language of war is employed by deity who claims Ephraim as his helmet ("the stronghold of My head") and Judah as his "scepter" (60:7bc). But "whereas Ephraim and Judah are honorable parts of the warrior's equipment, Moab is simply the basin in which he washes

---

2. deClaissé-Walford et al., *Book of Psalms*, 508 (italics original).

his mucky feet . . . [and] Edom is where the warrior throws his [dirty] shoes as he does so."[3] Philistia is only said to be thoroughly defeated (60:8).[4]

All that to say, since God is utterly dominant both over Israel and over these foreigners and their territories, his people—represented by "Ephraim" and "Judah": God's helmet and his scepter, no less—need not expect any trouble from non-Israelite foes who are thoroughly discomfited. This is in complete contrast to what the psalmist and his cohort seem to have been experiencing, as described in their first utterance in 60:1–5. In God's eyes, his people apparently are both ignorant of his sovereignty and untrusting of his providence, for he asks, in a twofold question, who would lead him to conquer these foreign lands (60:9).[5] All he needs, apparently, is cooperation from his people. Would that God's people take the initiative and boldly go with him (or "lead" him) in victory. After all the land is all his to allocate as he sees fit (with a little help from God's friends!).[6] In other words, "God seeks to call the people who are God's weaponry [helmet and scepter: his people] or army to be about their work," side-by-side with God's sovereign power.[7] Why are they complaining of rejection? God is still preeminent, exercising dominion over every nation, and his purposes for his people still hold good. It is they who need to buckle up their faith and pull up their boots for action. God's answer thus gets to the root of the problem—he has not rejected his people; in fact, it is the other way: his people, failing to take bold initiative with faith in their God, are rejecting him. That this section is introduced as God speaking "in His holiness" (60:6a) suggests that this faithless inaction on the part of his people falls short of the holiness of God and what he expected of them—in short, a moral failure. Yet, though it is a rebuke of sorts, this response of God to his people's accusation is a reassurance that he has not rejected them. But God's closing questions lead God's people to reply . . .

God's People to God (60:10–12)

However, the people seem incredulous at God's double question in 60:9. They reply with a corresponding twofold question of their own in 60:10, employing the vocative, "God," twice. The emphatic fronted pronoun "You" in 60:10a expresses their incredulity: "Have *You* not Yourself . . . ?" In other words, they are accusing *God* (again) of failing to meet his obligations to lead them to victory. Thus, the theme of God's apparent rejection of them is reasserted (in their minds God has "rejected," them; 60:1a, 10a). The people feel spurned, while God implies that it is his people who are faithless. No doubt, the latter is right in his assessment, but he does not return to the table to answer for himself.

3. Goldingay, *Psalms*, 2:231.

4. The MT of 60:8c has an imperative verb ("shout triumphantly"; and עָלַי, *'alay*, "over me"). The corresponding verse, 108:9, has the first-person imperfect ("I will shout triumphantly"; and עָלֵי, *'ale*, "over," without the first-person suffix); this is followed in the translation of 60:8c here.

5. I take 60:9 to be part of the quote of God's speech, considering the persistence of the first person singular and the geographical referents, carried over from 60:6–8.

6. The verbs "portion out" (חלק, *chlq*; 60:6b) and "measure off" (מדד, *mdd*; 60:6c) are employed in the Pentateuch to describe God's apportionment of the land (Num 26:53, 55, 56; 35:5; etc.).

7. Goldingay, *Psalms*, 2:232. He imagines the admittedly odd picture of God being led, and deity as "a commander in chief asking where the scouts are to show the way to a city"; this, of course, is not any more anthropomorphic or incongruous than deity wearing a helmet and wielding a scepter (60:7b) (Goldingay, *Psalms*, 2:232). Perhaps the oddity emphasizes the important role of God's people as they participate with him in his endeavors.

Nonetheless, God's accusation in 60:6–9 seems to have prodded his people to rethink their rejection, for in 60:11 they make another request for his aid, but this time acknowledging their own helplessness ("worthless is deliverance [from] a human," 60:11b). And in 60:12, they seem to have regained their confidence to maintain that with God's help they can overcome all odds and all adversaries, for "He—He tramples underfoot" all their enemies.[8] And with that the psalm concludes, leaving readers with a strong hope that God will deliver . . . if they do their part![9]

Sermon Map

I. Rejection by God?
    Failure and distress of God's people (60:1a–bα; 2a, 2bβ; 3, 10)
    Move-to-relevance: When we feel God has rejected us

II. Reassurance of God
    Divine sovereignty over all (60:6–8)
    Call for faith and action (60:9)
    Move-to-relevance: How God is in control of all today

III. Reliance upon God
    Calling upon God confidently (60:1bβ, 2bα, 4–5, 11–12)

IV. *Faithfully Forward!*
    Specifics on faith-filled, bold action with God for success

---

8. Again we have the emphatic fronted third-person pronoun in 60:12a. Also 60:12a has human action; 60:12b has divine action. Both work in tandem: faith in divine action, and bold execution of human initiative.

9. "God helps those who help themselves" may not be far from wrong!

PSALM 61:1–8

Psalm of Disorientation

Security under God's King

PSALM 61 IS A psalm of prayer and confidence in God. There is apparently a faintness of heart (61:2) that prompts this utterance.[1] However, the focus is more on the refuge that God is than on the distress the psalmist is in.

Translation

61:1 Hear, God, my lament;
       attend to my prayer.
61:2 From the end of the earth, to You I call when my heart is faint;
       to the rock higher than I, lead me.
61:3 For You are a refuge for me,
       a tower of strength against the face of the enemy.
61:4 Let me sojourn in Your tent forever;
       let me take refuge in the shelter of Your wings.
61:5 For You, God, You hear my vows;
       You give [me the land of] inheritance,
       [the possession] of those who fear Your name.
61:6 Add days upon days to the King['s life],
       His years like generation to generation.
61:7 May He sit [enthroned] forever before the face of God;
       appoint lovingkindness and truth—they will preserve Him.
61:8 Then I will make music to Your name for always,
       as I fulfill my vows day after day.

---

1. The cause of this languor is indeterminate, though enemies may have been involved (61:3b).

Structure

The structure of the psalm recognizes its two parts:

> **Appeal for Refuge; Assurance** (61:1–5)
>   *Appeal* (**61:1–3**)   "hear, God" (61:1a); "for You" (61:3a)
>   *Assurance* (**61:4–5**) "God, You hear" (61:5a); "for You" (61:5a)
>
> **Appeal for Ruler; Adoration** (61:6–8)
>   *Appeal* (**61:6–7**)   "days upon days" (61:6a)
>   *Adoration* (**61:8**)   "day after day" (61:8b)

Theological Focus

> In the face of terminal oppression, producing woes psychological and physiological, the people of God rest confidently in the refuge of deity and in the eternal reign of the divine King that is characterized by God's lovingkindness and truth, resulting in eternal praise.

Commentary

Appeal for Refuge; Assurance (61:1–5)

As was noted, the distress of the psalmist does not get any elaboration here: there is no lament, besides the declaration that the psalmist finds himself "faint" of heart, at the "end of the earth" (61:2a)—"in the twilight zone, in the foyer of the area of Death."[2] "Enemy" is mentioned (61:3b), but there no description of that foe, other than an implication that they are powerful and that they cause cardiac weakness. Such non-specificity lends the psalm the capacity to be relevant in situations of difficulty of various kinds. This enemy could even be the approaching specter of death.[3] No wonder the emphasis here is on God as a "refuge," for no human effort will yield success against this final archenemy. And so, since God alone is a "refuge" for the oppressed always (as implied by the perfect form of the verb הָיִיתָ, *hayita*, "are" (61:3a)—"the rock" that is high and "a tower of strength" (61:2b, 3b)—therefore, he should be a "refuge" for the oppressed now and onwards, too (as implied by the imperfect form of the verb, "to take refuge," 61:4b), as they find a shelter under his wings. The structure of 61:1–5, below, keeps the focus on God as "refuge."[4]

---

2. Brueggemann and Bellinger, *Psalms*, 271.

3. So, Brueggemann and Bellinger, *Psalms*, 271. The collapse of heart (61:2a) is congruent with this assumption. "The phrase suggests a person's whole being running out of energy; it is not merely a statement about how one feels inside" (Goldingay, *Psalms*, 2:237).

4. Modified from Auffret, "Alors je jouerai," 170.

A "hear" (61:1aα)		
B "God" (61:1aβ)		Vocative
C "For You" (61:3a)		
D "refuge" (61:3a)		Noun
D' "take refuge" (61:4b)		Verb
C' "For You" (61:5aα)		
B' "God" (61:5aβ)		Vocative
A' "hear" (61:5aγ)		

And so 61:1–5 ends as it began, with an utterance to "God" (61:1a, 5a, in the vocative). But what began with an appeal to deity to "hear" (imperative in 61:1a) concludes here with an assurance that God *does* "hear" (perfect in 61:5a). There is strong assurance here that this hearing God will be a "rock," a "refuge," a "tower," a "shelter" beneath his wings (61:2b–3)—accomplishing a remarkable translocation of the psalmist from a scary locus at "the end of the earth" (61:2a) to a secure one, "Your tent" (61:4a), and that forever!

> Prayer suspends the distantness between the supplicant and the deity. Breaking down a perceived distance and the creation of sense of nearness and presence is a major function of prayer. The Psalms are of great importance in the recognition of distantness, which results from various kinds of stress and distress, and in the closing of that gap, which threatens spiritual health and even life itself. The very recitation of psalms like 61 serves to diminish distance and enhance nearness and presence.[5]

Being in the presence of God ("in Your tent," 61:4a) is the essence of safety, security, and salvation from the threats of enemies and the evil one.

The section ends with a declaration that deity has heard the supplicant's promises of sacrifices upon deliverance (61:5a) and has, or soon will, grant him his inheritance, the stability of land,[6] as he does to all who fear God's name (61:5bc).

Appeal for Ruler; Adoration (61:6–8)

Psalm 61:5 could have moved seamlessly into 61:8 with the repetition of "my vows" (61:5a, 8b) and "Your name" (61:5c, 8a), but there is a seeming interpolation of 61:6–7 that deals with the ruler of the land. Yet, the construction of the entirety of the psalm demonstrates its integrity in the vocabulary shared between the two sections: "face" (61:3b, 7b) and "forever" (61:4a, 7a).

And there is also a coherent "story" in the movement of the psalm as it arrives at 61:6. The closing confidential assertion of the previous section, 61:5bc, dealt with the "inheritance" that is due to those who fear God. This mention of "inheritance" and the implication of it being land reminds the psalmist that such a possession cannot be secure without a divinely appointed regent to govern and defend this blessing of territory. And so the poem moves into an appeal for this ruler in 61:6–7. So also, for all of God's people, in every age and in every place, the finality of divine blessing can be indemnified and ensured only if a godly ruler reigns. Therefore

---

5. Tate, *Psalms 51–100*, 116.

6. While יְרֻשָּׁה, *yrushshah*, "inheritance," occurs only here in the Psalter, elsewhere it implies the land granted by God to his people (see Num 24:18; Deut 2:5, 9, 12; 3:20; Josh 1:15; 12:6, 7). Metaphorically, this might well indicate divine blessings of any kind for God's people of another day and dispensation.

61:6–7 is an appeal for such a regent with a longevity that extends from "days" to "years" to "generations" (61:6) and even to "forever," whose reign is located and conducted before the very "face" (i.e., presence) of God (61:7a), who will personally enable this ruler to manifest divine "lovingkindness and truth" (61:7b). The language may be moving towards hyperbole, but exaggeration it is not, if a divine Ruler is being conceived of here—the Messiah.[7]

> Undoubtedly the language is drawn from prayers by and for contemporary kings, language which could be extremely exalted. Nevertheless, we must ask why such prayers were added to psalms, or kept in psalms, during the post-exilic period when there were no kings. Surely they were retained to express the hope for a future king, whose reign would manifest the qualities of true monarchy, qualities longed for through so many disappointments . . . . The words of the text convey a latent hope which transcends their finite limits.[8]

In fact, the Targum interprets 61:5 as referring to the מלכא משיחא, *mlk' mshych'*, "King Messiah," and the supplicant's vows being fulfilled "*day* after *day*" (61:8b) as "in the *day* of the redemption of Israel and in the *day* of the magnification of the מלכא משיחא as king."[9] This is the one who will "sit [enthroned]" before "the face of God" (61:7a), so that his people oppressed by "the face of the enemy" (61:3b) will no longer be terrorized. Then will the righteous abide in the divine presence "forever" (61:4a), because their King sits in the divine presence "forever" (61:7a). These, the ones who fear "Your name" (61:5) will exult in "Your name"—the name of God—eternally (61:8). And all this is directly linked to the longevity of the King's reign: as he rules "days upon days" (61:6a), his people serve God "day after day" (61:8a)—blessing forever, bliss forever!

Sermon Map

    I. Opposition

        Deadly danger (61:1, 2a, 3b)

        Move-to-relevance: The dangers of death besetting us

    II. Protection

        Divine refuge (61:1, 2b, 3–4)

        Divine blessing (61:5)

        Move-to-relevance: How God protects us

    III. Dominion

        Divine ruler securing divine blessing (61:6–7)

        Divine name praised (61:8)

    IV. *Experience the Refuge, Expect the Ruler*

        How to access the refuge now; how to anticipate the ruler soon

---

7. Therefore I have chosen to capitalize "King" (61:6a) and the pronouns referring to this ruler.
8. Tate, *Psalms 51–100*, 115.
9. My translation of the Aramaic.

PSALM 62:1–12

Psalm of Orientation

Only Trusting in God Always

God, in Psalm 62, is directly addressed only in its final verse (62:12; vocative "Lord"), after the composition has explicitly addressed persecutors (62:3; enemies in the second person), the psalmist himself (62:5–7; vocative "my soul," 62:5a), and the community of God (62:8, 10; vocative "people," 62:8a[1]). In any case, the psalm as a whole is a poem of confidence, expressing the way things usually are in a difficult life; an admixture of assurance, admonition, and adjuration (to self or to members of the community). Notably, there is no express petition herein. Thus it prescribes a stance of orientation for God's people in a messy world, particularly in 62:9–12 that sounds like a verset of wisdom, employing characteristic terminology, "breath," "vanity" of hope (both words from the root הבל; 62:9c, 10b), and a numerical idiom (62:11).[2]

Translation

62:1 Only for God in silence [awaits] my soul;
    from Him is my deliverance.

62:2 Only He is my rock and my deliverance;
    my stronghold: I shall not be greatly shaken.

62:3 Until when will you assail a person,
    that you may destroy [him], all of you,
    as [you would] a leaning wall, a tottering fence?

62:4 Only to thrust [him] down from his dignity did they deliberate;
    they delight in falsehood;
    with their mouth they bless, but inwardly they curse.

62:5 Only for God be in silence, my soul,
    for from Him is my hope.

---

1. There is also a single instance of a first-person plural in 62:8c.
2. See Job 33:14; 40:5; Prov 21:6; 30:15, 18, 21, 29; 31:30.

62:6   Only He is my rock and my deliverance;
          my stronghold: I shall not be shaken.
62:7   Upon God [is] my deliverance and my honor;
          the rock of my strength, my refuge [is] in God.
62:8   Trust in Him at all times, people;
          pour out your heart before His face;
          God [is] a refuge for us.
62:9   Only a breath are humans; a falsehood are persons;
          in the balances they go up;
          they are together less than a breath.
62:10 Do not trust in oppression,
          and in robbery do not be vainly confident;
          if wealth increases, do not set heart [on it].
62:11 Once God has spoken;
          twice I have heard this, that strength [belongs] to God.
62:12 And to you, Lord, [belongs] lovingkindness,
          for You—You recompense a person according to his work.

Structure

The psalm is divided into two sections, 62:1–7 (with every verse beginning with either אַךְ, עַד, or עַל, 'ak, 'ad, or 'al; "only," "until," or "upon") and 62:8–12. The first section is an *Expression of Trust* primarily directed to the individual self (though the enemy is also addressed in 62:3); the second, an *Exhortation to Trust*, is essentially to the community (though God is also addressed in 62:12). The adjuration (self-exhortation) and resulting assurance of the psalmist in 62:5–7 is thus passed on the community in 62:8, with appropriate admonitions to assailants (62:3–4) and to those who would dare mistrust God (62:9–10). Overall, the structure might be considered chiastic, with assurance bookending the entirety of the psalm (62:1–2, 11–12):

> **Expression of Trust** (62:1–7)
>   *Assurance* (**62:1–2**)
>   *Admonition* (**62:3–4**)
>   *Adjuration* (**62:5**); *Assurance* (**62:6–7**)
>
> **Exhortation to Trust** (62:8–12)
>   *Adjuration* (**62:8ab**); *Assurance* (**62:8c**)
>   *Admonition* (**62:9–10**)
> *Assurance* (**62:11–12**)

Theological Focus

An exclusive and unceasing trust in a personal God, the strong and loving One who is a refuge for, and a rescuer of, his community, marks the attitude of the people of God, rendering them unshakable, particularly in times of oppression and distress, as they anticipate God's ultimate just recompense, in contrast to those who fail to trust God and instead trust humanity and its sinful contrivances.

Commentary

Expression of Trust (62:1–7)

Striking in this section is the repetition of the particle אַךְ, translated "only," in 62:1a, 2a, 4a, 5a, 6a; in every instance, it is emphatic, fronting the clause.[3] Four of the five instances of "only" in this first part of the psalm deal with the exclusivity of God—the *only* one worth waiting for/ trusting in (62:1a, 5a), and the *only* one who can deliver (62:2a, 6a). The fifth instance points out that enemies and assailants have *only* one goal—to destroy the righteous (62:4a). Clearly, the psalmist is interested in making a strong case for his adjurations to wait on God alone and to trust him (62:5, 8ab). This focus upon God as the "only" trustworthy being is also emphasized in the creative employment of prepositions: "*for* God" the righteous wait (אֶל, 'el; 62:1a; and לְ, *l*; 62:5a); "*from* Him" comes their deliverance and hope (מִן, *min*; 62:1b, 5b); "*upon* God" is their deliverance and honor (עַל; 62:7a); and "*in* God" is their refuge (בְּ, *b*; 62:7b).[4]

The need for these utterances of assurance is the presence of assailants who attack the righteous—they are directly addressed in 62:3. Utterly evil, their only desire is to "destroy" (רצח, *rtsch*; 62:3b) the psalmist and his cohort; and to further that nefarious goal, they "delight" in falsehood (also רצה; 62:4b). They were "thrusting down" God's people (לְהַדִּיחַ, *lhaddiach*; 62:4a) as if they were knocking over a "tottering" wall (הַדְּחוּיָה, *haddchuyah*; 62:3c). With their inclination towards "falsehood" (62:4b), it might well be that this assault (verbal?) was more devious machination than dangerous mauling, more psychological than physical. Either way, the psalmist was in danger of being "destroyed" (62:3b).

Also note the intensely personal references to God in this section: he is "*my* deliverance" (62:1b, 2a, 6a, 7a); "*my* rock" (62:2a, 6a); "*my* stronghold" (62:2b, 6b); "*my* hope" (62:5b); the "rock of *my* strength" (62:7b); and "*my* refuge" (62:7b). Yes, indeed, this God can be trusted because he is a personal God, actively and deeply and intensely involved with the life and circumstances of every one of his children! Therefore, the psalmist adjures himself (his "soul," 62:5a) to "be in silence" (i.e., wait or hope) for deity. No doubt, his "silence" before God (62:1a, 5a) reflects the absolute and exclusive sufficiency of this divine refuge ("only" ×4 in 62:1a, 2a, 5a, 6a): there is nothing left to say when God is trusted totally—one may well remain silent.[5]

---

3. Another occurrence is found in 62:9a; see below. Also of note is the fact that the first words of ten of the twelve verses of the psalm (except for 62:8, 12) begin with a consonant (either א or ע) followed by a short vowel, *patakh* (אַךְ, עַד, עַל, אַל, *'al*, or אַחַת, *'achat*: "only," "until," "upon," "[do] not," or "once").

4. Another: the righteous trust "*in* Him" (בְּ; 62:8); see below.

5. Perhaps it is because of this self-imposed silence that deity is not addressed directly in this psalm until it gets to the last verse (62:12). "The usual response to that awareness [of God as the source of deliverance] is to make a loud noise to God, not to be silent … Yet the psalm as a whole bears out this opening claim, for

There is a greater degree of assurance in 62:6b ("I shall not be shaken") than was visible in 62:2b ("I shall not be *greatly* shaken"). The psalmist's own trust, it appears, has been growing: once he was not *greatly* shaken; now he will not be shaken *at all!* Indeed, whereas 62:1 is an expression of assurance, 62:5—quite similar to 62:1—becomes an adjuration, with the psalmist addressing himself, exhorting his soul to trust in God. The chiastic structure of 62:7 (a verbless verse) again emphasizes the sufficiency of God:

"Upon God	*Prepositional phrase*
[is] my deliverance and my honor;	*Two attributes*
the rock of my strength, my refuge [is]	*Two attributes*
in God."	*Prepositional phrase*

"Structurally and theologically, the reality of God encompasses the psalmist"—his assurance begins and ends with God.[6] "Honor," כָּבוֹד, *kavod*, in 62:7a is related to the adjective "heavy," כָּבֵד, *kaved*.[7] Thus it indicates, in this case, all those "weighty" things—each person's importance and significance—discovered and maximized only when one's life is utterly laid "upon God" (62:7a).

Exhortation to Trust (62:8–12)

The first verse in the psalm that does not commence with either אַךְ, עַד, or עַל is 62:8, and this syntactical shift indicates a conceptual shift: the psalmist turns his attention to his community, the people of God. The same elements in 62:1–7 (adjuration and assurance, admonition, and assurance) are present in 62:1–8, too, but in reverse order.[8] An adjuration to trust God at "all times" comes first, with an appeal to pour out one's heart before him (62:8ab). "The time reference perhaps takes up the fact that for anyone there are times when it is tempting not to trust, and these are the moments when it is most important to do so . . . . Any fool can trust when there is no pressure."[9] "All times" (62:8a) and the repeated "only" (62:1a, 2a, 5a, 6a) combine in this psalm to create an urgent appeal to God's people to trust him unceasingly and exclusively.

But the people of God might not do so, so the psalmist introduces an admonition in 62:9–10 (this time to the community of God's people, unlike in 63:3–4 that was directed to assailants). Trusting in anyone else or anything else is folly: humans are but a "breath" and even "together [they are] less than a *breath*" (62:9a, 9c), thus drawing attention to the total insubstantiality and weightlessness, so to speak, of humankind—"in the balances they go up" (62:9b).[10] Besides, persons are but "falsehood" (62:9a): thus those who trust in such evildoers

---

the suppliant is silent toward God throughout the psalm until the statement of faith in the last line . . . Being silent to God is a novel way of declaring trust" (Goldingay, *Psalms*, 2:246). Also, the four other instances of "until when [עַד־אָנָה, *'ad-'anah*]" in the Psalms address God (13:1 [×2], 2 [×2]); only in 62:3a is it addressed to humans. All that to say, "the psalm is silent to God but noisy to human beings" (Goldingay, *Psalms*, 2:246).

    6. Goldingay, *Psalms*, 2:249.

    7. Of God, כָּבוֹד indicates "glory," God's substantiality and weightiness.

    8. Note also the shared vocabulary between the two sections: "falsehood" (62:4b, 9a); "refuge" (62:7b, 8c); "strength" (62:7b, 11b); and "person(s)" (62:3a, 9a, 12b).

    9. Goldingay, *Psalms*, 2:249.

    10. Perhaps there is an implied contrast here with the "weightiness" or "honor" (כָּבוֹד) that God alone

are as bad as the assailants of 62:4c who "delight in *falsehood*." "Trust" in God (62:8a) is then opposed to "trust" in oppression, or even in robbery (62:10ab). That attitude is only to be "vainly confident" (62:10b)—and the wordplay is pungent: "breath" in 62:9a, 9c is the noun הֶבֶל, *hevel*, and "vainly confident" in 62:10b is the cognate verb הבל, *hvl*. The sole occurrence of "only" in 62:8–12 occurs in 62:9a: "*only* a breath are humans." Therefore trusting in them is futile. Neither are the people of God to "set *heart*" on wealth (62:10c); rather, they are to "pour out" their "heart" before God (62:8b), for he alone is a refuge. It is easy to turn away from God in times of trouble and do what everyone else is doing, seeking recourse in others for extrication from trouble, transacting acts of sin to preclude trouble, and relying upon one's own wealth, might, and cunning to bribe, coerce, and finagle one's way out of trouble.[11] All objects of trust outside God, the psalmist is asserting, are pure folly.

The psalm then draws to a close with a proverbial statement in 62:11: it has a "once …; twice …" idiomatic utterance (i.e., "many times"), and a gnomic report that "strength" and "lovingkindness" belong to God (62:11b–12a), as well as the lapidary inscription about God's just recompense (62:12b).

"Strength" (62:11b) was already predicated of God in 62:7b. And we saw earlier, with the many first-person-suffixed descriptions of God, that this deity was a personal one, caring not only about his people as a community, but also about his children as individuals. In other words, God's "lovingkindness" (62:12a) to one and all is, like his strength, never in question. Both belong to God, both come from God, and both are the prerogative of God, and God alone:

> "strength
>   [belongs] to God.
>   And to you, Lord, [belongs]
>   lovingkindness."

Therefore, he "only" is to be trusted, not anyone else or anything else, to meet the needs of his people in every circumstance ("at all times," 62:8a). One is assured that those who trust in God will be blessed—God's just recompense in action (62:12b). On the other hand, in the context of the admonition of 62:9–10, there is also the implication that those who do *not* trust God in this fashion will face the consequences, too.

In sum, "the psalm is not simply the prayer of a persecuted person, but an explicit exhortation embedded in a self-motivating and accusing monologue. It is also not a legal document, but an ideological document," and thus a psalm of orientation, dictating how things ought to be: the righteous trusting exclusively and constantly in their God, no matter how dire the situation.[12]

---

grants (62:7a).

11. The word חַיִל, *chayil*, translated "wealth" in 62:10c, can also mean "might/power."
12. Botha, "Psalm 62," 43.

Sermon Map

I. Opposition's Gambit
   Assault (62:3–4)
   Move-to-relevance: The assaults we face in life

II. Overconfident Godlessness
   Trusting in everything but God (62:9–10)
   Move-to-relevance: Our tendency to look away from God

III. Only God
   Exclusively God (62:1–2, 5–7)
   Constantly God (62:8)
   Gracious God (62:11–12)

IV. *Go for God and God Alone!*
   How keep one's focus on God alone

PSALM 63:1–11
Psalm of Orientation

Yearning for God and His Lovingkindness

THE PREVIOUS PSALM, PSALM 62, had only verse directly addressing God (62:12). In contrast, this psalm, Psalm 63, is almost entirely addressed to God (with perhaps the exception of the last verse, 63:11). It is possible that the entire psalm was uttered by an Israelite king, who then refers to himself in the third person in 63:11. In any case, this prayer of orientation is for all of God's people (perhaps especially their leaders).

As a psalm of orientation, Psalm 63 demarcates the expected and "normal" attitude of the child of God towards deity. There is no specific lament, though a violent opposition lurks in the background (63:9–10), as also does a less than ideal world that is dry and parched (63:1c)—but perhaps this is only metaphorical (see below). The psalm is also devoid of any specific petition. Further substantiating Psalm 63 as a psalm of orientation are the many imperfect verbs, most likely describing ongoing aspects of the supplicant's life in divine presence—how life ought to be lived in the divine economy: "earnestly longing," "thirsting," "yearning" (63:1), "beholding," "seeing" (63:2), "blessing," "lifting up hands" (63:4), "being satisfied," "joyfully shouting," "offering praise" (63:5), "remembering," "meditating" (63:6), "shouting with joy" again (63:7), and "cleaving" (63:8)—all that the psalmist (or any child of God) is doing, does, and will/should do.[1] In any case, "the one praying is firmly rooted in God's world and confident of God's power and love."[2] The poem therefore begins and ends with a naming of "God" (63:1a [×2], 11), the only instances of "God" in the composition.

Translation

63:1 God, You are my God; I earnestly long for You;
   my soul thirsts for You, my flesh yearns for You,
   in an earth dry and desolate, without water.
63:2 Thus in the holy place I have beheld You,
   to see Your power and Your glory.

---

1. Modified from Goldingay, *Psalms*, 2:255.
2. deClaissé-Walford et al., *Book of Psalms*, 519.

63:3 Because Your lovingkindness is better than life,
       my lips laud You.
63:4 So I bless You for [all] my life;
       in Your name I lift up my hands.
63:5 As with fat and richness [of food] my soul is satisfied,
       and with lips joyfully shouting my mouth offers praise.
63:6 When I remember You on my bed,
       in the night watches I meditate on You.
63:7 For You have been a help to me,
       and in the shadow of Your wings I shout with joy.
63:8 My soul cleaves unto You;
       Your right hand holds me.
63:9 But they—those seeking to destroy my soul—
       will go into the depths of the earth.
63:10 They who pour it out upon the hand of the sword—
       a portion for foxes they will be.
63:11 But the king will rejoice in God;
       everyone who swears by Him will offer praise,
       for the mouths of those who speak falsehood will be stopped.

Structure

All that the psalmist is doing in relation to God may be utilized to create a structure for the psalm:[3]

> **Running to God's presence (63:1–2)**
> "my soul" (63:1b)
> "God" (63:1a [×2]); "earth" (63:1c)
>
> **Revering God's kindness (63:3–5)**
> "my soul" (63:5a)
>
> **Remembering God's faithfulness (63:6–8)**
> "my soul" (63:8a)
>
> **Rejoicing in God's protection (63:9–11)**
> "my soul" (63:9a)
> "God" (63:11a); "earth" (63:9b)

---

3. From Martin, "Longing for God," 62–63.

As indicated by the recurrence of "my soul" in each of these sections of the composition, the entirety of the psalmist's being is (to be) involved with his running to God, revering God, remembering God, and rejoicing in God—a wholistic, consolidated, total, and exhaustive alliance with deity.[4]

Theological Focus

The lives of the people of God, and of their leaders, living in a less than ideal world and beset by opposition and trauma, are characterized by a fervent and incessant yearning for the presence of God, satisfied on this side of eternity by his lovingkindness revered, his faithfulness remembered, and his protection rejoiced in—a blissful cleaving to God as he holds them in his grasp.

Commentary

Running to God's Presence (63:1–2)

The parched nature of the "earth" (or "land") is likely to be metaphorical, in conjunction with the "thirst" of the psalmist's soul for God (63:1). No doubt, all of life this side of eternity can be characterized as "dry and desolate, without water." And in such a constrained life, the norm for the people of God must be a soulful and intense yearning for God. This ardent desire was temporarily satisfied in the sanctuary/temple (63:2) where, with the community of God, the power and glory of God was comprehended "in the splendor of worship with its sacrifices, processions, and rituals," and heard in the recounting of divine acts of wonder performed for his people.[5]

Revering God's Kindness; Remembering God's Faithfulness (63:3–8)

And there in the sanctuary, the psalmist becomes acutely aware of God's lovingkindness—"better than *life*" (63:3)—and so he breaks out in praise, not just for the duration of the worship, but "all my *life*" (63:4).

> "So I bless You
> for [בְּ, *b*] [all] my life;
> in [בְּ] Your name
> I lift up my hands."

---

4. "Soul," נֶפֶשׁ, *nephesh*, refers to the entirety of one's being; it does not have the exclusive sense of immateriality as it does in English.

5. Goldingay, *Psalms*, 2:257.

In 63:4a there may be a subtle play on words: "to bless" is בָּרֵךְ, *brk*, while בֶּרֶךְ, *berek*, means "knee." The proximity to "hands" is telling (63:4b): thus hands lifted and knees bowed, in total commitment and dependence upon God.

"The psalmists often plead for divine help in trouble. This confession [of God's loving-kindness] suggests that divine loyalty is a deeper reality than wilderness experiences and the opposition of evildoers."[6] The earth, dry and desolate, is made livable by the lovingkindness of God! A rich feast it becomes, with an abundance of culinary delicacies (63:5a). Indeed, because he is now "satisfied" with God's kindness (63:5a), his lauding "lips" (63:3b) become "joyfully shouting *lips*" that move his mouth in praise (63:5b). Thus "the mouth that began dry and dusty is now full of praise and blessing for God," and those same organs are involved in the gratifying divine banquet.[7]

The scene then seems to shift in 63:6. Earlier, at daytime and in the sanctuary, the psalmist was employing his "joyfully shouting [רְנָנָה, *rnanah*] lips" (63:5b); here at nighttime and in his bed, he is still "shouting with joy [רנן, *rnn*]" (63:7b). Both day and night, therefore, the longing of the psalmist for his God is manifest in his exclusive focus upon deity and his exulting joy in him. Thus the indicated time and space is representative of what should happen in the life of every child of God: an unceasing concentration upon the mercies of God that leads to greater joy: the remembrance is, no doubt, that of the experience of God's faithfulness in the past. And why not jubilate? God has been the help of the psalmist who continues to abide in the shadow of divine wings (63:7). And so his soul "cleaves" to God (63:8a): deity will be the sole resource for help at all times. But there is a mutuality in this grasping relationship: God's right hand, in turn, holds his child (63:8b).[8]

Rejoicing in God's Protection (63:9–11)

On the other hand, enemies—and 63:9 begins with a disjunctive "but they"—will only go away from God and "into the depths of the earth," headed into Sheol, dead presumably (63:9b). These adversaries may have thought they were impaling ("pour[ing] ... out") the righteous on "the hand [יָד, *yad*] of the sword" (63:10[9]), but little did they know that they were the ones headed downward. In contrast, the "right hand [יָמִין, *yamin*]" of God (63:8b) upheld those who lifted their "hands [יָד]" to his name (63:4b): God was protecting his own. Foes would "be [היה, *hyh*]" food for foxes (63:10b),[10] for God had "been [היה]" a help to his people (63:7a). On the other hand, in a stark contrast, the righteous would be as ones feasting and being sated on "fat and richness" (63:5a).

When all is said and done, the king, representing the people—and perhaps this ruler is the psalmist obliquely referring to himself—will rejoice in God and "offer praise" to him (63:11b). Of course, it is not just the regent who has occasion and reason to exult and exalt: all of God's people who long earnestly for him, satisfied with his presence, also "offer praise"

---

6. Brueggemann and Bellinger, *Psalms*, 278.

7. deClaissé-Walford et al., *Book of Psalms*, 520.

8. This reciprocity is further (and amply) reflected in the entirety of the psalm by its thirteen first-person suffixes (signifying "I"/"me"/"my") and fifteen second-person suffixes (signifying "You"/"Your").

9. "Hand of the sword" is an idiom for the weapon's power.

10. Tate notes the shameful end of these wicked ones—"unattended and unburied" (Tate, *Psalms 51–100*, 128).

(63:5b). "Swearing by Him" (63:11b) is another manifestation of the loyalty and commitment of the people of God to, and their absolute trust in, their deity.[11] And thus, basking in divine protection, and even as their "mouths" offer praise (63:5b), the righteous (and their rulers), i.e., those who "earnestly long [שׁחר, *shchr*]" for God (63:1a), will behold the "mouths" of their adversaries—organs that produce "falsehood [שֶׁקֶר, *sheqer*]"—being "stopped [סכר, *skr*]" (63:11c; the wordplays are powerful). And with another mention of "God" in the last verse (63:11a), the psalm concludes as it began. God wins . . . and so do his people!

Sermon Map

I. Starved

    A less-than-ideal world (63:1c)

    A less-than-healthy opposition (63:9a, 10a, 11cα)

    Move-to-relevance: Life is not perfect

II. Sated

    A more-than-enough lovingkindness (63:3a, 5a)

    A more-than-expected faithfulness (63:6–7bα)

    A more-than-adequate protection (63:9b, 10b, 11abcβ)

    Move-to-relevance: God is all we need

III. *Seek and Sing!*

    Seeking God (63:1ab, 2, 8)

    Singing of God (63:2, 3b–4, 5b, 7bβ)

    How to seek always and to sing everywhere

---

11. While swearing by the king is noted in the OT (1 Sam 17:55; 2 Sam 15:21), here it is likely to indicate swearing by God (the nearest antecedent to "him" in Ps 63:11b is "God" in 63:11a), the one to whom his people "offer praise" (63:5b, 11b).

PSALM 64:1–10

Psalm of Disorientation

Rejoicing in the Refuge

PSALM 64 "COMMUNICATES A sense of anxiety and perplexity about the nature of human society that is at home in every generation. The supposed sophistication of modern society is not immune to deep awareness of destructive forces which threaten to reduce our semi-ordered world to chaos," whether it be from medical, political, economic, or social causes, not to mention the deprivations of one's own personal sins.[1] Nevertheless, there appears to be a focus in the psalm on thought and word. A number of words kin to those semantic fields attests to this emphasis: God is asked to "hear" the "voice" of the psalmist's "lament" (64:1) that bemoans the oppressors' "secret counsel" (64:2), their sharp "tongues," and their weaponized "bitter word," (64:3), for they cunningly "calculate" and derisively "say" that their misdeeds will escape notice (64:5); they "conceive" a "well-conceived conception," the outcome of their dark, inner "thought" and "heart" (64:6). Yes, these oppressors may wax eloquent and wreak havoc, but to no avail: God's punitive action will make them trip on their own "tongue" (64:8), causing all mankind to penitently "fear" and "proclaim" God and "understand" his deeds (64:9), while the righteous "rejoices" and finds refuge in God, uttering "praise" to him (64:10).[2] But the emphasis on thinking and speech does not make matters any less serious.[3] In any case, the psalm is, in sum, a declaration of confidence in the protection and deliverance of God.[4]

---

1. Tate, *Psalms 51–100*, 135.

2. Modified from Botha, "Textual Strategy," 73. That being said there is actual action here as well: "doers [from פעל, *p'l*] of harm" (64:2b) who "shoot" (×2; 64:4) the upright with an "arrow" (64:3b). As well, there is the "doing [also from פעל]" of God (64:9b), who recompenses the wicked by "shooting" the wicked (64:7a) with his "arrow" (64:7a).

3. It is also possible that supernatural forces are being considered as operating in all of those wicked enterprises.

4. Tate, *Psalms 51–100*, 135.

Translation

64:1 Hear, God, my voice, in my complaint;
    from terror of the enemy preserve my life.
64:2 Hide me from the secret counsel of evil ones,
    from the tumult of doers of harm,
64:3 who have sharpened their tongue like a sword;
    they aimed the arrow of the bitter word
64:4 to shoot the blameless from hiding places—
    suddenly they shoot at him, and they do not fear.
64:5 They strengthen themselves [for] an evil purpose;
    they calculate to set snares covertly;
    they say, "Who will see them?"
64:6 They conceive injustices: "We have perfected a well-conceived conception,
    for the inward thought and heart of a person are deep."
64:7 But God will shoot them with an arrow—
    suddenly they are wounded.
64:8 And Yahw[eh] will make [them] stumble upon their own tongue;
    all who see them will shake their head.
64:9 Then all mankind will fear,
    and they will proclaim the doing of God,
    and His works they will understand.
64:10 The righteous one rejoices in Yahweh,
    and seeks refuge in Him;
    and they will praise—all the upright of heart.

Structure

As might be expected, Psalm 64 follows the characteristic pattern of a lament:

Petition and Persecution (64:1–6)
    Petition (**64:1–2**)
    Persecution (**64:3–6**): "shoot" (64:4a, 4b); "suddenly" (64:4b)

Punishment and Penitence (64:7–9)
    Punishment (**64:7–8**): "shoot" (64:7a); "suddenly" (64:7b)
    Penitence (**64:9**)

Praise (64:10)

Theological Focus

Caught unawares in the midst of, and terrified by, treacherously scheming and arrogant predators, the righteous petition God against their persecution, and expect divine punishment for those evildoers commensurate with their wickedness, that brings all mankind to penitence, and culminates in the praise of God by his people.

Commentary

Petition and Persecution (64:1–6)

Psalm 64 commences with a staccato of urgent appeals: "hear," "preserve" (64:1), and "hide" (64:2a). Correspondingly, there is a trio of adversaries: "enemy" (64:1b), "evil ones," and "doers of harm" (64:2), and a triplet of effects—they cause "terror" (64:1b), concoct "secret counsel," and create "tumult" (64:2). It appears that there may be more going on than just the foes' antagonistic thoughts and words: the supplicant's very life seems to be in grievous danger from persecution. Of course, lethality comes in many varieties, and thoughts leading to words can cause serious harm of a psychological kind. A hint that that may be the case is seen in the wordplay: the enemies shoot arrows of the "bitter word" (דָּבָר מָר, *davar mar*; 64:3b), even as they proceed to transact an "evil purpose" (דָּבָר רָע, *davar ra'*; 64:5a).

At any rate, the petition has ominous overtones with verbal assaults likened to swords and arrows (64:3) aimed at their prey from concealment and undertaken brazenly (64:4). The psalmist and his righteous cohort are "blameless" (תָּם, *tam*; 64:4a),[5] but the opponents have "perfected" (תמם, *tmm*; 64:6a) their wicked plots against the former, emphasized in the threefold occurrence of the root חפשׂ, *chps*, in "conceive," "well-conceived," and "conception" (64:6a). So these opponents are not just conceiving, they are conspiring and maneuvering and scheming and acting to take down the righteous. And all this talk of "secret counsel" (64:2a), "hiding places" (64:4a), the unexpected suddenness of the attacks (64:4b), the covert traps (64:5b), and the claim that no one will see them (64:5c), means that God's people are unable "to discover the quarter from which the weapon was shot, nor to detect the hand which forged the arrowhead, or tinged it with the poison," making these assaults all the more treacherous.[6]

> The sinister nature of the activity of the evildoers in these verses suggests to the reader that superhuman forces, or even agents, are at work, ... [particularly in] a culture pervaded by awareness of the harmful powers of speech, combined with a sense of superhuman powers and demons. The sudden arrow, which comes silently and opens deadly wounds ... , and the sense of traps and snares contribute to a feeling of anxiety and apprehension of the uncanny.[7]

---

5. The community of God in this psalm are labeled equivalently as the "blameless" (64:4a), the "righteous" (64:10a), and the "upright of heart" (64:10c). These attributions do not indicate absolute holiness, of course, but a steadfast loyalty and commitment to their God.

6. Spurgeon, *Treasury of David*, 3:83.

7. Tate, *Psalms 51–100*, 133–34. Moving to spiritual warfare in application may not be a bad approach at all.

No wonder the psalmist pleads that God may "hide" him (סתר, *str*; 64:2a); after all, these sinister antagonists are discharging their weapons from "hiding places" (מִסְתָּר, *mistar*, also from סתר; 64:4a).

The arrogance of these nefarious ones is obvious: not only do they lack fear (ostensibly of both humans and God, 64:4b), they are haughtily insensible enough to congratulate themselves that no one will spot their vile strategies—"Who will see them?" (64:5c): "Our plans are too well-laid in the depths of our intelligence to be foreseen or even detected." Notice the contrast between the psalmist's plea (64:1a) and the wicked ones' puffery (64:5c):[8]

64:1a	"Hear, God, my voice, in my complaint."
64:5c	"They say, 'Who will see them?'"

The righteous go humbly to God, petitioning him to hear their voice; the unrighteous proclaim hubristically that no one will see them—they are wrong!

Punishment and Penitence (64:7–9)

The beginning of 64:7, "but God . . . ," indicates that a turning point has been achieved with the appearance of deity. He shows up in this psalm only in 64:7 and 64:8 as a subject, distributing just deserts as punishment to the wicked who dare oppress God's people. The opponents "shoot" their "arrow" (64:3b–4), and God, in return, "shoots" an "arrow" (64:7a). But that is about all he has to do, apparently—one shot with one arrow and the wicked are instantly laid low (64:7). And even as the wicked discharged their weapons at the righteous "suddenly" (64:4b), so also God's unerring aim will pierce the attackers "suddenly" (64:7b).[9] The difficult verse, 64:8, is best seen as the malefactors stumbling (and supposedly falling[10]) on their own tongue—their own weapon, a metaphorical "sword" (64:3a).[11] Another case of tit-for-tat, though what exactly the divine retribution is remains unspecified. Indeed, just as "the psalm portrays the work of evildoers as secret and mysterious," so also "the anticipated judgment of God . . . has some of the same mystery."[12]

Whatever the divine punishment is, the consequence is that *"all* mankind" will "fear" (64:9a) as they see what has now befallen the wicked—the ones who themselves had no "fear"

---

8. From Auffret, *Voyez de vos yeux*, 130.

9. These are the only instances of "suddenly," פִּתְאֹם, *pit'om*, in the Psalter.

10. Stumbling and falling is a common pairing in the OT: Ps 27:2; Prov 24:16, 17; Isa 3:8; 8:15; 31:3; Jer 46:6, 12, 16; 50:32; Dan 11:19.

11. The verse, 64:8, is quite undecipherable in the MT as it is. I follow the minimal emendation of Barré, "Proposal on the Crux," 115–19, changing וַיַּכְשִׁילוּהוּ, *wyykshylwhw*, to יַכְשִׁיל יהו, *wykshyl yhw* ("and Yahu/Yahw[eh] will make [them] stumble"), and considering עָלֵימוֹ, *'lymw*, as עָלֵים, *'lym* (with the מ, *m*, enclitic: "upon"). Thus: "And Yahw[eh] will make [them] stumble upon . . . ."

12. Tate, *Psalms 51–100*, 132.

(64:4b). They who thought no one would "see" their camouflaged immoralities (64:5c) are themselves "seen" (64:8b) by the rest of humanity who "shake their head," either in approval of the fate of the wicked or with apprehension of the justice of God. In any case, humanity will be struck by God's justice and they will proceed to announce his works, as they comprehend his actions (64:9). Interestingly enough, there is a wordplay with the various verbs: "shoot" is ירה or ירא (*yrh* or *yr'*; 64:4a, 4b and 64:7a); "fear" is ראה, *r'h* (64:4b and 64:9a); and "see" is ירא (64:5c and 64:8b). There is also the labeling of the wicked as "*doers* of harm" (from פעל; 64:2); in contrast, and at the end of it all, mankind, seeing God's punishment of those evil ones, will proclaim deity's "doing" (also from פעל; 64:9b). The untenable situation of persecution has been turned to punishment, and the petition of the psalmist has been heard, seemingly converting all mankind, and generating, in the righteous, praise for this great God.

Praise (64:10)

"All" mankind will fear, proclaim, and understand God (64:9), but "all" the righteous (64:10c) will "rejoice" in Yahweh, "seek refuge" in him, and "praise" him—a parallel trio of actions (64:10). Indeed, this threefold response ought to be how God's people live in a world beset by evil: with joy at God's hearing of their petition; in safety under God's protection in times of persecution; and with exultation at God's restoration of order and the penitence of all humankind. Whereas the wicked boasted of the depth of their "heart" (64:6) and of the clever plots emanating from it, the last laugh—or more accurately, the last *Hallelujah* (הלל, *hll*, "praise")—will be had by the "upright of *heart*" (64:10c). The structure of 64:10 emphasizes the relationship of the people of God with their deity, and the consequences thereof:[13]

> "The righteous one
>   rejoices
>   in Yahweh,
>   and seeks refuge
>   in Him;
>   and they will praise—
> all the upright of heart."

The psalm's systematic use of paronomasia, repetition, irony, metonymy, and metaphor [not to mention number: see the various triplets] presupposes a sense of the unity of reality that is grounded in God. Everything connects. The law of reality is the law of correspondence, because one God's being lies behind it. We can look for connections even where things look unconnected or conflicted and can believe there is meaning and coherence even where things look meaningless and fragmented.[14]

After all, God is for his people, so they can rejoice, trust, and praise him, no matter what the circumstances!

---

13. From Auffret, *Voyez de vos yeux*, 132.
14. Goldingay, *Psalms*, 2:271.

PSALM 64:1–10

Sermon Map

I. Persecution
    Treacherous and terrifying attacks (64:1–6)
    Move-to-relevance: Manifest evils around us—demonic, social, etc.

II. Punishment
    Divine retribution that is commensurate (64:7–8)
    Move-to-relevance: But God is all we need

III. Praise
    Widespread acknowledgment of God by mankind (64:9)
    Joy, protection, and praise for the righteous (64:10)

IV. *Take Refuge and Give Reverence!*
    Specifics on seeking safety in God and praise him

PSALM 65:1–13

Psalm of Disorientation

God's Blessings: Spiritual, Social, Physical

PSALM 65, ADDRESSED ENTIRELY to God, is like "a play with three acts."[1] Each act concerns a spatial entity: Zion, the cosmos, and the earth, respectively, and furthermore, each act deals with the work of God in that particular locus: forgiving, ordering, and blessing, respectively.

Translation

65:1 To You, praise [awaits] in silence, God, in Zion,
 and to You the vow will be fulfilled.
65:2 The One who hears prayer—
 unto You all flesh comes.
65:3 The records of iniquities, they prevail against me;
 [but] our rebellions, You—You forgive them.
65:4 Blessing [upon] the one You choose and draw near [to You]:
 he abides in Your courts.
 We will be satisfied with the goodness of Your house,
 Your holy temple.
65:5 [With] awesome acts, in righteousness You answer us, God of our deliverance,
 the trust of all the ends of the earth and the distant seas—
65:6 the One who establishes the mountains by His power,
 the One girded with might;
65:7 the One who stills the roaring of the seas,
 the roaring of their waves, and the tumult of the peoples.

---

1. deClaissé-Walford et al., *Book of Psalms*, 527.

65:8   And they will be awed—those dwelling in the ends [of the earth]—by Your signs;
     [from] the going out of the morning and [of] the evening
     You make [them] shout for joy.
65:9   You have visited the earth and made it overflow;
     You have greatly enriched it.
     The stream of God is full of water;
     You prepare their grain, for thus You prepare it.
65:10 Its furrows to drench, to saturate its ridges,
     with great showers You soften it; its growth You bless.
65:11 You have crowned the year with Your goodness,
     and Your tracks, they drip fatness.
65:12 The pastures of the wilderness drip,
     and with jubilation the hills, they array [themselves].
65:13 The meadows clothe [themselves] with flocks,
     and the valleys drape [themselves] with grain;
     they shout triumphantly; indeed, they sing.

Structure

The structure follows the three spatial loci and the three acts of God therein/thereof:

God and Zion (65:1–4): *God's gracious forgiveness*
  "goodness" (65:4c)
  "praise" (65:1a)

God and Cosmos (65:5–8): *God's powerful ordering*
  "awesome," "ends" (65:5a)
  "awed," "ends" (65:8a)

God and Earth (65:9–13): *God's bountiful provisioning*
  "goodness" (65:11a)
  "shout triumphantly," "sing" (65:13c)

Ultimately, Psalm 65 is a paean to the graciousness, greatness, and goodness of God, all directed primarily towards humanity. And such a deity, who governs Zion, the cosmos, and the earth and acts mightily in each arena for the sake of his people, is a God worthy of praise (65:1a) in shouting and song (65:13c), by beings both animate and inanimate, sentient and non-sentient. Interestingly, enough, God is not called "Yahweh" in this psalm, despite the presence of Zionic elements, thus maintaining its focus upon a deity who superintends everyone and everything in every space and every time.

Theological Focus

The goodness of God—graciously forgiving mankind (their spiritual need), powerfully maintaining order in his creation (their social need), and bounteously provisioning them (their physical need)—evokes joyous praise from an awed and trusting humankind and from creation itself.

Commentary

God and Zion (65:1–4)

The first two lines of the psalm each begin directly with "to You" (65:1a, 1b), a clear indication that this psalm is going to be God-directed. And the structure of 65:1–4 shows the focus to be on the God of grace who forgives his people's sins, literally blockading those "iniquities" and "rebellions" by his prayer-hearing and forgiving intentions:

A	"Praise" to God "Zion" (65:1a)	
	B	"one who hears prayer" (65:2a)
		C "unto You" (65:2b)
		D "iniquities" (65:3a)
		D' "rebellions" (65:3bα)
		C' "You" (65:3bβ)
	B' "You forgive" (65:3bγ)	
A'	"Blessed[ness]" to mankind God's "courts," "house," "temple" (65:4)	

So much so, "praise" to God from mankind (65:1a) is reciprocated by "blessedness" to mankind from God (65:4).

Silently, praise waits to be voiced and uttered before God in Zion, i.e., in the temple, and a vow awaits fulfillment (65:1[2])—referring to the offering of thanks intended to be made for God's goodness (65:4a, 11a), likely for the forgiveness of sin. One of the main functions of the temple was to mediate God's mercies to his people who had broken his laws, and so, to a prayer-hearing God, "all flesh" comes (65:2b). These are God-seekers, people who worship him, having access to his "courts," his "house," and his "temple" (65:4bcd). But later this cohort also seems to include "those dwelling in the ends [of the earth]" (65:8a).

In any case, these worshipers of God come bearing not offerings and sacrifices, but apparently their own sins (65:3). The parallel between God as "one who hears prayer" (65:1b)

---

2. As it is, the Hebrew text of 65:1a reads, "To You, silence, praise, God." It is best to see "silence" as a predicate, thus: "To You, praise [awaits] in silence, God." That would make the construction similar to that of 62:1a: "Only for God in silence [awaits] my soul."

and who "forgives" (65:3bγ) makes it clear that the approach of "all flesh" to God is for the purpose of seeking his pardon.[3]

This arrival of humanity was not simply "to" (לְ, *l*) God, but "unto" (עַד, *'ad*) God (65:2b), signifying a deliberate approach towards deity, to get right with him. While it is "all flesh," a plurality, that comes to God (65:2b), 65:4a points to a singular individual who is blessed by God.[4] That simply asserts that each and every confessing individual who seeks divine pardon will be blessed by this prayer-hearing, sin-forgiving God, one by one, one and all. No one is rejected. The consequence is the blessing of abiding with God (65:4b), enjoying the goodness of God's house and temple. That is to say, the forgiven sinner will be satisfied by the very presence of God.

And thus, "praise" [תְּהִלָּה, *thillah*) from mankind goes to God (65:1a), the "prayer [תְּפִלָּה, *tphillah*]"-hearing, forgiving deity and, in the other direction, blessedness from God comes to forgiven mankind (65:4a)! God is good, indeed!

God and Cosmos (65:5–8)

The second section, 65:5–8, looks both forwards and backwards—it acts as a hinge (see below). It is bookended by "awesome/awed" and "ends," and delineates what is described in between as God's wondrous, numinous, and stupendous acts:

65:5	"awesome" (65:5a); "ends" (65:5b) "answer" (65:5a) *links to* "hear" (65:2a)
65:6–7	**Acts of God**
65:8	"awed"; "ends" (65:8a) "shout for joy" (65:8c) *links to* "shout triumphantly" (65:13c)

After the parochial activities of God in Zion, 65:5–8 outlines his works, expanding its scope to the cosmos as a whole.[5] While "earth" is mentioned in *God and Cosmos* (65:5b), as well as components thereof ("mountains," "seas," and "peoples" and "those dwelling"; 65:5b–8a), the metaphorical focus appears be upon the divine subduing of the chaos that still continues to stain an ungodly and disorderly cosmos post-fall. The participles in 65:6–7 ("the One who establishes," "the One girded," "the One who stills") indicate that the activities described are ongoing: God continues to restrain and constrain chaos, whether natural (of the mountains and seas; 65:6–7bα) or national ("the tumult of the peoples"; 65:7bβ). He is after all, the God of order. Iniquities of humanity may "prevail" (גבר, *gvr*; 65:3a), but God is the one girded with "might" (גְּבוּרָה, *gvurah*; 65:6b), well able to overcome the forces of disorder in nature as well as in nations (and in individuals as was seen in the first section, *God and Zion*). No wonder inhabitants even to the ends of the earth are awed by those "signs" (65:8a), whether they dwell in the east ("[from] the going out of the morning") or in the west ("and [of] the

---

3. "Record" translates דָּבָר, *davar*.

4. And 65:4c returns to the plural "we."

5. Notice also the movement from the specific people of God, the ones in view in 65:1–4, to all humanity in this section: "all the ends of the earth and the distant seas" (65:5b), and "those dwelling in the ends [of the earth]" (65:8a).

evening") (65:8bc). The structuring of 65:8 re-emphasizes what was stated in 65:6–7, about the greatness of God:[6]

> "And they will be awed—
>   those dwelling in the ends [of the earth]—
>   **by Your signs;**
>   [from] the going out of the morning and [of] the evening
>   You make [them] shout for joy."

Thus, this central section, *God and Cosmos*, declaring the continuing exhibition of divine power and might, provides the basis for the previous section: why this awesome deity can pardon sin (65:1–4[7]). It also delineates the grounds for the following section: how this powerful God can grant incredible fertility to the earth (*God and Earth*, 65:9–13; see below).[8] Therefore, these redoubtable deeds ("awesome acts" [from ירא], 65:5a; and "signs" that "awe" [ירא], 65:8a) evoke "trust" (65:5b) in the greatness of this sovereign God who has all things in the cosmos under his absolute control.

God and Earth (65:9–13)

From the general involvement of God in maintaining order from disorder in the cosmos comes a specific consequence—his beneficence towards his creation, demonstrated in the bounty of his provisioning on earth.

This final section of Psalm 65, *God and Earth*, is firmly linked to all what preceded it. The same "earth" that God ordered (65:5b) is the "earth" that God renders fecund (65:9a); the powerful one who "establishes" mountains (כון, *kwn*; 65:6a) also "prepares" the earth for grain (also כון [×2]; 65:9d); both Zion and earth manifest the "goodness" of God (65:4c, 11a);[9] and God's people enjoy "blessing" (אַשְׁרֵי, *'ashre*; 65:4a) and the earth He "bless[es]" (ברך, *brk*; 65:10b). "Thus, the presence of God in the temple [*God and Zion*], and the 'awesome deeds' in ordering creation [*God and Cosmos*], are continuous with the work of God in and with Earth [*God and Earth*]."[10] Though in this final section humans have disappeared, there can be no question that God's provisioning on earth is for their sake, to meet all their physical needs. All that to say, this deity is not just an abstraction hovering disinterestedly

---

6. See Auffret, *Voyez de vos yeux*, 144. The morning and evening events might also signify time—from sunrise to sunset, i.e., all day, all the time, always!

7. God "answers" his people, but what the question (or plea) was is unclear. It might well have been a prayer for forgiveness (65:2–3). In that case, the "answer" of God, "in righteousness," was his bestowal of forgiveness (65:5a).

8. Wallace, "*Jubilate Deo*," 58.

9. If the "stream of God" (65:9c) is issuing from the temple, this blessing of bounty in nature coheres even more precisely with *God and Zion* (65:1–4).

10. Wallace, "*Jubilate Deo*," 58. Wallace ("*Jubilate Deo*," 59–60) also points to Canaanite and Syrian texts that describe gods enabling agricultural fertility. However, significantly absent from all of them is the motif of joy found in 65:1a, 4, 8, 12b–13. Of course, neither is there any indication of those deities forgiving sin or overwhelming chaos.

over his creation, but one who is actively working for its benefit and for the goodness of his people—a God of grace (65:1–4), power (65:5–8), and bounty (65:9–13).

With nine verbs having God as the direct or indirect (in the case of infinitives) subject in 65:9-10, the earth is prepared by deity with an abundance of rain for the bumper crop described in 65:11-13: he "greatly" (רַב, *rav*; 65:9b) enriches the earth with "great" (רְבִיבִים, *rvivim*; 65:10b) showers.[11] Thus, the earth's "pastures," "the wilderness," "hills," "meadows," and "valleys" (65:12–13b) overflow with an agricultural extravagance and prodigality, such that even the divine footprints—"Your tracks," i.e., wherever God goes—oozes with abundance ("fatness"), as the year is crowned with "goodness" (65:11b).

And the rightful response of praise to this magnificence of divine provision (65:13c) portrays nature itself (indicated by "they") joining a ringing worship of this bountiful, blessing God![12] While much of this irruptive praise will be fully manifested only in the eschaton as the kingdom of God is consummated with its new heavens and new earth, there should be no doubt about what this composition is asserting: "Earth's fruitfulness is itself its act of praise. It is through its fruitfulness that it glorifies God. This link between its fruitfulness and its praise extends the link between the earth and humanity, since there is a sense in which the fruitfulness of our lives of faithfulness is an aspect of our worship."[13]

And so God's people are impassioned by this text about the magnificent blessings they have been granted by their God, the One who cares for them personally (graciously forgiving them), who cares for his cosmos (powerfully ordering it), and who cares for the very environment in which his community lives (bountifully provisioning it), as he provides for *all* needs: forgiveness beyond sin, peace beyond chaos, and fertility beyond barrenness. Spiritual life, social life, and physical life—all taken care of by the "goodness" of God (65:4c, 11a)!

Sermon Map

I. Gracious Forgiving
    God's acquittal (65:2–4)
    Move-to-relevance: The reconciliation of God

II. Powerful Ordering
    God's control (65:7–8)
    Move-to-relevance: The constraint of God

III. Bounteous Provisioning
    God's bestowal (65:9–13b)
    Move-to-relevance: The provision of God

IV. *Join Nature's Noise!*
    Praise (65:1, 13c)
    Specifics on the appreciation of nature's noise and our participation

---

11. Psalm 65:10a is chiastic: "Its furrows / to drench, // to saturate / its ridges."
12. Such a response of nature is not entirely unusual in the Psalter; see 89:12; 96:11–12; 98:7–8; etc.
13. Goldingay, *Psalms*, 2:283.

PSALM 66:1–20

Psalm of Orientation

Faithfulness of God; Faithfulness of His People

PSALM 66 BEGINS EXACTLY where Psalm 65 ended: the latter concluded with nature "shouting triumphantly" (65:13); the former begins with humans called to "shout triumphantly" (66:1), followed by an exhortation to "make music" to glorify God (66:2). One could therefore see this psalm as being quite hymnic, with a focus first on the community (66:1–12) and then on the individual (66:13–20).[1]

Translation

66:1 Shout triumphantly to God, all the earth;
66:2 make music to the glory of His name;
make glorious His praise.
66:3 Say to God, "How awesome [are] Your works.
Because of the greatness of Your strength
Your enemies will cringe before You.
66:4 All the earth will worship You,
and will make music to You;
they will make music to Your name."
66:5 Come and see the works of God
that are awesome in action unto humanity.
66:6 He turned the sea into dry land;
they passed through the river on foot;
there let us rejoice in Him.

---

1. However, the magnitude of the offerings in 66:13–15 seem to exceed the possibilities for a single individual; the supplicant may have been a community leader of significant means, or perhaps was resolving to join a communal offering of sacrifice.

66:7 The One ruling by His might forever,
    His eyes take notice of the nations:
    let not the rebellious exalt themselves.
66:8 Bless our God, peoples,
    and make heard the voice of His praise—
66:9 the One keeping our souls in life,
    and He does not let our feet slip.
66:10 For You have tried us, God;
    You have refined us as refined silver.
66:11 You brought us into a net;
    You laid hardship upon our hips.
66:12 You made mortals ride on our heads;
    we went through fire and through water;
    yet You set us forth into a wide place [of flourishing].
66:13 I will enter into Your house with whole-offerings;
    I shall fulfill my vows to You,
66:14 which my lips opened [to speak]
    and my mouth spoke in my narrow place [of distress].
66:15 Whole-offerings [of] fatlings I shall offer to You
    with the smoke of rams;
    I shall prepare bulls with male goats.
66:16 Come, hear, and I will recount, all who fear God,
    what He has done for my soul.
66:17 To Him with my mouth I cried,
    and extolled [Him] on my tongue.
66:18 If I regard harm in my heart,
    the Lord will not hear.
66:19 But truly God heard;
    He attended to the voice of my prayer.
66:20 Blessed be God,
    who has not turned aside my prayer
    or His lovingkindness from me.

Structure

Each part, community-related and individual-related, goes through a similar sequence of exalting God (his praise), exulting in God's deeds (his performance), and extolling him for his deliverance (preservation):[2]

COMMUNITY (66:1–12)		INDIVIDUAL (66:13–20)	
66:1–4	God's Praise 1	66:13–15	God's Praise 2
66:5–7	God's Performance 1 "Come and see" (66:5a) Warning (66:7)	66:16–19	God's Performance 2 "Come, hear" (66:16a) Warning (66:18–19)
66:8–12	God's Preservation 1 "Bless our God" (66:8a)	66:20	God's Preservation 2 "Blessed be God" (66:20a)

For both the larger community and for the anonymous individual, God is worthy of praise, his performances are worthy to be testified to, and he is worthy of blessing because of his preservation of all his people and of each one singly. "Individual deliverance and communal deliverance are included in the Psalter not merely for balance, but of necessity. Each needs the other."[3] "Shout triumphantly to God" the community is exhorted (66:1a); and "I will . . ." asserts the individual (66:13a). Thus, "worship is set forth as both communal and individual. The individual experience of worship properly belongs in the context of the corporate."[4]

Theological Focus

> The recollection of God's past performances of might in the preservation of his people as they remain faithful to him in and through their present, sovereignly ordained adversities moves God to hear their prayers, and results in both individual and communal praise for deliverance, the adumbration of a global celebration of this awesome God.

Commentary

Community (66:1–12)

The entirety of the earth is called to make a triumphant shout to God (66:1).[5] And praise needs to be commensurate to the status of the person being praised: the "glory" of God's name

---

2. Modified from Gaiser, "'I Will Tell You,'" 140. The categories, however, are not airtight: praise pervades the entire composition.
3. Gaiser, "'I Will Tell You,'" 141.
4. Tate, *Psalms 51–100*, 151.
5. "All the earth" bookends the *Praise 1* section (66:1a, 4a); it is also unified by the repeat of "make music" (66:2a, 4b, 4c) and "name" (66:2a, 4c).

(66:2a) demands "glorious" praise (66:2b). Besides, his works are "awesome" and his strength "great" (66:3ab), so much so the defeat of his enemies is absolute (66:3c). All this calls for praise because God's mighty deeds are undertaken for the benefit of his people: in fact, "all the earth," it is recommended, should engage in the worship of God (66:4).

Though the "works" of God were mentioned in 66:3a, more detail is provided in 66:5-7.[6] "Sea" and "river" (66:6ab) are likely to refer to the same entity (as in 93:3-4; Jonah 2:3), with Ps 66:6a indicating the exodus and 66:6b referring to the crossing of the Jordan. These "works" of God are directed "unto humanity," the rescue of God's people (66:5b). In any case, the exultation is for God's overcoming the forces of chaos indicated by those waters. Strikingly, there is an anachronous relocation of the psalmist's generation to the day of the exodus: while the earlier band of Israelites ("they") crossed the waters (66:6b), it is the current crop ("us") that is called to rejoice "there" (66:6c) in a present reality, thus assimilating the community of Psalm 66 with the broader group of God's people of all time. And so, all are invited to "come and see" God's performance (66:5a).[7]

There is also a warning to the wicked embedded here (66:7); he who made his enemies cringe (66:3c) will surely not look askance at the rebellion and self-exaltation of the nations (66:7bc). So while this psalm is essentially a hymn of praise, it is also an exhortation to the unruly to learn from the experience of God's triumph over his foes. After all he is the King of the universe "ruling by His might forever" (66:7a).

While the mighty works of God are exulted in, in 66:5-7, the consequence of those divine performances is brought home to the community in 66:8-12, as they proclaim their preservation by God.

There is an ironic anguish in the psalm: the people of God "make" (שִׂים, *sym*) his praise glorious (66:2b), and God "keeps" (שִׂים) their souls in life (66:9a), but it is he himself who "lays" (שִׂים) hardship upon his community (66:11b). While that perplexity is not solved in this psalm, there is no question that God's people do go through considerable angst (66:10-12b). Perhaps there is some consolation in recognizing that even those trials are a work of a sovereign God: "*You* have tried us," "*You* have refined us" (66:10), "*You* brought us into a net," "*You* laid hardship upon our hips" (66:11), and "*You* made mortals ride on our heads" (66:12a). But there is hope for those in a "narrow place [of distress]" (66:14b): God ultimately delivers them into "a wide place [of flourishing]" (66:12c).[8]

As was noted, the "they" in 66:6b becomes "us" in 66:6c; likewise in this section, the preservation described (66:8-12) relates to the community of God ("our" [66:9a, 9b, 11b, 12a]; "us" [66:10a, 10b, 11a, 12c]; and "we" [66:12b][9]), but it is the "peoples" who are called to bless God (66:8a). "Here the world praises and so becomes a part of this central confession. Israel's story has become a reality for the world."[10] The distinction between the righteous and the erstwhile wicked have been dissolved[11]—the latter have become part of the people of God, it seems:

6. Both 66:3a and 66:5b label God's deeds as "awesome."

7. Such time-space travel, so to speak, is not uncommon in the Torah: Deut 5:2-3; 6:20-22; 26:5-9. Also, whereas it was the "foot" of their ancestors that passed through the Red Sea (Ps 66:6b), it will be "our feet" that do not slip (66:9b).

8. The MT's רְוָיָה, *rwayah*, "abundance" (66:12c) is best read as רְוָחָה, *rwachah*, "wide place," i.e., respite/relief, as do the Targums (also attested to by the LXX that has ἀναψυχή, *anapsychē*, "relief," and by the Syriac versions that have ܪܘܚܬܐ, *rwcht'*, "an expanse/space").

9. Thus every line of 66:9-12 has a first-person plural.

10. deClaissé-Walford et al., *Book of Psalms*, 536.

11. This is not very different from the dissolution of the distinction between the first generation of the

all are praising deity. This is the anticipated result of God's praise for God's performance that results in God's preservation of his people—and the universe acclaims this great God!

Individual (66:13–20)

The second half of the psalm turns from the response of the community to God to that of the individual towards God. This person, perhaps a leader in the assembly, resolves to praise God by fulfilling promises of sacrifice that were made in the hour of crisis from which divine deliverance was granted (66:13–15). He who, with his peers, had been "brought [בוא, *bw'*]" into a net (66:11) and who "went through [בוא]" fire and water (66:12b), now declares that he will "enter [בוא]" into God's house to fulfill his promises of sacrifice (66:13a) post-deliverance. The employment of the same verb in those three instances suggests that adversities sovereignly ordained by God are no obstacle to the supplicant's grateful offerings to that same God: his preservation from those malignities, it is implied, far overwhelms the vexations he was led through. And so, because of God's "works" (from עשה, *'sh*; 66:3a), the psalmist himself resolves to "prepare" (also עשה; 66:15c) sacrifices for God. Worship, thus, is a response to God's performance of preservation—for the great things God has done!

And so, as in the case of the community ("come and see," 66:5a), the individual worshiper bids all to "come, hear" his recounting of God's performance: "what He has *done* [again עשה]" (66:16b). The psalmist's "mouth" had made vows to sacrifice (66:14b); now his "mouth" cries out in praise to God (66:17a). God who had attended to the sufferer's "voice" of prayer (66:19b) is to be glorified with a global "voice" of praise (66:8b). Testifying to what God has done, then, is an integral part of worship that engenders communal praise.[12]

Here also there is a warning (as there was in the previous section, 66:7): a condition to God's answering of prayer is given in 66:18. He will *not* "hear" those who are wicked (who "regard harm in . . . heart"). In context, such wickedness in heart could well be the result of a loss of faith in God when he permits difficulties in one's life (66:10–12b): it is easy in such situations to slip into an attitude of distrust in God. In the psalmist's case, that God *did* "hear" him and attend to his prayer (66:19b) establishes the supplicant's innocence with regard to such rebellious thoughts. Indeed, no defiant word was uttered by him; his lips and mouth only promised sacrifice for deliverance even in the midst of his disasters (66:14). All that to say, it is required of God's people that they remain faithful to him, no matter what.

And so the psalm comes to a close with a blessing pronounced upon God ("blessed be God," 66:20a), paralleling that in the corresponding section ("bless our God," 66:8a). His lovingkindness is poured out for his people, as he preserves them, even through difficulties, by his mighty performances. Therefore, all praise by all people in all places is due him!

---

exodus Israelites and those currently uttering the psalm, the "they" becoming "us"!

12. In light of "*all* the earth" in 66:1a, 4a, "*all* who fear God" in 66:16a is likely to include everyone who has seen or heard of God's remarkable performances, a striking expansion of the cohort of the devout to people of every tribe, tongue, and nation.

Sermon Map

I. God's Performance
   Exulting in God's deeds (66:5–6)
   Warning to the rebellious (66:7)
   Move-to-relevance: The unassailable power of God

II. God's Preservation
   Adversities assail (66:10–12b)
   Warning to the rebellious (66:18–19)
   Extolling God's deliverance (66:9, 12c)
   Move-to-relevance: How God delivers us

III. God's Praise
   Individual praise (66:13–16)
   Communal praise (66:1–4, 8, 20)
   Move-to-relevance: The provision of God

IV. *Persevere in Praise through Plight*
   Praising God, communally and individually, despite predicaments

PSALM 67:1–7

Psalm of Orientation

Covenant Keeping and Global Praising

PSALM 67 IS A request for divine blessing upon the community of God, but with a specific purpose: that God may, thereby, earn worldwide respect and recognition for his rulership over all things and all people.[1] The blessing asked for, anticipated, or even already obtained is at least both martial ("deliverance," 67:2b[2]) and agricultural (67:6a); perhaps the psalm was employed at a festival celebrating these blessings.

Translation

67:1 God, may He be gracious to us and bless us;
  may He shine His face with us;
67:2 that Your way may be known on the earth,
  Your deliverance among all nations.
67:3 May the peoples give You thanks, God;
  may all the peoples give You thanks.
67:4 May the populace be glad and shout for joy,
  for You judge the peoples with uprightness
  and the populace on the earth You lead.
67:5 May the peoples give You thanks, God;
  may all the peoples praise You.
67:6 The earth, it has yielded its produce:
  may God bless us—our God.
67:7 May God bless us,
  and all the ends of the earth will fear Him.

---

1. The request for blessing in 67:1 follows right after "blessed be God" in 66:20.
2. But, in such an unspecified description, it likely involves more than military liberation.

Structure

The psalm is carefully structured, with a central tricolon (67:4) surrounded by bicola comprising an identical refrain (67:3, 5) and two requests at either end of the song (67:1–2, 6–7):[3]

67:1–2	**Request 1**: *blessing; worldwide respect of God* "bless" (67:1a); "earth" (67:2a); "shine [יָאֵר, ya'er]" (67:1b) "*all* nations" (67:2b)
67:3	**Refrain 1**: *worldwide recognition of God* "peoples" (67:3a, 3b); "give You thanks" (67:3a, 3b) "*all* the peoples" (67:3b)
67:4	**Rationale**: *worldwide rulership of God* "populace" (67:4a, 4c); "peoples" (67:4b); "earth" (67:4c)
67:5	**Refrain 2**: *worldwide recognition of God* "peoples" (67:5a, 5b); "give You thanks" (67:5a) "*all* the peoples" (67:5b)
67:6–7	**Request 2**: *blessing; worldwide respect of God* "bless" (67:6b, 7a); "earth" (67:6a, 7b); "fear [יִירְאוּ, yir'u]" (67:7b) "*all* the ends of the earth" (67:7b)

There is a substantial focus on "peoples" and the "populace," with those terms arranged in chiastic fashion in 67:3–5:

67:3a	"peoples"	
67:3b	"peoples"	
67:4a		"populace"
67:4b	"peoples"	
67:4c		"populace"
67:5a	"peoples"	
67:5b	"peoples"	

Perhaps because of the emphasis on a worldwide recognition of God, there is no explicit mention of Israel, Jerusalem, the temple, or Zion; instead "all" occurs four times (67:2b, 3b, 5b, 7b; see above) to encompass humankind globally.[4]

---

3. From deClaissé-Walford et al., *Book of Psalms*, 538; Talstra and Bosma, "Psalm 67," 302. Spero calls it a "menorah psalm," from its seven verses (branches), with a patterned number of Hebrew words in each line: 7, 6, 6, 11, 6, 6, 7, respectively—thus seven verses with forty-nine words (Spero, "Menorah Psalm," 11–16).

4. Yet see below, on 67:6a, for a specific aspect of Israel's relationship with God.

Theological Focus

The people of God, faithful to their deity in obedience to divine demand, can expect his gracious blessing upon them and their undertakings, including fruitfulness of the earth, with the anticipated result of global recognition and fear of God, as well as grateful acknowledgment of his rulership, filling the ends of the earth.

Commentary

Request 1 (67:1–2)

Three of the six verbs from the Aaronic benediction (Num 6:24–26) are reused here—"be gracious" (Ps 67:1a); "bless" (67:1a; also in 67:6b, 7a); and "shine" (67:1b). There is also the shared divine "face" in 67:1b, which, it is hoped, will be shining "with us" (67:1b), rather than "upon us" as in Num 6:25, perhaps indicating a more relational interaction between the two parties of the psalm.[5] But God here is אֱלֹהִים, *'elohim*, not יְהוָה, *yhwh*, as in the earlier text, likely an accommodation to the breadth of the human populace mentioned in Psalm 67. It is also the speakers of this song—"us," i.e., the people of God (three first-person plural suffixes in 67:1)—who are asking to be blessed themselves (unlike the benediction pronounced upon the congregation by the priest in Numbers 6). The shining of God's face upon humanity is idiomatic for divine benevolence and blessing,[6] perhaps indicating divine pleasure. On the other hand, the hiding of his face is ominous.[7] This divine grace and blessing indicates, in this psalm, "deliverance" (Ps 67:2b) as well as the productivity of the earth (67:6a), but encompasses "every good given and every perfect gift" coming from God (Jas 1:17).

After an indirect address in Ps 67:1, God is directly addressed in 67:2, detailing the purpose for the request for grace and blessing. The parallelism of 67:2a and 67:2b are obvious:

67:2a	"that	Your way	may be known	on [בְּ, *b*]	the earth,
67:2b		Your deliverance		among [בְּ]	all nations."

God's people seek his God's gracious blessing of them so that the earth and all nations may come to know him as they recognize his faithfulness and commitment to his own—a worldwide respect of deity.

> While the Aaronic blessing is located in the broad context of Yhwh's purpose that the whole world should seek blessing like Israel's, that context and purpose receive no mention in the blessing itself. It focuses simply on Israel. In contrast, here the aim of God's being gracious to "us" and blessing "us" (that is, the aim of God's

---

5. Goldingay, *Psalms*, 2:300.
6. Psalms 4:6; 31:16; 80:3, 7, 19; 119:135.
7. Psalms 13:1; 27:9; 44:24; 51:9; 69:17; 88:14; 102:2; 104:29; 143:7.

involvement in Israel's historical or political life and of God's involvement in nature [seen later in 67:6]) is that the world as a whole should come to acknowledge God.[8]

Refrain 1; Rationale; Refrain 2 (67:3–5)

The expected result of the nations knowing God's way and his deliverance is expressed in a repeated refrain (67:3, 5): the gratitude of these peoples and their praise for God's actions—a global recognition of deity that acknowledges that his blessing of Israel (the "us" of 67:1) is good news for everyone. This is the Abrahamic blessing coming to fruition: "in you [through God's people] all the families of the earth shall be blessed" (Gen 12:3). This refrain (in the form of *Refrain 1* and *Refrain 2*; Ps 67:3, 5) bookends the central core of the psalm, 67:4, its only tricolon, in which the worship of the peoples in 67:3, 5 overflows into gladness and shouts of joy of the populace (67:4a) as they accept God's universal rulership: he "judges" with "uprightness" and he "leads" (67:4bc).[9] This is the only instance in the OT of the verb "lead" with God as the subject and the nations as object.[10] Considering the divine shepherd motif linked with "leading" in the Psalter (23:2; 77:20; 78:72), 67:4c takes on a richer hue: the nations, too, are to be God's flocks!

Request 2 (67:6–7)

The final section of the psalm introduces what at first blush seems to be a divergent topic—the fruitfulness of the earth. Of note, "earth" carries the article in 67:2a, 4c (= habitation of humans) but is inarticular here in 67:6 (= cultivated land[11]); "earth" is also fronted in its clause in 67:6a, giving it emphasis. Besides, "has yielded" is the only perfect verb in Psalm 67 and seems to be looking back to the past; all the others, imperfects, look to the future. How does one put all that together to comprehend the "storying" of this psalm?

Direct parallels to 67:6a (employing "earth," "yield," and "produce") include: Lev 26:4, 20; Ps 85:12; Zech 8:12.[12] All deal with future blessing (or cursing) of Israel contingent upon its keeping of the covenant with Yahweh. Indeed, one may go so far as to say that covenant-keeping would have been understood to be the basis of Ps 67:6a: "the *earth* has *yielded* its *produce*" would be equivalent to saying Israel had been faithful to its God.

> In the context of Psalm 67, therefore, this phrase apparently does not declare primarily that the harvest was gathered in, but that nature is a witness to the fact that Yahweh has indeed blessed his people and his land in response to their compliance with the stipulations of the covenant. On the basis of this evidence that God is satisfied with their devotion to him, the community prays that God will bless them even more so that all the world will come to acknowledge his saving power

---

8. Goldingay, *Psalms*, 2:301.

9. There is probably no distinction between "peoples" and "populace," though the former may point to people *groups*, and the latter to a more indiscriminate collection of humankind.

10. In Job 12:23, the nations are the object of God's leading, but as captives. Elsewhere in the Psalter, both individuals (5:8; 23:2; 27:11; 31:3; 43:3; 61:2; 73:24; 139:10, 24; 143:10) and community (77:20; 78:14, 53, 72) are led by God.

11. Though in the translation I have added the article.

12. Also see variants: Lev 25:19; Deut 11:17; 32:22; Ps 78:46; Ezek 34:27; Hag 1:10.

(his salvation). They ask that all the world will know his requirements for worship (his way [67:2a]) and will gladly join in with reverence, praise, and respect (fear [67:7b]) for him alone. In this way, all the inhabitants of the earth will become partners in a covenant with Yahweh, the God of Israel.[13]

Remarkably, God hiding his face from his people (Deut 31:17, 18; 32:20) shows up in proximity to the "earth" not "yielding" its "produce" (32:22)—both are results of the breach of covenant. This, in light of the opening request to have God shine his face upon them (Ps 67:1a), is telling, for that makes the request sections of the psalm (67:1-2 and 67:6-7) tightly linked with covenant terminology. If the "earth . . . has yielded its produce," then covenant keeping, or living a life by divine demand, the inhabitation of an ideal *world in front of the text*, is taking place among God's own people. May God continue to bless "us," the supplicants request in 67:7, so that such covenant keeping with God would spread worldwide "and all the ends of the earth will fear Him." And we join in that prayer: May that begin with the community of God and may its global consummation happen soon!

Sermon Map

I. Communal Grace

God's blessing (67:1, 6b–7a)

Move-to-relevance: The abundant grace of God in our lives

II. Universal Governance

Recognition and respect of God's rulership (67:2–5, 7b)

Move-to-relevance: Why a global respect of God is lacking

III. Individual Goodness

Condition for communal grace: faithful obedience (67:6)

IV. *Faithfulness Leads to Favor for Foreigners*

Specifics on faithful obedience, that God's favor would spread to others

---

13. Botha, "Psalm 67," 374–75.

PSALM 68:1–35
Psalm of Orientation

God: Provider, Warrior, Ruler

THIS PSALM HAS A widespread reputation "as textually and exegetically the most difficult and obscure of all the psalms."[1] Hapaxes aplenty and vexing syntaxes galore combine to create perplexities rendering much of its translation tentative. However, the thrust and pericopal theology of the psalm is quite discernible.

Rather than commence with an address to God or an exhortation to the community of God's people, Psalm 68 opens with a declaration of what God does/has done. The only plea to God in the psalm comes near its end, in 68:28–30, and the only praise (or exhortation thereunto) in 68:4 and 68:32–35. Most of the psalm recounts, in narrative form, God's deeds on behalf of his people, making him worthy of praise.

Translation

68:1 God arises, His enemies are scattered,
    and those who hate Him escape from His face.
68:2 As smoke blown away, You blow [them] away;
    as wax melts from the face of fire,
    the wicked perish from the face of God.
68:3 But the righteous rejoice;
    they exult before the face of God;
    and they exult with rejoicing.
68:4 Sing to God, sing praises to His name;
    lift up [a song] to Him riding on the clouds;
    yes, Yah is His name: exult before His face.
68:5 Father for orphans and judge for widows—
    God in His holy habitation—

---

1. Dahood, *Psalms II*, 133.

68:6   God, the One settling the solitary [in] a house,
         the One leading out prisoners into prosperity:
         only rebels abide in a scorched land.
68:7   God, when You went forth before the face of Your people,
         when You marched through the wilderness,
68:8   the earth quaked, even the heavens flowed, before the face of God,
         the One of Sinai—before the face of God, the God of Israel.
68:9   You made to fall plentiful rain, God;
         Your inheritance, when it was parched, You established.
68:10 Your community dwelt in it;
         You established [her] in Your goodness to the afflicted, God.
68:11 The Lord, He gives the utterance:
         the women who proclaim [good] tidings [are] a great army;
68:12 kings of armies flee, they flee;
         and the beautiful one of the house—she will divide the spoil
68:13 (though you lie down among the sheepfolds):
         the wings of a dove covered with silver,
         and its pinions with glistening gold.
68:14 When the Almighty scattered the kings there,
         it snowed in Zalmon.
68:15 A majestic mountain is the mountain of Bashan—
         a mountain with peaks is the mountain of Bashan.
68:16 Why do you keep watch, mountains with peaks,
         at the mountain which God desires for His dwelling?
         Surely Yahweh will abide [in it] permanently.
68:17 The chariotry of God—myriads, thousands doubled;
         the Lord among them—Sinai, in holiness.
68:18 You ascended on high—You took captive captives,
         You received gifts among people,
         and even rebels—that Yah God may abide [in it].
68:19 Blessed be the Lord—day after day He bears our burden,
         God, our deliverance.
68:20 God is to us a God of deliverances;
         and to Yahweh the Lord belong escapes from death.
68:21 Surely God—He shatters the head of His enemies,
         the hairy crown of the one who goes about in his guilt.
68:22 The Lord said, "From Bashan I will bring [them] back;
         I will bring [them] back from the depths of the sea,
68:23 so that your foot may shatter [them] in blood,
         [that] the tongue of your dogs [may have] its portion from enemies."

68:24 They see Your processions, God,
    the processions of my God, my King, in holiness.
68:25 The singers went at the head, string-players after,
    in the midst of maidens playing tambourines.
68:26 In the congregation, bless God,
    Yahweh, the fountain of Israel.
68:27 There is Benjamin, the youngest, ruling them,
    the princes of Judah, their noisy throng,
    the princes of Zebulun, the princes of Naphtali.
68:28 Your God has commanded your strength;
    be strong, God, You who have acted for us
68:29   from Your temple;
    to Jerusalem kings will bring tribute to You.
68:30 Rebuke the creature in the reeds,
    the gathering of the bulls among the calves, the peoples.
Trampling the pieces of silver,
    He has dispersed the peoples who take pleasure in war.
68:31 Envoys will come from Egypt;
    Cush will hasten with her hands to[wards] God.
68:32 Kingdoms of the earth, sing to God,
    make music to the Lord.
68:33 To Him riding upon the ancient highest heavens—
    behold, He gives out His voice, a voice of strength—
68:34 give strength to God;
    over Israel is His majesty, and His strength in the skies.
68:35 Awesome [are You,] God, from Your sanctuaries.
    The God of Israel—He gives strength and great power to the people.
Blessed be God.

Structure

The structure of the psalm, though not easy to detect, may be organized as follows:[2]

> **Praise 1 (68:1–4)**
> *Theophany and Praise* (**68:1–4**)
>   "righteous" (68:3a)
>   "to Him riding on the clouds" (68:4bβ)
>
> **God the Provider (68:5–10)**
> *God and afflicted* (**68:5–6**)
> *God and procession* (**68:7–10**)
>
> **God the Warrior (68:11–23)**
> *God and spoils* (**68:11–13**)
>   "Lord ... utterance," אָמַר ... אֲדֹנָי, *'adonay ... 'omer* (68:11a)
> *God and dwelling* (**68:14–18**)
>   "Lord" (68:17b)
> *God and blessedness* (**68:19–20**)
>   "Lord" (68:19a)
> *God and victory* (**68:21–23**)
>   "Lord"; "Lord said," אָמַר אֲדֹנָי, *'amar 'adonay* (68:20b, 22a)
>
> **God the Ruler (68:24–32)**
> *God and procession* (**68:24–27**)
> *God and tribute* (**68:28–32**)
>
> **Praise 2 (68:33–35)**
> *Theophany and Praise* (**68:33–35**)
>   "to Him riding upon the ... heavens" (68:33a)
>   "Israel" (68:34b, 35b)

One may consider the psalm as beginning and ending in a theophany (68:1–2, 4bβ; 68:33) accompanied by hymnic praise (68:3–4bα; 68:34–35). The middle section, forming the bulk of the composition, deals mostly with God the Warrior (68:11–23), on either side of which is pictured God the Provider (68:5–10) and God the Ruler (68:24–32). Thus there is a hint here of cyclical worship (from *Praise 1* to *Praise 2*) centered upon God the Warrior. In any case, all of the poem focuses upon God, described in a variety of terms: besides the numerous instances of "God [אֱלֹהִים, *'elohim*]," there is also "God [אֵל, *'el*]" (68:19b, 20a [×2], 24b, 35b); "Yah" (68:4c, 18c); "Yahweh" (68:16c, 20b, 26b); "Lord" (68:11a, 17b, 19a, 20b, 22a, 32b); "Almighty" (68:14a); as well as "the One of Sinai" (68:8b, also see 68:17b); "Him riding on the clouds/heavens" (68:4b, 33a[3]); "father for orphans" (68:5a); "judge for widows" (68:5a);

---

2. See Knohl, "Psalm 68," 5–10.

3. This is a standard description of the storm god Baal in Ugaritic mythology (see for example, "Poems about Baal and Anath," III AB A 29 [*ANET* 131]), and polemically applied to Yahweh here, as well as in Deut 33:26; Isa 19:1. Usually, עֲרָבָה, *'aravah*, indicates "wilderness," but in Ps 68:4b it is likely to be a homonym meaning "clouds" (especially considering 68:9, 33). In light of the fact that Deut 33:26 shows Yahweh "riding" upon the "heavens" and through the "skies" in "majesty" (see Ps 68:33a, 34b for the same terms), it is likely that the imagery of Psalm 68 borrows from the Torah and not from period literature. Also Deut 33:2

"the One settling the solitary" (68:6a); "the One leading out prisoners" (68:6b); and "King" (68:24b). "The 'disconnectedness' of the psalm . . . is transformed into a 'connectedness' by its concentration on God and his praise."[4]

The "storying" of the psalm, within the opening and closing praise sections, involves God establishing his afflicted people in stability, both socially and economically (68:5–10: *God the Provider*), followed by his winning battles for his besieged people (68:11–23: *God the Warrior*), and then by God's supremacy and dominance, bringing him, the rightful King, laud and tribute from every earthly kingdom and all humanity (68:24–32: *God the Ruler*). Such a movement is not necessarily chronological, but it is logical, delineating the initial establishment of God's people, their triumph over their enemies, and God's ultimate rulership over all. The sequence of the occurrences of "K/king" and "kingdom" in the Psalm suggests this "storying":

"kings" fleeing (68:12a)
"kings" scattered (68:14a)

"King" (68:24b)

"kings" submitting (68:29b)
"kingdoms" praising (68:32)

Theological Focus

God—the provider, who cares for his afflicted people in his goodness, the warrior who defends them with his might, and the ruler who maintains the cosmos in order under his dominion—is worthy of praise from all humanity.

Commentary

Praise 1 (68:1–4)

The cause for praise at the beginning of the psalm is God's defeat of the enemies of the "righteous," and it is structured in 68:2–3 as an *inclusio*:

Extermination of the wicked (68:2ab)
"wicked perish" (68:2c)
"righteous rejoice" (68:3a)
Exulting of the righteous (68:3bc)

---

has "Sinai" (as in Ps 68:8b, 17b) and "myriads [רְבָבָה, *rvavah*]" of God's holy ones in his attendance (and 68:17a has "myriads [רִבֹּא, *ribbo'*]" of divine chariots, driven, ostensibly, by an equal number of angelic charioteers). See Scacewater, "Divine Builder," 119–21. Note that in 68:4c, "Yah" is prefixed with the preposition בְּ, *b*, that emphasizes the essence of the object modified (*beth essentiae*): thus "yes, Yah."

4. Tate, *Psalms 51–100*, 184.

While the wicked perish "before the face of God" like wax in the "face of fire" (68:2bc), the righteous exult "before the face of God" (68:3b).[5]

Psalm 68:1a is similar to Num 10:35b (uttered by Moses as the ark was being moved). "The association with the ark in the context of the enemies of God clearly recalls the early battles in Israel's history, and just as with those battles, the outcome of the wicked against God is never a question."[6] All deity has to do is "arise," and his foes are "blown away," they "melt," and they "perish" (Ps 68:1–2). This God, *their* God ("Yah," 68:4c), is surely worthy of praise.

The next three sections of the psalm elaborate the reasons for such joyous praise.

God the Provider (68:5–10)

The main body of the psalm opens with God as Provider, demonstrating his care for his "people" (68:7)—the "orphans," "widows," (68:5); "prisoners" (68:6); and "afflicted" (68:10). It is a "father" dwelling in a "habitation" who cares for the "orphans" (68:5) and who "settles the solitary [in] a house" (68:6): the parental and domestic side of God's providence brings out a personal touch to his care. Considering the oppression of widows, he is to them a "judge" (68:5), and to prisoners, perhaps those figuratively persecuted (and not for felonies), a liberator (68:6).[7] "Ordinary potentates give their attention to the rich and powerful; but the LORD champions the helpless."[8] Yes, Yahweh "riding on the clouds" (68:4c) becomes one with his people on the earth!

Then God is directly addressed in 68:7–10; the subsection is neatly laid out (see below), beginning and ending with "God" and centering on his "face" (i.e., his presence).[9]

---

5. Indeed, the five occurrences of "face" (68:1b, 2b, 2c, 3b, 4c) unite the section, as well as the repetitions of "blow" (68:2a [×2]), "rejoice/rejoicing" (68:3a, 3c), "name" (68:4a, 4c), and "exult" (עָלַץ, *'lts*; 68:3b; עָלַז, *'lz*; 68:4c).

6. deClaissé-Walford et al., *Book of Psalms*, 548.

7. There are several allusions to the exodus here: "Yah[weh] is his name" (68:4c and Exod 15:3; the first instance of "Yah" in Scripture is in Exod 15:2); "leading out [יצא, *yts'*]" (Ps 68:6b and Exod 6:6, 7; 7:4, 5; 12:17, 41, 42, 51; etc.; and in the *hiphil*, as in Ps 68:6b, in Deut 5:6, 15; 6:12); "inheritance" (Ps 68:9b and Deut 4:21, 38; and God's "inheritance," in Deut 4:20; Pss 28:9; 33:12; 74:2 [all referring to God's people; but "Your inheritance" in 68:9b refers to God's land]); and women announcing battle triumph (68:11b and Exod 15:20–21). There are also references to "Sinai" and "wilderness" in Ps 68:7b, 8b, 17b (see 78:40; 106:14; 107:4). However, there is no mention of rain in the exodus narrative, as there is in 68:8–9; that is perhaps a conflation of what happened later—divine agricultural blessing for covenant keeping.

8. Ross, *Psalms*, 2:476. The "rebels" in 68:6c are likely to be foreigners (as in 68:18bc), perhaps those who caused God's people to be orphans, widows, solitary, and imprisoned.

9. See Vincent, "From Sinai to Jerusalem," 121–22; and Auffret, *Merveilles à nos yeux*, 9.

```
A    "God" (68:7aα)
          "You went forth" (68:7aβ)
     B    "Your people" (68:7aγ)
          "You marched" (68:7bα)
          C    "wilderness" (68:7bβ)
               D    "earth" (68:8aα)
                    E    "heavens flowed" (68:8aβ)
                         F    "before the face of God,
                              the One of Sinai" (68:8aγ–8bα)
                         F'   "before the face of God,
                              the God of Israel" (68:8bβ)
                    E'   "plentiful rain" (68:9a)
               D'   "Your inheritance" (68:9bα)
          C'   "parched" (68:9bβ)
          "You established" (68:9bγ)
     B'   "Your community" (68:10a)
          "You established" (68:10b)
A'   "God" (68:10b)
```

It details a procession of emancipation, God "marching" through the wilderness, leading "Your people" (68:7), establishing "Your community" (68:10[10]) in "Your goodness" (68:10b), into the land of promise, "Your inheritance" (68:9b), with abundant fertility—God's comprehensive care and concern.[11] Notice that the elements B and B' each have the people of God sandwiched between two actions of God—they are protected and provided for, secured and settled, by their deity!

God the Warrior (68:11–23)

The chronology (or "history," if you will) of the section God the Warrior may be sequenced thus: the defeat and fleeing of enemy armies and the commandeering of spoils (68:11–13); God choosing Mount Zion as his dwelling—the victorious King taking occupancy of his palace (68:14–18); the blessing of his people, the citizenry (68:19–20); and a resumption of the divine warrior motif as the kings and armies that fled in 68:12 are captured and exterminated (68:21–23). God is in focus throughout, with his speech opening and closing the section ("Lord . . . utterance," אֹמֶר . . . אֲדֹנָי, 68:11a; and "Lord said," אָמַר אֲדֹנָי; 68:22a). Besides, five of the six occurrences of "Lord" in the psalm are found in this section (68:11a, 17b, 19a, 20b, 22a; also see 68:32b).

With the God-as-Warrior motif we are pointed to another aspect of the flourishing of God's people (besides the fertility of the land in the previous section)—the downfall of enemies. However, strikingly, we are never provided details of the battle or how exactly this divine defeat

---

10. Literally, "your creatures."

11. "If there is rain, there is life; if there is no rain, there is death . . . And God does give this gift, in abundance. It is rain of great generosity, as generous ["plentiful," נְדָבָה, ndavah; 68:9a] as the love of God . . . [described in Hos 14:4 as being "freely/limitlessly (נְדָבָה)" offered] . . . Only in these two passages is . . . [נְדָבָה] applied to God" (Goldingay, Psalms, 2:320). The goodness of God, abundant, plentiful, gracious, and free!

of adversaries was accomplished. Indeed, the battle appears to be already over when we arrive on the scene in 68:11, and the women are proclaiming the glad tidings of victory. In all likelihood, that omission is deliberate, letting the narrative extend its validity for all God's people for all time in all potential situations of conflict and hostility with foes.[12]

While the meaning of 68:11-13 is rather opaque, the gist is that what the Lord announces (68:11a), the women proclaim—no doubt the good news of victory (68:11b; as also in Exodus 15; Judges 5) and, though they remain in the "house," "lying down among the sheepfolds" (Ps 68:12b, 13a), they too participate in the "spoils" of wars that are exemplified by "silver" and "gold" ornaments (68:12b, 13bc). In any case, the enemies and their leaders are put to flight—mentioned twice, in rapid succession (68:12a), as the "Almighty"[13] scatters them like snow on the slopes of the hill of Zalmon (near Shechem; Jdg 9:48). And with that victory, the conquering hero, God, takes over another mountain, his dwelling (Ps 68:15-18), in the process rescuing prisoners ("taking captive captives"; 68:18a) and receiving gifts from them, likely tribute (68:18b).

But deity's choice of (ostensibly) Mount Zion has evoked some anthropomorphic envy among more "majestic"[14] peaks (68:15-16). "Bashan" was well known for its fine cattle (Deut 32:14; Ps 22:12; Ezek 39:18; Amos 4:1), not to mention fierce lions (Deut 33:22) and noble trees (Isa 2:13), thus making the location "a symbol of that which was lofty, rich, and powerful."[15] But these other peaks can only look on in frustration as God battles for and abides with his people, choosing Mount Zion for his abode. Notice that the God who "settles" (ישׁב, *yshv*) the solitary in homes (Ps 68:6a), and who enables his community to "dwell" (ישׁב) in his land (68:10a), now makes Mount Zion/the temple his own "dwelling" (ישׁב, 68:16b). "Yahweh tents forever among his people. The true God dwells with Israel. All other peoples ['mountains'] are jealous."[16] It is not only God who dwells in Mount Zion (the temple, with his community), there are also innumerable divine chariots, a mighty host, in attendance (68:17a)![17]

At any rate, with all that God has done, is doing, and will do for his people, the psalmist cannot but pour out a blessing upon God (68:19-20), echoing with the name of God:

> "Lord" (68:19a)
> "God our deliverance" (68:19b)
> "God" (68:20aα)
> "God of deliverances" (68:20aβ)
> "Yahweh the Lord" (68:20b)

---

12. Besides, there is also the implication that God's people need not worry about martial and military details: God has it all under control!

13. Only here and in 91:1 in the Psalter.

14. "Majestic" in 68:15a is literally "of God," the divine name being used as a superlative designating a high mountain.

15. Tate, *Psalms 51-100*, 180.

16. LePeau, "Psalm 68," 140-41.

17. It is quite appropriate for one "riding [רכב, *rkv*]" clouds and skies (68:4b, 33a) to be the commander of uncountable "chariots [רֶכֶב, *rekev*]" (68:17a). "Sinai" in 68:17b, as in 68:8b, is likely a divine epithet, considering the parallel structure of the phrases: "the Lord among [בּ, *b*] them" (68:17bα) and "Sinai in [בּ] holiness" (68:17bβ). As well, the fact that that would give 68:17b two synonymous notions in parallel: "Lord" and "Sinai," as also in 68:17a that has "chariotry" and "myriads, thousands doubled."

And the poet also introduces a first-person plural for the first time in this psalm: "day after day He bears *our* [לָנוּ, *lanu*] burden" (68:19a), with a parallel "God is *to us* [לָנוּ] a God of deliverances" (68:20a[18]). *Our*-burden Bearer, *our* Deliverer! And with yet another paralleling of prepositions in 68:20a, 20b, the psalmist underscores the nature of this divine deliverance:[19]

68:20a	"God is *to* [לְ] us	a God *of* [לְ, *l*]	deliverances;
68:20b	and *to* [לְ] Yahweh	belong escapes *from* [לְ]	death."

The section concludes with some violent images portraying the defeated and discomfited state of the enemies of God and of his people (68:21–23), much of it the words of God, and corresponding to his utterances earlier in 68:11–13.[20] Such graphic descriptions are not unique in the literature of the ancient Near East; for instance, "Poems about Baal and Anath" (V B 19–20, 27–29) has:[21]

> Now Anath goes to her house,
> The goddess proceeds to her palace.
> Not sated with battling in the plain ...
> She plunges knee-deep in knights' blood,
> Hip-deep in the gore of heroes.

All that to show that the guilty oppressors of the community of God will find no escape by fleeing (68:12a); wherever they may be,[22] God will "bring [them] back" to suffer their just deserts (68:22), to pay the price for their offences against God's community. And the recompense of these felons appears to occur at the hands of God's people (68:23a).

God the Ruler (68:24–32)

Now that the victor, God, has been established (or remains established) as universal ruler in his palace (the temple) in his capital (Jerusalem), a festal, triumphal procession of his people and of foreigners ensues, streaming into his presence, bearing tribute and singing praise. In a sense, this procession of victory in 68:24–32 is a response to the earlier procession to war in 68:7–10. The rulership of God commences the section with "my King" (68:24b), and the mention of other "princes," "kings," "envoys," and "kingdoms" (68:27bc, 29b, 31a, 32a), all of them submissive to God, emphasizes the totality of divine dominion.[23]

---

18. "Our deliverance" in 68:19b has the first-person plural suffixed to "deliverance."

19. God "leads out" prisoners (יצא; 68:6b), and he himself "went forth" (יצא; 68:7a) with his people—those were the "escapes" from death (תּוֹצָאוֹת, *totsaot*, also from יצא; 68:20b).

20. Both those divine utterances have duplications of verbs: "flee" (×2, 68:12a) and "bring ... back" (×2, 68:22a, 22b), and "shatter" (×2, 68:21a, 23a).

21. *ANET* 136.

22. "Bashan" here (68:22) stands for the east, and the "sea" (68:22b), the Mediterranean, for the west.

23. Notice the "going about" (הלך, *hlk*; 68:21b) of the once-active enemy; now they get to watch, with frustration, the "procession" (הֲלִיכָה, *halikah*; 68:24a, 24b) of God's people, the victors.

After the initiation of the procession (68:24) and the detailing of the musicians parading (68:25), 68:26 provides, with emphasis upon God, the goal of the entire endeavor: that God may be blessed![24] The reason for the specific mention of Benjamin, Judah, Zebulun, and Naphtali (68:27) might be because "they embrace all Israel, North and South, with Benjamin being first because of . . . the location of Jerusalem in its borders."[25]

With that, the psalmist directly addresses the people of God in 68:28a, reminding them that their God had commanded (and thus endowed) strength for them. "Yet the psalm's presupposition is not that God gives this gift and then stays in the sanctuary, leaving Israel to go out to fight. God goes out and gets involved in the battle, giving the gift in its midst as the people fight and discover that they achieve more than they could have dreamed because God is acting for/with them."[26] Therefore, in 68:28b, God is urged to continue to "be strong" for his people. In other words, God's bestowal of strength parallels his own being strong and acting for the sake of his people: God works in and with his own:[27]

> "He has commanded,
> your God,
> your strength;
> be strong,
> God,
> You who have acted for us."

The demonstration of God's strength and his acting is symbolized in the overpowering of the "creature in the reeds" (a hippopotamus? 68:30a) that, like Leviathan and the sea dragon, stands for the chaos and disorder against the *shalom* and order of God, perhaps stand-ins for rogue nations and/or demonic entities.[28] "It is such power that is embodied in the earthly powers that assert themselves against Israel. So the psalm urges God to put them down," with a note about the destruction of the wealth of the warmongers (68:30cd).[29] This rebuke of the unruly and the fractious (those *not* submitting to God, 68:30) is surrounded on either side by the convocation of those who submit to God's rulership (68:29, 31; below).[30]

---

24. The "fountain of Israel" that Yahweh is (68:26b) indicates his founding of that nation and his choice of that people.
25. Goldingay, *Psalms*, 2:330.
26. Goldingay, *Psalms*, 2:330.
27. The structure follows the Hebrew word order; see Vincent, "From Sinai to Jerusalem," 114.
28. See Job 40:15—41:34; Pss 74:13-14; 89:10-11; Isa 27:1; etc.
29. Goldingay, *Psalms*, 2:331.
30. Vincent, "From Sinai to Jerusalem," 116. "Cush" (68:31b) is the region south of Egypt.

68:29b	*Those submitting to God, bringing tribute*
68:30a	"rebuke the creature in the reeds"
68:30b	rebellious "gathering"
68:30bβ	"bulls"
68:30bγ	"calves"
68:30bδ	rebellious "peoples"
68:30cd	"dispersed the peoples who take pleasure in war"
68:31	*Those submitting to God, bringing tribute*

All that to say, 68:29b–32 underscores the responses of the peoples of the world: some submit to God, others do not. The latter are rebuked and dispersed, perhaps constituting a final disposition of these insurrectionary and mutinous elements.

The psalm has come full circle: *God the Provider*, caring for his own, fought for them as *God the Warrior*, and continues to bless them and receive the submission of the universe as *God the Ruler*.

Praise 2 (68:33–35)

And so the psalm concludes, as it commenced, with a call to praise. Both these sections of praise, *Praise 1* and *Praise 2*, share the theophanic concept of the divine rider on the clouds/heavens (68:4b, 33a[31]), and in their hymnic praise both have particular labels for God's people ("righteous," 68:3a; "Israel," 68:34b, 35b).

The "awesomeness" of God the Provider, God the Warrior, and God the Ruler is emphasized in the structure of 68:34–35:[32]

A	"*Give strength* to God;	
	B	over *Israel* is His majesty,
		C and His strength in the *skies*.
		C' Awesome [are You,] God, from Your *sanctuaries*.
	B'	The God of *Israel*—
A'	He *gives strength* and great power to the people."	

All praise is certainly due him!

---

31. "Riding upon the ancient highest heavens" likely indicates God's dominion of the heavens from earliest times (from eternity past, perhaps, or at least after the creation of space).

32. From Vincent, "From Sinai to Jerusalem," 118. The giving of strength to God (68:34a) is a worshipful ascription of might to deity, an element of praise.

Sermon Map

I. God Provides
   God's care for his afflicted people: his goodness (68:5–10)
   Move-to-relevance: God's provision in our lives

II. God Protects
   God's defense of his people: his might (68:11–23)
   Move-to-relevance: God's protection in our lives

III. God Presides
   God's rulership of the cosmos: his dominion (68:24–32)
   Move-to-relevance: God's presidency over all

IV. *God's Praise*
   The praise of God (68:1–4, 33–35)
   Specifics on praising God for his activities towards us

PSALM 69:1–36

Psalm of Disorientation

Devastation to Deliverance

PSALM 69, ONE OF the longest pleas for help in the Psalter, is an individual lament with imprecations and thanksgiving.[1] The woes besetting the psalmist are many: enemies (69:4, 14, 18–19, 21), guilt (69:5), shame (69:6–7, 19), alienation (69:8, 11–12), grief (69:10, 29), discouragement (69:20bc), discipline (69:26), and perhaps illness (69:20a). "This psalm shows just how complicated life can be and that one can suffer because of God's action and/or inaction and that the enemies can threaten because of personal pain, sin, or because of the person's faithfulness—or in this case, all of the above at the same time."[2] There seems to be no specific precipitating cause of the psalmist's anguish; that is perhaps intentional, lending the poem versatility for use in a number of distressing situations particular to the human condition.

Translation

69:1 Deliver me, God,
      for the waters have gone in, [up] unto my neck.
69:2 I have sunk in deep mire, and there is no foothold;
      I have gone in to depths of waters, and a torrent has flooded me.
69:3 I have been wearied with my crying; my throat is hoarse;
      my eyes have failed while hoping for my God.
69:4 More than the hairs of my head are those hating me without a cause;
      powerful are those destroying me—my enemies, falsely;
      what I did not plunder, I then have to restore.
69:5 God, You—You know my foolishness,
      and my guilty acts are not concealed from You.

---

1. It is traditionally considered one of the six imprecatory psalms, along with Psalms 55; 59; 79; 109; and 137.
2. deClaissé-Walford et al., *Book of Psalms*, 553.

69:6 May they not be ashamed through me,
>> those who hope in You, Lord Yahweh of Armies;
> may they not be disgraced through me,
>> those who seek You, God of Israel.

69:7 For I have borne reproach for Your sake;
>> disgrace has covered my face.

69:8 I have become alienated from my relatives,
>> and a foreigner to the children of my mother.

69:9 For zeal for Your house has consumed me,
>> and the reproaches of those reproaching You have fallen upon me.

69:10 And I weep in my soul with fasting:
>> and it becomes a reproach to me.

69:11 And I give sackcloth [for] my garment;
>> and I become to them a byword.

69:12 Those sitting in the gate complain about me,
>> and [I am] the mocking song of the drinkers of beer.

69:13 But as for me, my prayer is to You, Yahweh,
>> at a time of goodwill.
> God, in the greatness of Your lovingkindness,
>> answer me with Your truth in deliverance.

69:14 Rescue me from the mud and do not let me sink;
>> may I be rescued from those hating me and from the depths of waters.

69:15 May it not flood me, the torrent of waters;
>> and may it not swallow me, the deep;
>> and may it not close its mouth upon me, the pit.

69:16 Answer me, Yahweh, for Your lovingkindness is good;
>> according to the greatness of Your compassions, face towards me.

69:17 And do not hide Your face from Your servant,
>> for I am in distress; quickly answer me.

69:18 Draw near to my soul, redeem it;
>> because of my enemies, ransom me.

69:19 You—You know my reproach and my shame and my disgrace;
>> before You are all those distressing me.

69:20 Reproach—it has broken my heart and I am sick;
>> and I hope for sympathy, but there is none;
>> and for comforters, but I have not found [any].

69:21 They also give me bitterness in my food,
>> and for my thirst they pass a drink to me of vinegar.

69:22 May their table before their face become a snare;
    and to [their] friends, a trap.
69:23 May their eyes be darkened [to keep them] from seeing,
    and make their loins shake continually.
69:24 Pour out Your indignation upon them,
    and Your burning anger, may it overtake them.
69:25 May their encampment become desolate;
    in their tents may none be dwelling.
69:26 For the one You Yourself have struck down, they pursued,
    and the suffering of those You wounded, they proclaimed.
69:27 Add iniquity to their iniquity,
    and may they not go in to Your righteousness.
69:28 May they be wiped out of the book of life
    and with the righteous may they not be recorded.
69:29 But I am afflicted and suffering;
    may Your deliverance, God, secure me on high.
69:30 I will praise the name of God with song
    and magnify Him with thanksgiving.
69:31 And it will please Yahweh better than an ox,
    [even a] young bull with horns and hoofs.
69:32 The afflicted see; they rejoice;
    those seeking God, may their heart become revived.
69:33 For Yahweh hears the needy,
    and His prisoners He does not despise.
69:34 Let heaven and earth praise Him,
    the seas and all that teems in them.
69:35 For God will deliver Zion and build up the cities of Judah,
    and they will dwell there and possess her.
69:36 The descendants of His servants, they will inherit her,
    and those loving His name, they will abide in her.

Structure

In structure, one can discern the psalm going from protest to plea, and then concluding with a praise:[3]

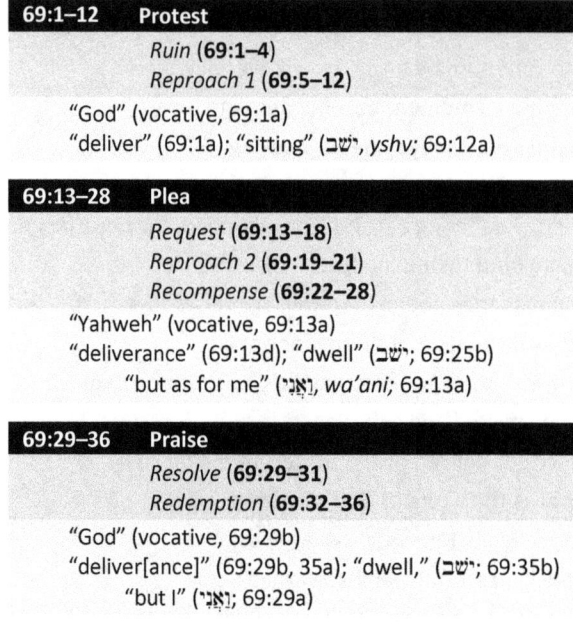

Strikingly, the protest and plea sections share a number of elements, particularly between 69:1–12 and 69:13–21 (below).

---

3. Of course, the categories are not watertight; for instance, there are pleas in the protest (69:1a, 6) and praise sections (69:29).

Psalm 69:1–12	Psalm 69:13–21
"deliver me" (69:1a)	"deliverance" (69:13d)
"I have sunk" (69:2a)	"do not let me sink" (69:14a)
"deep" (69:2a)	"deep" (69:15b)
"depths of waters" (69:2b)	"depths of waters" (69:14b)
"torrent" (69:2a)	"torrent" (69:15a)
"flooded me" (69:2b)	"flood me" (69:15a)
"those hating me" (69:4a)	"those hating me" (69:14b)
"my enemies" (69:4b)	"my enemies" (69:18b)
"You—You know" (69:5a)	"You—You know" (69:19a)
"be ashamed" (69:6a)	"my shame" (69:19a)
"be disgraced," "disgrace" (69:6c, 7b)	"disgrace" (69:19a)
"reproach[ing]" (69:7a, 9b [×2], 10b)	"reproach" (69:19a, 20a)
"and I weep" (וָאֶבְכֶּה, wa'evkeh; 69:10a)	"and I hope" (וָאֲקַוֶּה, wa'aqawweh; 69:20b)
"I give" (69:11a)	"they … give" (69:21a)
"[they] complain about me" (יָשִׂיחוּ בִי, yasichu bi; 69:12a)	"they pass a drink" (יַשְׁקוּנִי, yashquni; 69:21b)

One might thus "story" this prayer psalm as commencing with a protest of the dire situation the psalmist is in (ruin; 69:1–4), as he pays special attention to the insults and shame he has to face (reproach; 69:5–12). The protest then turns into a plea, employing the same verbiage, but now refocused as a request to God (69:13–18) that continues to lament the disgrace brought upon him by others (reproach again; 69:19–21). But this plea section is followed by a unique set of verses, 69:22–28—an imprecation condemning the evildoers who harangue the supplicant (a desire for their recompense). Then, with confidence that deity will hear his protest and heed his plea, the psalmist concludes with a section of praise, resolving to be grateful (69:29–31) for the redemption and final security granted him (and his community) by God (69:32–36).

Theological Focus

When devastated by dire circumstances—assailed without cause by their enemies, abused for their devotion to God, and abandoned by their kin—God's people remain confident in his goodness, lovingkindness, truth, and compassion, expecting and praying for God's deliverance that includes appropriate recompense for oppressors, and that is consummated in the safety and security of the community of God for generations to come.

Commentary

Protest (69:1–12)

Chaos (ruin) threatens the supplicant: waters have gone in, [up] unto [his] neck" (69:1b) and he has "sunk" down where there is no "foothold," in to the "depths" of waters (69:2). The "waters" have "gone in" (69:1b) and he has "gone in" to the "waters" (69:2b).[4] This mutual "going in" and the oppositions of up vs. down and neck vs. foot(hold) paint a picture of total devastation. Besides, the sufferer's throat is hoarse, and his eyes have failed (likely by the throes of weeping—a "torrent" of a different kind; 69:3). Every body part is seemingly affected. Even the hairs on his head are outnumbered by his enemies who seek to destroy him for no reason (69:4a).[5] And all this even as he was "hoping for my God" (69:3b) who, it seems, has not shown up! Yet, despite the graphic images, the reader is not given any specifics of the situation, leaving it to one's imagination to fill in the details and apply it to oneself.

Though there is a plea in 69:5–6, the bulk of 69:5–12 continues the protest, mostly dealing with the "reproach" (as a noun, 69:7a, 9bα, 10b; and as a verb, 69:9bβ) he was facing.[6] The confession of his own guilty acts in 69:5 is more likely to be the psalmist's protestation of his own innocence and an implicit call for vindication: God surely knows the supplicant's foolishness and guilt (or the absence thereof); and just as confidently, the supplicant is claiming that what he is being put through is entirely undeserved. In any case, the psalmist's woes are threatening: earlier, waters had gone in, up to his "neck" (נֶפֶשׁ, nephesh; 69:1b); here it is the waters of weeping that are flooding his "soul" (also נֶפֶשׁ, 69:10a).

The disgrace and insults ("reproach") he is facing are being borne for God's sake (69:7, 9: both verses begin with כִּי, ki) and therefore the psalmist pleads that his humiliation may not negatively affect others who seek God, as they become discouraged at his plight (69:6).[7] Likewise, the supplicant also prays that the "disgrace" that covered his face (69:7b) may not be the cause of others' "disgrace" (69:6c).

That God is the "Lord Yahweh of Armies" and the "God of Israel" (69:6a, 6c), the powerful and personal deity of his people, makes it incumbent upon God to intervene on behalf of the sufferer, one of his own. "The prayer leaves Yhwh with no way out."[8] The rest of 69:5–12 deals with the psalmist's emotional suffering (69:1–4 recollected his physical woes): within the home (69:8) and even without (69:10–12[9]). The supplicant is all alone—his "commitment to God has cost everything."[10]

---

4. Note also the assonance of "I have sunk in . . . ," ". . . טָבַעְתִּי בְ, tava'ti b . . . (69:2a), and "I have gone in . . . ," . . . בָּאתִי בְ, ba'ti b . . . (69:2b).

5. In all likelihood, 69:4c details the demands of these extortionist adversaries, numerous and rapacious.

6. This reproach no doubt involved the opponents' ridiculing his sufferings and especially the seeming incapacity of his God to extricate him from his woes.

7. This might be a hint that the speaker is a leader of some sort in the community of God. As well, it is likely that "zeal for Your house" was the cause of the opposition that has "consumed me" (69:9), making his devotion the direct cause of his reproach (69:10b).

8. Goldingay, *Psalms*, 2:340.

9. "Members of the community mock and humiliate the speaker . . . [69:10–12], who becomes even the subject of drunkards' songs . . . [69:12b] and of the scurrilous talk of those who sit in the town gate" (Tate, *Psalms 51–100*, 197).

10. deClaissé-Walford et al., *Book of Psalms*, 559.

Plea (69:13–28)

Employing much of the same language and metaphors from the *Protest* section (see figure above), 69:1–12 is now transformed into a plea, with a request (69:13–18), and a reprisal of the supplicant's reproach (69:19–21). An indication of this transformation from *Protest* to *Plea* is found in a wordplay: "and I weep" (וָאֶבְכֶּה; 69:10a) is, in construction, person, number, and verb form, similar to "and I hope" (וָאֲקַוֶּה; 69:20b). Weeping and protesting might still be continuing, but it is waiting and pleading that now takes precedence. But, in addition, the plea also is a call for the recompense of enemies (69:22–28).

A request for God to "answer" is made twice in 69:13–18 (69:13d, 16a, 17b); each time the psalmist adduces the ground for why deity should do so, and follows up with a request for action in both instances:[11]

69:13	*Request for "answer" (69:13)* Divine "goodwill," "lovingkindness," "truth"
69:14–15	**Request for action**
69:16–17	*Request for "answer" (69:16–17)* Divine "lovingkindness," "good[ness]," "compassions"
69:18	**Request for action**

Thus there is an emphasis here on the attributes of God, the bases for the psalmist's plea: indeed "greatness" describes both God's lovingkindness (69:13c) and his compassions (69:16b).[12] The requests for action (69:14–15, 18) convey the seriousness of the situation, with death imminent in the form of chaotic waters consuming and a miry pit engulfing (as in 69:1–2).

The chiastic structure of 69:16–17 concentrates on the divine "face" (i.e., presence; once as a verb, then as a noun):

69:16aα	"answer me"	
69:16aβ	"for"	
69:16b		"face" (פְנֵה, *pnh*: verb)
69:17a		"face" (פָּנֶיךָ, *paneh*; noun)
69:17bα	"for"	
69:17bβ	"answer me"	

"When Yhwh's face turns, that means action: God sees and acts."[13] On the other hand, when deity hides his face, his wrath is manifest.[14] In fact, the instances of "face" (as a noun or as a verb) in the psalm are themselves structured in a pattern.

---

11. From Goldingay, *Psalms*, 2:345.

12. Oppressors may "be more [רבב, *rbb*]" than the hairs of one's head (69:4a), but "great [רֹב, *rov*]" are God's lovingkindness and compassions (69:13c, 16b)! The "time of goodwill" in 69:13b indicates the moment of God answering/accepting the plea (as in Isa 49:8; 58:5). The "deliverance" in Ps 69:13d is one that is grounded in a familiar OT pair of divine attributes: "Your lovingkindness" and "Your truth" (69:13cd).

13. Goldingay, *Psalms*, 2:347. See Pss 22:24; 25:16; 119:132.

14. See Pss 13:1; 27:9; 30:7; 44:24; 88:14; 89:46; 102:2; 104:29.

Psalmist's	"face"	69:7b
God's	"face"	69:16b
God's	"face"	69:17a
Enemies'	"face"	69:22a

In 69:18, the request is specified as the supplicant's redemption and ransoming from enemies. That involves punishment of those foes (69:22–28; below), but not before the psalmist points out emphatically to God ("You—You know"), once again, the "reproach" and "shame" and "disgrace" he is facing (69:19a).

For the ones who gave him food of "bitterness" and drink of "vinegar" (69:21), the psalmist wishes a dinner table that is a "snare" for them and "a trap" for their friends (69:22).[15] He was wearied with crying and his "eyes" were failing (69:3b); now he hopes his enemies' "eyes" will be darkened and unseeing (69:23a). The supplicant was sinking without a "foothold [מָעֳמָד, ma'amad]" into the waters of chaos (69:2a); now he wishes that the loins of his foes would "shake [הַמְעַד, ham'ad]" unceasingly (69:23b).[16] He who was alienated from family (69:8) prays that his adversaries would be rendered homeless (69:25). All of this points out that the imprecation is for just deserts to be visited upon persecutors—"add iniquity to their iniquity" (69:27a).[17] While 69:29 commences a new section with וַאֲנִי (as also did 69:13), 69:26–29a creates a textual structure that emphasizes the fate wished upon the psalmist's oppressors:[18]

69:26b	"suffering" (מַכְאוֹב, mak'ov)	
69:27a	"iniquity" (עָוֺן, עֲוֺנָם, 'awon, 'awonam)	
69:27bα	"not"	
69:27bβ		"righteousness"
69:28a		"wiped out"
69:28bα		"righteous"
69:28bβ	"not"	
69:29aα	"afflicted" (עָנִי, 'ani)	
69:29aβ	"suffering" (כְאֵב, k'v)	

The enemies who "proclaimed" (סָפַר, sphr; 69:26b) the psalmist's woes with glee would themselves be eradicated from the "book" of life (סֵפֶר, sepher; 69:28a) of life. Inasmuch as the waters

---

15. "Food" in 69:21a translates an uncommon word that indicates sustenance for the sick and unfortunate (as in 2 Sam 13:5, 7, 10).

16. "The loins are a symbol of strength and the place on which one girds one's weapons (e.g., Ezek 29:7; Job 40:16), so that disabling the loins means disabling the warrior (e.g., Deut 33:11; Isa 45:1)" (Goldingay, *Psalms*, 2:350).

17. Note that there is a hint in the background of divine chastisement upon the psalmist and his cohort (69:26). Whatever that is, "the acts of God are not lamented; they are simply stated. The complaint is not against God here but against the enemies who further persecute and tell of the victim's pain" (deClaissé-Walford et al., *Book of Psalms*, 561).

18. Modified from Allen, Leslie C., "Value of Rhetorical Criticism," 579.

have "gone in" to the psalmist and he has "gone in" to the waters (69:1b, 2b), the enemies will *not* "go in" to divine righteousness (69:27b; all using בוא, *bw'*). Such imprecations, though they appear to be wishes and pleas by the psalmist, are essentially consequences of iniquitous behavior, punitive measures decreed by God. Thus the psalmist, in praying such maledictions, is simply agreeing with God: "add iniquity to their iniquity" (69:27a).[19]

Praise (29:29–36)

After an outpouring of *Protest* (69:1–12) and a poignant *Plea* (69:13–28), the *Praise* section begins appropriately with a confident resolve (69:29–31[20]), for a "song [שִׁיר, *shir*]" is better than an "ox [שׁוֹר, *shor*]" (69:30a, 31a).[21] The chiastic structure of 69:30–36 is centered upon God:[22]

69:30aα	"name"	
69:30aβ	"God"	
69:31a		"Yahweh"
69:32b	"God"	
69:33a		"Yahweh"
69:35a	"God"	
69:36b	"name"	

The prayer closes with a picture of the redemption accomplished by God and its ramifications for the entire cosmos (69:32–36). The afflicted will "see" and rejoice (69:32a) at the divine workings on their behalf (69:33[23]), while the enemies' eyes are going to be darkened by God to prevent them from "seeing" (69:23). The "heart" of the psalmist was once broken by reproach and ridicule (69:20a), but the "hearts" of these people of God will one day be revived (69:32b). But it is not only the individual and/or the community of God that is engaged in praise for redemption; "heaven and earth . . . , the seas and all that teems in them" are, too (69:34)—i.e., *all* of creation. And with that the psalmist fades into the background as God's deliverance of his community and their cities takes the foreground (69:35a): his people and their descendants will "dwell" and "abide" therein (69:35b, 36b), "possessing"

---

19. The supplicant "gives [נתן, *ntn*]" sackcloth as he mourns in a religious devotion for God (69:11a); in return, his enemies "give [נתן]" him bitterness and vinegar for provender (69:21a); as a result, he wishes that God would "add [נתן]" iniquity to their iniquity (69:27a). Also: It was his devotion that "became" his reproach (69:10b), as he "became" a byword, a ridicule, to his opponents (69:11b), now causing him to "become" alienated from his kin (69:8a). No wonder he execrates those foes with the same verb: "may . . . become," 69:22a, 25a; and "may . . . be," 69:25b. One day, however, with divine intervention, the hearts of God-seekers will "become" revived (69:32b; all employing the verb היה, *chyh*)!

20. The section commences with a plea for deliverance (69:29), but one that is linked to praise suggesting: "When you deliver me, I will praise . . ."

21. This relativizes the value of heartfelt thanks over blood-shedding sacrifices (also see 1 Sam 15:22–23; Pss 50:7–15, 23; 51:18–19; Isa 1:10–17; 66:1–6; etc., for the same sentiments).

22. From Allen, Leslie C., "Value of Rhetorical Criticism," 580.

23. "*His* prisoners" in 69:33b is surprising, but likely parallels "needy" in 69:33a, both equivalent to the people of God. Thus it indicates those among the prisoners (of the enemies) who are God's people, not that God was the agent of their imprisonment.

and "inheriting" Judah and Zion (69:35b, 36a[24])—forever safe, forever secure![25] The prayer "deliver me" (69:1a) has been answered: God will "deliver" (69:35a; also see "deliverance," 69:13d, 29b). Indeed, God has not hidden his face from his "servant" (69:17a); the lineage of God's "servants" will dwell in their own land, by the grace of God (69:36).

Sermon Map

I. Assailed by Enemies

   The psalmist's distress (69:1–4, 21)

   Move-to-relevance: Enemies in our lives, spiritual/otherwise

II. Abused for Devotion

   The psalmist's faithfulness (69:5–7, 9–11)

   Move-to-relevance: Affliction despite our faithfulness to God

III. Alienated from Kin

   The psalmist's abandonment (69:8, 12, 19–20)

   Move-to-relevance: Even kith and kin disdain us

IV. Answered by God

   The psalmist's prayer (69:13–18)

   The psalmist's imprecation (69:22–28)

   The psalmist's deliverance (69:29–36)

V. *Alone in Affliction? Anticipate Aid!*

   How to keep trusting God even when desolate in distress

---

24. "Her" in 69:35b, 36a, 36b is Zion, indicated by the feminine singular suffix.

25. Those townsfolk "sitting [ישׁב, *yshv*]" at the gate scorn the psalmist (69:12), but one day their tents will have no one "dwelling [ישׁב]" in them (69:25b). And, instead, it will be the people of God and their descendants who "dwell [ישׁב]" in their own cities, established by God himself (69:35b).

PSALM 70:1–5

Psalm of Disorientation

Help!

PSALM 70 IS ONE of those OT texts which are part of the "double traditions": its five verses are almost totally identical to Ps 40:13–17.[1] Both Psalms 40 and 70 are found towards the end of a major division of the Psalter: Book I ends with Psalm 40; Book II with Psalm 72.[2]

> Psalm 40 expresses the psalmist's need for deliverance from those who seek to snatch away her life by recalling—if not the details—the actuality of a prior deliverance: "The Lord takes thought for me." This is how the Lord is: thoughtful, mindful of the psalmist. Psalm 70, without the remembered past to call upon, makes of the same sense expressed in the final colon of the poem, "You are my helper and deliverer," an elongated plea: "Hasten to me, O God!" The tension of the *Sitz-im-Leben* of the psalmist, one of interpersonal trial, is responded to and expressed differently, despite many shared notes, rills, and flourishes. Psalm 40 is an expression of patient confidence. Psalm 70 is an expression of impatient pleading... Psalm 70 does not afford that luxury of time. There is no recourse to the past, no flipping through the pages of one's life to find the evidence of Gods fidelity; there is only urgent need.[3]

---

1. Jacobson, Karl N., "Dualing," 290. Another example of such twinning songs includes the pair of Psalms 14 and 53; there is also the use of Psalm 18 in 2 Samuel 22; and parts of Psalms 57 and 60 appear to have been employed in Psalm 108.

2. Besides, the respective portions preceding each member of this duo, i.e., Ps 40:1–12 and Ps 69:1–36, are similar. Both these antecedent sections have God's deliverance celebrated in praise (40:3, 9–10; 69:30–31; 34) and obedience/thanksgiving declared to be better than sacrifice (40:6; 69:30–31). As well, a number of words are shared between 40:1–12 and 69:1–36: "hope" (40:1a; 69:6a); "he heard/Yahweh hears" (40:1c; 69:33a); "clay/mud [טִיט]" (40:2b; 69:14a); "mouth" (40:3a; 69:15c); "many/great(ness)" (רַב, *rav*; 40:3c, 5a, 9a, 10d; 69:13c, 16b); "see" (40:3c, 12b; 69:23a, 32a); "turn [his] face/face" (40:4b; 69:16b); "count/proclaim" (סָפַר, *sphr*; 40:5f; 69:26b); "book" (סֵפֶר, *sepher*; 40:7b; 69:28a); "what is acceptable/goodwill" (רָצוֹן, *ratson*; 40:8a; 69:13b); "righteous(ness)" (40:9a, 10a; 69:27b, 28b); "You Yourself know/You—You know" (אַתָּה יָדַעְתָּ, *'attah yada'tta*; 40:9c; 69:5a, 19a); "hidden/covered" (כסה, *ksh*; 40:10a; 69:7b); "Your deliverance" (40:10b; 69:29b); "concealed" (40:10c; 69:5b); "lovingkindness" (40:10c, 11b; 69:13c, 16a); "truth" (40:11b; 69:13d); "compassion(s)" (40:11a; 69:16b); "continually" (40:11c; 69:23b); "iniquities" (40:12b; 69:27a [×2]); "hairs of my head" (40:12c; 69:4a); and "heart" (40:12d; 69:20a, 32b). However, the superscriptions (untranslated in this work) of those two psalms differ: Psalm 40 has "The Music Director's. David's. Psalm." Psalm 70 has "The Music Director's. David's. For a memorial." Thus, at least for the Masoretes, the intended use of these two psalms was different.

3. Jacobson, Karl N., "Dualing," 297.

In that sense, Psalm 70, an abbreviated version of Psalm 40, takes its own place in the Psalter, as a prayer uttered at a time of greater urgency and in a tone of greater stress. It begins and ends with a plea that God move quickly to deliver the supplicant—unlike other prayer psalms that conclude with thanksgiving. And every verse of Psalm 70 has one or more imperatives (70:1, 5) or jussives (70:2–3, 4)—this psalm is petition exclusively.

Translation

70:1 God, to rescue me—
 Yahweh, to my help, hurry.
70:2 May they be ashamed and humiliated,
 those seeking my soul;
 may they be driven back and disgraced,
 who take pleasure in my harm.
70:3 May they be turned around according to their shame,
 those saying, "Aha, aha."
70:4 May they exult and rejoice in You,
 all those seeking You;
 and may they say continually, "May God be magnified"—
 those loving Your deliverance.
70:5 But I [am] afflicted and needy;
 God, hurry to me.
 My help and my savior You [are];
 Yahweh, do not delay.

Structure

The psalm is structured as follows and is similar to that of 43:13–17:[4]

	70:1	**Deliverance 1**: *Hurry to help and rescue, God!* "God," "Yahweh" (both vocatives) "rescue"; "my help"; "hurry"
	70:2–3	**Defeat**: *Let my enemies be negated!* "seeking my soul"; "saying"
	70:4	**Delight**: *Let the righteous be joyful!* "seeking You"; "say"
	70:5	**Deliverance 2**: *Hurry to help and save, God!* "God," "Yahweh" (both vocatives) "savior"; "my help"; "do not delay"

"The psalm is almost a staccato of images.... There is no guide as to how to read the gaps. It is as if the prayer was lifted in such a hurry that there is no time to explain in more detail... Here there is no resolution, for sometimes real life is exactly that way. We cry out for answers, we cry out for God to hurry, and all we hear back is a deafening silence."[5]

Theological Focus

The only hope for the people of God in times of emergent crisis is God who can defeat their enemies and command their deliverance resulting in their joyous exultation of God.

Commentary

Deliverance 1 (70:1)

Clearly, the psalmist is in urgent need of help. He calls upon "God" and "Yahweh" (70:1a, 1b, 5b, 5d) asking him to come to "my help" (70:1b, 5c), to "rescue" him as his "savior" (79:1a, 5c): "hurry" and "do not delay," he pleads (70:1b, 5d).

---

4. From Auffret, "'Les oreilles, tu me (les) as ouvertes,'" 235. It is notable that while Psalm 69 explicitly voiced the concern that the righteous and the community of God were being "reproached" (69:6–7, 9, 19–20), there is no imprecatory utterance in the composition that the enemies would be reproached reciprocally. That "missing" aspect of the prayer of Psalm 69 is complemented in Psalm 70 (70:2–3). Indeed, these two psalms also share vocabulary: "rescue" (69:14a; 70:1a); "seek" (69:6d; 70:2b, 4b); "rejoice" (69:32a; 70:4a); "loving" (69:36b; 70:4d); "afflicted" (69:29a, 32a; 70:5a); "needy" (69:33a; 70:5a). See Goldingay, *Psalms*, 2:358.

5. deClaissé-Walford et al., *Book of Psalms*, 565.

Defeat for Enemies; Delight for Righteous (70:2–4)

How the help requested in 70:1, 5 should manifest, according to the psalmist's desire, is described in 70:2–4, regarding both enemies and righteous—the community of God. Both parties are directly quoted (70:3b, 4c). The foes go "Aha, aha!" in derision and ridicule (70:3b). Upon them the psalmist wishes shame, disgrace, and humiliation, as they are "driven back" and "turned around" in utter defeat (70:2c, 3a). The point is emphatically asserted in the wordplay: "may they be ashamed" is יֵבֹשׁוּ, *yevoshu* (70:2a), and "may they be turned around" is יָשׁוּבוּ, *yashuvu* (70:3a).

On the other hand, the people of God go "May God be magnified" (70:4c). Upon them the psalmist wishes joy and exultation in their continual praise of God in utter delight (70:4ab, 4d). These wishes for the enemies and righteous (all jussives) are neatly interspersed with their respective actions:

	Psalmist's Wishes	Enemies' Action
70:2ab	"may they be ashamed and humiliated,	those seeking my soul"
70:2cd	"may they be driven back and disgraced,	who take pleasure in my harm"
70:3ab	"may they be turned around …,	those saying, 'Aha, aha!'"

	Psalmist's Wishes	Righteous' Action
70:4ab	"may they exult and rejoice in You,	all those seeking You"
70:4cd	"may they say continually …,	those loving Your deliverance"

The enemies are "seeking my soul" (70:2b), whereas the righteous are "seeking You" (70:4b). And the enemies "take pleasure in my harm" (70:2d), while the righteous are "loving Your deliverance" (70:4d). Two peoples, two worldviews, two lifestyles, . . . and two fates.

Yet, even after these desires are expressed for the fates of the two discrete cohorts, the psalmist is still suffering. So he pleads again for deliverance.

Deliverance 2 (70:5)

A symmetrical alignment in 70:5 between supplicant and deity gives the second plea for deliverance pathos (with both 70:5a and 70:5c being verbless):

> "but I [am]"
> "afflicted and needy"
>
> "my help and my savior"
> "You [are]"

The structuring of 70:1 and 70:5bcd also appears to be deliberate:[6]

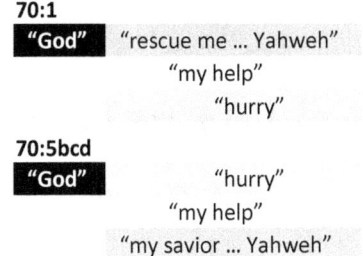

70:1
"God"   "rescue me ... Yahweh"
         "my help"
         "hurry"

70:5bcd
"God"   "hurry"
         "my help"
         "my savior ... Yahweh"

The entire emergency prayer thus begins and ends with God! John Cassian (ca. 360–435) in an extended meditation on his version of 70:1 ("O God, make speed to save me: O Lord, make haste to help me") comments:

> This verse ... embraces all the feelings which can be implanted in human nature, and can be fitly and satisfactorily adapted to every condition, and all assaults. Since it contains an invocation of God against every danger, it contains humble and pious confession, it contains the watchfulness of anxiety and continual fear, it contains the thought of one's own weakness, confidence in the answer, and the assurance of a present and ever ready help ... This verse, I say, will be found helpful and useful to every one of us in whatever condition we may be.[7]

"God, hurry ... , do not delay!"

Sermon Map

I. Deliverance Pled

    Emergent crisis (70:1, 5)

    Move-to-relevance: Our emergent crises

II. Defeat Prayed

    Enemies' fate (70:2–3)

    Move-to-relevance: How God overcomes our enemies

III. Delight Predicted

    Enthusiastic praise (70:4)

    Move-to-relevance: How God stimulates our praise

IV. *Run to God!*

    Specifics on committing to God totally and confidently in crises

---

6. Modified from Auffret, "'A Mon Aide Hâte-toi!,'" 287.
7. Cassian, *Conferences* 10.10 (*NPNF*[2], 11:405–6).

PSALM 71:1–24

Psalm of Disorientation

God for the Entirety of Life

PSALM 71 REFERS EXPLICITLY to various stages of the supplicant's life: youth, including birth (71:5–6, 17) and old age (71:9, 18; see below). It likely that at the time of utterance of the song, the psalmist is in his middle age, looking both backwards to his birth and youth, and forwards to his old age. While Psalm 71 is a prayer psalm, its pleas are less urgent than those of Psalm 70, giving it more of a tone of confidence as the entirety of a life is envisaged.[1] Thus, while the psalm is a lament, "it is a kind of confident, even jubilant, psalm of lament. The reason for this may be that the speaker in the psalm addresses God from the viewpoint of one who has attained mature adulthood and who is approaching old age . . . . The suppliant manifests a serenity often denied to the young" (see below).[2]

Translation

71:1 In You, Yahweh, I have taken refuge;
    let me not be ashamed ever.
71:2 In Your righteousness rescue me and save me;
    incline to me Your ear and deliver me.
71:3 Be to me a rock of habitation
    to which I may continually come.
A house of steadfastness to deliver me—
    indeed, my cliff and my steadfastness You are.
71:4 My God, save me from the hand of the wicked,
    from the palm of the wrongdoer and the oppressor.

---

1. In light of the plea for an increase in "greatness" (71:21a), this psalm may have been the sentiments of a king or a community leader. The "sign" that the psalmist becomes, as a result of his deliverance (71:7a), may also suggest such a representative and modeling role for the poet, since elsewhere in the Psalter "signs" are extraordinary wonders performed by God for the benefit of his nation (78:43; 105:5, 27; 135:9).

2. Tate, *Psalms 51–100*, 211.

71:5 For You are my hope,
> Lord Yahweh, my trust from my youth.
71:6 Upon You I have been supported from birth;
> You are the One who separated me from my mother's womb;
> of You is my praise continually.
71:7 A sign I have become to many,
> for You are my refuge of strength.
71:8 My mouth is filled with Your praise
> [and] all day Your splendor.
71:9 Do not cast me away in the time of old age;
> when my strength fails do not abandon me.
71:10 For my enemies have said [things] against me;
> and those who watch for my soul have counseled together,
71:11 saying, "God has abandoned him;
> pursue and seize him, for there is no one who is rescuing [him]."
71:12 God, do not be far from me;
> my God, hurry to my help.
71:13 Let them be ashamed, let them be consumed,
> those harboring animosity [towards] my soul;
> let them be covered with reproach and disgrace,
> those seeking my evil.
71:14 But I—continually I will wait,
> and add to all your praise.
71:15 My mouth will recount Your righteousness,
> [and] all day Your deliverance;
> for I do not know their count.
71:16 I will come with the mighty deeds of the Lord Yahweh;
> I will remember Your righteousness, Yours alone.
71:17 God, You have taught me from my youth,
> and until now I announce Your wonders.
71:18 And even unto old age and grayheadedness,
> God, do not abandon me,
> until I announce Your strength to [that] generation,
> [and] to all who are to come, Your mighty deeds,
71:19 and Your righteousness, God, unto the height [of heaven].
> You who have done great things—
> God, who is like You?
71:20 You who have caused me to see many distresses and evils,
> You give me life once again,
> and from the depths of the earth
> will bring me up once again.

71:21 May You increase my greatness,
       and turn around [and] comfort me.
71:22 Yes, I—I will give You thanks with an instrument, the harp,
       [I will praise] Your truth, my God;
       I will make music to You with the lyre,
       Holy One of Israel.
71:23 My lips will shout for joy when I make music to You—
       and my soul, which You redeemed.
71:24 My tongue also will utter Your righteousness all day;
       for they are ashamed, for they are humiliated,
       those seeking my evil.

Structure

The three expressions of praise, in 71:8, 16, 24, lend the psalm a tripartite structure, with each part having an appeal regarding the distress, assurance of God's deliverance, and adoration promised when that deliverance occurs:[3]

	71:1–8	**71:9–16**	**71:17–24**
	Youth	Middle Age	Old Age
Appeal	71:1–4	71:9–13	71:17–19a
Assurance	71:5–7	71:14a	71:19b–21
Adoration	71:8	71:14b–16	71:22–24

Though the utterance of the psalm is at a single instant, likely in middle age (the present), looking back to youth (the past) and forward to old age (the future), the psalm is essentially moving through time as shown above: from youth (71:1–8; see 71:5–6, appreciating God's trustworthiness in the past), through middle age (71:9–16; see 71:9, anticipating aging in the future), into old age (71:17–24; see 71:17a, 18c, announcing God's greatness in the latter days of life). And along that temporal axis, as was noted, there is an increasing equanimity and confident quietude: as the psalm progresses, the number of personal wishes for aid decrease,[4] and foes are seen as defeated (71:24, as opposed to 71:4, 10–11, 13). Incidentally, the number

---

3. From Goldingay, *Psalms*, 2:366. The division is not entirely watertight: for instance, adoration ("praise") also occurs in the assurance section (71:6c); neither is 71:1–4 necessarily a part of the psalmist's "youth," despite references to "womb," "birth," and "youth" in this section (71:5–6).

4. Seven such wishes are found in 71:1–8: "let me not be ashamed" (71:1b), "rescue me," "save me," "incline to me Your ear," "deliver me" (71:2), "be to me a rock" (71:3a), "save me" (71:4a); four in 71:9–16: "do not caste me away," "do not abandon me" (71:9), "do not be far from me," "hurry to my help" (71:12); and three in 71:17–24: "do not abandon me" (71:18b), "increase my greatness," "turn around [and] comfort me" (71:21).

of direct addresses to God in the vocative reaches a peak in that last portion of the psalm:[5] experience, apparently, teaches one to call upon God and become serene as a result.

> The psalm invites all who enter its poetic words to take a long view when trouble surrounds .... Today's world travels at warp speed, and the long view of life is rarely the norm when one is struggling with accusations and fears of God's absence. The prayer's message can teach us, just as it did an ancient audience, to take the long view of God's path in our lives, to look from birth to the age of gray hair and see where God has been a refuge and protector.[6]

No wonder "hoping" (71:5a) and "waiting" (71:14a), in "youth" and "middle age," disappear in "old age": God has become a concrete and very present reality!

Theological Focus

Through the span of life, from birth to old age, the righteousness of a God faithful to his people continues to build their confidence in his strength to deliver them from all their distresses, even those divinely ordained, making the courses of their lives a stage for God's mighty deeds, thereby evoking their praise for him.

Commentary

Youth (71:1–8)

Like the other sections, this one also goes through an appeal for help (71:1–4), a statement of assurance in God's trustworthiness (71:5–7), and a pledge of adoration (71:8).

As do Psalms 69 and 70, this psalm commences with an address to God, but not with an imperative plea as in 69:1a or 70:1; rather, a perfect verb, "I have taken refuge," is used to declare the poet's haven in Yahweh (71:1a). It is then followed by a number of imperatives expressing wishes for deliverance (71:1b–4[7]), albeit with a note of confidence in Yahweh being—or becoming—the psalmist's "rock of habitation," "house of steadfastness,"[8] "cliff" and "steadfastness"—a secure dwelling, indeed (71:3). The ground of these appeals is God's "righteousness" (71:2a): that makes him just and the seeker of justice for his persecuted people. This divine righteousness will be manifest when the supplicant is saved from "the wicked," "the wrongdoer," and "the oppressor" (71:4).

This "youth" section, though largely a plea for help (71:1–4, and likely uttered after the psalmist has passed his youth), is undergirded by a reflective gaze upon the psalmist's early years (71:5–6) that proves to him that God is even now a true "hope" and "trust," the one who

---

5. Thrice in 71:1–8 (71:1a, 4a, 5b); twice in 71:9–16 (71:12a, 12b); and six times in 71:17–24 (71:17a, 18b, 19a, 19c, 22b, 22d).

6. deClaissé-Walford et al., *Book of Psalms*, 571.

7. Being "rescued," "saved," "delivered" (71:2) are equated with "not being ashamed" (71:1b), such shame being the loss of face incurred if God does not liberate his own.

8. I emend לבוא תָּמִיד צִוִּיתָ, *lvo' tamid tsiwwita*, to לְבֵית מְצוּדוֹת, *lvet mtsudot*, "house of steadfastness" (71:3c, as in 31:2).

had "supported" him even before his birth (71:5). Emphasizing divine sustenance, the pronoun "You" echoes in 71:5a, 6b, 7b, in addition to the second-person suffixes in 71:6 ("upon *You*," "of *You*") and 71:8 ("*Your* praise," "*Your* splendor"). This divinely wrought deliverance—how and when this is accomplished we are not told—is a marvel, a wonder of God, so much so the delivered one becomes a "sign" to others (71:7a), an exemplum of God's providence and protection. God would "be [היה, *hyh*]" a rock of habitation to the psalmist (71:3a) and he, in turn, would "become [היה]" a portent to others (71:7a).

Thus the psalmist who began by taking "refuge" in God, not wanting to be ashamed before others (71:1a), ends up becoming a testimony and a marvel to many, as he makes God his "refuge" (71:7b). No wonder the psalmist can come to God "continually" (71:3b), resulting in praise "continually" (71:6c), even "all day" (71:8b).[9]

Middle Age (71:9–16)

In this section also there is an appeal for aid (71:9–13), an expression of assurance that God will show up (71:14a), and a promise of adoration (71:14b–16).

The psalm is likely to have been uttered in the psalmist's middle age: he has looked towards the past in 71:1–8; he now looks towards the future, anticipating old age and the failure of strength, in 71:9:

"Do not cast me away	*Negation + imperfect verb + first-person suffix*
in the time of old age;	*Prepositional phrase*
when my strength fails	*Prepositional phrase*
do not abandon me."	*Negation + imperfect verb + first-person suffix*

The pathos is patent: the plea to God that the psalmist not be abandoned bookends the manifestations of a senescent and impotent future that he expects to enter into. As it is, he is in trouble *now*; surely, come a few more years/decades hence, he will be in no position to withstand the assault of "enemies" and "those who watch for my soul [i.e., life]," all scheming and plotting against him (71:10). These are the ones reporting with derision, "God has *abandoned* him" and "there is no one who is *rescuing* [him]" (71:11). And that is precisely the psalmist's plea: "do not *abandon* me" (71:9b), and earlier, "*rescue* me" (71:2a). He does not want to be "ashamed" by the suggestion that his God has left him and cares not for him (71:1b); he asks, instead, that his enemies be the ones who are "ashamed" (71:13a). His own strength may "fail" (כלה, *klh*; 71:9b), but he pleads that it will be his enemies who are "consumed" (also כלה; 71:13a). His adversaries show him animus and seek his harm (71:13d);[10] in contrast (expressed with an emphatic fronted pronoun), "I—continually I will wait," ostensibly upon God, promising to add to deity's praise upon deliverance (71:14). So the psalmist who "continually" comes to God (71:3b) "continually" praises God (71:6c) and "continually" waits for God (71:14a). And he promises he will "recount [ספר, *sphr*]" divine "righteousness"

---

9. Each of the adoration sections contains "all day" (71:8b, 15b, 24a), the continuous praise of the psalmist for God's splendor, righteousness, and deliverance, respectively. All three attributes/actions are synonymous with the manifestation of divine work as God saves his people.

10. Incidentally, "harbor animosity" (71:13b) translates the verb שטן, *stn*, from which we get "Satan." Also, note that 71:13ab is parallel to 71:13cd.

(including God's deliverance) "all day" (71:15ab), the manifestations of which he does not know the "count [סְפֹרוֹת, sphorot]" (71:15c). This is the very "righteousness" that was the ground of God's saving activity (71:2a), the magnificence of which "righteousness"—"Yours alone"—the supplicant promises to remember when delivered (71:16b).[11]

Old Age (71:17–24)

This final section is also patterned after the preceding ones: appeal (71:17–19a), assurance (71:19b–21), and adoration (71:22–24). It begins in 71:17 with another invocation to God, asserting with a perfect verb that God had been the psalmist's teacher from his youth.

Notice the supplicant's claim: "until now I announce [עַד־הֵנָּה אַגִּיד, 'ad-hennah 'aggid]" God's wonders (71:17b). With that time-stamped summary of his declaration, the psalmist's middle age appears to have come to its close; he now turns his gaze even further forward than before to his golden years.[12] And, on the verge of entering "old age and grayheadedness" (71:18a), he expects to continue his proclamations of God's acts: he appeals to God not to abandon him "unto [עַד] old age" and "until [עַד] I announce" God's greatness to the next generation and "unto [עַד] the height [of heaven]" (71:18a, 18c, 19a). It appears that the psalmist wants to extend his promise of adoration in his middle age—to "*come* with the *mighty deeds*" of God and "Your righteousness" (71:16)—into his old age, when he will declare, again, "to all who are to *come*," God's "*mighty deeds*, and *Your righteousness*" (71:18d–19a).

That is not surprising, for there is no one like God: "God, who is like You?" (71:19c). Though this God is the one "who has caused me to see [אֲשֶׁר הִרְאִיתַנִי, 'asher hir'itani] many distresses and evils" (71:20a), he is also the one "who has done [אֲשֶׁר־עָשִׂיתָ, 'asher-'asita] great things" (71:19b), and will assuredly revive him again (71:20b).[13] Thus, in the long run of human life, the supplicant of this psalm expects God, the doer of "great [גָּדוֹל, gadol]" things, to increase the psalmist's own "greatness [גְּדוּלָּה, gdullah]" (71:19b, 21a), perhaps by making him and his community unashamed and prospering them in the strength of their God.[14]

The psalmist then concludes this section, and the psalm, with a vow of future adoration (71:22–24). This pledge is emphatic, with a fronted pronoun: "Yes, I—I will give You thanks" (71:22a), as emphatic as his earlier determination to wait for God in his dire situation: "But I—continually I will wait" (71:14a). He who was once "ashamed" (71:1b) prayed that it would be his enemies who would be "ashamed" (71:13a); that petition was answered: his enemies did become "ashamed" (71:24b). And so, the psalmist's "soul" that had been chased by enemies (71:10b), the "soul" against which animosity was directed (71:13b)—that "soul," now redeemed, sings praises (71:23b). "Your righteousness," asserted to be the basis of

---

11. The psalmist's "coming with the mighty deeds" (71:16a) might well be a leader's prepared remarks for public delivery regarding Yahweh's great works, as also indicated by "announce" (7:17b, 18c).

12. That 71:18 looks farther than 71:9 is clear from the addition of "grayheadedness" in the former. Also, the double use of "until/unto [עַד]"—"*until* now" in 71:17b and "*unto* old age and grayheadedness" in 71:18a—seems to signal the entry into another phase of life in 71:17. In fact, there are two more instances of the preposition—"*until* I announce" in 71:18c and "*unto* the height [of heaven]" in 71:19b—which may move the clock even further ahead, perhaps pointing to his final days, after he has accomplished his goals to the fullest extent possible.

13. The verb, תָּשׁוּב, tashuv, literally "You return" (71:20b, 20d), is read adverbially, indicating a repetition of action—thus, "once again."

14. And the one who led the psalmist into "many [רַב, rav]" distresses is now asked to "increase [רבה, rvh]" the psalmist's greatness (71:20a, 21a).

God's deliverance (71:2a), is to be recounted by the supplicant (71:15a), remembered by him (71:16b), declared by him (71:17b, 18cd, 9a), and now to be praised by him (71:23).[15]

> The psalm expounds ... [God's grace/righteousness] in the context of looking over a life as a whole: birth and youth, middle age and old age. It looks back to a life upheld by God from youth, indeed from its very beginning, from birth.... It has been a life of learning about God's awesome deeds and a life of proclaiming them.... As a middle-aged person, the supplicant stands between youth and old age. Will life continue to be like that into old age, when one lacks the strength to defend oneself...? Will God continue to be faithful so that the supplicant can continue to proclaim God's acts...? The psalm looks forward to making a difference even after one's life is over.[16]

Indeed, for one observes that the psalmist's vocalizations of the greatness of God are for the benefit of a generation to come (71:18cd). It is not at all surprising that each of the three sections of the psalm end in praise (adoration) that is promised to be uttered "all day" (71:8b, 15b, 24a). For God is faithfully righteous, and worthy of praise in every era.

In sum, whether looking backwards or forwards, to the past or to the future, the people of God remain confident in the present, in a God who is righteous and faithful to them throughout life. Looking *upwards* is what matters!

Sermon Map

I. Distresses of Life
   Crises threaten in every age (71:4b, 9–11, 13b, 13d, 20a, 24c)
   Move-to-relevance: Our crises, irrespective of age
II. Deliverance of God
   God as the refuge (71:1–4a, 5–7, 12, 13a, 13c, 14a, 18a, 18b, 20b–21)
   Move-to-relevance: God's rescue of his people
III. Devotion of People
   Praise for deliverance (71:8, 14b–17, 18c–19, 22–24b)
   Move-to-relevance: Praising God in every age of life
IV. *Glory to the God of All Generations!*
   Specifics on praising God in every age of life, even through crises

---

15. These are not essentially different ascriptions of praise, but likely to be synonymous.
16. Goldingay, *Psalms*, 2:378.

PSALM 72:1–20

Psalm of Orientation

God Bless the King!

PSALM 72 IS TRADITIONALLY considered one of the royal psalms.[1]

Translation

72:1   God, Your justice, to the King give,
      and Your righteousness to the Son of the King.
72:2   He will pass verdict [for] Your people with righteousness
      and [for] Your afflicted ones with justice.
72:3   The mountains will bear peace to the people,
      and [also] the hills, with righteousness.
72:4   He will judge the afflicted of the people,
      He will deliver the children of the needy,
      and He will crush the oppressor.
72:5   They will fear You as [long as] the sun [shines],
      and before the moon—generation after generation.
72:6   He will come down like rain upon the mown grass,
      like great showers drenching the earth.
72:7   In His days the righteous will flourish,
      and [be in] abundance of peace until the moon is no more.
72:8   And may He rule from sea unto sea,
      and from the River unto the ends of the earth.
72:9   Before Him they will kneel, the desert-dwellers,
      and His enemies, the dust they will lick.
72:10   The kings of Tarshish and the islands, they will bear tribute;
      the kings of Sheba and Seba, they will bring gifts.

---

1. The others are Psalms 2; 18; 20; 21; 28; 45; 101; 110; 132; and 144.

72:11 And they will bow to Him, all kings;
       all nations, they will serve Him.
72:12 For He will rescue the needy one crying for help,
       and the afflicted, and the one for whom there is no helper.
72:13 He will have pity on the weak and needy,
       and the souls of the needy He will deliver.
72:14 From oppression and from violence He will redeem their soul,
       and their blood will be precious in His eyes.
72:15 And may He live [long], and may the gold of Sheba be given to Him;
       and may they pray for Him continually;
       all day may they bless Him.
72:16 May there be a spreading of grain in the earth,
       on top of the mountains may it sway—
       its fruit like Lebanon;
       and may they bloom—[its] crops—like vegetation of the earth.
72:17 May His name be forever;
       before the sun may His name increase;
       and may they bless themselves by it;
       may all nations call Him blessed.
72:18 Blessed be Yahweh God, God of Israel,
       alone working wonders.
72:19 And blessed be His glorious name forever;
       and may His glory fill all the earth.
       Amen and amen.
72:20 The prayers of David son of Jesse are ended.

Structure

The psalm begins with a request in 72:1 (an imperative), adds another in 72:8 (a jussive), and then ends with a series of wishes in 72:15–17 (jussives), followed by a doxology, 72:18–19, and a colophon, 72:20, that concludes Book II of the Psalter. Thus one might see the psalm structured on the basis of these three sets of requests to God (*Request 1*; *Request 2*; *Request 3*), what the responses of the king will be when the requests (the first two) are granted (*Response 1*; *Response 2*), and the results of the king's responses (*Result 1*; *Result 2*), organized as shown below.[2]

---

2. Modified from Heim, "Perfect King," 228.

72:1	**Request 1**: *King's justice and righteousness*
72:2–4	**Response 1**: *Protection of people* "afflicted," "deliver," "needy," "oppressor" (72:4)
72:5–7	**Result 1**: *Righteous' fear and flourishing*
72:8	**Request 2**: *King's global rule*
72:9–11	**Result 2**: *Rulers' subjugation and tribute*
72:12–14	**Response 2**: *Protection of people* "needy," "afflicted," "deliver," "oppression" (72:12, 13, 14)
72:15–17	**Request 3**: *King's longevity, honor, and blessing*
72:18–19	Doxology
72:20	Colophon

In sum, this psalm is all about the king and the magnificence of his reign, and a yearning for him and for it![3]

However, no Israelite king in history (at least those depicted in 1–2 Samuel, 1–2 Kings, 1–2 Chronicles, and the books of prophecy) ever attained to such exalted levels of regency, greatness, or global span of kingdom as described in Psalm 72. Thus, the song appears to be expressing an eschatological hope, to be fulfilled in the Messiah, the Lord Jesus Christ.[4]

> Historically, the kingdom of Israel, even in the days of the united monarchy, was never a ranking power.... Moreover its career was short-lived; the combined rule of David and Solomon totals about seventy-five years. The divided kingdoms were soon to be fighting for existence, much less proclaiming world rule. Psychologically, it was impossible for such an Israel to entertain grandiose ideas of world empire apart from Yahweh's direct Messianic intervention.... Unless seen in the light of Yahweh's Messianic economy, world dominion was too removed from reality for the sober Hebrew to contemplate.[5]

Albeit from a later era, rabbinic exegesis has also traditionally seen Psalm 72 as messianic. The Targum on 72:1 has the plea: "God, give the decree of Your judgment to the King Messiah [מלכא משיחא, *mlk' mshych'*], and Your righteousness to the son of David the king."[6] The Talmud has Rabbi Yehdua HaNasi calculating the length of the messianic era from 72:5: "The messianic era will last three generations, as it is stated: 'May they fear You as long as the sun and moon endure, throughout the generations'" (72:5; *b. Sanh.* 99a).[7] On the endurance of the regent's name forever (72:17), the Midrash on the Psalms declares, "the King Messiah will never know the taste of death," and also interprets the rule in 72:8 as that of the "King

---

3. It is impossible to guess who is uttering the psalm: there is no first person at all in the entire composition.

4. For this reason, in my translation I have capitalized "King," "Son," and the pronouns referring to this messianic ruler.

5. Murphy, *Study of Psalm 72 (71)*, 74–75. Besides Pss 89:25–29, 36–37, several other prophetic words also reflect the sentiments of the rule of God's King that are described in Psalm 72: Isa 2:2–4; 9:7; 11:1–5; 32:1, 16–18; 45:14; 49:23; 60:1–12; Jer 3:17; 23:5–6; 33:15–16; Ezek 34:25–27; Mic 4:1–3; Zech 8:12; 9:10; etc. The notion of nations being blessed through Israel was adumbrated in Gen 12:3; 18:18; 22:18; 26:4; 28:14; 49:10.

6. My translation from the Aramaic.

7. Calculated as דּוֹר, *dor*, singular, i.e., *one* "generation"; and דּוֹרִים, *dorim*, plural (though translated singular to conform to English felicities), i.e., *two* "generations."

Messiah."[8] All that to say, historically there has been a tendency in ancient Judaism to view the king in Psalm 72 as the Messiah. Christian interpreters, of course, have freely taken that stance, and with justification.

Theological Focus

The deliverance of God's people from all their ills and woes (and the destruction of their oppressors) will be accomplished by the compassionate and powerful Messiah-King, whose eternal and global reign will be marked by justice, righteousness, and abundant peace and prosperity, and who will be recognized as absolutely supreme by all other rulers, as this King continues to bless all who joyfully receive his rulership.

Commentary

Request 1; Response 1; Result 1 (72:1–7)

The manifestation of the King's justice and righteousness are requested right at the start (72:1[9]) for, of course, the ruler's attributes and character qualities are intimately linked to the well-being of his people. Therefore, the request is followed by the King's response (72:2–4; voiced by the psalmist) and the results thereof (72:5–7).

That this King is a critical intermediary between God and the people of God is immediately apparent. The regent receives *God's* "justice" and "righteousness" (72:1) and channels them to *God's* community, as he "passes verdict [for] Your people with *righteousness* and [for] Your afflicted ones with *justice*" (72:2):[10] "both the attributes and the people belong to God, and the king is the instrument that brings them together."[11] Indeed, even inanimate nature participates in directing "righteousness" to the people of God (72:3b) and bringing peace. Thus the entire globe is suffused with the justice and righteousness of God mediated by this messianic ruler. An integral part of this exercise of divine justice and righteousness is the deliverance of the afflicted and the destruction of the afflicters (72:4). That "people" are mentioned in succession in three consecutive verses (72:2a, 3a, 4a[12]) underscores the goodness of God to his community, through the reign of this King.

---

8. Braude, *Midrash on Psalms*, 562, 563. Likewise, *Midrash on Numbers* 13.14 (Freedman and Simon, *Midrash Rabbah*, 528).

9. "Give" is, incidentally, the only imperative in the poem, and "God" the only invocation therein. The parallelism in 72:1 between "King" and "Son of the King" likely identifies the same person, qualified in the second phrase as being of royalty himself. This messianic "King" is the "Son of the [ultimate] King"—God himself.

10. The four attributes occur chiastically in 72:1–2: "Your justice" / "Your righteousness" // "Your people with *righteousness*" / "Your afflicted ones with *justice*." Also see 72:4a for yet another expression of divine justice—"judge," from the same root.

11. Tate, *Psalms 51–100*, 223.

12. They are also referred to in 72:2b, 4a ("afflicted"), 4b ("children of the needy"), 7a ("righteous").

The result of this rule by the divine representative, this messianic King, is that "they [the delivered ones] will fear You," revering God "generation after generation," and for what seems like a reign of eternity by this ruler (72:5).[13] His abundant beneficence towards his people is described with an agrarian simile: "like rain on the mown grass" and "like great showers drenching the earth" (72:6). The "*Son* of the King" (בֵּן, *ben*; 72:1b) brings blessing to the "*children* of the needy" (from בֵּן; 72:4b); and divine "righteousness" (צְדָקָה, *tsdaqah*; 72:1b, 2a, 3b) blesses the "righteous" (צַדִּיק, *tsaddiq*; 72:7a). And no wonder, for the "great showers" (רְבִיבִים, *rvivim*; 72:6b) of this Messiah produces an "abundance" (רֹב, *rov*; 72:7b) of "peace"—and God's people flourish forever (72:3a, 7b).

Request 2; Result 2; Response 2 (72:8–14)

While the justice and righteousness of the King (and his response to, and the result of, the first request) were in focus in the first section, here it is upon the actual reign and its extent (and the results of [72:9-11], and the ruler's response to [72:12-14], the second request [72:8]).

The section is delineated by the first explicit jussive, "And may he rule" (72:8a). The extent of the rule is worldwide, "from [Mediterranean] sea unto [Dead] sea, and from the [Euphrates] River unto the ends of the earth" (72:8). The one who "will come down" (יֵרֵד, *yered*; 72:6a) with blessing—"may He rule" (יֵרְדְּ, *yerd*; 72:8a). The result of the King's global reign is the subjugation of, and tribute paid by, all foreign kings, as depicted in a remarkable triple chiasm of 72:9-11, all to emphasize the latter's submission, and thus the former's absolute dominion, with a resolute finality:[14]

    A   "they will kneel" (72:9aα)
        B   "desert dwellers" (72:9aβ)
        B'   "enemies" (72:9bα)
    A'   "they will lick" (72:9bβ)

            C   "kings of Tarshish and the islands, they will bear tribute" (72:10a)
            C'   "kings of Sheba and Seba, they will bring gifts" (72:10b)

    A"   "they will bow" (72:11aα)
        B"   "all kings" (72:11aβ)
        B'''   "all nations" (72:11bα)
    A'''   "they will serve Him" (72:11bβ)

Again, we are directed to the response of this global ruler, that prompts such prostration and tribute from foreigners and even enemies: the protection of his people, in 72:12-14, as also in 72:2-4.[15] While the earlier, 72:2-4, dealt with the ruler's justice and righteousness, here in 72:12-14 it appears to be his compassion ("pity," 72:13a) that is in view—it impels his "rescue,"

---

13. Or that their fearing of this King is ceaseless, occurring all day and all night (in relation to the sun and the moon respectively).

14. "Serve" in 72:11b, עָבַד, *'vd*, can also carry the connotation of "worship" (see 2:11; 97:7; 100:2; 102:22; 106:36; 134:1). This may very well be the case, since the regent is the Messiah!

15. Indeed, the verbal parallels between these two portions are considerable (see structure of the psalm above).

"deliverance," and "redemption" (72:12a, 13b, 14a). So much so, their "blood" (i.e., lives) is "precious in his eyes" (72:14b).

Continuing the theme of messianic rule for all time ("*until* [עַד, *'ad*] the moon is no more," 72:7b) from the previous section, 72:8 adds the notion of his rule in all lands and all space ("from sea *unto* [עַד] sea," and "*unto* [עַד] the ends of the earth"). This is surely no ordinary human governor!

Request 3 (72:15–17)

The free-standing set of requests in 72:15–17 begins with a standard blessing upon the King: "may He live [long],"[16] complemented by a wish that he continue to receive foreign tribute (72:15a). And thus is the Messiah-King prayed for by his people (72:15bc[17]), who are themselves blessed by the name[18] of the one who is himself called blessed by all humanity (72:17). All of this indicates the intensity of joy and immensity of gratitude for the reign of the God-King. It is perhaps not a coincidence that the doxology actually prays a "blessing" upon Yahweh God, the God of Israel (72:18a); so in 72:15 this messianic King turns out to be receiving the blessing reserved for God! In fact, both his "name" and the "name" of Yahweh are ascribed to be "forever" (72:17a, 19a), conflating God's King with God's Person.[19]

In between these exclamations of blessing and being blessed is an adumbration of the prosperity of the earth and its produce (72:16).[20] The structure of 72:15–17 (below) shows that "the fertility of the land is part of God's blessing on Israel, but it is not because of a good harvest that the people increase and grow strong. It is because the king is truly God's agent, giving hope and fullness to their lives, that the people flourish."[21] That the description of the King surrounds (and precisely matches) the description of the land's prosperity validates this conclusion (see below).

---

16. This is essentially a cheer being raised for the ruler, "Long live . . . !" (see 1 Sam 10:24; 2 Sam 16:16; 1 Kgs 1:25, 34, 39; 2 Kgs 11:12).

17. "Praying for Him" either describes the people blessing their King, or it is a request being made to God to bless his regent.

18. "May they bless themselves" (72:17c) is the *hithpael* form of בְרךְ, *brk*, "bless." See Gen 22:18; 26:4; Jer 4:2 that also employ the *hithpael* form of the verb.

19. The nomen "Yahweh" is Trinitarian in connotation, and includes the Messiah-King, the Lord Jesus, of course. See Eldhose, "Trinitarian Interpretation."

20. The MT's מֵעִיר, *me'ir* ("from the city") is emended to עָמִיר, *'amir* ("crops"), keeping the agricultural picture intact.

21. Tate, *Psalms 51–100*, 224–25. The structure is modified from Barbiero, "Risks of a Fragmented Reading," 75.

King (72:15)

72:15a	*Begins with* וִיחִי, *wichi,* "may he live"
72:15bc	*Begins with* וְ, *w + imperfect third-person plural:* וְיִתְפַּלֵּל, *wyitpallel,* "and may they pray"

Land (72:16)

72:16abc	*Begins with* וִיהִי ("may there be")
72:16d	*Begins with* וְ *+ imperfect third-person plural:* וְיָצִיצוּ, *wyatsitsu,* "and may they bloom"

King (72:17)

72:17ab	*Begins with* וִיהִי ("may ... be")
72:17cd	*Begins with* וְ *+ imperfect third-person plural:* וְיִתְבָּרְכוּ, *wyitbarku,* "and may they bless"

The final request (*Request 3:* 72:15–17) thus seeks to bless the messianic ruler, and be blessed by him, with a bounty of provision. The King rules "unto the ends of the *earth*" (72:8b), with his goodness like showers "drenching the *earth*" (72:6b), resulting in an abundance of grain "in the *earth*" (72:16a) proliferating like the grassy vegetation "of the *earth*" (72:16d): thus God's glory fills "all the *earth*" (72:19b). This is nothing but a vision of the kingdom of God among mankind: "Thy Kingdom *has* come!"[22]

Doxology; Colophon (72:18–20)

Appropriately enough, the psalm concludes with a doxology that closes Book II of the Psalter (72:18–19), adding, as well, a colophon, a statement denoting the author (72:20).[23] In the context of the characteristics and actions of the messianic King detailed in Psalm 72, the doxology serves to link this regent with Yahweh, with the verbal repetitions noted above (blessing, "name forever"). May the reign of this God-King be consummated soon!

---

22. Incidentally, the first word of Book I of the Psalter (1:1a) is "blessed," and the last word of Book II (72:19; leaving aside the doxology and colophon) is also "blessed" (72:17d).

23. However, the prayers of David are *not* ended; see Pss 86; 138–145. It is only the current collection of psalms, Psalms 51–72, that have been completed.

Sermon Map

I. Ruin of the Righteous
   Afflicted and oppressed by violence (72:2b, 4ab, 12, 13, 14)
   Move-to-relevance: Our potential ruinous circumstances

II. Reign of the King
   Justice, righteousness, peace, pity—global and eternal (72:1–3, 6–8, 17ab)
   Defeat of oppressors (72:4c), subjugation of kings (72:9–11, 15a)
   Move-to-relevance: The promised Messiah

III. Response of the People
   Fear and worship (72:5), flourishing and gratitude (72:15b–16, 18–20)
   Move-to-relevance: Praise for the Messiah-King

IV. *Rejoice in the Reign of the Ruler!*
   Specifics on praising God for his soon-coming King

PSALM 73:1–28
Psalm of Reorientation

Peace and Prosperity of the Wicked

WHILE PSALM 73 DOES mention the distress of God's people (73:2, 14, 21, 26a), its focus is primarily the seeming prosperity and immunity to affliction of those perpetrators of oppression and wickedness, and the response of God's people to this apparent disparity. Thus, the psalm borrows a theme common to wisdom literature. Ultimately, however, the composition deals with a problem of the "heart" (73:1b, 7b, 13a, 21a, 26a, 26b).

Translation

73:1 Surely God is good to Israel,
    to the pure in heart.
73:2 But as for me—close to stumbling came my feet;
    all but slipped, [did] my steps.
73:3 For I was envious of the boastful:
    the peace of the wicked I saw.
73:4 For there are no pangs unto their death,
    and fat is their belly.
73:5 They do not have the trouble [of other] people,
    and [as it is] with [other] mortals they are not afflicted.
73:6 Therefore pride has become their necklace;
    a garment of violence is a covering for them.
73:7 Their eye bulges with fatness;
    the imaginations of [their] heart overflow.
73:8 They mock and speak in wickedness;
    of oppression they loftily speak.
73:9 They set their mouth against the heavens,
    and their tongue, it struts on earth.

73:10 Therefore they are satisfied with food,
    and waters of abundance are imbibed by them.
73:11 And they say, "How does God know?
    And is there knowledge with the Most High?"
73:12 Behold, these are the wicked;
    and forever at ease, they increase wealth.
73:13 Surely in vain I have kept my heart clean,
    and washed my hands in innocence;
73:14 And I have become afflicted all day,
    and my rebuke [happens] every morning.
73:15 If I had said, "I will reckon like that,"
    behold, the generation of Your children I would have betrayed.
73:16 When I considered to understand this,
    [it was] troubling in my eyes,
73:17 until I went into the sanctuary of God:
    I perceived their outcome.
73:18 Surely skiddy places You set for them;
    You cause them to fall into ruin.
73:19 How they become desolated in a moment;
    they are completely terminated by sudden terrors.
73:20 Like a dream upon waking,
    Lord, upon being roused, You will despise their shadow.
73:21 When my heart was embittered,
    and [in] my innards I was pierced,
73:22 then I was senseless and unknowing—
    a beast I was with You.
73:23 But I am continually with You;
    You hold my hand, [on] the right.
73:24 By Your counsel You guide me,
    and afterward You will bring me honor.
73:25 Who is there for me in heaven?
    But with You, I desire nothing on earth.
73:26 It may come to an end—my flesh and my heart,
    [but] the strength of my heart and my portion is God, forever.
73:27 For, behold, those far from You perish;
    You terminate all those who are unfaithful to You.
73:28 But as for me, the nearness of God is my good;
    I have set the Lord Yahweh [as] my refuge,
    that I may recount all Your acts.

Structure

The composition is "narratival" and story-like in its layout. The confidence in divine goodness in the introduction of 73:1 is questioned, bemoaned, and besieged in 73:2–12 (the *Perplexity* of the psalmist: the "I" chafing about the "they" [the wicked]), a correction occurs in 73:13–17 (the *Pivot* of the psalmist: the "I"), and a reorientation closes out the rest of the psalm, 73:18–26 (the *Perception* of the psalmist: but now the standalone "they" and "I" of the *Perplexity* section has become "they" + "You" [God], and "I + You," respectively), before an emphatic conclusion, 73:27–28:[1]

Introduction	Proverb ("*God* is *good* to Israel")	**(73:1)**
Perplexity	Plight of the psalmist ("I")	**(73:2–3a)**
	Prosperity of the wicked ("they")	**(73:3b–12)**
Pivot	Penitence of the psalmist ("I")	**(73:13–17)**
Perception	Plight of the wicked ("they" + "You")	**(73:18–20)**
	Portion of the psalmist ("I" + "You")	**(73:21–26)**
Conclusion	Proverb ("the nearness of *God* is my *good*")	**(73:27–28)**

Theological Focus

> The prosperity and peace of the wicked can lead the righteous to envy them—thus causing God's people to suspect the goodness of God and his care for them—until they come to recognize the true state of affairs: the presence of God and his goodness with them forever, their divine refuge satisfying all their needs and bringing them ultimate vindication over their enemies who are punished.

Commentary

Introduction (73:1)

The psalm begins and ends with assertions of God's "goodness" (73:1, 28). Between these two declarations is the struggle of the psalmist to answer *how* God is good to his people. Indeed, until the turning point of the psalm (73:13–17, Pivot), God is not mentioned after 73:1.[2] However, at the end of the psalm, divine goodness is defined as the "nearness of God," as the psalmist comes to recognize that the abiding presence of God with the divine community is the ultimate and critical reality to be attended to and sought!

---

1. Modified from Tate, *Psalms 51–100*, 232; Allen, Leslie C., "Psalm 73," 4–5; and Wendland, "Aspects of the Structure," 139.
2. He is derisively referred to in 73:11 by the wicked.

Perplexity (73:2–12)

The psalmist commences the account of his *Perplexity* with a plaintive voice of contrast, lamenting his plight (73:2–3a): God might be good to his people (73:1), "but as for me ..." (73:2). It is almost as if he is suggesting a "surely not!" to the "surely" in 73:1. Yes, God is good, *but* "I" am "slip slidin' away" (73:2), envious of the boastful and thriving wicked (72:3a).[3] They are psychologically peaceful in mind (73:3b), physically prosperous in body (73:4–5), pridefully predatory in action (73:6–7), and perniciously profane in utterance (73:8–9). Having all they want in provisions, they claim God does not know (or care) about their nefarious undertakings (73:10–11).[4]

These malefactors take up most of the section (73:3b–12, their prosperity): they are explicitly labeled "wicked" at the beginning and end, their peaceful and "forever-at-ease" state being particularly galling for the psalmist:[5]

```
"peace" (שָׁלוֹם, shalom; 73:3b)
   "wicked" (73:3b)
      "people," "mortals" (73:5)
         "therefore," "them [לָמוֹ, lamo]" (73:6)
            "eyes," "heart" (73:7)
               "they speak in wickedness" (73:8a)
               "of oppression they speak loftily" (73:8b)
            "mouth," "tongue" (73:9)
         "therefore," "them [לָמוֹ]" (73:10)
      "God," "Most High" (73:11)
   "wicked" (73:12a)
"at ease" (שָׁלֵו, shalew; 73:12b)
```

Such are the wicked, and not only do they seem to inhabit *shalom*, "they increase wealth" (73:12b).[6] This, the perplexed psalmist implicitly declares, is both incomprehensible and unfair.

---

3. Paul Simon, "Slip Slidin' Away," in *Greatest Hits, Etc.* (New York: Columbia, 1977). The fronted pronoun ("but as for me"), "close to," and "all but" are emphatic in 73:2. "Steps" translates אֲשֻׁרָי, *ashuray*; one remembers that a similar word אַשְׁרֵי, *ashre* ("blessing") commenced the Psalter. Perhaps this is a hint that the supplicant's "blessedness" is vanishing even as his "steps" are faltering. See deClaissé-Walford et al., *Book of Psalms*, 589.

4. Following Dahood (*Psalms II*, 190), 73:10a is emended from יָשִׁיב עַמּוֹ הֲלֹם [יָשִׁיב / יָשׁוּב], [yashiv / yashuv] *'ammo halom*, "his people return here," to יִשְׂבְּעוּם לֶחֶם, *yisv'um lechem*, "they are satisfied with food," a phrase that is not uncommon in the Psalter (78:25, 29; 132:15). In 73:11, "God" is אֵל, *'el*, and "Most High," עֶלְיוֹן, *'elyon*. Both carry connotations of deity's power and might: perhaps the claim is that this numinous being has better things to do than deal with the trivial transactions of mere mortals—i.e., practical or functional atheism.

5. Structure modified from Auffret, "Et moi sans cesse avec toi," 250. The "belly" (אוּלָם, *'ulam*) of the wicked is full (73:4b), and at ease they are, seemingly "forever" (עוֹלָם, *'olam*; 73:12b).

6. "Wealth," חַיִל, *chayil*, can also mean "power."

Pivot (73:13–17)

This section begins with "surely" (73:13a), demarcating it from the next that also commences with "surely" (73:18a[7]). In effect, this pivot is a penitential response on part of the psalmist, regarding his earlier feelings of envy towards those thriving evildoers.

In his frustration, he had initially felt his all his uprightness was in vain, for those who were *not* upright appeared to be prospering (73:13), an incongruent state of affairs.[8] The contrast with 73:1 is striking:

73:1	"*Surely* God is good to Israel, to the *pure* in *heart*!"
73:13	"*Surely* in vain I have kept my *heart clean*, and washed my hands in innocence."

Such a voicing of doubt regarding the declaration of 73:1 is essentially identical to the assertion of the wicked in 73:11: "How does God know?" Does he know? Does he care? Is he really "good" (73:1a)? After all, the wicked were "not afflicted" (73:5b), but the psalmist was "afflicted"—and that "all day" (73:14a); the "eyes" of the evil ones were contented and satiated (73:7a), while the "eyes" of the psalmist were bothered by these perplexities (73:16b); the wicked "do not have … trouble" (73:5a), but the psalmist found God's apparent unfairness "troubling" (73:16b).

Nevertheless, in this *Pivot* section, the psalmist, in penitence, comes to the realization that voicing his pique and envy in this fashion would be a betrayal of God and his people (73:15) for, in effect, such an attitude was one that amounted to a distrust of God, his sovereignty, and his providence, a sentiment that could, if publicly voiced, endanger the faith of "Your children" (73:14b). Yes, the wicked could spout out their disdain of deity (they "say," אמר, *'mr*; 73:11a), but the righteous one felt the constraint to maintain a judicious silence (refusing to "say [said]," אמר; 73:15a), at least for the sake of his community.

So all of this festered like a wound, "until I went into the sanctuary of God" (73:17).[9] This is the first mention of God after 73:1 (and 73:11, where "God" is used disdainfully[10]), and with that, the psalmist's perspective changes. What he had mistakenly "reckoned," "considered," and "understood" (73:15a, 16a) is now corrected in the presence of God, perhaps in worship. As a result of this pivot in 73:13–17, the perplexing dissonance of 73:4–12 becomes a perceptional consonance in 73:18–26.

---

7. That was also the first word of the psalm (73:1a).

8. The psalmist is not making a claim of sinlessness here, of course. Such predications of non-culpability, scattered throughout the Psalter, indicate "the innocence of a relatively righteous person of honorable life" (Goldingay, *Psalms*, 2:407).

9. Literally, 73:17a has "sanctuaries," perhaps referring in general to the larger precincts of the temple/tabernacle, as in Lev 21:23; Jer 51:51.

10. A pronominal suffix indicating God ("*Your* children") also showed up in 73:15b.

Perception (73:18–26)

This perception is a reorientation of the psalmist with regard to the plight of the wicked (73:18–20). Prominent here is "they" (the wicked) and "You" (God), unlike the earlier *Perplexity* section that had only "I" (in the plight of the psalmist, 73:2–3a) and "they" (in the prosperity of the wicked (73:3b–12). That is to say, *Perplexity* occurs when "God" is not in the equation. However, here in the *Perception* section, there is "they" + "You" (in the plight of the wicked, 73:18–20) and "I" + "You" (in the portion of the psalmist, 73:21–26). In other words, proper *Perception* begins with "God" in the picture. It is to such a divine point of view that the psalmist's perception now aligns.

The commencement of 73:18 with "surely" and the *Perception* of the psalmist create a contrast with the earlier "surely" in 73:13 (and the *mis*perception of the psalmist). Once it was the psalmist who was in danger of "stumbling" and "slipping" (73:2); now he sees that it is the wicked who have "skidded" and "fallen" (73:18). And the ones who had "set" their mouths arrogantly against God (73:9a) are now the ones who have been "set" by God in unsecure places (73:18a); those who were at "peace" (שָׁלוֹם; 73:3b) and "at ease" (שָׁלֵו; 73:12b) would become instantly "desolated" and "completely terminated" (73:19). A garment of violence had been the cover "for them" (לָמוֹ; 73:6b), and waters of abundance had been drunk "by them" (also לָמוֹ; 73:10b). But now God sets up "for them" disaster (again לָמוֹ; 73:18b); yet for the psalmist, "for me" (לִי, *li*; 73:25a), there is God and so there would be bliss forever. And thus, the nightmare of the prosperity of the wicked ends (73:20).

Now that the malefactors have been dealt with, there still remains the issue of the psalmist's wrong attitude and estrangement from God—his earlier doubts about divine providence and justice. To that he now turns: the portion of the psalmist (73:21–26).

Once the supplicant was "un*know*ing" (from ידע, *yd'*; 73:22), harking back to his days of trying "to understand" (also ידע, 73:16a) the whole perplexing situation. Indeed, he had been tempted to believe those evildoers' claim that God does not "know" and there is no "knowledge" with him (ידע and דֵּעָה, *de'ah*; respectively; 73:11). But after the sanctuary experience (73:17a), everything changed. Once the psalmist was a beast "with You" (73:22b),[11] but he realized that, in fact, he was continually "with You"—in the presence of God (73:23a, 25b). And being "with You" is all he needs, for God is the strength of his "heart" (73:26b). Once that same "heart" had been embittered (73:21a), akin to the "heart" of the wicked overflowing with arrogance (73:7b). No longer! Guided and counseled by God, "with God," the psalmist would ultimately be vindicated and honored (73:24), though he is "mocked" and "rebuked" now (73:8a, 14b). The "outcome" (אַחֲרִית, *acharit*; 73:17b) of the wicked was desolation and destruction; the fate of the psalmist "afterward" (אַחַר, *achar*; 73:24b) is honor in the presence of God.[12] The wicked would be set on "skiddy places" (חָלָק, *chalaq*; 73:18a); the "portion" of the righteous (חֵלֶק, *cheleq*; 73:26) would be God himself. The gang of the nefarious speak against the "heavens" and their tongues parade arrogantly on "earth" (73:9); for the psalmist, he has God in "heaven," and he wants nothing more on "earth" (73:25). "For

---

11. In his ignorance and his misperception, no better than an irrational animal.

12. In 73:24b there may be a hint of an eschatological *ultimate* vindication, especially in a psalm following one about the Messiah, the eschatological King (Psalm 72). Indeed, the same verb, לקח, *lqch*, translated "bring" in 73:24b, was used of Yahweh "taking/bringing" Enoch and Elijah into his presence (Gen 5:24; 2 Kgs 2:3, 5, 9, 10; also see Ps 49:15, 17). Besides, there is the claim that God is the psalmist's portion *forever* even when his life fails him (73:26b). Nonetheless, it must be noted that לקח can also be used of the rescue accomplished by God in this life (as in 18:16).

them" (לָמוֹ, 73:18a) is ruin; "for me" (לִי, 73:25a) is God! Even if his life came to an end, his portion would be God "forever" (73:26), in contrast to the apparent (but mistaken) ease of the wicked "forever" (73:12b). Dramatically illustrating this assertion, "it may come to an end" (the single word כָּלָה, kalah) begins 73:26a, and "forever" ends 73:26b.

> "It may come to an end—
>   my flesh
>   and my *heart*,
>   [but] the strength of my *heart*
>   and my portion is God,
> forever."

It is the contrast between everything else in the cosmos and God himself! He is all one needs—forever!—no matter what the circumstances appear to be. In the long run, in the ultimate reckoning, the people of God are on the right side, because God is with them!

Conclusion (73:27–28)

The psalm ends with a conclusion that reprises the fate of the wicked (73:27) and that of the righteous (73:28). The former are those "far from You" (73:27a),[13] the latter those who experience the "nearness of God" (73:28a). The contrast is further sharpened with the somewhat redundant, but emphatic, וַאֲנִי, wa'ani, "but as for me" (73:28a). The long and short of it is that the psalmist will "recount" the acts of God (ספר, sphr; 73:28c)—perhaps the deliverance of the righteous and the destruction of the wicked. This is quite a shift from his earlier petulant and unperceiving "reckoning" (also ספר; 73:15a) of divine unfairness. And all because the supplicant had "set" God as his refuge (73:28b), unlike the wicked who "set" their mouths to speak against God (73:9a), and who would, in turn, be "set" up by God for a downfall (73:18a). Yes, he will take care of his own—that he will, forever!

---

13. And who "are unfaithful" to God (73:27b); that verb commonly labels illicit sexual activity (זנה, znh; see 106:39) and metaphorically also can indicate the worship of false gods (particularly in the prophetic tradition; e.g., Jer 2:20; 3:1, 3, 6, 8).

Sermon Map

I. Prosperity of the Wicked
   They do evil (73:3, 6–9, 11, 12a)
   Yet they thrive (73:4–5, 10, 12b)
   Move-to-relevance: The seeming flourishing of evildoers

II. Plight of the Righteous
   God's people are upright (73:1, 13)
   Yet they suffer, leading to skepticism and envy (73:2, 14, 21–22)
   Move-to-relevance: The suffering of the righteous

III. Plight of the Wicked
   Evildoers will be punished (73:15–20, 27)
   Move-to-relevance: Praise for the Messiah-King

IV. Prosperity of the Righteous
   God is enough (73:23–26, 28)

V. *Sufficiency of the Sovereign!*
   Specifics on resting in God's sufficiency for all things, for all time

PSALM 74:1–23

Psalm of Disorientation

Lament in Chaos and Destruction

PERHAPS THE ORIGINS OF Psalm 74 date back to the destruction of Jerusalem (587–586 BCE; see references to the temple: 74:2c–7). "The psalm returns again and again to the concern that all that Israel has come to depend on for stability is gone."[1] The song sounds like a communal lament, but there is only one verse with a first-person plural, 74:9; for that matter, there is only one verse with a first-person singular, too, 74:12.

Translation

74:1 God, why have You rejected [us] permanently?
    Your anger smokes against the sheep of Your pasture.
74:2 Remember Your congregation, which You acquired of old,
    [which] You redeemed as the tribe of Your inheritance,
    [and] this Mount Zion, where You have abided.
74:3 Lift Your footsteps toward the permanent ruins,
    all the damage wrought by the enemy in the holy place.
74:4 Your adversaries have roared in the midst of Your meeting place;
    they have set their signs as signs.
74:5 It seems as one lifting up axes in a thicket of trees.
74:6 And now its engraving—completely,
    with hatchet and crowbars—they smash.
74:7 They sent to the fire Your sanctuary, [down] to the earth;
    they profaned the abode of Your name.
74:8 They said in their heart, "Let us completely suppress them";
    they have burned all the meeting places of God on earth.

---

1. deClaissé-Walford et al., *Book of Psalms*, 594.

74:9 Our signs we do not see;
>there is no longer a prophet,
>and there is not any with us who knows until when.

74:10 Until when, God, will the adversary revile,
>[and] the enemy spurn Your name permanently?

74:11 Why do You turn back Your hand, even Your right hand?
>From the midst of Your bosom, destroy.

74:12 But God is my King from of old,
>the One accomplishing deliverance in the midst of the earth.

74:13 You—You divided the sea by Your strength;
>You broke the heads of the sea monsters on the waters.

74:14 You—You crushed the heads of Leviathan;
>You gave it as food for the people dwelling in the desert.

74:15 You—You split spring and stream;
>You—You dried up ever-flowing rivers.

74:16 To You is the day; to You also is the night;
>You—You determined the light and the sun.

74:17 You—You established all the boundaries of the earth;
>summer and winter, You—You shaped them.

74:18 Remember this: the enemy has reviled, Yahweh,
>and a foolish people has spurned Your name.

74:19 Do not give to the wild beast the soul of Your turtledove;
>the life of Your afflicted do not forget permanently.

74:20 Look upon the covenant;
>for the dark places of the earth are filled by the abodes of violence.

74:21 Let not the oppressed turn back disgraced;
>let the afflicted and needy praise Your name.

74:22 Arise, God, dispute Your [own] dispute;
>remember Your reviling from a foolish one all day.

74:23 Do not forget the voice of Your adversaries,
>the uproar of those rising against You, ascending continually.

Structure

Psalm 74 can be structured according to God's (in)actions in time—present, past, and future:

> **Plaint: God's Inaction in the Present**
> (74:1–11; God and Enemy: lament)
>
> Protest (**74:1–3**)
> Prosecution (**74:4–9**)
> Perplexity (**74:10–11**)
>
> "permanent/ly" (74:1a, 3a); "remember" (74:2a); "enemy" (74:3b, 10b)
> "adversary" (74:4a, 10a); "revile" (74:10a); "Your name" (74:7b, 10b)
>
> **Praise: God's Action in the Past**
> (74:12–17; God and Chaos: hymn)
>
> **Petition: God's Action in the Future**
> (74:18–23; God and Enemy: lament)
>
> "permanently" (74:19b); "remember" (74:18a, 22b); "enemy" (74:18a)
> "adversary" (74:23a); "revile" (74:18a, 22b); "Your name" (74:18b, 21b)

Theological Focus

> When it appears that God has angrily rejected his people, letting them suffer and their institutions be ruined for no obvious reason, and there seems to be no end in sight to their malignant oppression by ungodly and uncouth foes, the people of God appeal to him as his own inheritance, redeemed and blessed by his presence, and they find consolation in the history of God's powerful defeat of chaos and his establishment of creation in the past, resting in the hope that their divine King will act equally mightily on their behalf in the future, to result in his praise.

Commentary

Plaint: God's Inaction in the Present (74:1–11)

This *Plaint* section begins and ends with the question "Why?" (74:1a, 11b), the first addressing God's relationship to his people, the second his relationship to the enemy.[2]

The psalmist commences with a protest of God's treatment of his own (74:1–3), bounded by "permanently" (74:1a) and "permanent" (74:3a[3]): God's rejection of his people "permanently" has resulted in the "permanent" ruins of his sanctuary. Ironically it is not the enemy

---

2. And there is "until when . . . ?" (74:10). Also note: "permanently," 74:1a, 10b, acting as a bookend for the section. There is also the chiastic appearance of foes: "enemy" (74:3b) / "adversaries" (74:4a) // "adversaries" (74:10a) / "enemy" (74:10b).

3. I keep 74:3 as part of the protest also because it points out God's apparent failure to "lift [His] footsteps" towards the ruins.

that has been the subject of his smoking anger (74:1b), but his own flock, those to whom he bears a responsibility as their shepherd, those he himself had redeemed.[4] The chiastic structure of 74:2ab brings the pathos of the situation to the fore:

> "Remember Your congregation,
>   which You acquired of old,
>   [which] You redeemed
> as the tribe of Your inheritance."

How could God do this to the people he had rescued? He had even permitted the manifestation of his presence with them, his own dwelling ("Mount Zion," "where You have abided" [74:2c], "holy place" [74:3b], "Your meeting place" [74:4a], "Your sanctuary," "the abode of Your name" [74:7], and "the meeting places of God" [74:8b]), to be deracinated. "Come and see for yourself," the psalmist exhorts ("lift Your footsteps . . . ," 74:3a), "at all the horror that has been perpetrated."

Then comes the poet's prosecution of the violence and terror wrought by the enemies, their malevolence described graphically in 74:4-8, with them serving as the subjects of seven verbs: "Your adversaries have roared" (74:4a), "they have set their signs" (74:4b[5]), "they smash" (74:6b[6]), "they sent to the fire" (74:7a), "they profaned" (74:7b), "they said" (74:8a), "they have burned" (74:8b). Not only does seven symbolize a totality, but "all" and "completely" occur in chiastic order declaring the consummation of the total destruction and utter desecration![7]

> "*all* the damage" (74:3b)
>   "*completely* ... they smash" (74:6)
>   "'*completely* suppress'" (74:8a)
> "burned *all* the meeting places" (74:8b)

What God had once done is pictured as now coming entirely undone, as the three lines of description in 74:2 are literally and literarily reversed in 74:7-8.[8]

---

4. The two verbs "You acquired" and "You redeemed" (74:2a, 2b) are redolent of the exodus: see Exod 15:13, 16.

5. The "signs" of the foes (74:4b) erected in the temple precincts were likely symbols of their victory. Indeed, Israel's own "signs" had disappeared (74:9a).

6. Likely the destruction is that of the woodwork of the temple (74:5) and its decorations (74:6).

7. As well, the dreadful scope of the arson: "[down] to the earth" (74:7a); "all" the damage (74:3b) that has affected "all" the meeting places of God (74:8b); destruction is "completely" accomplished (74:6a); the people are "completely" suppressed (74:8a).

8. See Sylva, "Procreation Discourse," 253. The cognate words, "congregation" and "meeting places" occur at the beginning and the end, respectively (74:2a, 8b; as shown), as well as in the middle—"meeting place" (74:4a).

God's Work
"Your congregation" (עֵדָה, 'edah; 74:2a)
"Mount Zion, where You have *abided* [שָׁכַן, shkn]" (74:2c)

Enemies' Work
"Your sanctuary ..., the *abode* [מִשְׁכָּן, mishkan] of Your name" (74:7b)
"meeting places [מוֹעֵד, mo'ed] of God" (74:8b)

It is as if God's people have gone from redemption (74:1–3a) to *non*-redemption (74:3b–9)! To make matters worse, Israel is now bereft of signs and prophets, and no one knows "how long" the agony will last (74:9); it is seemingly endless!

This is a matter of serious perplexity for the psalmist (74:10–11), and indeed, for all God's people in similar crises throughout the ages. How long is this going to go on, and why? "Until when" (עַד־מָה, 'ad-mah) commences 74:10 (and concludes 74:9 [עַד־מָתַי, 'ad-mati][9]), and "why" commences 74:11. In fact, 74:10 has a rather ironic chiastic structure:

> "Until when,
>   God,
>   will the adversary revile,
>   and the enemy spurn
>   Your name
> permanently?"

Everything is unintelligible and incomprehensible—that God's people should suffer so and God's own name be besmirched thus.[10] And "forever"? "Does it have to be so?" the psalmist asks befuddled. Surely "Your right hand" (74:11a)—the symbol of God's power—if wielded can set right this untenable situation. Yet it seems that that divine extremity "sits there in Yhwh's pocket, withheld" (or withered).[11] Instead, the supplicant pleads, God should demolish the enemy, taking out his hand "from the midst of Your bosom" (74:11b).

Praise: God's Action in the Past (74:12–17)

The closing verse of the previous section, 74:11, urged God to act against the enemy. The current section of *Praise* recollects how God had once acted against another foe, the age-old enemy, chaos, as he created the heavens and the earth in the past.[12] This argument is deployed

---

9. There is also "no longer" (עוֹד, 'od; 74:9b).
10. "Name" indicates the person of God (74:10b).
11. Goldingay, *Psalms*, 2:430.
12. The section begins and ends with a mention of "earth" (74:12b, 17a). The description of divine action in 74:13–14 is somewhat parallel to the mythology of the Babylonian creation story *Enuma Elish* where Marduk kills a sea goddess and other assorted beasts before fashioning the heavens and the earth (*ANET* 60–72). Ugaritic literature of cosmogony also tells of a battle between Baal and Yam (sea) and its demonic monsters; the victorious Baal is enthroned king (see Grønbæk, "Baal's Battle," 27–44). The divine action in 74:15 appears to be the act of creation in which the covering waters were drained away into some kind of

by the supplicant to motivate God to repeat his ancient performance against modern foes. One observes seven discrete actions of God in 74:13a, 13b–14, 15a, 15b, 16, 17a, 17b, each marked by an emphatic and redundant pronoun, אַתָּה, *'attah*, preceding a second-person suffixed verb ("You—You . . ."). No doubt, this parallels—and counters—the seven destructive actions of the enemy in 74:4–8 (noted above).

The enemies were wreaking havoc "in the midst" of the sanctuary (74:4a), so the psalmist urged God to draw out his hand "from the midst" of his bosom to destroy these foes (74:11b), essentially to act with power to destroy the enemy, just as he had once defeated chaos "in the midst" of the earth (an action labeled "deliverance," 74:12b).[13] If he can annihilate disorderly monsters and regenerate space and time from chaos to establish the cosmos in security, why does he not eliminate those diabolic enemies currently overrunning and infesting his sanctuary? Surely, "all" the damage wrought by those foes in "all" the meeting places (74:3b, 8b) can be remedied in an instant by the Creator who set "all" the boundaries of the earth (74:17a). This is, of course, grounded in the acclamation of God as "my King," in 74:12, the central verse of Psalm 74.[14] Indeed this regent's divine dominion is "of old" (74:12a), extending from way before the current crisis.

Petition: God's Action in the Future (74:18–23)

Following that recollection of God's mighty acts of the past (in the preceding *Praise* section), the psalmist ends the poem with a poignant section that is almost a lament, a *Petition* to God to act in the future.[15] For the first and only time in Psalm 74, "Yahweh" is employed (74:18), a powerful motivation to the personal deity that he is to his people.

This section is also laid out with its opening (74:18–19) and closing (74:21–23) sections bearing verbal parallels, intensifying the *Petition* as it urges divine intervention:[16] "remember" (74:18a, 22b); "reviled/reviling" (74:18a, 22b); vocative for deity ("Yahweh," 74:18a; "God," 74:22a); "foolish" (74:18b, 22b); "Your name" (74:18b, 21b); "afflicted" (74:19b, 21b); "do not forget" (74:19b, 23a); and "permanently/continually" (74:19b, 23b). Adding to the pathos is

---

abyss to cause the appearance of land. Indeed, there are a number of verbal parallels between this psalm and the creation and flood stories (in Genesis 1–11): "earth" (Ps 74:7a, 8b, 12b, 17a, 20b and Gen 1:1–2); "sea" (Ps 74:13a and Gen 1:10); "sea monsters" (Ps 74:13b and Gen 1:21); "waters" (Ps 74:13b and Gen 1:2); "food" (Ps 74:14b and Gen 2:9); "split" (Ps 74:15a and Gen 7:11); "spring" (Ps 74:15a and Gen 7:11; 8:2); "dried up/dry" (Ps 74:15b and Gen 1:9; 8:7, 14); "river[s]" (Ps 74:15b and Gen 2:10, 13); "day" and "night" (Ps 74:16a and Gen 1:5); "light" (Ps 74:16b and Gen 1:14–16); "summer" and "winter" (Ps 74:17b and Gen 8:22); and "shape/form" (Ps 74:17b and Gen 2:7–8, 19). See Michael, "Works of God's Salvation," 12. It is not surprising then, that as in the creation account of seven days with its allusion to the dedication of the temple (see Kuruvilla, *Genesis*, 29–49), here in Psalm 74 also, God's creative activities are closely linked to the temple. "The destruction of the temple as described in the opening verses of Ps 74 would then be an assault not simply on the physical building established for the worship of YHWH but on YHWH's very sovereignty and the entirety of the created order as well" (Greene, "Creation, Destruction," 99–100).

13. "While the enemy claimed his stake in the temple, the psalmist finds hope in the God who has acted in the whole earth . . . Whereas the enemy's actions are limited in time and space [74:3b], Yhwh has been king before time and in all the earth [74:17a]. Therefore, the hymn in Ps 74:12–17 presents an answer to the apparent triumph of evil described in Ps 74:3b–9" (Cunha, "Creation, Kingship," 141).

14. The introduction of the first-person singular in 74:12 (after the first-person plurals in 74:9) is a hint that the psalmist was himself a leader-spokesman addressing the divine King on behalf of the community.

15. As was shown earlier, a number of verbal parallels link this section with the first, *Plaint* (74:1–11).

16. Modified from Girard, *Les Psaumes Redécouverts: De la Structure au Sens: 51–100*, 305–6.

another wordplay: "God has used his power to form winter (חֹרֶף [*choreph*, 74:17b], but he remains silent while foolish foes taunt (חֵרֵף [*chereph*, 'reviled/reviling'; 74:18a, 22b])."[17] The "earth" established by God (74:17a) is now an "earth" filled by the dwellings of these violent ones (74:20b). They are "rising" against God (קוּם, *qwm*; 74:23b), so would that God in turn "arise" (קוּם; 74:22a) against them.[18] Many are the references here to the tumultuous noise of the enemies: "reviled," "spurned" (74:18), "reviling" (74:22b), "voice," "uproar" (74:23)—and this infernal din is occurring "all day" and "continually" (74:22b, 23b). Also note the emphasis on these foes lining up to dishonor the Creator (74:18a, 18b, 22b, 23b): these scoffing buffoons, the psalmist argues, must be silenced. What began as "God, why . . . ?" (74:1a) and moves into "Until when, God . . . ?" (74:10a), now ends with "Arise, God . . ." (74:22a).

God's people thought they had been rejected by God "permanently" (74:1a), as the enemy made the sanctuary a "permanent" ruin (74:3a), spurning the divine name "permanently" (74:10b). Would that God not forget his afflicted "permanently" (74:19b). Indeed, in light of 74:12–17, the psalmist is "implying that all God has to do is act as God has done in the past."[19] And the result would be that the delivered community of God would "*praise* Your name" (הלל, *hll*; 74:21b), as opposed to the destroyers and vandals "profaning" (also חלל; 74:7b) the abode of "Your name."[20]

Yet the lament ends quite abruptly. "The psalm stops rather than finishes. Its rhetoric thus reflects the situation it presupposes. It achieves no closure, as the people's experience has achieved no closure."[21] And the "Why?" and "Until when?" questions of the psalm (74:1a, 10a) remain unanswered. All that remains is trust and hope in a God gracious and mighty. And that is the attitude he calls his people to adopt.

---

17. Tate, *Psalms 51–100*, 252. As well, note the image of a ferocious "wild beast" consuming an innocent "turtledove," God's precious possession (74:19a).

18. The "disputing of Your [own] dispute" (74:22a) is also an exhortation to God to defend his own (just) cause.

19. deClaissé-Walford et al., *Book of Psalms*, 600. The reference to a "covenant" in 74:20a is unlikely to indicate any specific biblical treaty between God and humanity; rather, it is simply an appeal to God to remember his promises to his community—"commitments to his people which he should not forget" (Tate, *Psalms 51–100*, 252–53).

20. And the "spurning" of "Your name" (74:10b, 18b).

21. Goldingay, *Psalms*, 2:436.

Sermon Map

I. Present: God's Inaction Expostulated
   God's rejection of them (74:1, 3–9)
   God's relation to them (74:2, 10–11, 19)
   Move-to-relevance: The apparent rejection by God of his people

II. Past: God's Action Extolled
   God's reputation (74:12–17)
   Move-to-relevance: God's inimitable defeat of chaos

III. Future: God's Action Expected
   God's response hoped for (74:18, 20–23)

IV. *Consolation in the Conquering of Chaos!*
   Specifics on waiting upon God, trusting in his defeat of chaos

PSALM 75:1–10

Psalm of Orientation

Praise to the Exalting Judge

THIS PSALM OF ORIENTATION begins with a human first-person plural "we" (75:1), moves to a divine first-person singular "I" who is the judge (75:2-3), then to a human first-person singular "I" admonishing the wicked (75:4-5), followed by a restatement of God's judgeship (75:6-8) that then reverts to a human "I" praising God (75:9), before closing with another divine first-person utterance with "I" (75:10; see below). While Psalm 74 sought God's intervention, Psalm 75 depicts a God who is ready to act.

Translation

75:1   We give thanks to You, God, we give thanks,
           and Your name is near;
           they [Your people] recount Your wonders.
75:2   [God:] "For I take [hold of] the appointed time,
           I—I judge with uprightness.
75:3   When the earth and all its dwellers are swaying,
           I—I steady its pillars."
75:4   I [the psalmist] said to the boastful, "Do not boast,"
           and to the wicked, "Do not exalt the horn.
75:5   Do not exalt on high your horn;
           [or] speak with a forward neck."
75:6   For not from the east, nor from the west,
           and not from the wilderness; [from] the mountains [is exaltation].
75:7   For God is the judge;
           one He humbles, and another He exalts.

75:8   For a chalice is in the hand of Yahweh,
           and the wine ferments, full of spices.
       And He pours from this; surely the dregs are drained,
           and all the wicked of the earth have drunk.
75:9   But I—I will announce forever;
           I will make music to the God of Jacob.
75:10 [God:] "And all the pairs of horns of the wicked ones I will shatter;
           they will be exalted, the horns of the righteous one."

Structure

The psalm is chiastically laid out, with a concluding summary from God:

Acclamation 1 (**75:1**)	Praise for God's imminent action
Arbitration 1 (**75:2–3**)	God as "judge" (first person; 75:2a)
Admonition (**75:4–5**)	Warning to the "wicked"
Arbitration 2 (**75:6–8**)	God as "judge" (third person; 75:7a)
Acclamation 2 (**75:9**)	Praise for God's action
Conclusion (**75:10**)	

Theological Focus

Despite adverse circumstances caused by the wicked, the righteous are grateful to God and praise him, for they are confident that their sovereign God is just and that his justice will honor the righteous and abase the wicked.

Commentary

Acclamation 1 (75:1)

After the lamenting and lugubrious conclusion of Psalm 74 that has no resolution in sight (74:22–23), 75:1 comes as a surprise. The people of God are thanking him (75:1a; though it was his smoking anger against them that introduced the prior psalm, 74:1b), for his name is near (75:1b; though they had accused earlier God of rejecting them permanently, 74:1a),[1] and they are recounting his wonders (75:1c; though in Psalm 74 it was the wicked who were demolishing everything, including God's own dwelling, 74:3–9)! Thus, the *Acclamation 1* of

---

1. The nearness of God's name indicates the proximity of his person to his people, actualized, perhaps, in his "name established in his dwelling" (Deut 12:5, 11).

God in 75:1 occurs without any intimation to the readers of this psalm that God had actually done something about those wicked ones of Psalm 74 or the oppression they had unleashed on his people, including the reviling of his own name (74:10–11, 18–23).

Of course, the editors of the Psalter are not trying to imply that something miraculous has happened between 74:23 and 75:1.[2] Rather, the change has been in the minds of God's people. While in the previous psalm the focus was on trusting God even when he was seemingly inactive, here the emphasis is on trust in God because of the certainty of his action, especially his performance as a judge against malefactors and evildoers (see *Arbitration 1* and *Arbitration 2* below). Though deliverance and judgment may not have happened yet, God's people are confident in the justice of their deity; so much so, they can already give thanks.[3]

Arbitration 1 (75:2–3)

After the exclamation of thanks by the community of God, deity shows up, agreeing with the mindset of his people. Yes, he will judge as the sovereign one who controls and sustains the entirety of the earth and all of its inhabitants (75:2–3): "Yahweh is the basis of both the world's stability and of the moral order. If either is challenged, chaos may erupt, but Yahweh's steadying hand will be there to restore order."[4] The cosmos in its physicality and in its morality is dependent on God for its solidity and fixity. And that, God seems to imply, is enough reason for his people to trust him. The mention of "appointed time" in 75:2a is notable: the psalmist had grieved in 74:10, "*Until when*, God . . . ?" noting also that "there is not any with us who knows *until when*" (74:9c). To that, God replies here in 75:2a: "at the appointed time,"[5] he will judge (an emphatic fronted pronoun with a first-person suffixed verb confirms this: "I—I judge . . ."), for he is totally sovereign, even over time (75:2).[6] And over space, too: with another emphatic "I—I steady . . . ," God declares himself as the one who stabilizes the earth and its denizens (75:3). The people of God do not have to worry: God's got this!

Admonition (75:4–5)

The psalmist then takes over, quoting himself and warning the unrighteous. The "horn" in 75:4b, 5a, 10a, 10b indicates the power and honor of the bearer.[7] "In an animal such as an ox, the neck is a locus of strength, and it suggests the capacity to decide the direction one will take or to walk head high."[8] In any case, self-sufficiency and an utter lack of dependency on anyone or anything, least of all on God, is implied by the idiom. The arrogant wicked are thereby warned that self-exaltation is foolish and insolent, nothing but the adoption of a god-complex.

---

2. And one should not necessarily read other adjacent psalms to create a sequential story.
3. Later in 75:9, we see that this praise (*Appreciation 2*) is explicitly in the future, as also is God's action of judgment (75:10).
4. Tate, *Psalms 51–100*, 259.
5. Which he "takes [hold of]"—*carpe diem* at its best!
6. Indeed, even the intentional alternation of א- and מ-words ('- and *m*- words) in 75:2 (כִּי אֶקַּח מוֹעֵד אֲנִי מֵישָׁרִים אֶשְׁפֹּט, *ki 'eqqach mo'ed 'ani mesharim 'eshpot*) suggests the perfection of divine order.
7. Also see Ps 89:17, 24; 92:10; 112:9; 132:17; 148:14.
8. Goldingay, *Psalms*, 2:444.

The psalmist's utterance in 75:4–5 is created carefully in an almost reverse-staircase pattern, with progressive gapping in each of the four lines, adding to the power of his direct speech:[9]

74:4a	אָמַרְתִּי 'amarti "I said	לַהוֹלְלִים lahollim to the boastful,	אַל־ 'al 'Do not	תָּהֹלּוּ tahullu boast,'
74:4b		וְלָרְשָׁעִים wlarsha'im and to the wicked,	אַל־ 'al 'Do not	תָּרִימוּ קָרֶן tarimu qaren exalt the horn.
74:5a			אַל־ 'al Do not	תָּרִימוּ לַמָּרוֹם קַרְנְכֶם tarimu lammarom qarnkem exalt on high your horn;
74:5b				תְּדַבְּרוּ בְצַוָּאר עָתָק tdabru btsawwa'r 'ataq [or] speak with a forward neck.'"

Arbitration 2 (75:6–8)

With three uses of the conjunction כִּי, *ki*, "for," in 75:6a, 7a, 8a, the point is affirmed: exaltation will not come from any time or from any space (75:6[10]), but from God alone who judges (75:7), and he will put down every mutiny against his authority (75:8[11]). In sum, it is best to let *God* be the one who handles horns!

Acclamation 2 (75:9)

And the psalmist's own final word makes up the emphatic *Appreciation 2* with a conjunction + fronted pronoun and a first-person verbal suffix: "But I—I will announce . . ." (75:9). Because God was, likewise, emphatically the judge ("I—I judge . . . ," 75:2b) and because he was emphatically sovereign ("I—I steady . . . ," 75:3b), the child of God can emphatically praise ("I—I will announce . . . ," 75:9a), and that this devout one does forever! So, the psalm concludes as it began, with thankfulness and praise.

---

9. Modified from Auffret, "C'est Dieu qui juge," 387. The utterance in 75:4 is unlikely to be God's: the *Selah* that follows 75:3 (untranslated) is unusual in the middle of a speech; besides, "I said [אָמַרְתִּי, *'amarti*]" in the Psalms always refers to the psalmist (75:4a; also see 30:6; 31:14, 22; 32:5; 38:16; 39:2; 40:7, 10; 41:4; 73:15; 89:2; 94:18; 116:11; 119:57; 140:6; 142:5), except in 82:6 (deClaissé-Walford et al., *Book of Psalms*, 605). In any case, 75:4–7 hangs together, unified with the motif of "exalting."

10. In 75:6b, the word הָרִים, *harim*, is a polysemantic pun: it can be both the plural of הַר, *har*, "mountain" (thus, "mountains"), as well as the *hiphil* infinitive construct of רוּם, *rwm*, "exalt" (thus, "exaltation/to exalt," as in 1 Chr 15:16; 25:5; Ezra 3:12; 9:6) (Jensen, "Psalm 75," 418). I have attempted to give the sense of the pun with: "[from] the mountains [is exaltation]." That exaltation comes "not from the east, nor from the west" (75:6a) likely indicates sunrise and sunset, i.e., exaltation does not come from any *time*. And "wilderness" and "mountains" (75:6b) complement that declaration: neither does exaltation come from any *space*. Another possibility is to have all four references indicate *regional* space, particularly in relation to Palestine's geography: east and west, south ("wilderness") and north ("mountains") (Jensen, "Psalm 75," 424). All that to say, exaltation cometh solely from God.

11. A chalice of wine symbolizing the wrath of God is a familiar prophetic metaphor: Isa 51:17, 22; Jer 25:15–17; 49:12; 51:39; Ezek 23:31–35; Hab 2:16.

Conclusion (75:10)

God has the last word. Summarizing divine judicial policy, he affirms that the horns of the wicked will be destroyed, while those of the righteous will be exalted (75:10): the right, and only, way to gain exaltation is at God's hands. The divine oracle in 75:10 is strikingly constructed to bring out the contrast between the demolishing of the wicked (75:10a) and the distinguishing of the righteous (75:10b): every grammatical facet of each of the two lines is different (bolded), affirming that nothing and no one can escape the Great Arbitrator who grants just deserts to one and all:[12]

"'And all the **pairs of horns**	*feminine dual noun*
of the **wicked ones**	*masculine plural noun*
I will shatter;	*active verb, first-person singular common*
they will be exalted,	*passive verb, third-person feminine plural*
the **horns**	*feminine plural noun*
of the **righteous one**.'"	*masculine singular noun*

Thus, "the poem confirms . . . that there are two ways of life: one lived with God and one lived against God," ways that have diametrically opposing fates.[13] Those living righteously will be exalted—their expected deliverance will come, but those living wickedly will be destroyed. All because "Your name is near" (75:1b).

Sermon Map

I. Fear
   Move-to-relevance: Our fear of our dire circumstances
II. Faith
   The nearness of God (75:1b–c)
   The sovereignty of God (75:2–3)
   The response of praise (75:1a, 9)
III. Fate and Fortune
   The fate of the wicked (75:4–8, 10a)
   The fortune of the righteous (75:10b)
   Move-to-relevance: The justice of God is coming
IV. *Be Faithful: God Is Fair!*
   Specifics on resting in God's gracious justice

---

12. From Jensen, "Psalm 75," 427.
13. deClaissé-Walford et al., *Book of Psalms*, 607.

PSALM 76:1–12

Psalm of Orientation

Fearsome Deity Defeats Foes

PSALM 76 IS ESSENTIALLY a call to worship, the tangible expression of fealty to God: the "fear" of God resounds in this psalm (76:7a, 8b, 11b, 12b). Ultimately, despite the ubiquity of evil, God triumphs in judgment and "the psalm invites the reader to join the company of those who affirm, in the teeth of seemingly overwhelming evidence, that there is a judgment which sets right the horrible endemic evil in human existence."[1]

Translation

76:1 Known in Judah [is] God;
    in Israel great is His name.
76:2 His shelter came to be in Salem;
    and His dwelling in Zion.
76:3 There He smashed the flames of the bows,
    and shield and sword and [weapon of] war.
76:4 Resplendent [are] You,
    [more] majestic [than] the mountains of prey.
76:5 The strong of heart let themselves be plundered,
    they slumbered in sleep;
    and all of the warriors could not find their hands.
76:6 At Your rebuke, God of Jacob,
    both chariot and horse were stupefied.
76:7 You [are] to be feared—You;
    and who can stand before You in the time of Your anger?
76:8 From the heavens You made Your verdict heard;
    the earth feared and kept still

---

1. Tate, *Psalms 51–100*, 267–68.

76:9   when God rose to judgment,
           to deliver all the afflicted of the earth.
76:10 For fury [towards] man shall praise You;
           with the remainder of furies You gird Yourself.
76:11 Make vows to Yahweh your God and fulfill [them];
           let all those around Him bring tribute to the One who is to be feared.
76:12 He humbles the spirit of princes;
           feared [He is] by the kings of the earth.

Structure

Psalm 76 describes Yahweh directly by means of four *niphal* participles—"*known* in Judah [is] God" (76:1a); "*resplendent* [are] You" (76:4a); "You [are] to be *feared*" (76:7a); and "*feared* [He is]" (76:12b). We may thus see four sections to the psalm: the first forms an introduction addressed to people about the *Renown of God*; the second and third form the body of the psalm, respectively describing the *Resplendence of God* and the *Reverence for God* (both addressed to God); the fourth forms a conclusion, again addressed to the people, exhorting them to worship him, to show *Respect towards God*:[2]

> **Renown of God (76:1–3)**: *Address to People*
> "known" (*niphal* participle, 76:1a)
> Liturgical terms: "shelter," "Salem," "dwelling," "Zion" (76:2)
>
> > **Resplendence of God (76:4–6)**: *Address to God*
> > "resplendent" (*niphal* participle, 76:4a)
> > "You" (76:4a)
> >
> > **Reverence for God (76:7–10)**: *Address to God*
> > "feared" (*niphal* participle, 76:7a)
> > "You" (×2; 76:7a)
> >
> > **Respect towards God (76:11–12)**: *Address to People*
> > "feared" (*niphal* participle, 76:12b)
> > Liturgical terms: "vows," "fulfill," "tribute" (76:11)

Overall, it is the mighty power of God against his enemies that serves to express his renown, his resplendence, and his reverence, and to excite respect for him. In all four sections martial activities of deity predominate: "smashed," "flames of the bows," "shield," "sword," "[weapon of] war" (76:3), "prey" (76:4b), "be plundered," "warriors" (76:5), "chariot," "horse" (76:6); "anger" (76:7b), "fury," "furies" (76:10), "princes," "kings of the earth" (76:12). "The imagery is a poetic depiction of the terrible evil which pervades life in this world [and God's firm response to it]. Ours is not a utopian world devoid of the power of chaos, free of the demonic, and basically

---

2. Another *niphal* participle, though not describing deity, is found in 76:6a ("stupefied," the response of enemy armies to God).

loving ... The world groans in its suffering and cries out for judgment."[3] But there is a God who is willing to take action against these evils on behalf of his people. Thus, the response of his people to their renowned, resplendent, reverence-inspiring, and respect-worthy deity is to express their commitment to him in worship. Indeed, this expectation is suggested in liturgical terms in every section: "shelter," "Salem," "dwelling," "Zion" (76:2), "resplendent," "majestic" (76:4), "feared," "stand before You" (76:7), "vows," "fulfill," "tribute" (76:11).

Theological Focus

The renowned, resplendent, and revered God's defeat of his foes and the deliverance of his people motivate all the earth to respect him.

Commentary

Renown of God (76:1–3)

In the locus of his operations, "Judah," "Israel," "Salem," "Zion" (76:1–2), God is renowned. And it was "there" that he defeated his enemies (76:3a). This is God's victory sourced in his command-and-control center, the temple, "there" wherein he dwells.[4] Thus God is the one who brings שָׁלוֹם to שָׁלֵם (*shalom* to *shalem*), the warrior who is the Peace-Maker par excellence.[5] That is why he is renowned! The reason for this fame of God is explicated in the body of the psalm, in the next two sections (76:4–6, 7–10).

Resplendence of God (76:4–6).

This God is renowned, because he is also "resplendent" (76:4a), fiery, and bright and shining in all his glory.[6] So much so his foes are stunned and undone: they "let themselves be plundered"[7] as they reclined in the arms of Morpheus—in fact, they couldn't even find their hands (76:5). And not just human foes, even the beasts of the animal kingdom ("horse") and inanimate objects ("chariot"), were benumbed and befuddled ("stupefied," 76:6b). This was God, the "God of Jacob" (76:6a), the God of his people, the "majestic" one (אַדִּיר, *'addir*; 76:4b) who could decimate even the "strong" of heart (אַבִּיר, *'abbir*; 76:5a) without engaging in a fight, apparently! All deity does in 76:4–6 is issue a "rebuke" (76:6b) and the rest is history!

---

3. Tate, *Psalms 51–100*, 267.

4. The word for "shelter," מְעֹנָה, *m'onah*, can also mean "lair," particularly associated with lions (Pss 10:9; 104:21–22; Jer 25:38; Amos 3:4). That would make God "a leonine warrior who takes a powerful position in Jerusalem on Mount Zion and defeats all attackers" (Tate, *Psalms 51–100*, 261). "Flames of the bows" pictures arrows as fire, or perhaps even flaming arrows.

5. Goldingay, *Psalms*, 2:452.

6. The second line of 76:4 is unclear: it might indicate the enemy predators, now dead prey themselves, dotting the mountainside, a consequence of the battle waged by this renowned and resplendent deity.

7. The verb is in a rare form of the *hithpolel* and is reflexive.

Reverence of God (76:7–10)

Then comes the third *niphal* participle, "feared," נוֹרָא, *nora'* (76:7a)—clearly linked to the preceding participle, "resplendent," נָאוֹר, *na'or* (76:4a), as is evident from the wordplay and the emphatic constructions with the second-person pronoun, "You":

76:4a נָאוֹר אַתָּה
na'or 'attah
"Resplendent [are] *You*"

76:7a אַתָּה נוֹרָא אַתָּה
'attah nora' 'attah
"*You* [are] to be feared—*You*"

Yahweh is renowned, not only because he is resplendent but also because he inspires reverential awe, fear. God's resplendence, divine fire, his awe-inspiring, wonder-striking, breathtaking glory that discomfits all his foes, is cause for fear of God, a source of dismay to his enemies (but a delight to his people, of course). He acts from the "heavens" (76:8a), he "rises to judgment" (76:9a), he "makes ... heard" his verdict (76:8a), and the anti-God populace can only "fear" and "keep still" in reverence for this great deity (76:8b), as God accomplishes deliverance for his people, "the afflicted" (76:9b). This, too, is an act in accordance with his glory: even his "fury [towards] man" redounds to his praise (76:10a).[8]

Respect towards God (76:11–12)

The concluding section, *Respect towards God*, points to the response of God's people to their great deity—submissive worship. To the One who dwells in שָׁלֵם (76:2a), to him his own people "fulfill [שׁלם, *shlm*]" their vows (76:11a). Indeed, it is not just his own people, but also "all those around Him," ostensibly including even defeated foes (76:11b[9]), who demonstrate their respect to Yahweh by paying tribute to this feared One who humbles earth's human royalty (76:12). How then can God's own people fail to worship him? "All" of the warriors were defeated (76:5c), "all" of the afflicted were delivered (76:9b), and "all" around bring tribute to this God (76:11b). And thus, this God of renown, resplendence, reverence, and respect is glorified in all the earth!

---

8. The second line of 76:10 is also unclear. Either it means that the defeat of his enemies does not involve all his anger; the remainder he girds on (puts in reserve?). Or it might mean that he girds on his fury as if donning armor, using it all against his foes. In any case, the gist of the verse is obvious: even the intimidating and menacing wrath of God (towards his adversaries) is worthy of praise (by his devout).

9. Enemies are designated as "those around" also in 44:13; 79:4.

Sermon Map

I. Renown of God; Resplendence of God
   The smashing (76:1–3)
   The stupefying (76:4–6)
   Move-to-relevance: The one who fights against foes

II. Reverence for God
   The saving (76:7–10)
   Move-to-relevance: The one who fights for his own

III. Respect towards God
   The serving (76:11–12)

IV. *Serve the Smashing, Stupefying, Savior!*
   Specifics on praising/serving the God who fights for us

PSALM 77:1–20

Psalm of Disorientation

Remembering the Shepherd

PSALM 77 MOVES FROM *Lamenting* (77:1–10) to *Lauding* (77:11–20): complaints about distress and remembrances of doubt give way to remembrances of divine doings and praise as God's dramatic remedying of chaos is rehearsed.

Translation

77:1 My voice to God—and I will wail;
    my voice to God—and He gives ear to me.

77:2 In the day of my distress the Lord I sought;
    my hand, in the night, was stretched out and is not feeble;
    it refused to be comforted—my soul.

77:3 I will remember God, and I will groan;
    I will complain, and my spirit grows faint.

77:4 You held the lids of my eyes [open];
    I was troubled and I could not speak.

77:5 I considered the days of old,
    the years of forever.

77:6 I will remember my song in the night;
    with my heart I will complain,
    and my spirit searches out:

77:7 Will the Lord reject forever
    and [will He] not continue be pleased anymore?

77:8 Has His lovingkindness ceased eternally
    [and His] utterance ended for generation to generation?

77:9 Has God forgotten to be gracious,
    or has He withdrawn, in anger, His compassions?

77:10 And I said, "This is to hurt me,
>   the changing of the right hand of the Most High."
77:11 I will remember the actions of Yah;
>   yes, I will remember Your wonders of old.
77:12 I will meditate on all Your doing,
>   and on Your actions I will muse.
77:13 God, Your way is of holiness—
>   what god is great like God?
77:14 You are the God who works wonders;
>   You have made known among the peoples Your strength.
77:15 You have redeemed with Your arm Your people,
>   the children of Jacob and Joseph.
77:16 The waters saw You, God;
>   the waters saw You, they convulsed;
>   indeed, the deeps trembled.
77:17 They poured forth water—the clouds;
>   a sound they gave out—the skies;
>   indeed, Your arrows flashed about.
77:18 The sound of Your thunder was in the whirlwind;
>   lightnings lit up the world;
>   it trembled and shook—the earth.
77:19 In the sea was Your way,
>   and Your paths in the mighty waters,
>   and Your footprints not known.
77:20 You led like a flock Your people,
>   by the hand of Moses and Aaron.

Structure

The structure of the psalm follows two major movements, *Lamenting* and *Lauding*. The central sections of the composition (77:3–10, 11–15) thus deal with the psalmist's memories and concerns, "I will remember . . ."—the first is negative (recalling doubts about God), the second, positive (recollecting doings of God).[1]

---

1. That six terms synonymous with reflecting are employed in this psalm, for a total of eleven instances, is not insignificant: "remember" (77:3a, 6a, 11a, 11b); "concerned" (77:3b, 6b, 12b); "considered" (77:5a), "searches out" (77:6c); "meditate" (77:12a), and "forgotten" (77:9a). Staircase parallelisms of Hebrew poetry also link the lamenting and lauding sections (77:1, 11, 16).

PSALM 77:1-20

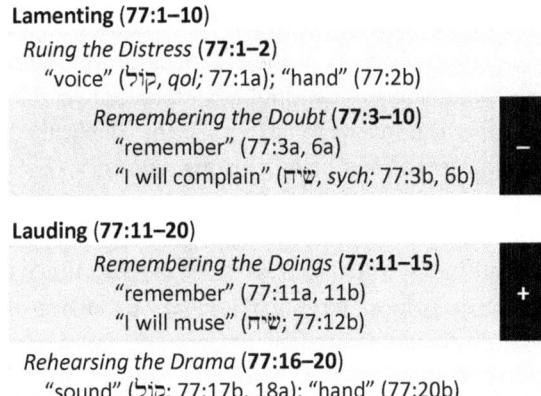

Though at the end of the psalm the lament is not resolved, hope rises with the recollection of God's past deeds. "At the close of the psalm the reader senses that a theophanic intervention of the wonder-working God of creation and exodus is imminent, though the worshiper waits for it to come."[2]

Theological Focus

Doubts about God's care in the day of distress are dispelled by the remembrance of his dramatic doings in the conquering of chaos and of his providential and pastoral care for his flock.

Commentary

Lamenting (77:1-10)

This *Lamenting* section (77:1-10) is united by the mentions of a number of words and notions arranged in parallel:[3]

77:2a	"day"	77:5a	"days"
77:2b	"night"	77:6a	"night"
77:3bα	"I will complain"	77:6b	"I will complain"
77:3bβ	"my spirit"	77:6c	"my spirit"
77:4b	"I could not speak"	77:10	"I said"

---

2. Tate, *Psalms 51–100*, 276.
3. From Auffret, "La droite du très-haut," 103.

Clearly, the psalmist is in considerable crisis as he sobs his "voice to God" (77:1a, 1b), "wailing" in the hope that God would listen.[4] Indeed, in the psalmist's elliptical utterances in 77:1, coherent speech appears to be collapsing in the face of calamity. The sufferer had begun his moans "in the day" of distress and was continuing with an unrelenting stretching out of his hand "in the night" (77:2ab): he is inconsolable (77:2c). The supplicant "remembers" God, but he is "groaning," he is "concerned," and he is "growing faint" (77:3).[5] So while there is some hope that God would "give ear" to him (77:2b), this remembering of deity does not brim with confidence, but is beset by doubt: "the very thought of God, who is the hope of deliverance, has become a source of pain and spiritual distress."[6] Yes, the psalmist "remembers" (77:3a, 6a), but God, unfortunately, seems to have "forgotten" (77:9a). So much so, the prayer moves from talking about God (77:1–3) to addressing God (77:4–6), almost confronting him, and then turning in complaint to the community (77:7–10).

Perhaps it was the inaction of God and his lack of response to the psalmist's distress (his "forgetting," 77:9a) that was keeping the supplicant's eyes open in sleeplessness (77:4a), and his mouth closed in speechlessness (77:4b). In any case, the poet's remembering (77:6a)—perhaps the divine acts of deliverance in the past marked by God's "pleasure," "lovingkindness," "grace," and "compassions" (77:7–9)?—does not seem to give him any relief.[7] His recollection of times of "forever" (77:5b), i.e., forever *past*, only leads him to a fearful suspicion that God has now abandoned him, also "forever" (77:7a), i.e., forever *future*. Doubt continues to reign,[8] as he hurls a series of questions at God (77:7–9).[9] Even the attributes of deity foundational to a relationship with his people (Exod 34:6) have apparently vanished. God, the psalmist feels, has rebuffed his own, and retreated from his past relationship with them. Besides, any word God may have had for his people also seems to have disappeared (Ps 77:8b). The gravity of God's seeming distance spans all of time—"forever" (77:7a), "anymore" (77:7b), "eternally" (77:8a), and "for generation to generation" (77:8b).[10] This is indeed a dire circumstance; these are dreadful straits that the supplicant is drowning in.

Though God's "utterance [אֹמֶר, 'omer]" (77:8b) may have ceased, the psalmist "says [אמר, 'mr]" something (77:10a), his earlier troubled silence (77:4b) now turning into a testy spiel, as his doubt (and frustration) reaches a climax! The supplicant concludes his lament with a direct accusation: the powerful "right hand" of the "Most High," once a saving force, has now "changed" to become an oppressive one (77:10). The problem is entirely God himself—there are no enemies in sight, no obvious sin on the part of the psalmist, and no other external source of this distress. The ancient "days [יָמִים, yamim]" and "years [שְׁנוֹת, shnot]" (77:5) have now "changed [שְׁנוֹת]" into an insufferable age under God's "right hand [יְמִין,

---

4. The same verb, צָעַק, tsa'aq, "wail," was employed of the Israelites' lament in Egypt: Exod 3:7, 9; Deut 26:7.

5. The verbs in 77:1a, 3a, 3b, 6a, 6b are cohortatives and are thus translated "I will . . ."

6. Tate, *Psalms 51–100*, 274.

7. The "searching out" by the supplicant's spirit (77:6c) is likely a seeking for answers, or even for an acknowledgment from God of having heard his prayer for help.

8. It not only reigns, it pours!

9. Of the six questions, the first and last (77:7a, 9b) deal with God's rejection of his people and his withdrawal from them, underscoring (the felt) divine abandonment.

10. Goldingay, *Psalms*, 2:466, notes that "nowhere else does a psalm ask whether Yhwh's commitment ['lovingkindness'] has ceased. Its question is an unthinkably earth-shattering one, literally . . . [33:5]; even heaven-shattering . . . [36:5; 57:10] . . . It seems that God's word could not be relied on, and not just temporarily but for all time."

ymin]."[11] The right hand of God was usually protective,[12] but not for the psalmist, not here, not now. An agonizing lament, indeed!

Lauding (77:11–20)

After the *Lamenting*, the composition takes a remarkable turn to *Lauding*, though still focusing on "remembering" (77:11a, 11b) and employing related cognitive verbs (see above). The wordplays here are poignant:[13]

77:11aα	"I will remember"	
77:11aβ		"the *actions* of Yah"
77:11b	"Yes, I will remember"	Your *wonders* [פִּלְאֶךָ, *pil'eka*] of old"
77:12a	"I will meditate"	on all Your *doing* [פָּעֳלֶךָ, *pa'aleka*]"
77:12bα		"and on Your *actions*"
77:12bβ	"I will muse"	

One notices that the numerous first-person references in 77:1–6 gave way to more of a focus on God in 77:7–10—albeit all accusatory. However, in 77:11–16, it seems to be all second-person references to deity, but now they are all acclamatory. Apparently, the inward look and *Lamenting* has been transformed to an upward look and *Lauding* (between 77:10 and 77:11, it seems). "We are not told how or why this happens. The Psalm moves beyond a pitiful, shriveled, self-contained present tense [of distress and doubt—the *Lamenting*] to a large, dense past peopled by God's reality and transformative action [doings and drama of God's intervention—the *Lauding*] . . . The Psalm's clear implication is that the powerful memory of God's transformative act decisively alters the present."[14] In other words, the positive "remembrance" of divine intervention in the distresses of the past (77:11a, 11b) is intended to counter the negative implications of the "remembrance" of the seeming divine inaction in the distresses of the present (77:3a, 6a). Once the psalmist considered God's deeds "of old" (77:5a) with skepticism ("Why don't you act now?"); now he is considering the doings of God "of old" (77:11b) with surety ("Of course you are going to act now!"). Once he was "complaining [שׂיח]" pessimistically about God not helping him (77:3b, 6b); now he is "musing [שׂיח]" optimistically about God's deeds (77:12b).

In the subsequent verses, the supplicant focuses on God's "actions," "wonders," and "doings" (77:11–12), rehearsing the drama of God overcoming the forces of chaos (77:16–20).[15] These exploits are carefully recounted, with the magnificence and grandeur of the theophany

---

11. From Auffret, "La droite du très-haut," 100.
12. See Pss 17:7; 18:35; 20:6; 44:3; 63:8; 73:23.
13. Figure modified from Auffret, "La droite du très-haut," 101.
14. Brueggemann and Bellinger, *Psalms*, 741.

15. A number of verbal similarities with Exod 15:11–16 also makes it possible that this "drama" is alluding to the Exodus event (see Ps 77:13 with Exod 15:11; Ps 77:14–15 with Exod 15:14, 16; Ps 77:16, 18 with Exod 15:8; Ps 77:20 with Exod 15:13). "In Exod 15 and here the poems superimpose onto the exodus story the imagery of a divine victory over forces of disorder, embodied in and symbolized by the sea. Thus the sea takes over much of the place of the Egyptian army" (Goldingay, *Psalms*, 2:468).

taking centerstage (*C* and *C'*; below), bounded at either end by God's powerful deliverance and his pastoral direction of his people (*A* and *A'*):[16]

A	*God's powerful deliverance* (77:15): "You have redeemed" "Your people"; "arm"; "Jacob and Joseph"	
	B Triumph over "waters" (77:16)	
		C Thunder–lightning theophany (77:17) "sound"; "arrows flashed about"
		C' Thunder–lightning theophany (77:18) "sound"; "lightnings lit up"
	B' Triumph over "waters" (77:19)	
A'	*God's pastoral direction* (77:20): "You led" "Your people"; "hand"; "Moses and Aaron"	

And, the entire cosmos is responding in submission to this divine undertaking:

77:17a	"They poured forth water—	the clouds"
77:17b	"A sound they gave out—	the skies"
77:18b	"Lightnings lit up	the world"
77:18c	"It trembled and shook—	the earth"

Nothing is exempt—clouds, skies, world, and earth, all respond with reverent obeisance as they convulse, tremble, and shake, with their waters, deeps, thunders, whirlwinds, and lightnings (77:16–18).

And thus, the twofold "voice [קוֹל]" of the psalmist's lament in 77:1a, 1b is now answered by the twofold "sound [also קוֹל]" of the divine drama in 77:17b, 18a. Now the "hand" stretched out in prayer in times of darkness (77:2b) can now be at rest, for God is caring for his people by the "hand" of his appointed leaders (77:20). And with that the psalm concludes, rather abruptly but with the implied question: God is totally sovereign over every part of the cosmos—even the elements prostrate themselves before him—and he leads his people as a shepherd does his flock. So will he not care for his people in their day of distress? And the expected answer is, "Of course, he will!"

---

16. Modified from Weber, "'They Saw You, the Waters,'" 112.

Sermon Map

I. Distress and Doubt
   Psalmist's Distress (77:1–2)
   Psalmist's Doubt (77:3–10)
   Move-to-relevance: Our distresses cause us to doubt God
II. Doings and Drama
   God's Doings (77:11–15)
   God's Drama (77:16–20)
   Move-to-relevance: God's doings lead us to trust God
III. *Rightly Remember God's Reliability for Reassurance!*
   Specifics on rightly remembering

PSALM 78:1–72

Psalm of Disorientation

Perceiving the Past to Preclude Punishment

AFTER PSALM 119, THIS one is the longest composition in the Psalter, seemingly "endless," according to Jerome.[1] That it does not address God directly is also remarkable, seeking rather to rehearse at length certain events in the lives of God's people.[2] But however long and historical the psalm appears to be, as in all other psalms and indeed as in every pericope of Scripture, the author is *doing* something with the text. "It is designed not merely to record the past but to change people for the future. The psalm is an exhortation in poetic form."[3]

Translation

> 78:1 Give ear, my people, to my law;
>   turn your ears to the words of my mouth.
> 78:2 I will open my mouth in a parable;
>   I will pour out mysteries of old,
> 78:3 which we have heard and known,
>   and [which] our fathers recounted to us.

---

1. Jerome, *Homilies*, 88.

2. Over half the verses deal with the period of the exodus and desert wanderings. And yet, even Moses is never mentioned. Likely, the intention is to keep the focus on God himself, rather than on his agents. "It is God alone who directs the event at the sea . . . [78:12–13, 53], who functions as the leader and provider in the desert . . . [78:14–16, 23–29, 52], and who conducts the entrance to the land . . . [78:54–55]" (Kugler, "Not Moses, but David," 126).

3. Goldingay, *Psalms*, 2:479. Deliberate authorial design to *do* things with what is said is evident: "The stories . . . are not in the order in which they are found in the Pentateuch, nor do they function in the same way. The desert wanderings come *before* the exodus from Egypt. The miracle of water in the desert is bound in with the crossing of the Red Sea, unlike the Pentateuchal tradition. The story of manna, which in the Pentateuch is a story of grace, is joined to the narrative about the quail, becoming the instrument of God's punishment upon disbelief," by having God "rain down upon them" both victuals (78:24, 27) (Clifford, "In Zion and David," 124–25 [italics original]).

78:4   We will not hide [them] from their children,
>   recounting to the generation after, the praises of Yahweh,
>   and His strength and His wondrous workings which He has done.

78:5   For He established a decree in Jacob
>   and law He placed in Israel,
>
>   which He commanded our fathers
>   to make them known to their children,

78:6   so that the generation after might know—
>   children to be born;
>
>   they will arise and recount to their children,

78:7   and they will place their confidence in God
>   and will not forget the actions of God,
>   and observe His commandments,

78:8   and they will not be like their fathers,
>   a generation stubborn and rebellious,
>
>   a generation that did not prepare its heart,
>   and it was not faithful to God—their spirit.

78:9   The children of Ephraim, the ones armed, shooters of bows,
>   turned [back] in the day of battle.

78:10   They did not keep the covenant of God
>   and in His law they refused to walk;

78:11   and they forgot His actions
>   and His wondrous workings that He had shown them.

78:12   Before their fathers He did wonders,
>   in the land of Egypt, the field of Zoan.

78:13   He split the sea and caused them to pass through,
>   and He stood the waters like a heap.

78:14   And He led them with a cloud by day
>   and all the night with a light of fire.

78:15   He split rocks in the wilderness
>   and gave [them] to drink like the depths, abundantly.

78:16   And He brought forth streams from the cliff,
>   and caused waters to run down like rivers.

78:17   And they still continued to sin against Him,
>   to rebel against the Most High in the desert.

78:18   And they tested God in their heart
>   by demanding food for their soul.

78:19   And they spoke against God;
>   they said, "Is God able to prepare a table in the wilderness?

78:20 Behold, He struck the rock and they flowed—waters,
    and streams—they flooded.
  Also bread—is He able to give,
    or prepare meat for His people?"
78:21 Therefore Yahweh heard and was furious;
    and a fire was kindled against Jacob,
    and anger also mounted against Israel.
78:22 For they did not have faith in God,
    and did not trust in His deliverance.
78:23 And He commanded the skies above,
    and the doors of heaven He opened.
78:24 He rained down upon them manna to eat
    and grain from heaven He gave to them.
78:25 The bread of the mighty ones people ate;
    provision He sent to them in fullness.
78:26 He set out the east wind in the heavens
    and He guided by His strength the south wind.
78:27 And He rained down upon them like dust—meat,
    and like the sand of the seas—winged birds.
78:28 And He made [them] fall in the midst of His camp,
    around His abodes.
78:29 And they ate and they were very full,
    and their desire He brought to them.
78:30 And they had not turned aside from their desire,
    their food still in their mouths,
78:31 and the anger of God mounted against them
    and He killed some of their sturdiest ones,
    and the young men of Israel He brought to [their] knees.
78:32 In all this they sinned still,
    and they did not have faith in His wondrous workings.
78:33 And He made their days end in futility,
    and their years in sudden terror.
78:34 When He killed them, then they sought Him,
    and they turned back and they searched for God.
78:35 And they remembered that God was their rock,
    and God Most High their redeemer.
78:36 And they deceived Him with their mouth
    and with their tongue lied to Him.
78:37 And their heart was not steadfast with Him,
    and they were not faithful in His covenant.

78:38 And He, being compassionate,
    forgave iniquity and did not destroy,
  and often turned back His anger
    and did not stir all His wrath.
78:39 And He remembered that flesh they were,
    a wind that passes and does not turn back.
78:40 How much they rebelled against Him in the wilderness,
    [and] grieved Him in the wasteland.
78:41 And they turned back and tested God,
    and the Holy One of Israel they pained.
78:42 They did not remember His hand [of power],
    the day when He redeemed them from the adversary,
78:43 when He placed His signs in Egypt,
    and His portents in the field of Zoan,
78:44 and He turned to blood their great rivers,
    and their streams, they could not drink.
78:45 He sent among them swarms [of insects] and they consumed them,
    and frogs and they destroyed them.
78:46 And He gave to the caterpillar their crops,
    and their labor to the locust.
78:47 He killed with hailstones their vines,
    and their sycamore trees with flood.
78:48 And He handed over to hailstones their cattle,
    and their livestock to flashes of lightning.
78:49 He sent upon them His burning anger,
    fury and rage and distress—
    a band of angels of disaster.
78:50 He cleared a path for His anger;
    He did not spare their soul from death,
    and their life to the plague He handed over,
78:51 and He struck all the firstborn in Egypt,
    the first [issue] of [their] virility in the tents of Ham.
78:52 And He set out His people like sheep
    and He guided them like a flock in the wilderness.
78:53 And He led them in safety, and they did not dread,
    and their enemies the sea covered.
78:54 And He brought them to His holy territory,
    this mountain [that] His right hand acquired.
78:55 And He banished the nations before them,
    and caused them to fall as a share of [their] inheritance,
    and made the tribes of Israel abide in their tents.

78:56 And they tested and rebelled against God Most High.
        and His decrees they did not keep,
78:57 and they deviated and were deceitful like their fathers;
        they turned like a treacherous bow.
78:58 And they provoked Him with their high places,
        and with their idols aroused His jealousy.
78:59 And God heard, He was furious,
        and He utterly rejected Israel.
78:60 And He abandoned the abode at Shiloh,
        the tent [in] which He abided among people,
78:61 and gave to captivity His strength,
        and His splendor into the hand of the adversary.
78:62 And He handed over to the sword His people,
        and at His inheritance He was furious.
78:63 His young men fire consumed,
        and His virgins, they were not praised.
78:64 His priests by the sword, they fell,
        and His widows, they could not weep.
78:65 And the Lord, He awoke like [from] sleep,
        like a warrior overcome by wine.
78:66 And He struck His adversaries backward;
        an eternal reproach He gave to them.
78:67 And He rejected the tent of Joseph,
        and the tribe of Ephraim He did not choose.
78:68 And He chose the tribe of Judah,
        Mount Zion which He loved.
78:69 And He built His sanctuary like the heights,
        like the earth [that] He founded forever.
78:70 And He chose David His servant
        and He took him from the pens of sheep,
78:71 from [following] after ewes He brought him,
        to shepherd Jacob, His people,
        and Israel, His inheritance.
78:72 And he shepherded them according to the integrity of his heart,
        and with skillfulness of hands he led them.

Structure

The structure of the psalm is not easy to visualize, but clearly there are two historical recitals, *Recital 1* and *Recital 2*, both recounting the recidivism of God's people (78:9–31; 40–64), at the center of which stands an ahistorical summary of the recurrence of sin and the reprieve of grace (*Recurrence-Reprieve*; 78:32–39). The whole song is bounded by an introductory *Reason* for the psalm (78:1–8) and a concluding *Result* of blessing (78:65–72).[4]

Reason (78:1–8)
"Jacob," "Israel" (78:5)

Recital 1 (mostly post-exodus, in the wilderness; **78:9–31**)
Rebellion (78:9–11)
Rescue (78:12–16) ["Egypt," "Zoan," 78:12; "And He led them," 78:14a]
Rebellion (78:17–31) ["rebel," "tested God," 78:17–18]
  Recalcitrance of sin (78:17–20)
  Retribution for sin (78:21–31)

Recurrence–Reprieve (78:32–39)
Recurrence (78:32–37)
Reprieve (78:38–39)

Recital 2 (mostly exodus, from Egypt into Canaan; **78:40–64**)
Rebellion (78:40–42) ["rebel," "tested God," 78:40a, 41a]
Rescue (78:43–55) ["Egypt," "Zoan," 78:43; "And He led them," 78:53a]
Rebellion (78:56–67) ["tested and rebelled against God," 78:56a]
  Recalcitrance of sin (78:56–58)
  Retribution for sin (78:59–64)

Result (78:65–72)
"Jacob," "Israel" (78:71)

The psalm . . . reflects the frustrated and tortured way that God's grace and love went on, even in the face of constant disobedience from the ones God chose to love. It is about God working out why the people will not accept God's gifts to them in the wilderness and of the land and love God with all their hearts and follow the covenant. It is about God trying to figure out why the people only return when God destroys . . . [78:30–31, 60–64]. It is about God finding a way to have a relationship with a humanity that *grieves* and *causes God pain* . . . [78:40]. Psalm 78 is not one of the penitential psalms, but maybe it should be, because it tells of God's great passion for humans, even when those humans turn away. It also tells the sad story of human determination to ignore the good gifts of God and to remember God only when the way becomes hard or violent . . . It shows the long, long struggle that God has had with humanity.[5]

---

4. Modified from Kim and van Rooy, "Reading Psalm 78," 287.
5. deClaissé-Walford et al., *Book of Psalms*, 625 (italics original).

The long and short of it is that the failure of God's people (Ephraim) necessitated a replacement (Judah/David). How and why this happens—pointing, of course, to how such faithless failures should *never* happen again—is the thrust of Psalm 78.

Theological Focus

> Attending to the histories of the past—of God's marvelous workings and provisions of grace and of his people's miserable failings of faithlessness and disobedience—enable the community of God in the present to remain faithful to him, lest they exhaust divine patience and compassion, and be rejected from positions of leadership and influence.

Commentary

Reason (78:1–8)

The reason for this psalm forms the introduction to the rest of the composition. Whereas in other psalms such reasons are often an appeal to God to "give ear" and "turn ... ear," here it is the people's organ of hearing that is being talked about (78:1). They are to attend to the psalmist's "law" (תּוֹרָה, *torah*, or "instruction," ultimately comes from God, of course; 78:1a). But the content of the pedagogy is not something new: it has been passed down and recounted and made known from generation to generation (78:3–4)—the "wondrous workings" of God (78:4c). Indeed such a trans-generational sharing of vital information was commanded by God (78:5)—"not merely a cultural tradition but especially a divine obligation"—so that all future peoples of God may trust him, never forgetting the deeds and decrees of God, and obeying his laws (78:7).[6] Yahweh "established" (קוּם, *qwm*; 78:5a) and "placed" (שִׂים, *sym*; 78:5b) these injunctions upon his people; therefore the children of the next generation, in turn, "arise" (קוּם; 78:6c) and "place" their confidence and trust in God (שִׂים; 78:7a), unlike their ancestors, starkly described in 78:8:

"a generation	stubborn and rebellious,		
a generation	that did not	prepare	its heart,
	and it was not	faithful to God—	their spirit"

And with that the psalmist launches into *Recital 1* of historical events, mostly dealing with the time post-exodus, in the "wilderness" (78:15a, 19b).

---

6. Goldingay, *Psalms*, 2:486. The emphasis on such an ongoing communication from one generation to the next is evident from the repeats of words: "fathers" (78:3b, 5c, 8a); "generation" (78:4b, 6a, 8b, 8c; "generation after" in 78:4b, 6a); "children" (78:4a, 5d, 6b, 6c; "to their children" in 78:5d, 6c); "know/make known" (78:3a, 5d, 6a); "law" (78:1a, 5b); "recount" (78:3b, 4b, 6c); "mouth" (78:1b, 2a); and "command/commandment" (78:5c, 7c).

Recital 1 (78:9–31)

Both *Recital 1* and *Recital 2* emphasize God's anger at the waywardness and unfaithfulness of his people (78:18–21, 31–34, 59–67).[7] Ephraim is the tribe and their unfaithfulness the main issue that are focused upon in both recitals. It is likely that, being the largest tribe in the North, Ephraim stood for all God's people in those precincts. The generic references to "fathers" in 78:1–8 indicate that the problems pointed out were not unique for any given tribe.[8]

The rebellion of 78:9–11 does not specify any particular biblical event. But the divine covenant, the mutual agreement of relationship between deity and his people, had been broken by the human party (78:10a, 37b). This despite all the "wondrous workings" and "wonders" God had performed for the Israelites in rescuing them (78:11b, 12a).[9] Of his ability to provide for their every need, they should have had no doubt, as the textual structure of 78:18–20 depicts, centered as it is upon God's bounty:[10]

> "food for their soul" (78:18b)
> "is God able to prepare" (78:19bα)
> "table" (78:19bβ)
> "they flowed" (78:20aα)
> "waters" (78:20aβ)
> "streams" (78:20bα)
> "they flooded" (78:20bβ)
> "bread" (78:20cα)
> "is He able to give" (78:20cβ)
> "meat for His people" (78:20d)

They who were supposed not to "forget" the doings of God (78:7b) promptly "forgot" them (78:11a). And, sadly, their response to those divine marvels was only to "rebel" against God and "test" him (78:17b, 18a). The consequence of such human recalcitrance is divine fury at the faithlessness exhibited (78:21–22, 31). Again, the wrath of God is validated by the textual arrangement of 78:17–32: despite all that God had done for them (D, D'), the people continued to sin (A, B, B', A'), provoking God (C, C'; see below).[11]

---

7. God's anger consumes a lot of space in this psalm: "anger," 78:21c, 31a, 38c, 49a, 50a; "furious/fury," 78:21a, 49b, 59a, 62b; "rage," 78:49b; and "wrath," 78:38d.

8. Likewise, in 78:21, 31, 59, 71, "Jacob" and "Israel" designate the larger body of the people of God. The destruction of the cultic center at Shiloh (78:60) was clearly a blow to all Israelites.

9. Several of the exodus-related events are telescoped together in these recitals: God "split" the sea and God "split" the rocks (78:13a, 15a); he controlled the large body of "waters" as well as the small rivulets of "waters" (78:13b, 16b). "Zoan" (78:12b, 43b) was likely the storage city where the Israelite slaves were in forced labor during their captivity.

10. From Auffret, *Que seulement de tes yeux*, 260.

11. From Clifford, "In Zion and David," 128.

```
A    "still continued" (78:17aα)
  B    "to sin" (78:17aβ)
    C    "anger ... mounted against Israel" (78:21c)
      D    "heaven," "He rained down upon them" (78:23b, 24a)
      D'   "heavens," "He rained down upon them" (78:26a, 27a)
    C'   "anger ... mounted against them ... Israel" (78:31)
  B'   "they sinned" (78:32aα)
A'   "still" (78:32aβ)
```

That God's provision (78:23-30) is sandwiched between mentions of his anger (78:21-22, 30-31) indicates that his donation of victuals to his people was not all of grace—God's fury had not abated when he provisioned his people. "It is thus by no means to be taken for granted that something descending from the open heavens is a blessing rather than a curse. Nor is it to be taken for granted that a sentence beginning 'he rained' will convey good news [see Gen 7:4, 19:24; Exod 9:23]."[12] Yes, he rained "upon them [עָלָה, *'alah*]" manna, and he rained "upon them [עָלָה]" quail (Ps 78:24a, 27a), but with that his anger also rose "against them [עָלָה]" (78:31a). Indeed, the God who had led his people by night with "fire" (78:14b) was now sending "fire" against them (78:21b).

Recurrence-Reprieve (78:32-39)

This central section of the psalm is almost ahistorical, compared to the historical *Recital 1* and *Recital 2* preceding and following, respectively. It designates the pattern of the recurrence of sin among the people (78:32-37[13]) and the response of compassionate reprieve from God (78:38-39), making *Recurrence-Reprieve* rightly placed in the middle of the composition. Even divine wrath, it appears, did not accomplish a transformation in their behavior—at least not for long (see 78:34-35 for the people's brief moment of lucidity): insincerity and infidelity continue to grow rampant and become brazen (78:36-37).

The Israelites' hypocrisy, however, did not nullify divine compassion (78:38-39) that God extended "often" (78:38c), even with each failure on the part of his people: they "remembered" God (78:35a), and he "remembered" they were but flesh (78:39a); they "turned back" to seek God (78:34b), and he "turned back" his anger (78:38c) because they were like a transient wind that does not return—"turn back" (78:39b). And yet, in the very next instant, as will also be seen in the following *Recital 2*, the people would "turn back" again, but this time to sin (78:41a), as they "do not remember" God's power (78:42a).

---

12. Goldingay, *Psalms*, 2:494. The "mighty ones" (78:25a) could well be angelic beings, and thus manna the food of the gods.

13. This chunk of text, 78:32-37, begins with "they did not have faith" (78:32b) and ends with "they were not faithful" (78:37b). A sad commentary on the attitudes of God's people!

Recital 2 (78:40–64)

This second recital, somewhat anachronously, deals mostly with the events of the exodus (particularly the plagues[14]) and the settlement of Israel in Canaan.[15] As with the *Recital 1*, this one, too, has the people's rebellion (78:40–42), God's rescue of them (78:43–55), and their rebellion again (78:56–58[16]), resulting in God's retribution (78:59–64).

Once again, there is a "turning back" by the people and their "testing" of God (78:41a), along with a failure to "remember" the doings of God in the past (78:42a), thus grieving the Holy One of Israel—a serious sin, indeed! What they had forgotten was that God, in his rage against the tormentors of his people, the Egyptians, "sent" (שלח, *shlch*; 78:49a) upon them "a band [from שלח] of angels of disaster" (78:49c),[17] delivering his own. And when all was said and done in Egypt (and in the subsequent wilderness meanderings, for which see *Recital 1* [78:9–31]), God brought his people to his "holy territory, this mountain" (78:54), likely his abode at Shiloh (see 78:60).[18] All forgotten!

God "hearing" is overwhelmingly considered good news in the Psalter (6:8, 9; 10:17; 18:6; 22:24; 28:6; 31:22; 34:6; etc.), but not here. In 78:59 (as in 78:21), God "heard" and became furious at his people's unfaithfulness. Though it incorporates part of the concluding section, the structure of 78:59–67 is enlightening:[19]

A "rejected" (78:59b); "tent" (78:60b)
  B "gave" (78:61a); "adversary" (= *enemies of Israel;* 78:61b)
    C "sword" (78:62a)

    C' "sword" (78:64a)
  B' "adversaries" (= *Israel itself;* 78:66a); "gave" (78:66b)
A' "rejected"; "tent" (78:67a)

The first four elements, *A*, *B*, *C*, and *C'* (78:59–64) show God more passive than active, abandoning his presence among his people,[20] giving them over to the enemy and their sword,

---

14. *Recital 2*, 78:43–51, is neatly bounded by "Egypt" (78:43a, 51b), with the plagues listed in between (78:44–50).

15. There is considerable similarity between 78:44–55 and Exod 15:1–18, with Ps 78:44–51 corresponding to Exod 15:1–12, and Ps 78:52–55 to Exod 15:13–18: "sent," Exod 15:7; Ps 78:49a; "streams," Exod 15:8; Ps 78:16a, 44b; "You/He led," Exod 15:13; Ps 78:53a; "people/His people," Exod 15:13, 16; Ps 78:52a; "holy," Exod 15:13; Ps 78:54a; "You/He brought them," Exod 15:17; Ps 78:54a; "inheritance," Exod 15:17; Ps 78:55b; and "which Your [right] hand[s] acquired/established," Exod 15:17; Ps 78:54b. However, Moses and Aaron do not show up in this recital—"in this assault against the land of Egypt the Lord alone is the warrior" (Clifford, "In Zion and David," 134).

16. The "they" in 78:57 is likely a return reference to Ephraim, the ones with "bows" who "turned [back]" (employed both in 78:9 and 78:57). Besides, there is also "shooters [רמה, *rmh*]" in 78:9a and "treacherous [רְמִיָּה, *rmiyyah*]" in 78:57b.

17. Sending "distress [צָרָה, *tsarah*]" upon that "adversary [צָר, *tsar*]" (78:49b).

18. Jerusalem shows up only later, in 78:68–69, though of course "His holy territory" and "this mountain" (78:54) could include Jerusalem and Mount Zion anachronously. Or "this mountain" (78:54b) could be referring to the "mountain of Your inheritance," as in Exod 15:17, where God chose to meet with his people.

19. From Girard, *Les Psaumes Redécouverts*, 368.

20. The unfortunate loss of Shiloh (78:60).

quenching all the joys of the people, and even seeing the deaths of his priests.[21] But in *B'* God awakens to take direct action against his *own* people—now *they* are the "adversaries"!—whom he strikes and eternally reproaches (78:66). He then proceeds, in *A'*, to reject Ephraim (78:67). Thus the reaction of God becomes progressively more direct and active and, needless to say, more dire and grievous. A sorry state, indeed!

His people did not acknowledge God's powerful "hand" (78:42a); as a result, they were given into their adversaries' "hand" (78:61b). Once it was Israel's enemies whose chattel was "handed over" for destruction (78:48a), and whose lives were "handed over" to the plague (78:50c). But soon it was God's own people who were "handed over" to the sword (78:62a). Likewise, earlier it was Egypt that was "consumed" by insects (78:45a); after their sin, it was Israel's young men who were "consumed" by fire (78:63a). The one who led his people at night with the light of "fire" (78:14b) would kindle a "fire" against those same people (78:21b), to destroy their youth in the "fire" (78:63a). At one point in time, it was quail that were "falling" around Israel's camp (78:28a); then it was their enemies that God caused to "fall" as an inheritance to his people (78:55b); afterwards, sadly enough, even God's own priests, the leaders of his people, would "fall" to the sword, in retribution from deity (78:64a). The progression was downward and inexorable: they who "remembered" God (78:35a) were "remembered" by God who had compassion on them (78:39a); but it was all to no avail: they quickly forgot and "did *not* remember" God's powerful work on their behalf (78:42a).

Result (78:65–72)

The psalm concludes with the *Result* of the of the failures of God's people recounted in *Recital 1* and *Recital 2*.[22] In short, Ephraim was rejected, and Judah was chosen (78:67–68a). Shiloh may have been abandoned (78:60), but Mount Zion was now chosen (78:68b). This turning of a new page is pictured as though God were stimulated by wine, "roused with the sudden unstoppable vigor of the intoxicated" (78:65).[23] As was noted earlier, once God's "adversaries" were the foes of his people (78:42b), and he defeated them; but then he gave his own people into the hand of the "adversary" (78:61b); now his people themselves had become God's "adversaries" (78:66a). So he struck them and put upon them an eternal reproach (78:66b).[24] Once it was a rock God had "struck" to produce water for his people (78:20a); then it was their enemies' firstborn that were "struck" (78:51a); now it is his own who are divinely "struck" (78:66a). Those who had questioned God's ability to "give" them the essentials they needed (78:20c), to them God "gave" in abundance (78:15b, 24c), and even "gave" obnoxious plagues to their enemies (78:46a), but they still refused to trust God. So he "gave" up his people (i.e., "His strength," 78:61a) unto captivity, and finally he "gave"

---

21. Young men were killed, virgins were not fêted—there were no wedding songs to be sung to them (78:63).

22. The psalm began with a mention of "Jacob" and "Israel" (78:5a, 5b); it now ends likewise (78:71bc).

23. Tate, *Psalms 51–100*, 294.

24. I.e., long-lasting recrimination for their failure to walk with God, trusting him. This "eternal reproach" is not necessarily related to the afterlife, though, from our post-cross point of view, shoddy Christian lives, we know, will result in loss of eternal rewards (but not loss of salvation). Besides, there is always earthly discipline that God can lay upon his wayward children.

them an eternal reproach (78:66b). It is almost as if God is completely "giving" up, washing his hands of his recalcitrant and refractory people.[25]

Enough was enough and a change was going to be brought about, starkly depicted in the structure of 78:67–68:

> "And He rejected
> the tent of Joseph,
> and the tribe of Ephraim
> He did not choose.
> And He chose
> the tribe of Judah,
> Mount Zion
> which He loved."

And from Judah, David was chosen, from the sheep pens where he led ewes (78:70–71a), to shepherd God's "people," the divine "inheritance," the very possession of God (78:71bc). That David was now doing (78:71–72) what God had once done (78:52–53a)—both texts have "His people," "H/he led them," and "flock"—suggests that this new leader/shepherd was one that God approved of and one who would walk in God's paths, unlike the Israelites' ancestors and predecessors.

Rejection would be the fate of peoples who failed to have faith in God despite all that he had done for them in the past. New peoples and new leaders would be chosen. And this is a lesson for all of God's people of all time in all places. May we listen to the recitals and never be like those "fathers."

Sermon Map

I. Faithfulness
   History of divine action (78:11–20b, 23–29, 38–39, 42b–55)
   Move-to-relevance: God's faithfulness in our lives

II. Faithlessness
   History of human action (78:9–10, 20c–22, 32, 34–37, 40–42a, 56–58)
   Move-to-relevance: Our faithlessness

III. Fallout
   History of divine reaction (78:30–31, 33, 59–72)
   Move-to-relevance: Fallout in our lives

IV. *Don't Forget, Be Faithful, and Avoid the Fallout!* (78:1–8)
   Remembering God's faithfulness and being faithful to him

---

25. Of course, that is never the case: God never gives up. Yet, the recounting of the events of Psalm 78 are intended to move us to acknowledge divine frustration and displeasure with the ways of sinful mankind, particularly in God's own community, by those who ought to have known better.

PSALM 79:1–13

Psalm of Disorientation

Confession amidst Calamity

THIS PSALM IS ESSENTIALLY a community lament pleading with God to divert his anger away from his people and their sin, and, instead, to direct it towards oppressing powers so that the righteous may be delivered.

Translation

79:1	God, the nations have come into Your inheritance;
	they have defiled Your holy temple;
	they have put Jerusalem in ruins.
79:2	They have given the dead bodies of Your servants
	as food to the birds of the heavens,
	the flesh of Your devout ones to the beasts of the earth.
79:3	They have poured out their blood like water around Jerusalem,
	and there was no one burying [the dead].
79:4	We have become a reproach to our neighbors,
	derision and ridicule to those around us.
79:5	Until when, Yahweh? Will You be angry eternally?
	Will Your jealousy burn like fire?
79:6	Pour out Your wrath upon the nations which do not know You,
	and upon the kingdoms which upon Your name they do not call.
79:7	For they have consumed Jacob,
	and his habitation they have desolated.
79:8	Do not remember against us the iniquities of the earlier [generation];
	quickly let Your compassion come to meet us,
	for we have become very low.

79:9   Help us, God of our deliverance, for the matter of the glory of Your name;
       and rescue us and forgive our sins for the sake of Your name.
79:10 Why should the nations say, "Where is their God?"
       May there be known among the nations in our sight
       vengeance for the blood of Your servants which has been poured out.
79:11 May the groaning of the prisoner come before You;
       according to the greatness of Your arm [of power]
       preserve the people doomed to death.
79:12 And return to our neighbors sevenfold to their bosom—
       the reproach with which they have reproached You, Lord.
79:13 And we, Your people and the sheep of Your pasture
       will give thanks to You forever;
       from generation to generation we will recount Your praise.

Structure

The poem moves from the *Pain* of an invasion (79:1–4), through *Penitence* for sin (79:5–9) and *Petition* for punishment (79:10–12), to a *Promise* of praise for deliverance (79:13):

Pain (**79:1–4**)
Penitence (**79:5–9**)
Petition (**79:10–12**)
Promise (**79:13**)

What is striking is the alternation of references throughout the psalm between the afflicting invaders (represented below as "they") and the afflicted people of God (represented below as "we"), a rather unusual sequencing of a lament psalm:

79:1–3	They	
79:4–5		We
79:6–7	They	
79:8–9		We
79:10	They	
79:11		We
79:12	They	
79:13		We

While this back-and-forth turbulence is to be expected in an utterance born out of chaos and catastrophe, it is not just the enemies who are guilty: Israel herself is! So this psalm turns out to be a plea to God to redirect his wrath from against his people to against their enemies.

Theological Focus

> Confident in God's compassion and willingness to forgive their sins, the people of God appeal to him to relent from his wrath for their failures and to redirect his opposition to invading and violating enemies to pay them back in kind, promising to praise him forever.

Commentary

Pain (79:1–4)

It is possible that 79:1 refers to the invasion of Jerusalem by the Babylonians in 587 BCE (Lam 4:12): the enemies, of course, "made straight for the palace where the King lived" (Ps 79:1).[1] But this is as much detail of the disaster faced by the psalmist that we can extract from his composition: invaders have sacked Jerusalem and the temple. The attackers are pillaging and defiling (79:1a), shedding the blood of God's people (79:2a, 3a). The slaughter is horrific, but it is the outcome thereof that is described—the fate of the corpses (they remain unburied) and of the blood (it floods the city; 79:2–3). The actual massacre is left to the imagination.

It appears that even Israel's neighbors (Moab? Edom? Ammon?) were complicit in this attack, or at least participating in the derision of the foes against the Israelites (79:4).[2] The reason for the ridicule was that God's people had trusted in a seemingly impotent deity, incapable of protecting his own. "Around" Jerusalem was the blood of the Israelites (79:3a), and "around" them were these sneering neighbors (79:4b).

Penitence (79:5–9)

Yet a self-conscious note of guilt and penitence pervades the psalm. The questions put to God in 79:5 appear at first blush to be protesting a delay in God's avenging himself on the enemy. In fact, as subsequent verses show, it is actually the extent and duration of divine anger directed against God's *own* people (through the hand of violent aggressors) that is being questioned. Was God going to be angry with them eternally, and would his jealousy continue such that he would persist in punishing Israel for its disloyalty to him? Remarkably, divine jealousy is "like fire" (79:5b), while its outcome is a cascade of blood "like water" (79:3a): an inferno and a deluge at the same time! Would that God, instead, turn his wrath upon the rampant besiegers, those who do not know him (79:6–7)—the ones who had "consumed [אכל, *'kl*]" Jacob (79:7a), just as the birds devoured as "food [מַאֲכָל, *maʾakal*]" the corpses of the Israelites (79:2b). These attackers do not call on "Your name" (79:6b), so God is urged to decimate them; and, correspondingly, for the glory of "Your name" and the sake of "Your name," God is pressed to deliver his people (79:9a, 9b).

---

1. Goldingay, *Psalms*, 2:520. "This psalm continues to be recited at the Western Wall (Wailing Wall) of the temple in Jerusalem on Friday afternoons and ... is used in the liturgy of the Ninth of Ab, a fast day which commemorates the destruction of the temple" (Tate, *Psalms 51–100*, 303).
2. See 2 Kgs 24:2; Ezek 35:10, 15; 36:5.

Accompanying this penitence and a call for the redirection of divine anger is an explicit request that God not remember the sins of their fathers (79:8a) or even their own sins (79:9b). "The hope of the psalm is that although the community might have to grant the appropriateness of Yhwh punishing it for its waywardness, surely there comes a time when enough is enough."[3] Indeed, there are a number of resonances of Psalm 79 with Leviticus 26, particularly the section that deals with the consequences of the disobedience of God's people (26:14-46): "Your holy temple [הֵיכַל קָדְשֶׁךָ, hekal qadsheka]," Ps 79:1b, and "Your sanctuaries [מִקְדְּשֵׁיכֶם, miqdshekem]," Lev 26:31; "Jerusalem," Ps 79:1c, and "cities," Lev 26:31, 33; "flesh," Ps 79:2c and Lev 26:29 (×2); "desolate," Ps 79:7b and Lev 26:22, 31, 32, 34, 35, 43; "remember," Ps 79:8a and Lev 26:42 (×3), 45; "seven[fold]," Ps 79:12a and Lev 26:18, 21, 24, 28; and "give thanks [ידה]," Ps 79:13b, and "confess [ידה]," Lev 26:40.[4] Clearly a chagrined consciousness of their own failings and a haunted recognition of God's wrath against his people drives their lament in the face of disaster.

Petition (79:10-12)

"Where is their God?" the occupying foes ask contemptuously (Ps 79:10a). God, it seemed, had decamped, admitting defeat, as invaders overran his country, conquered his capital, captured his palace, and slaughtered his people. "To the nations, Israel is [now] a people without king, nation, home, or deity . . . [And] to hear her deepest doubts and fears echoed sarcastically by her enemies was painful."[5] The psalmist therefore petitions God that these wicked be punished: those attacking nations do not "know" God (79:6a), but may they come to "know" the vengeance of God for the blood of his saints (79:10b).[6] Would that the "reproach" they, the Israelites, were "to our neighbors" (79:4a) be returned "to our neighbors" in kind, but manifold[7]—i.e., with the "reproach" with which they had "reproached" God himself (79:12). Any attack on the reputation of God's people was ultimately an attack on God's own reputation, they argue.

Early in the psalm, the violators had "come" (79:1a) and "poured out" the "blood" of "Your servants" (79:2a, 3a). Here in the petition section those phrases are repeated (79:10c), but what "comes" now is the agonizing plea of the sufferers before God (79:11a; below).

---

3. Goldingay, *Psalms*, 2:525.
4. From Ho, "Leviticus 26 in Psalm 79," 10.
5. Tate, *Psalms 51-100*, 301.
6. Note that the call is for *God* to act; the people do not intend to take action themselves—the focus is entirely upon deity to whom alone vengeance belongs. Besides, even in their call for the punishment of their foes, the endpoint is their own deliverance from divine punishment, rather than any triumph over enemies. See Introduction for more on imprecations.
7. "Sevenfold" in 79:12a indicates an infinite amount.

79:1a	"come"—nations' invasion
79:2a–3aα	"Your servants ... *poured out*"
79:3aβ	"blood"
79:6a	"*pour out* Your wrath"
79:10cα	"blood"
79:10cβ	"Your servants ... *poured out*"
79:11a	"come"—sufferers' plea

Will he hear?

Promise (79:13)

The situation seems hopeless, with no end or remission of the violence in sight, nonetheless the psalm concludes with a promise of praise in the future—indeed, the last word of the psalm is תְּהִלָּתֶךָ, *thillateka*, "Your praise" (79:13c). "Your inheritance," "Your holy temple" (79:1), "Your servants," and "Your devout ones" (79:2) were being destroyed. But, on the other hand, if God would relent and turn back the anger directed against his own, thus protecting these institutions and entities, "Your servants" (79:10c), "Your people," and the flock of "Your pasture" (79:13a) would sing "Your praise" (79:13c). In other words, "even in the darkest of days, there is a future with God for the people."[8] And if the extent of the thanksgiving ("forever," 79:13b) is any indication, that future is going to be long lasting!

Sermon Map

I. Pain
    Chaos and catastrophe (79:1–4)
    Move-to-relevance: Chaos and catastrophe afflicting us

II. Penitence
    Recognition of failure and sin (79:5–9)
    Move-to-relevance: Failure and sin in our lives

III. Petition
    Confident prayer for deliverance (79:10–12)
    Move-to-relevance: Confidence in a compassionate God's hearing prayer

IV. *Praise!* (79:13)
    Praising God for his forgiveness of sin and powerful deliverance

---

8. deClaissé-Walford et al., *Book of Psalms*, 629.

PSALM 80:1–19

Psalm of Disorientation

Plea for Deity to Relent and Rescue

PSALM 80 IS A communal lament, but unlike the preceding psalm and many other laments in the Psalter, there is no call for divine action towards, or retribution upon, enemies. But it begins with calling God a shepherd in 80:1; Psalm 79, one remembers, left off with its closing reference to God's shepherding of his flock, his people (79:13).[1] And, as in 79:5a, this psalm, too, asks God "until when?" (80:4b). However, Psalm 80 is less pointed about the sin of God's people being complicit in their disaster (as was Psalm 79), though 80:4 implies God's displeasure, and 80:16b does mention the "rebuke" of God of his own.

Translation

80:1   The One shepherding Israel, give ear;
        the One driving Joseph like a flock,
        the One sitting [enthroned above] the cherubim, shine forth.

80:2   Before [the face of] Ephraim and Benjamin and Manasseh,
        stir up Your might,
        and come for deliverance to us.

80:3   God, restore us,
        and cause Your face to shine, and we will be delivered.

80:4   Yahweh, God of Armies,
        until when will You fume at the prayer of Your people?

80:5   You have fed them the bread of tears,
        and You have made them drink tears by [large] measure.

80:6   You set us [as an object of] contention to our neighbors,
        and our enemies mock [us] to themselves.

---

1. So did Psalm 78, concluding with a note about David, God's agent, shepherding God's people (78:71–72); as well, Psalm 77, with God leading his people "like a flock," through Moses and Aaron (77:20).

80:7 God of Armies, restore us
    and cause Your face to shine, and we will be delivered.
80:8 A vine from Egypt You uprooted;
    You drove out the nations and You planted it.
80:9 You cleared [the ground] before it[s face],
    and it rooted its roots and filled the land.
80:10 The mountains were covered with its shadow,
    and with its branches the great cedars.
80:11 It was sending its boughs unto the sea
    and to the river its shoots.
80:12 Why have You broken down its walls,
    and all who pass [that] way pluck it?
80:13 A wild boar from the forest ravages it,
    and the creature of the field feeds on it.
80:14 God of Armies, do turn;
    look down from the heavens and see,
    and attend to this vine
80:15 and the stock which Your right hand has planted,
    and unto the child You have strengthened for Yourself.
80:16 Burned with fire, cut down,
    from the rebuke of Your face they perish.
80:17 May Your hand be upon the person of Your right hand,
    upon the human child whom You have strengthened for Yourself.
80:18 And we will not deviate from You;
    revive us, and upon Your name we will call.
80:19 Yahweh, God of Armies, restore us;
    cause Your face to shine, and we will be delivered.

Structure

The psalm is marked by similar refrains in 80:3, 7, 19 that divide it into a *Petition*, a *Plaint*, and a *Parable*:

> **Petition (80:1–3)**
> Refrain (80:3): "God …"
>
> **Plaint (80:4–7)**
> Refrain (80:7): "God of Armies …"
>
> **Parable (80:8–19)**
> *Past:* God's saving acts (80:8–11)
> *Present:* Vine's current state (80:12–16)
> *Future:* People's promised faithfulness (80:17–19)
> Refrain (80:19): "Yahweh, God of Armies …"

Theological Focus

God's people are confident in their personal and powerful God's favorable turning towards them from his anger to restore them from their calamities in the present, because of the intimate relationship they have had with this God of the universe in the past, as they promise to serve him faithfully in the future.

Commentary

Petition (80:1–3)

The *Petition* commences with an address to God, invoked by three participles (80:1): "the One shepherding," "the One driving" his flock, and "the One sitting [enthroned]." Thus, the Shepherd of his people is also the King of the universe, located above the cherubim, both figuratively and literally in the temple, and "shining forth" in his glorious resplendence (80:1c).

After the mention of Joseph in 80:1, the other son of Rachel and her two grandchildren are also noted in 80:2a: Benjamin, and Ephraim and Manasseh. As in Psalm 79, these Northern tribes seem to be in focus here as well, and the poem is recounted from their viewpoint. Or perhaps, these tribes have already been exiled and are giving their suffering voices to the psalmist. In any case, God is called upon to deliver his people, and four imperatives beseech him: "stir up," "come" (80:2), "restore," and "cause Your face to shine"[2]—deliverance

---

2. An idiom for finding favor with deity. And notice that "cause … to shine [הָאֵר, ha'er]," the imperative addressed to God in the refrains (80:3b, 7b, 19b), is equated, by paronomasia (a palindrome), to "see [ראה, r'h]," another plea to God in 80:14b.

is assured then (80:3). "The psalm has no doubt of Yhwh's might . . . ; the problem is getting Yhwh to activate it."[3]

The petition that God would come "before [the face] [לִפְנֵי, *liphne*]" of his people (80:2a), is based on the fact that long ago, "before it[s face] [לְפָנֶיהָ]" God cleared a path for that parabolic vine, his people, to flourish (80:9a). Surely after that, God owed them allegiance and loyalty. But, no, this same people of God are perishing from the rebuke of "Your face [פָּנֶיךָ, *paneka*]" (80:16b). Hence the petition in the refrains: would that God cause "Your face [פָּנֶיךָ]" to shine upon them and deliver them (80:3b, 7b, 19b).

Plaint (80:4–7)

The God who is supposed to hear and answer the prayers of his people "fumes" at their approaches to him (80:4b). The psalmist hints that this ire is well-deserved, and only wants to mitigate its extent: "until when?" (80:4b). "Tears" are their food and "tears" are their drink (80:5)—indeed, they are fed these victuals by God himself, who is held responsible for the current dire situation.[4] And as if that were not enough, God's people are the object of their foes' ridicule (80:6). While the people of God implore him to come for deliverance "to us [לָנוּ, *lanu*]" (80:2c), their enemies deride their victims "to themselves [לָמוֹ, *lamo*]" (80:6b)—likely casting aspersions on the futility of devotion to a God who apparently does not care for his own.

A rhetorical cascade of countering second-person verbs, all negative in their impact, follows after "You fume" (80:4b): "You have fed," "You have made them drink" (80:5), "You set us" (80:6). How long can this anger burn, his people ask. The plaint ends with the same refrain, though with some differences (80:7). The first refrain invoked "God" (80:3a). This one invokes the "God of Armies" (80:7a). Surely this is a powerful deity capable of doing something about the serious predicament of his people.

With that, the psalmist moves to an extended parable, in a continuing attempt to ameliorate God's wrath and to motivate his action on their behalf.

Parable (80:8–19)

In Psalm 79, the question of how long ("until when"; 79:5a) God would be angry with his people led to a plea for forgiveness and a petition for enemies to be punished (79:6–9). Here, the same question in 80:4b leads to a pathos-laden *Parable* of the vine, describing God's people and how close they were to him once (80:8–19).[5] How, then, could they be treated thus by God in his implacability?

The parable is historical, beginning with the exodus and the entry into Canaan, events orchestrated by God himself (80:8). The earlier series of negative actions in the second-person ("You . . ."; 80:5–6) becomes now, in this *Parable* section, a series of positive actions of God in the past—again a rhetorical attempt to move God to remedy the current crisis: "You uprooted," "You drove out," "You planted" (80:8), and "You cleared" (80:9). The structure of 80:8 emphasizes the divine action (below).

---

3. Goldingay, *Psalms*, 2:535.

4. "By [large] measure" (80:5b) translates an unclear phrase, literally "by . . . [the] third."

5. The "vine" is a standard biblical metaphor for the people of God: Gen 49:22; Isa 5:1–7; 27:2–6; Jer 2:21; 12:10; Ezek 15:1–8; 19:10–14; Hos 10:1.

> "A vine
> from Egypt
> You uprooted;
> You drove out
> the nations
> and You planted it."

Likewise, the wordplays in 80:9a, 9b:[6]

פִּנִּיתָ, pinnita	לְפָנֶיהָ, liphaneha
"You cleared [the ground]	before it[s face]"
וַתַּשְׁרֵשׁ, wattashresh	שָׁרָשֶׁיהָ, sharasheha
"and it rooted	its roots"

The "sea" in 80:11a is the Mediterranean (in the west), and the "river" in 80:11b, the Euphrates (on the east). Thus, with the "mountain" range in the south (Sinai; 80:10a) and the "cedars" in the north (Lebanon; 80:10b), all points of the compass are covered. This was a great work of God for his people across the land. And despite all that God had once done for his beloved, they still have to go through this suffering now? "The affliction is fundamentally a trial of faith ... Yet the people hope enough to offer this lament."[7]

As if to stress that incongruity of past divine action with present divine *in*action, the series of second-person positive verbs (80:8–9) and its manifest effects (80:10–11) are suddenly halted by "Why have You broken ..." (80:12a)! The devastation of the vineyard's walls leaves it susceptible to the rampages of passersby and the rapacity of predators (80:12b–13). Whereas the "One shepherding [רעה, *rʿh*]" (80:1a) was expected to feed his flock, it is, paradoxically, a wild beast that "feeds [רעה]" on the flock (80:13b). And in the end, what is left is only to be destroyed (80:16a).

Why was this happening? The reason, of course, was the unfaithfulness of the vine to its divine vinedresser, implied in the notion of God's "rebuke" (80:16b; and as Isa 5:1–7 explicitly declares). But obviously, not *all* were equally culpable, and perhaps the relatively innocent among people were justified in questioning God. In any case, the divine community recognizes that its fate lies in the hands of God and so God is appealed to, with vigor and pathos (Ps 80:14).

One notices that "turn" in the appeal of 80:14a shares the same root as "restore" in the refrains of 80:3, 7, 19 (שׁוב, *shwv*], making 80:14 effectively a variant of the latter refrains. Of course, Yahweh needs to "turn" before he can "restore," i.e., before he can cause his people to turn. But this makes the request rather unusual: rather than people needing to "turn" first to Yahweh, this request is directed to Yahweh; but it indicates here the sense that the punishment

---

6. From Auffret, "Fais luire ta face," 1057. Note also that each of the verses, 80:10 and 80:11, are chiastic. This is a remarkable cascade of artistic literary devices in 80:8–11. "Great cedars" in 80:10b is literally "cedars of God" (אַרְזֵי־אֵל, *arze-ʾel*), denoting their magnificence and might with a superlative.

7. Tate, *Psalms 51–100*, 314.

of his people had run its course (at least in the supplicant's mind), and that they had learned their lesson.[8] They had already "turned"; now it was God's turn to turn ("restore").

It had been God's right hand that planted this stock, and it was up to him to sustain it—"the child You have strengthened for Yourself" (80:15; repeated with minor changes in 80:17). This "child"/"human child" (80:15b, 17b) and the "person of Your right hand" (80:17a) most likely stands for the corporate entity of Israel, that singular vine, and the terms are intended to evoke an emotion of parental attachment from the deity who had ostensibly abandoned his offspring. In return, the psalmist, on behalf of his people, promises not to deviate from God and to call upon his name (80:18).

The song then ends with the refrain, expanding the appellative of God to "Yahweh, God of Armies," strengthening the plea with the composite name of deity (80:19) who is both the covenantal God of his people and the commanding general of his heavenly battalions. Notice the sequence of names by which God is addressed in the refrains:

80:3a	"God"
80:7a	"God of Armies"
80:19a	"Yahweh, God of Armies"

This God (80:3a), this *powerful* God (80:7a), this *their* powerful God (80:19a), was going to help them!

Sermon Map

I. Personal God
   God cares (80:1, 8–11)
   Move-to-relevance: How God has cared for us

II. Punishing God
   God chastises (80:4–6, 12–13, 16)
   Move-to-relevance: How God chastises us

III. Preserving God
   Confident in the custody of God (80:2–3, 7, 14–15, 19)

IV. *Promising God!* (79:13)
   Resolution to remain faithful to God

---

8. And this seemed to be the attitude of the psalmist in Psalm 79 as well.

PSALM 81:1–16

Psalm of Orientation

Plea of Deity That People Would Listen

PSALM 81 GOES FROM the worship of God (a hymn) in 81:1–5 to the wish of God (an oracle) in 81:6–16.[1] The bulk of the composition is in God's voice and ends with a note of wistfulness—God's unmet desires for his people. Thus it indirectly speaks to God's people everywhere, moving them to develop attitudes of trust in him, as he desires. This is therefore a psalm of orientation: how things are/ought to be in God's ideal world.

Translation

81:1 Shout for joy to God our strength;
    proclaim triumphantly to the God of Jacob.

81:2 Raise music, give timbrel,
    [and] a pleasant[-sounding] lyre with a harp.

81:3 Blow the horn at the new moon,
    at the full moon, on the day of our festival.

81:4 For it is a statute for Israel,
    a judgment of the God of Jacob.

81:5 A decree in Joseph He established
    when He went out against the land of Egypt.
    Lips I had not acknowledged I listened [to]:

81:6 "I relieved [him] from the burden of his shoulder;
    his palms from the basket were released.

81:7 In distress you called and I rescued you;
    I answered you in the secret place of thunder;
    I tried you at the waters of Meribah.

---

1. The psalmist here may be a priest/Levite/prophet or a leader, a spokesperson for the people of God and for God himself, as he channels the oracular utterance.

81:8 Listen, My people, and I will remonstrate with you—
       Israel, if you would [only] listen to Me.
81:9 Let there not be among you a strange god;
       and you shall not worship a foreign god.
81:10 I am Yahweh, your God,
       who brought you up from the land of Egypt;
       open wide your mouth and I will fill it.
81:11 And My people did not listen to My voice,
       and Israel did not [want to] submit to Me.
81:12 And I sent him [off] to the stubbornness of their heart:
       they can walk by their own plans.
81:13 Would that My people would listen to Me,
       [and] Israel would walk in My paths.
81:14 Quickly their enemies I would subdue,
       and against their adversaries turn My hand."
81:15 (Those hating Yahweh will cower before Him,
       and may their time [of punishment] be forever.)
81:16 "And I would feed you from the best of wheat,
       and [with] honey from the rock I would satiate you."

Structure

The psalm follows the outline noted above, the *Worship of God* followed by the *Wish of God*:

Worship of God (81:1–5b)
    Summons (**81:1–3**)
    Statute (**81:4–5**)

Wish of God (81:6–16)
    Salvation (**81:6–7**)   ["listen," 81:5c]
    Stipulation (**81:8–10**)   ["listen," 81:8a, 8b]
    Stubbornness (**81:11–12**) ["listen," 81:11a]
    Satiation (**81:13–16**)   ["listen," 81:13a]

The oracle, the *Wish of God* (81:6–16), alternates between God's indirect and direct addresses to his people, with a parenthetical interjection by the psalmist in 81:15:

81:6	Indirect
81:7–10	Direct
81:11–14	Indirect
81:15	Psalmist's Interjection
81:16	Direct

That further accentuates the desire of God for his people—as he employs different rhetorical means[2]—to get them to "listen" (see above for the echoes of this verb) and submit to his overtures and conditions; then, and then alone, would their lives be satiated, aligned to the call of God, and result in blessing.

Theological Focus

Listening to God and walking in his way—acknowledging his care and worshiping with joy, and not being stubborn and walking by one's own plans, all of which are willed and earnestly wished by God for his people—brings abundant blessing: protection from God and provision from God.

Commentary

Worship of God (81:1–5b)

At the outset, the psalmist calls for the worship of God (81:1–3). In connection with "statute," "judgment," and "decree" (81:4a, 4b, 5a), this worship is God-commanded, a manifestation of the submission and fealty of the people of God to their delivering deity. "The acknowledgment of God expressed in praise is not designed to make us feel good but to be an expression of that commitment, which then needs to affect life outside the church building as well as inside it."[3] In a sense, then, this worship of God *is* the wish of God, what he himself desires (81:6–16).

The psalmist admits that he had not attended to these statutes of God—he had not "acknowledged" what he had "listened" to (81:5c).[4] What he should have done, and the words he should have listened to with submission, form most of the remainder of the psalm (81:6–16).

---

2. Including literary art, such as the chiastic structure in 81:6 (verb / מִן [*min*] + noun / upper limb body part // upper limb body part / מִן + noun / verb).

3. Goldingay, *Psalms*, 2:557. The use of "Joseph" in 81:5a may indicate, as in Psalms 79–80, a focus upon the Northern tribes.

4. He *did* listen, but not with "acknowledgment," i.e., without submission or commitment (81:5c), a superficial listening: the psalmist's lip-service to God's lips, as it were.

The Wish of God (81:6–16)[5]

The wish of God in 81:6–16 becomes an expansion of the "statute," "judgment," and "decree" of God (81:4–5a) that stipulate the faithfulness of his people to him (expressed in their worship, but no doubt, extending into every corner of their lives, too). It begins with an account of God's salvation of his people from Egypt (81:6–7), described in what is almost a theophany: the oppressed called "in [בְּ, b]" distress, and God answered them "in [בְּ]" (i.e., from) the "secret place of thunder" (81:7ab)—"the place where Yhwh lives in the heavens, whence thunder comes."[6]

This relationship of aid and succor that they had established with their God at the exodus obligated his people to follow his dictates (81:7–10): they were to serve him exclusively and, as a result, they would be blessed (the filling of their mouths, 81:10c[7]). However, this did not come to pass because of their stubbornness (81:11–12), the consequence of which was an abandonment by God of his unfaithful subjects to their own devices.

God's desire is expressed again in 81:13–16—the satiation of his people, conditioned upon their "walk in [בְּ]" his paths (81:13b) as opposed to their "walk by [בְּ]" their own plans (81:12b). No wonder "listen" forms an important motif all throughout this section (81:8a, 8b, 11a, 13a; also in 81:5c; see psalm structure above, and figure below). Upon such listening (that includes, of course, the subsequent commitment and obedience to the one and only God) hinges the blessing of deity upon his people:

81:6–7	*Blessing past:* What God had done ["distress," צָרָה, *tsarah;* 81:7a]
81:8	"*Listen*, My people" "if you would [only] *listen* to Me" "Israel"
81:9–10	"I am Yahweh, your God" (81:10a)
81:11–13	"My people did not *listen*" (81:11a) "would that My people would *listen* to Me" (81:13a) "Israel" (81:11b, 13b)
81:14–16	*Blessing future:* What God would do ["adversary," צַר, *tsar;* 81:14b]

This is "the longing of God for a responsive people. There is a tone of lament in these verses, a reflection of the grief of God because of a wayward people."[8] If only they had walked in the divine way, they would have been protected (81:14[9]) and abundantly provided for (81:16[10]).

---

5. While the distinction is not precise, the will of God is noted in 81:9 and implied in 81:11, and the wish of God, a more subjunctive desire, is seen in 81:8b, and later in 81:13–14, 16.

6. Goldingay, *Psalms*, 2:552. For Meribah (81:7c), see Exod 17:7; Num 20:13–14; Deut 33:8. Generally, the OT saw the incident in this location as one where Israel "tried" God (Ps 95:8–9; see 95:9b), but here in this psalm, it is God "trying" the Israelites (81:7c).

7. Likely referring to the divine provision of food during the wilderness wanderings of the exodus generation.

8. Tate, *Psalms 51–100*, 324.

9. Emphasized by the psalmist's parenthetical imprecation upon enemies in 81:15.

10. The verb in 81:16a is a third-person masculine singular with a third-person masculine singular suffix

Indeed, just as God had fed his people once (81:10), he would feed them in plenty again (81:16).[11] Yes, obedience leads to blessing.

But, just as with Psalms 79 and 80, this one also ends without resolution. In the former pair, it was the people's desires that remained unresolved; here it is God's. "God is wishing for a different humanity, and there is no indication that the humans have responded in any way to God's plea. God remains at the table without any guests. What began as a great festival, with singing and dancing and joy, ends with God alone."[12] May that never be the case and may his people join him in the celebration, wholeheartedly listening to him always . . . and becoming satiated!

Sermon Map

I. Listening to the Past

    God's deliverance of his people (81:6–7, 14–16)

    Move-to-relevance: Listening to the past of God's deliverance

II. Listening in the Present

    His people's denial of God (81:5c, 11–12)

    Move-to-relevance: Our failure to listen to God in the present

III. Listening for the Future

    God's deliverance of his people (81:8–9, 12–16)

    Move-to-relevance: What we are missing by not listening

IV. *Listen!* (81:13)

    Listening to God better

("He would feed him"), but the verb in 81:16b is first-person common singular with a second-person masculine singular suffix ("I would satiate you"). The translation emends the former to align with the latter (thus: "I would feed you").

11. Alluding to Deut 32:13–14; Num 18:12. "Best" of wheat is literally "fattest" of wheat (Ps 81:16a).

12. deClaissé-Walford et al., *Book of Psalms*, 640.

PSALM 82:1–8

Psalm of Disorientation

Against Evil Heavenly Entities

FOR SEVERAL REASONS, PSALM 82 is unique—"*sui generis* in the Psalter; there is no other psalm like it."[1] It is almost entirely God's address (82:2–7; the psalmist/narrator makes introductory and concluding comments in 82:1, 8). But the divine words are not directed to humans; the events are entirely "unearthly" and the utterance is directed to beings that are god-like. However, these entities are nefarious practitioners responsible for evil on the earth and they are doomed to die. A divine council seems to be the best location where this divine address is taking place, with Yahweh depicted as sharing some ruling power with its members, though maintaining final say and sovereignty over the group.[2]

"The work of God is vast and unending, and this psalm that seems so odd to modern people can remind us of just that reality. God is God in places beyond our grasp."[3] All of this mysterious background is to be taken into account for the interpretation of Psalm 82. Therefore, how this rather obscure psalm, directly addressing some obscure entities, speaks today to its human readers, the people of God, will be the burden of its interpretation and its preaching.

---

1. Tate, *Psalms 51–100*, 332.

2. Such a council and its role is expressly found, or alluded to, elsewhere in the OT also: Gen 1:26; 3:22; 11:7 (the first-person plural references made by deity); Exod 15:11 ("gods," אֵלִם, *'elim*); Deut 4:19 ("army of heaven"); 10:17; 17:2–3 ("gods," אֱלֹהִים, *'elohim*, as here in Ps 82:1b); Deut 32:8–9 (a fragment from Qumran Cave 4, uniformly judged as superior to the MT here, reads בני האלהים, *bny h'lhym*, "sons of gods," instead of בני ישראל, *bny ysr'l*, "sons of Israel"; the LXX, agreeing, reads ἀγγέλων θεοῦ, *angelōn theou* [see Heiser, "Monotheism," 7n15]); 33:2–3 ("holy ones"); 1 Kgs 22:19–23 ("host of heaven" and "spirit"); 1 Chr 16:25 (אֱלֹהִים); Neh 9:6 ("army"); Job 1:6–12; 2:1–6 (בְּנֵי הָאֱלֹהִים, *bne ha'elohim*, "sons of the gods"; and "Satan"); 38:7 (בְּנֵי אֱלֹהִים); Pss 29:1 (בְּנֵי אֵלִים, *bne 'elim*, "sons of gods"); 58:1–2 ("gods," אֵלִם, *'elem*); 86:8 (אֱלֹהִים); 89:5–8 ("assembly/council of the holy ones"; בְּנֵי אֵלִים); 95:3; 96:4–5; 97:7, 9 (אֱלֹהִים); 148:2 ("hosts"); Isa 6:1–7 ("seraphim"); 14:13 (כּוֹכְבֵי־אֵל, *kokve-'el*, "stars of God"); 24:21 ("army of heaven" punished, as also here in Ps 82:6–7); Jer 8:2 ("host of heaven"); 23:18, 22 ("council [of Yahweh]"); Ezek 28:14 ("cherub"); Dan 4:13, 17, 23 ("watcher[s]," "holy one"); 10:13–21; 12:1 ("prince," "Michael," "chief princes"; "great prince"); Zech 14:5 ("holy ones"); also see Sir 17:17; Jub. 15:31–32; 35:17; 1 En. 10:9; 12:2, 4; 14:3; 15:2–3; 20:1–7 (not including other references to "angels," "angel of Yahweh," "Satan," etc.). "Each pagan nation was put under the administration of a being of inferior status to Yahweh, but Israel would be tended to by the 'God of gods,' the 'Lord of lords'" (Heiser, "Monotheism," 21–22; he argues that these other entities, especially those addressed in Psalm 82, are demons, fallen angels who have distorted their original God-ordained responsibilities over nations/peoples).

3. deClaissé-Walford et al., *Book of Psalms*, 641.

Translation

82:1 God, standing in the divine assembly—
   in the midst of the gods, He judges.
82:2 [God:] "Until when will you judge [with] injustice,
   and to the wicked show partiality?
82:3 Judge [for] the weak and the orphan;
   the afflicted and the destitute vindicate.
82:4 Save the weak and the needy;
   from the hand of the wicked rescue [them].
82:5 They do not know and they do not understand;
   in darkness they walk about;
   they are shaken—all the foundations of the earth.
82:6 I—I said, 'You are gods,
   and all of you are children of the Most High.
82:7 Nevertheless, like a human you will die,
   and like one of the princes, you will fall.'"
82:8 Arise, God, judge the earth,
   for You—You have inheritance in all the nations.

Structure

The structure of the psalm is straightforward:[4]

82:1	Assembly: *Rulership 1* ("standing," "judges") ("in [בְּ, b] the divine assembly")	*Psalmist*
82:2–4	Address: *Rebuke*	
82:5	Address: *Result*	*God*
82:6–7	Address: *Reprisal*	
82:8	Assembly: *Rulership 2* (to "arise," "judge") ("in [בְּ] all the nations")	*Psalmist*

---

4. Modified from Handy, "Sounds, Words and Meanings," 63. The psalm is replete with rhetorical figures, particularly chiastic structures, in 82:1, 2, 3, 4, each with alternating verbs and nouns; also note the parallelisms in 82:3–4a, 5ab, 6, 7.

Theological Focus

Since God, the cosmic sovereign, the possessor of all nations, takes drastic action against injustice- and evil-perpetrating members of his divine council in his wrath against them and in his concern for the weak, the people of God themselves attend carefully to matters of justice and to the welfare of the downtrodden.

Commentary

Rulership 1; Rebuke (82:1–4)

The psalm commences rather dramatically, with a snapshot of the divine council, wherein God, the ruler, is standing: the scene "transfers the reader to a space rarely seen by humans," and that without preamble or introduction.[5] In this assemblage, that permits even certain fallen spiritual entities access to him, God is undoubtedly sovereign and in charge: "standing, . . . He judges" (82:1). His standing, an unusual posture for an authority in a forensic setting,[6] indicates here that the protagonist is going to take extraordinary action (see 82:1, 8).

God wastes no time: he rebukes the miscreants in the council. Rather than be just and impartial, these beings have been governing (by means of sub-entities? directly?) with "injustice" and "partiality" towards the "wicked" (82:2; literally 82:2b reads: "and the face of the wicked lift"—an idiom for partiality, thus "show partiality"). The contrast between the activity of God and that of the wicked is starkly made with verbs and nouns chiastically arranged in 81:1, 2:

82:1 (God's Activity)		82:2 (Wicked's Activity)
"God, standing	Verb	[God:] "'Until when will you judge
in the divine [אֵל] assembly—	Nouns	[with] injustice,
in the midst of the gods [אֱלֹהִים],	Nouns	and to the wicked
He judges."	Verb	show partiality?'"

These evil "gods" ought to have been adjudicating in favor of the oppressed and suffering (82:3–4), liberating them from the "wicked" actants and agencies (82:4b). "Judge" resounds in 82:1b, 2a, 3a. God "judges" (82:1b), and the members of his council were to "judge" righteously (82:3a[7]), reflecting their sovereign but, instead, they "judge" unrighteously (82:2). Indeed, the structure of 82:2–4 literarily depicts the sufferers oppressively hemmed in by the body parts of the wicked (employing the literal wording of the Hebrew in 82:2b).[8]

---

5. deClaissé-Walford et al., *Book of Psalms*, 642.
6. See Exod 18:13; Jdg 4:5; Ruth 4:2; 1 Kgs 22:19–22; Isa 6:1; 16:5; 28:5; Ps 122:5; Prov 20:8.
7. That the judgment was to be "righteous" is evident from the occurrence of the root צדק, *tsdq*, in 82:3b, "vindicate."
8. From Dickson, "Hebrew Terminology for the Poor," 1038.

82:2b	"the *face* of the *wicked* lift"
82:3a	"the weak and the orphan"
82:3b	"the afflicted and the destitute"
82:4a	"the weak and the needy"
82:4b	"from the *hand* of the *wicked* rescue [them]"

And with these malevolent entities, God's patience is wearing thin: "Until when . . . ?" (82:2a).

Result; Reprisal (82:5–7)

The *Result* of the evildoing of those "gods" (82:1b) and their enabling of the "wicked" on earth (82:2b, 4b) by their partiality and inaction was disastrous for the weak, the orphan, the afflicted, the destitute, and the needy. They were like blind ones groping around in the blighted darkness in the absence of order, crushed by inequity and injustice, leading lives of miserable chaos. The consequent anger of God against the malfeasance of those powerful entities in the divine council would cause the very "foundations of the earth" to totter (82:5c).[9] God takes the charge of protecting the disenfranchised and marginalized of his people very seriously and expects his subordinates to have the same enthusiasm for that responsibility. They did not, and so, in his wrath, God was going to act.

He passes sentence on those vile ones with an utterance of *Reprisal* (82:6–7). Yes, those entities were "gods" and "children of the Most High" (בְּנֵי עֶלְיוֹן, *bne 'elyon*, 82:6b; akin to בְּנֵי אֵלִים, *bne 'elim*, "children of the mighty" or "heavenly beings," 29:1; 89:6, an appellation of power that far surpasses human might). But their immortality[10] as such "superhuman" beings was contingent and firmly in the control of that same Most High, Almighty God, Creator of the universe and sovereign over every power, the giver and taker of life. Here God decrees that they would die, like mortal "humans" and their rulers, "princes" (82:7).[11] Stripped of their immortality and condemned to the fate of death, they would be exalted no longer and would thus be deposed from the divine council and excluded from proximity to God.

This stunning reversal of events that leads even beings until now immortal to be punished with mortality for injustice and negligence of the weak and needy is a stern warning to human readers. If God took such serious action against those in his own council—"superhuman" entities—how much more of a precarious line would humans, already mortal, be treading on, if they were to engage in such wicked practices?

---

9. The only other use of "foundations" [מוֹסָד, *mosad*] in the Psalter is in 18:8 where, again, the wrath of God is on display. Also note Isa 24:21 that shows God punishing the heavenly host; 24:18 also has the "foundations of the earth" quaking. Hence my take of Ps 82:5c as depicting divine punitive action. But it is possible that this upheaval is simply the consequence of the injustices being perpetrated—society itself teetering on the verge of collapse.

10. Hinted at as an attribute of divine or heavenly beings in Gen 3:22.

11. Conceivably the "princes" (82:7b) could be angelic/demonic rulers as in Dan 10:13–21; 12:1. In any case, the reprisal for these evildoers of superhuman nature in Psalm 82 would be their demotion to the status of mortal beings. Whether this is a threat or an actual judicial verdict awaiting execution later (or even a recital of events already past) is unclear. "To fall" (82:7b) is often employed in the OT for catastrophic casualty: Exod 19:21; 32:28; Josh 8:25; Jdg 8:10; 12:6; 20:44, 46. So this was a prediction that had teeth and it seems that that dentition had taken, or soon would take, its bite.

Rulership 2 (82:8)

The psalm ends with a return to the divine regent. And no one is to forget: God *will* take action. The contrast between human rulers and heavenly ruler is made crystal clear in 82:7–8a:

> "human," "princes"
> "you will fall"
> "arise"
> "God"

God arises, so that perpetrators of wickedness fall![12]

Both 82:1 and 82:8 have "judge," a reference to God's posture, and nouns prefixed by the preposition בְּ. "Yhwh exercises authority among [בְּ, *in* the midst of] . . . the gods, and they rule the nations incompetently, but Yhwh has ownership among [בְּ, *in* all] . . . the nations."[13] And therefore, he can dispose of its leaders as he chooses! In a sense, this God who "judges" (82:1b, 8a) is effectively taking over the roles of those incompetent subordinates who were supposed to "judge" righteously but did not (82:2a, 3a). So now it is God himself, the heavenly sovereign and head of the divine council, who is going to do some judging of his own. The final verse of the psalm also declares "all the nations" (all peoples) as the possession of God: anyone who treats this divine "inheritance" with wickedness and injustice is in danger of being punished.

The thrust of the psalm is thus related to God's great concern for justice and the welfare of the disenfranchised and subjugated. If he would so dramatically and drastically punish heavenly beings for their role in the perpetration of evil among the peoples (including "all the nations," not just the community of God), there can be no doubt that he would view human participation in these nefarious activities equally seriously. Of course, those entities were working through their human agents,[14] those in control of the affairs of worlds, nations, societies. Therefore, the judgment on those "gods" will also be a judgment upon their human co-conspirators. Inscripturated as a psalm, this text thus also serves as warning to humans who may be tempted to commit such evils, becoming, knowingly or otherwise, pawns of satanic, anti-God operators in the heavenlies.

> The issue of governance of human affairs is a matter of life and death to God Almighty. He does not take lightly the mistreatment of the lowly and powerless in the world. Injustice shakes the very substructure of the cosmic order . . . The artistically constructed psalm . . . depicts judgment in the divine realm but we know as human beings that God does not intend to be any less rigorous with us. The responsibilities of the gods are ours . . . At the same time the psalm encourages us to keep our attention on heavenly matters as we conduct the business of the world. The gods are under a sentence of mortality; they have become no-gods. But the world is prone to believe that this is not true; it thinks that gods of indifference and injustice are still

---

12. Presumably it is the psalmist making the utterance. One might imagine him being privy to the goings on of the heavenly council, and taking part in the deliberations himself by urging God to take action and judge (82:8).

13. Goldingay, *Psalms*, 2:569. Interestingly enough, Deut 32:8–9, mentioned earlier in connection with the "sons of gods," has both "Most High" and "inheritance" (as in Ps 82:6b, 8b, respectively).

14. Including human institutions, no doubt.

in control. Ps 82 says that there is ultimate accountability. God is standing, even now, in the divine assembly and charges his agents, divine and human.[15]

God is concerned. God arises. God acts. And so must we!

Sermon Map

I. Rebuke

    God's rebuke of injustice (82:1–5b)

    Move-to-relevance: Injustice around us

II. Reprisal

    God's reprisal against perpetrators of injustice (82:5c–8)

    Move-to-relevance: Danger of punishment for injustice

III. *Reform!*

    How we can better care for the victims of injustice

---

15. Tate, *Psalms 51–100*, 341.

PSALM 83:1–18

Psalm of Disorientation

Foes Turned into God-Fearers

PSALM 83 IS A national cry,[1] a psalm of disorientation. One might see the composition as one long petition from beginning to end, without the usual affirmation of trust in God and the promise to praise him when he answers the prayer. In sum, it deals with "the general situation of Israel's vulnerability to the designs of surrounding peoples and its broader theological awareness that the world's attacks on Israel are attacks on Yhwh's purpose, Yhwh's sovereignty, and Yhwh's reputation."[2]

Translation

83:1   God, [let there be] no quiet with you;
      do not be silent and do not be still, God.
83:2   For behold, Your enemies create an uproar,
      and those who hate You have reared their head.
83:3   Against Your people they take crafty counsel,
      and they conspire against Your treasured ones.
83:4   They have said, "Come, and let us efface them as a nation,
      and the name of Israel will not be remembered again."
83:5   For they have conspired with one heart;
      against You they make a covenant:
83:6   the tents of Edom and the Ishmaelites,
      Moab and the Hagrites;
83:7   Gebal and Ammon and Amalek,
      Philistia with the inhabitants of Tyre.

---

1. However, there are no first-person singular or plural pronouns (except in 83:4 [quoting enemies] and in 83:13 [in a vocative]). Neither is there any mention of Jerusalem or the temple.

2. Goldingay, *Psalms*, 2:574.

83:8   Assyria also has joined with them;
          they have become an arm [of strength] to the children of Lot.
83:9   Deal with them as with Midian,
          as with Sisera, as with Jabin at the stream of Kishon,
83:10 the ones who perished at En-dor—
          they have became dung for the ground.
83:11 Make their nobles like Oreb and like Zeeb,
          and like Zebah and like Zalmunna all their leaders,
83:12 who have said, "Let us possess for ourselves
          the pastures of God."
83:13 My God, make them like tumbleweed,
          like chaff before the wind.
83:14 Like fire burning a forest,
          and like a flame scorching mountains,
83:15 so pursue them with Your tempest,
          and with Your storm terrify them.
83:16 Fill their faces with dishonor,
          that they may seek Your name, Yahweh.
83:17 May they be ashamed and terrified until always,
          and may they be humiliated and destroyed,
83:18 that they may know that You alone—Your name [is] Yahweh—
          [are] the Most High over all the earth.

Structure

The psalm is shaped as a lamentation followed by a supplication:[3]

Lamentation (83:1–8)
Appeal for divine intervention (83:1)
    Action of enemies expected (83:2–8)
        speech of enemies, 83:4a: "they have said [אָמְרוּ, *'amru*]"
        named peoples and places, 83:6–8

Supplication (83:9–18)
    Action of God exhorted (83:9–16a)
        named individuals and places, 83:9–11
        speech of enemies, 83:12a: "who have said [אָמְרוּ]"
Aftermath of divine intervention (83:16b–18)

---

3. From Costacurta, "L'aggressione contro Dio," 518–19.

Theological Focus

> When oppressed by the powers of the world, God's people, recognizing that their enemies are God's enemies, appeal with confidence to God for him to intervene as in the days of old, not only to defeat and punish those adversaries, but also to bring them, all over the earth, to a knowledge of, and submission to, himself.

Commentary

Lamentation (83:1–8)

The appeal for divine intervention (83:1) begins with "God" (אֱלֹהִים, *'elohim*) and ends with "God" (אֵל, *'el*). But the call to God is not that he listen or take action per se; rather it is phrased in the negative—that God *not* be quiet, and *not* be silent, and *not* be still. While it is Israel being beset by enemies, their foes are also God's foes, and this identification of common enemies is clear in the lamentation:[4]

83:2	Enemies of God: "Your enemies ... those who hate You"	
83:3		Enemies of people: "against Your people," "against Your treasured ones"
83:4		Enemies of people: "'let us efface them as a nation, ... Israel"
83:5	Enemies of God: "they have conspired ... against You"	

As well, in 83:3, we have "against Your people ... they conspire," and in 83:5 "they have conspired ... against You." Such an appeal to the confluence of enemies—God's and Israel's—is intended to motivate God into action. "Behold" (83:2): "Look, God, they're in front of you—our enemies *and* yours. You cannot afford not to act." The enemies consider Israel simply as a "nation [גּוֹי, *goy*]," like any other (83:4a), but Israel is quick to remind God that they are his "people [עַם, *'am*]" (83:3a).

A description of enemy action is found in 83:2–8, but it appears to be a threat that is imminent: the foes are only plotting and scheming so far (83:3). But they are "rearing their head" (83:2b) in anticipation of a strike. In addition, the adversaries have made a pact (perhaps with their god[s], 83:5b) against Israel, the only instance in the OT of someone "making a covenant" "against" another.[5] This covenant by enemies appears to be a conspiracy to counter the divine covenant between Yahweh and his people. Yet the irony is that despite all the machinations of the enemies who "create an uproar" (83:2a), God seems to have gone all "quiet" and "silent" and "still" (83:1). Truly a lamentable situation![6]

---

4. Also note that 83:3 is chiastic: "Against Your people / they take crafty counsel, // and they conspire / against Your treasured ones."

5. Goldingay, *Psalms*, 2:576.

6. The logic of listing of peoples in 83:6–8 is unclear, but the names appear to include nations all around Israel, from Tyre in the far northwest to Philistia, Amalek, and Gebal generally in the south, with the others occupying precincts more or less east of Judah. Some of them are actually distant relatives of Israel.

Supplication (83:9–18)

Named individuals and places show up again, this time in the supplication section (83:9–11), and all of them borrowed from the book of Judges: Sisera and Jabin from Judges 4–5; and Midian, Oreb and Zeeb, and Zebah and Zalmunna from Judges 6–8. Following this list of enemies and their utterances (Ps 83:12[7]), the supplication continues, but with items and events taken from nature (83:13–15). The structure of 83:9–14 is carefully undertaken:[8]

83:9	"as with" (כְּ, *ki* ×3)	
83:11a	"make"	
83:12b		"God"
83:13aα		"God"
83:13aβ	"make"	
83:13–14	"like" (כְּ ×4)	

In short, may God act in his wrath to decimate his (and their) foes to the same utterly defeated status of those historical adversaries in Judges, dissipating them like tumbleweed and consuming them like chaff, rendering them like a burnt forest, like a scorched mountain (83:13–15). May the God who "made" the enemies' leaders impotent long ago (83:11a) likewise "make" the current crop of anti-God potentates completely feckless (83:13). And with the tempest and storm in 83:15, the metaphors of fire and water are mixed, creating a vivid picture of the confusion and discomfiture of the objects of Yahweh's anger.[9]

But, in the end, we comprehend the psalmist's (and God's) ultimate goal in all of this: remediation. "This is complex theology, because what it ultimately declares is that what God desires is for all of God's acts to lead humans toward salvation and redemption."[10] The two pairs of retaliation-remediation statements in 83:16–18 reinforce the intent of God for all peoples, friends and foes alike, that they may "seek" his name and "know" it—i.e., acknowledge and submit to God's authority and sovereignty.[11]

---

7. This corresponds to the utterances in 83:4 of the earlier set of enemies in the lamentation section: all are out to finish off Israel.

8. From Auffret, "Qu'ils Sachent Que Toi," 54n21. Once "they [Assyria] had become" (from היה, *hyh*; 83:8b) aiders and abettors to Moab, but as the foes of God's people "[they] have become" (also from היה; 83:10b) fertilizer for the ground.

9. And 83:15 is chiastic: "so pursue them / with [בְּ] Your tempest, // and with [בְּ] Your storm / terrify them."

10. deClaissé-Walford et al., *Book of Psalms*, 648.

11. Goldingay notices the "strange tension that is a common feature of the OT. The psalmist wants people (a) to be killed, (b) to be humiliated, (c) to turn to Yhwh" (Goldingay, *Psalms*, 2:584). The dissolution of the tension in our psalm is achieved only with the recognition that poetry is rhetorical in intent, force, and impact, and is not necessarily literal.

83:16a	Retaliation	
83:16b	Remediation	
	"Your name, Yahweh" (שִׁמְךָ יְהוָה, shimka yhwh)	
83:17	Retaliation	
83:18	Remediation	
	"Your name [is] Yahweh" (שִׁמְךָ יְהוָה)	

Thus 83:17 is expanding/escalating 83:16a (retaliation), and 83:18 is expanding/escalating 83:16b (remediation).

Notice also how the situation at the commencement of the psalm has now, at its conclusion, been turned on its head, both literally and literarily:[12]

83:3a	"against [עַל, 'al] Your people"
83:4b	"name" (Israel's, effaced)
83:4b	"again [עוֹד, 'od]"
83:5a	"heart" (enemies')
83:16a	"face" (enemies')
83:17a	"until always [עֲדֵי־עַד, 'ade-'ad]"
83:18a	"name" (God's, reknowned)
83:18b	"over [עַל] all the earth"

The enemies were directed "against [עַל]" Israel (83:3a), but it will be God Most High "over [עַל]" the whole earth who will ultimately be victor; they sought to efface the "name" of God's people so that it would not be remembered "again [עוֹד]" (83:4), but, instead, it will be they who will be defeated "until always [עֲדֵי־עַד]" and who will, as a result, seek and know God's "name" (83:17–18). These enemies may have conspired in their "heart" (83:5a), but it will be another body part, their "faces," that would be filled with dishonor at the hand of God (83:16a). And, while the psalm began with "God" twice (83:1a, 1b: אלהים and אֵל), it ends with the covenant name, "Yahweh," precious to his people, also twice (83:16b, 18a). Thus, though this psalm, like several of the ones preceding it, ends without any obvious resolution to the dire situation of God's people, a satisfactory dénouement is no doubt forthcoming from "Yahweh, . . . the Most High over all the earth"!

---

12. From Auffret, "Qu'ils Sachent Que Toi," 54n21.

Sermon Map

I. Suffering
   The lament of God's people (83:1–8)
   Move-to-relevance: Distress in our days

II. Supplication
   The plea for God's intervention (83:9–15)
   Move-to-relevance: The kind of prayers we pray

III. Salvation
   The ultimate goal of enemies' conversion (83:16–18)

IV. *Request for Reformation!*
   How to seek the good of oppressors

PSALM 84:1–12

Psalm of Orientation

Pilgrimage of Life Towards the Presence of God

THIS PSALM IS TRADITIONALLY labeled a song of the pilgrim, in light of its references to the journey of the faithful to Jerusalem and the yearning to be in God's presence.[1]

Translation

84:1 How beloved are Your abodes,
      Yahweh of Armies.

84:2 It craved and also yearned—my soul—for the courts of Yahweh;
      my heart and my flesh shout for joy to the living God.

84:3 The bird also has found a house,
      and the pigeon a nest for itself, where she may lay her young,
      at Your altars, Yahweh of Armies, my King and my God.

84:4 Blessing [upon] the ones inhabiting Your house,
      they are continually praising You.

84:5 Blessing [upon] the person whose strength is in You,
      the highways [to Zion] are in their heart—

84:6 the ones passing through the valley of weeping.
      He makes it a spring;
      the early rain also covers it with water pools.

84:7 They walk from power to [more] power;
      [each] one appears before God in Zion.

84:8 Yahweh, God of Armies, hear my prayer;
      give ear, God of Jacob.

---

1. Psalms 42–43 is another composition (considered jointly as a single "pericope" or preaching text) that displays such a yearning, but its imperfect verbs signify a longing for God that has not been fulfilled, unlike the perfect verbs in Psalm 84 that indicate a consummation of that desire. Perhaps that is why "blessing [אַשְׁרֵי, 'ashre]" occurs thrice in this psalm, the most in any song of the Psalter.

84:9   At our shield look, God,
           and gaze upon the face of Your anointed.
84:10 For better is a day in Your courts than a thousand [elsewhere].
           I would prefer to stand at the threshold of the house of my God
           than live in the tents of wickedness.
84:11 For a sun and shield is Yahweh God;
           grace and glory Yahweh gives;
           He does not withhold good from those who walk uprightly.
84:12 Yahweh of Armies,
           blessing [upon] the person who trusts in You.

Structure

Essentially, Psalm 84 is a joyous journey—or at least potentially one—extolling the blessedness of the pilgrims *Aspiring* for, *Approaching* towards, and *Arriving* at the house of God.[2]

Aspiring (84:1–4)
  "blessing [upon]" (84:4a)
  "Yahweh of Armies" (84:1b, 3c)

Approaching (84:5–8)
  "blessing [upon]" (84:5a)
  "Yahweh, God of Armies" (84:8a)

Arriving (84:9–12)
  "blessing [upon]" (84:12b)
  "Yahweh of Armies" (84:12a)

Theological Focus

The people of God exult in God's presence and await with eagerness and yearning the day of being forever in his presence, as they undertake the journey of life in God's protection, God's provision, and God's power.

---

2. References to God's "abodes" (84:1a), "courts" (84:2a, 10a), "altars" (84:3c), and "house" (84:3a, 4a, 10b) punctuate the psalm—seven times. There are also seven occurrences of אֱלֹהִים, *'elohim*, (84:3c, 7b, 8a, 8b, 9a, 10b, 11a; and one instance of אֵל, *'el*, 84:2b).

Commentary

Aspiring (84:1–4)

The psalm launches immediately into an exclamation about the "beloved" nature of the temple precincts (84:1b).[3] Worship of God in his dwelling places goes far beyond obligation and obedience: it is "a transforming experience of joy and delight found only in the grandeur of God's presence."[4] So much so, the psalmist's soul "craved" and "yearned" with an *Aspiration* of profound intensity for the courts of God (84:2a). With a switch from these two perfect verbs in 84:2a to an imperfect in 84:2b ("shout for joy"), it is as if he is already there in the temple, shouting for joy to the living God.[5] The paralleling of 84:2a and 84:2b with alterations of verbs and nouns (plural/singular and masculine/feminine [see below]—indicating the experience this could potentially be for one and for all, for humanity universal) and the movement from desiring to be where God is to being with God himself powerfully conveys the sense of *Aspiring* to be in the very presence of deity:[6]

84:2a	*Feminine singular verbs* "It craved and also yearned"	*Feminine noun* —my soul—	**Where God is** for the courts of Yahweh"
84:2b	*Masculine nouns* "My heart and my flesh"	*Masculine plural verb* shout for joy	**God himself** to the living God"

So great is this aspiring pilgrim's anticipatory joy, he envies the birds who abide in God's presence constantly (84:3);[7] he, unlike those avian specimens, is not a permanent citizen of these divine precincts. Once again, the emotion of the psalmist overwhelms him as he personalizes this deity—"my King and my God" (84:3c).

Notice also the position of "Yahweh of Armies" (84:1b, 3c) around those who are potentially abiding and those who actually abide in his dwelling places:

"Yahweh of Armies" (84:1b)	**God**
"my soul," "my heart," "my flesh" (84:2)	*People: potentially abiding*
"bird," "pigeon," "her young" (84:3ab)	*Creatures: actually abiding*
"Yahweh of Armies" (84:3c)	**God**

---

3. The multiple buildings within the complex are denoted by the plural "abodes." "Beloved" is יָדִיד, *yadid*, and the word דּוֹד, *dod*, "lover," is employed in Song of Songs over thirty-five times. Alter remarks that in Psalm 84 it "conveys a virtually erotic intensity in the speaker's longing for the temple on Mount Zion" (*Book of Psalms*, 297n2).

4. Benedetto, "Psalm 84," 58.

5. This, of course, is the consummation of the journey described in 84:5–12, the *Approaching* and the *Arriving* of the pilgrim. That change of verb aspect may simply reflect the poet's fervent desire to be in the temple—it takes on an "already" tone, attesting to his certainty of reaching his destination soon. This makes the psalm somewhat dischronological, with 84:1–4 giving the impression of the journey being complete before it has begun. But in a sermon it is best to maintain the progressive chronology of a journey as suggested in the structure of the psalm (above).

6. From Jerome, Obiorah Mary, *"How Lovely Is Your Dwelling Place,"* 57.

7. Even "lowly birds [are] making their nests in lofty places" (Ross, *Psalms*, 2:758).

It is as if the commander of the hosts of heaven—"my King and my God" (84:3c)—is guarding the vulnerable ones who take refuge in his barracks, his palace, his temple! Not only are these inhabitants enthralled by the presence of Yahweh, they are also completely safe in his presence. And so the psalmist utters another benediction, blessing those who dwell with God; they cannot but continually praise him (84:4). All that to say, this is where the pilgrim is headed!

Approaching (84:5–8)

The notion of *Approaching* comes from the mention of the pilgrims in whose hearts are the "highways [to Zion]" (84:5b) and who are "passing through" (84:6a) and "walking" to come before God (84:7a). Thus 85:5–7 is a joyous expression of the Zion pilgrimage. The aspirational (and almost certain) pleasure of abiding, the zealous yearning of the "heart" (84:2b) to be with God, etches those highways to divine presence on the "heart" of the pilgrim (84:5b).

> Fundamentally then, worship, is not what is performed by those who are leading the service and observed by the congregation, but rather it is what emerges from the hearts of worshipers who are set on praising the Lord. Whether taken literally or figuratively, the focus in … [84:5] is upon the intense desire that delights the worshipers who approach the temple to worship the Lord. The sense of yearning introduced in the first strophe thus continues.[8]

Blessed is such a person, particularly one depending utterly on Yahweh, the life-pilgrim "whose strength is in You" (84:5a)!

However, this journey does not happen on a rose-strewn road, but on a tear-drenched track: "weeping" makes that valley that the pilgrim is traversing (84:6a) one of affliction and grief. But, though God may dwell in Zion, there can be no doubt he is with his people wherever they are—even the ones trekking through the Valley of Weeping (Slough of Despond?[9]) are in his care.[10] Defenseless birds "lay [שִׁית, *shit*]" their fledgling young in the presence of Yahweh (84:3b); in turn, God "makes [שִׁית]" springs of blessings for his faithful people, as they seek him on paths that are difficult (84:6b). That water of tears, the "valley of weeping," God converts into a water-spring of refreshment (84:6bc[11]), and thus the reinvigorated and well-hydrated pilgrims, "whose strength is in You" (84:5a), "walk from power to [more] power" (84:7a), in the might of their deity overcoming all odds, as they make their way to Zion, to the presence of God.

None the less, the prospect of weeping valleys causes the psalmist to break out into a petition that he be "heard," "given ear" to (84:8; and in the next section, that he be "looked" at, "gazed upon," 84:9b). Psalm 84:8 is chiastic, centered upon the psalmist's prayer, with the divine commandant and deity of Israel surrounding the petition (below).

---

8. Estes, "Psalm 84," 40.

9. The fictional bog of despair in John Bunyan's *Pilgrim's Progress* (1678).

10. Otherwise, a "Valley of Baca" (עֵמֶק הַבָּכָא, *'emeq habbaka'*, translated "the valley of weeping"; 84:6a) is unknown.

11. The MT has בְּרָכוֹת, *brakot*, "blessings," in 84:6c, but in the context of springs and rains, it is best emended to בְּרֵכוֹת, *brekot*, "water pools." Water in the Middle East is always a sign of divine blessing.

> "Yahweh, God of Armies,
> hear
> **my prayer**;
> give ear,
> God of Jacob."

In a sense then, "the psalm is about the pilgrimage itself which turns parched valleys into oases and clothes barren slopes with flowers whether it rains or not. Blessings are transmitted wherever the pilgrims go, because they are looking to God."[12] And so "walking" (84:7a) is not only an indication of the pilgrimage to Zion, but also a metaphor for the pilgrimage of life: God's people in worshipful living move from strength to strength daily.

Arriving (84:9–12)

The mention of standing at the threshold of the divine dwelling indicates the psalmist's arrival at his destination.[13] He now adds to the "prayer" mentioned in 84:8a. Not only does he desire that God hear this prayer, he also requests that God look with favor upon their leader. Notice that "shield" parallels "Your anointed" in a chiastic structure:[14]

> "At our shield,
> look,
> **God**,
> and gaze upon
> the face of Your anointed."

Later, it is God himself who is called his people's "shield" (84:11a).[15] "There is little tension between the king as 'our shield' ... and Yahweh as 'shield' ... , because the king embodied and exercised divine protective power ... The king was considered to be an 'extended arm' of Yahweh, who intervenes and establishes justice."[16] Thus, the call is essentially for continued protection (likely along the remaining journey, or even the trip back). In any case, the thrust of this section underscores the psalmist's preference to be at least colonizing the perimeter of God's house rather than to inhabit the tents of the wicked (84:10).

As God's people "walk" in worship (84:7), they walk not only in divine strength, but they also "walk" uprightly (84:11c). Thus they "appear" before God (ראה, *r'h*; 84:7b), they are "looked" upon by God (ראה, 84:9a), their "shield" (84:9a) becomes God's "shield" (84:11a), and their declaration of the "betterness" (טוב, *tov*) of the house of God (84:10a) is

---

12. Tate, *Psalms 51–100*, 359–60.

13. Or at least he is very close to his terminus.

14. "Shield" here, thus, indicates the one who protects the people of God making the pilgrimage, i.e., their leader. For "shield" as leader, also see 47:9; for "anointed" as leader, see 2:2; 18:50; 20:6; 89:18; etc.

15. For God as a shield, see 84:11a, and also 3:3; 18:2, 30; 28:7; 33:20; etc.

16. Tate, *Psalms 51–100*, 360.

reciprocated by God not withholding "good" (טוֹב, 84:11c) from these walkers of integrity, these worshipers of zeal![17]

84:5	"Blessing [upon] the person … in You"
84:7	"appears [ראה]"; "walk"
84:8–9	"look [ראה]"; "Yahweh," "God" (×3); "shield"
84:10–11b	"better [טוֹב]"; "Yahweh" (×2), "God"; "shield"
84:11c	"good [טוֹב]"; "walk"
84:12	"blessing [upon] the person … in You"

And thus, the psalm that commenced with a reference to divine "courts" (84:2a) concludes with a similar reference to God's "courts" (84:10a). To these locations, the people of God aspire, approach, and arrive, to abide therein. "People who walk the pilgrimage need to be people who walk their everyday lives with integrity; people who are to walk their everyday lives with integrity will be strengthened in doing so if they walk the pilgrimage. The two walks support each other."[18] Such a walk of integrity is not perfection, of course, but a consistent lifestyle of uprightness. All of this together conveys the sense that this pilgrimage—"concerned with the physical aspects of religion: journey, temple courts, feasting, liturgies, fellowship with fellow pilgrims, and the like"[19]—is symbolic of life as a whole, particularly its spiritual realities and the relationship of life-travelers with their God, as they enjoy God's protection, his provision, and his power. Though the presence of God is vitally experienced during this temporal trek, including the thrill and ecstasy of worshiping him, the journey for those on the trajectory of life is consummated only in eternity, towards which we move day by day, "craving" and "yearning" for divine presence!

Sermon Map

I. Presence of God in Abiding

    The yearning for and joy of God's presence (84:1–2, 4, 10, 12)

    Move-to-relevance: Our worship of God

II. Protection, Provision, and Power of God in Approaching and Arriving

    Protection (84:3, 8–9)

    Provision (84:6, 11)

    Power (84:5, 7)

    Move-to-relevance: Our trust in God

III. *Walk with God, to God!*

    Specifics on undertaking a walk with and towards God

---

17. Modified from Auffret, "Qu'elles sont aimables," 36.
18. Goldingay, *Psalms*, 2:599.
19. Tate, *Psalms 51–100*, 362.

PSALM 85:1–13

Psalm of Disorientation

Restoration to Divine Presence

PSALM 85 IS A prayer for God to act in the present as he has acted in the past, so that the people of God may enjoy his deliverance in the future.

Translation

85:1 Yahweh, You were pleased with Your land;
    You restored the restoration of Jacob.
85:2 You pardoned the iniquity of Your people;
    You covered all their sin.
85:3 You withdrew all Your fury;
    You turned away from Your burning anger.
85:4 Restore us [again], God, our deliverance,
    and end Your irritation with us.
85:5 Will You forever be angry with us,
    [and] extend Your anger from generation to generation?
85:6 Will You not Yourself return [to] revive us,
    [that] Your people may rejoice in You?
85:7 Show us, Yahweh, Your lovingkindness,
    and Your deliverance give us.
85:8 I will hear what God Yahweh will speak;
    for He will speak peace
to His people, and to His devout ones;
    and may they not return to folly.
85:9 Surely His deliverance [is] near to those who fear Him,
    that glory may abide in our land.

85:10 Lovingkindness and truth have met;
>   righteousness and peace have kissed.
85:11 Truth from the earth springs,
>   and righteousness from heaven looks down.
85:12 Indeed, Yahweh—He will give what is good,
>   and our earth will give its produce.
85:13 Righteousness will go before Him
>   and set a way for His footsteps.

Structure

The structure of the psalm follows a *Past Restoration* of divine action, a *Present Request* for divine action, and the *Future Rescue* by divine action, with the *Psalmist's Recommendation* before the final section:

85:1–3	Past Restoration
85:4–7	Present Request
85:8	**Psalmist's Recommendation**
85:9–13	Future Rescue

"The psalm thus starts as if it is going to be a praise hymn, segues into being a protest psalm, and ends up as a psalm of trust."[1] While it might be an exhortation to God to repeat the past (his mercy) in the present, it is also a warning to God's people *not* to repeat the past (their sin; see especially 85:8d). This is also evident in the psalmist's aside, 85:8. That this recommendation is a key verse seems obvious: it is the only time the first-person singular shows up in the psalm (perhaps the voice of a leader or priest). There is also a change from the imperatives of 85:7 to the cohortative and jussive of 85:8 creating a seam between 85:7 and 85:9. Besides, on the other side of 85:8, "surely" in 85:9 marks a transition from what just preceded.[2]

In any case, the psalm appears to be mostly one of disorientation: relief from distress is the trajectory of the poem, as 85:4–7 indicates. That being said, there is considerable reorientation in the final section of the psalm. Notable are the personifications of a number of nouns: "glory" that abides (85:9b); "lovingkindness," "truth," "righteousness," and "peace" that meet and kiss (85:10); "truth" that springs forth and "righteousness" that looks down (85:11); "earth" that gives (85:12b); and "righteousness" that goes before and trailblazes divine footsteps (85:13). The new world envisioned in a future deliverance is indelibly marked by these inanimate qualities and (divine) characteristics, that are, poetically speaking, thriving with vibrant vitality, bespeaking a new world of God.

---

1. Goldingay, *Psalms*, 2:604.
2. Also as will be shown below, 85:4–7 forms a compact rhetorical structure that stands alone.

Theological Focus

In the envisioned divine kingdom, ordained and directed by God, the sin of his people is pardoned, his discipline withdrawn, his demands met, and life is revitalized and marked by peace and harmony and plenty, as God himself dwells with his people.

Commentary

Past Restoration (85:1–3)

The first section, with its perfect verbs, deals with a historical restoration by God of his people. There is a double wordplay in 85:1: אַרְצֶךָ ... רָצִיתָ, *ratsita ... 'artseka* ("You were pleased with Your land") and שַׁבְתָּ שְׁבוּת, *shavta shvut* ("You restored the restoration"). With regards to the latter, scrutinizing the twenty-seven occurrences of שׁוּב שְׁבוּת, *shuv shvut*, in the OT, Bracke shows that the phrase "is associated with promises which indicate Yahweh's reversal of his judgment, and the restoration of a condition of well-being. Additionally, the vision of restoration . . . often includes Yahweh's correction of that which led to his judgment."[3] Essentially, it is a removal of God's wrath and a return of God's favor upon his people (also see 14:7; 53:6; 126:1, 4). This may also be a hint, albeit subtle, that some guilt of God's people had a role in their oppression (and exile). The hint of negativity in that phrase is manifested explicitly in 85:2–5: it was God's displeasure with their sin that led to all their problems in the first place. In sum, deliverance is what God's people sought then, and such a wish for deliverance is what has been universally voiced by the people of God of all times.

Obviously, the manner in which (or the grounds by which) this restoration would be accomplished was by God forgiving his people's sin (85:2). "*All* their sin" (85:2b) was mitigated by God's withdrawal of "*all* Your fury" (85:3a), that otherwise would have, no doubt, been destructive. His "restoring" of the "restoration" (both from שׁוּב, *shwv*, 85:1b) was paralleled by his "turning away" (also from שׁוּב, 85:3) from his incendiary anger.

Present Request; Psalmist's Recommendation (85:5–8)

If God did all that (85:1–3) once, why cannot he do so now? The *Present Request*, 85:4–7, reflecting that angst, is carefully structured:

85:4	Two imperatives (and "God, our deliverance")
85:5	Question (rhetorical)
85:6	Question (rhetorical)
85:7	Two imperatives (and "Yahweh ... Your deliverance")

---

3. Bracke, "*šûb šebût*: Reappraisal," 243.

The rhetorical questions serve to accentuate the request and motivate God to act and relent. Of course, what exactly the people are requesting deliverance from is not clear, though it is a fair guess that it is divine discipline (that can take various forms, including external oppression) that is in view.[4] Would that God "return" (from שׁוּב) to revive them (85:6a), just as he had once "turned away" (also from שׁוּב) from his anger in the past (85:3b) and had "restored" (again שׁוּב; 85:1) his people. "You turned away from your 'anger' once (אַף, 'aph; 85:3b), so please don't be 'angry' (אָנַף, 'nph) forever and extend your 'anger' (אַף) for generations now and forward (85:5)." There is a sense of hopelessness embedded even in the structure of 85:5, with God's anger bounded on either side by the interminable extent of that wrath:

> "Will you *forever*
> be **angry** with us,
> [and] extend your **anger**
> from *generation to generation*?"

Yet, there is a glimpse of future rescue (and relief) in the hope God's people have of rejoicing in him when his deliverance is accomplished and his "lovingkindness [חֶסֶד, *chesed*]" (85:7a) is displayed to his "devout ones [חָסִיד, *chasid*]" (85:8c).[5]

The aside of the psalmist (85:8)—perhaps a leader or a priest/Levite—declares his intent to attend to God's speech (and perhaps give up on his own accusatory speech, 85:5–6), anticipating the peace that will follow. God's "returning" (שׁוּב; 85:6a) from his anger and discipline is contingent upon his devout ones *not* "returning" (שׁוּב; 85:8d) to their folly and sin. "What better word is there for the Lord to speak to the people in answer to their pleading than 'shalom' . . . [85:8b]? *Shalom*, of course, is much more than the absence of war; it is the culmination of God's kingdom, where all have what they need and live in comfort without fear."[6] What God actually said is not stated, but it is likely to have been what is reported by the psalmist in the next section, 85:9–13—the future kingdom of God revealed.

Future Rescue (85:9–13)

"Given the fact that Yhwh is committed to them and they are Yhwh's committed people, deliverance must follow; indeed, it must be not merely certain but also imminent. Yhwh surely cannot allow calamity to continue."[7] And so the psalmist begins the final section of the psalm with that same certainty, "surely" (85:9), embracing a hearty sense of conviction about, and anticipation of, the future deliverance.

The verses, 85:10–11, are unusual. Not only are the nouns personified, the governing verbs in each of the four lines come at the end, emphasizing those actions. "Meet [פָּגַשׁ, *pgsh*]" and "kiss [נָשַׁק, *nshq*]" in 85:10 are rarely, if ever, employed in the OT in such a metaphorical

---

4. The vagueness of the threat also enables the utilization of the psalm in spaces and times far removed from those of the provenance of the composition.

5. This blessing of "lovingkindness" will show up again in 85:10.

6. deClaissé-Walford et al., *Book of Psalms*, 658. It is the state of blessedness consummated in the macrocosm of the kingdom of God in the future, but adumbrated in the microcosms of divine rule in the present in the lives of individuals and communities comprising the people of God, the body of Christ.

7. Goldingay, *Psalms*, 2:612.

fashion. The explanation that "truth" comes from the earth and "righteousness" from heaven in the second pair of personified nouns in 85:11 indicates that, in the first pair of the similarly personified nouns in 85:10a also, the first noun, "lovingkindness," must be heavenly in origin (as is explicitly noted in 85:7a), and the second, "truth," earthly (as is explicitly noted in 85:11a). As well, "righteousness" is thus heavenly, and "peace" earthly in 85:10b.

	Heavenly	Earthly
85:10a	Lovingkindness (also 85:7a)	Truth
85:10b	Righteousness	Peace
85:11	Righteousness	Truth

That suggests the role of God's people in the production of those earthly qualities, "truth" (85:10aβ, 11a) and "peace" (85:10bβ). "Truth" and "peace" are the manifest qualities of "His devout ones," "those who fear Him" (85:8c–9a). That this "truth," though springing from the earth, is ultimately God's is clear in the Psalter: 25:5, 10; 26:3; 31:5; 40:10, 11; 43:3; etc. "Peace," ostensibly emanating from earth (85:10bβ), is also God-spoken into existence (85:8b). Thus God's people living on the earth reflect those attributes of God, looking like God in his holiness, the ultimate goal of deity for humanity (Rom 8:29). This balance of the heavenly and earthly is extended further in Ps 85:12: Yahweh "gives" what is good and the earth "gives" its produce (agricultural bounty).

Then, in 85:13, the going forth of "righteousness" (from heaven, 85:10bα, 11b) before God, marking a path for his footsteps, bespeaks the arrival of God himself from heaven to earth, to dwell with his people, who now resemble him as they manifest "truth" and "peace" (85:10aα, 10bβ, 11a). This is a "meeting" and a "kissing" of the heavenly and the earthly (85:10). And then God will be with his own, and "Your land" (85:1a) becomes "our land" upon which rests the glory of God (85:9b). This is surely a picture of the kingdom of God, with everything in the heavens and earth coexisting in perfect harmony—particularly in the godliness of the divine community—and in peace and with plenty, disobedience reprieved, distresses removed, deliverance realized, demands met,[8] deity revealed![9]

---

8. Divine demands, the call of God for his people to be holy, to fear him, and to walk with him.

9. This deliverance is all encompassing—physical ("deliverance"; 85:9a), moral (production of God-likeness, i.e., "truth"; 85:10aβ, 11a), social (the establishment of "peace," 85:10bβ), and perhaps even agricultural (earth yielding "produce," 85:12b).

Sermon Map

I. God's Pardon
    What God had done in the past (85:1–3)
    What God hopefully will do in the present (85:4–7)
    Move-to-relevance: Our sin

II. God's Peace and Prosperity
    What God's people should do in the future: obedience (85:8)
    What God will do in the future (85:9–13)
    Move-to-relevance: Our trust in God

III. *Don't Return, People! Do Return, God!*
    Specifics on not returning to sin and hoping for the divine kingdom

PSALM 86:1–17

Psalm of Disorientation

Servants and Their Savior

PSALM 86 IS NOTABLE for its reuse of phrases from elsewhere in the Psalter and other books of the OT. Yet the prayer, even with all its allusions and recyclings, is a unique song composed by the poet.[1] "By using ways of speaking to God and of God that have been sanctified by their use over the centuries, individuals are able to articulate what they want to say to God . . . In a context of affliction, then, people who pray do not abandon the formulas of the faith; arguably these become more important."[2]

Translation

86:1   Incline, Yahweh, Your ear, answer me,
           for I am afflicted and needy.
86:2   Preserve my soul, for I am a devout one;
           deliver Your servant—You are my God—the one trusting in You.
86:3   Be gracious to me, Lord,
           for to You I cry all the day.
86:4   Rejoice the soul of Your servant,
           for to You, Lord, my soul I lift up.
86:5   For You, Lord, are good, and ready to forgive,
           and abundant in lovingkindness to all who cry to You.
86:6   Give ear, Yahweh, to my prayer;
           and attend to the voice of my supplications [for grace].
86:7   In the day of my distress I cry to You,
           for You answer me.

---

1. And it is the only psalm attributed to David in Book III of the Psalter (superscriptions are untranslated in this work; see Introduction).

2. Goldingay, *Psalms*, 2:618–19. That being said, the references to, and reutilizations of, other texts need not particularly concern the preacher focused on expositing the pericopal theology of this psalm.

86:8   There is no one like You among the gods, Lord,
           and there is nothing like Your doings.
86:9   All nations whom You have made,
           they will come and worship before Your face, Lord,
           and they will glorify Your name.
86:10 For You are great and the One doing wonders;
           You—You alone are God.
86:11 Teach me Your way, Yahweh;
           I will walk in Your truth;
           unite my heart to fear Your name.
86:12 I will give You thanks, Lord my God, with all my heart,
           and I will glorify Your name forever.
86:13 For Your lovingkindness is great toward me,
           and You rescued my soul from the depths of Sheol.
86:14 God, arrogant ones have risen up against me,
           and a crowd of violent ones have sought my soul,
           and they have not set You in front of them.
86:15 But You, Lord, are a God merciful and gracious,
           slow to anger and abundant in lovingkindness and truth.
86:16 Face towards me, and be gracious to me;
           grant Your strength to Your servant,
           and deliver the son of Your handmaid.
86:17 Do for me a sign for good,
           that those who hate me may see and be ashamed,
           for You, Yahweh, have helped me and comforted me.

Structure

As with all the other psalms, Psalm 86, too, is structured carefully, with sections dealing with pleas (*Plea 1*, 86:1–7; and *Plea 2*, 86:14–17) bookending the sections on the *Praiseworthiness* and *Praise* of God (86:8–10; and 86:11–13).[3] And within each plea section the arrangement is similar, with an *inclusio* surrounding a central plea for deliverance (86:2–5, 15–16). *Plea 1* has entreaties to God to consider the supplicant favorably (in 86:1, 6–7), and *Plea 2* has entreaties to God to consider the enemy unfavorably (86:14, 17; see below).[4]

---

3. Notice also the similarities between the central parts of the plea sections (86:2–5 and 86:15–16; see figure).

4. Tate labels 86:8–13 (*Praiseworthiness* + *Praise*) "a positive core" that sets up "a kind of dialectical tension" between its proclamation of God's praiseworthiness and promise of praise to him, and the pleas that precede and follow it (see Tate, *Psalms 51–100*, 377).

86:1–7	**Plea 1**	
	86:1	*Plea for hearing 1* "Yahweh"; "ear"; "answer me"
	86:2–5	*Plea for deliverance* "deliver" (86:2b); "Your servant" (86:2b, 4a) "be gracious to me" (86:3a) "abundant in lovingkindness" (86:5b)
	86:6–7	*Plea for hearing 2* "Yahweh"; "ear"; "answer me"
86:8–10	**Praiseworthiness** of God proclaimed "they will glorify Your name" (86:9c)	
86:11–13	**Praise** of God promised "I will glorify Your name" (86:12b)	
86:14–17	**Plea 2**	
	86:14	*Plea about enemies* "arrogant ones"; "violent ones"
	86:15–16	*Plea to God* "abundant in lovingkindness" (86:15b) "be gracious to me" (86:16a) "Your servant" (86:16b); "deliver" (86:16c)
	86:17	*Plea about enemies* "those who hate me"

The driving motif of the psalm is that of the Yahweh–servant relationship—"Lord" (×7: 86:3a, 4b, 5a, 8a, 9b, 12a, 15a) and "Your servant" (×3: 86:2b, 4a, 16b; also "son of Your handmaid," 86:16c). Equally significantly, the supplicant's "soul" is mentioned a number of times, underscoring the neediness of the one praying (86:2a, 4a, 4b, 13b, 14b). "The psalm thus works within the framework of the relationship of mutual 'commitment' between a master and a servant."[5] This theme is reinforced in the כִּי (*ki*)-clauses employed throughout the psalm, emphasizing the supplicant's commitment despite his distress and God's graciousness in rendering aid: "for" in 86:1b, 2a, 3b, 4b, 5a, 7b, 10a, 13a, 17c.[6] Also there is an unusually high frequency of the pronoun "You [אַתָּה, *'attah*]" addressing God (86:2b, 5a, 10a, 10b, 15a, 17c), as well as that of the second-person masculine suffix ךָ-, *-ka* (more than twenty instances).[7] It is therefore appropriate that Psalm 86 is characterized by a large number of imperative petitions—fifteen of them.[8]

---

5. Goldingay, *Psalms*, 2:619.

6. Thus, the last verse of each of the four sections contains such a clause (86:7b, 10a, 13a, 17c).

7. In "*Your*" (86:1a, 2bα, 8b, 9b, 9c, 11a, 11b, 11c, 12b, 13a, 16bα, 16bβ, 16c), "in *You*" (86:2bβ), "to *You*" (86:4b, 5b, 7a), "like *You*" (86:8a), "*You* alone" (86:10b), "I will give *You* thanks" (86:12a), and "set *You*" (86:14c).

8. In 86:1aα, 1aβ, 2a, 2b, 3a, 4a, 6a, 6b, 11a, 11c, 16aα, 16aβ, 16b, 16c, 17a.

PSALM 86:1–17

Theological Focus

The expectation of God's people that God will liberate them from their dire distress is grounded in their relationship as servants to this God, their master who, in his person and in his accomplishment of their past deliverance, is unique and incomparable, thus motivating them to praise him and to walk in his way uncompromisingly.

Commentary

Plea 1 (86:1–7)

Striking is the assonance of five consecutive Hebrew words in 86:1, employing six instances of נ:

... אָזְנְךָ עֲנֵנִי כִּי־עָנִי וְאֶבְיוֹן אָנִי

... 'aznka 'aneni ki-'ani w'evyon 'ani

"... Your ear, answer me, for I am afflicted and needy"

The echoing of the consonant accentuates the plea and the call for Yahweh to hear the supplicant. The request for hearing and answering is restated twice more in the first section (86:6, 7). We are not told what exactly the situation was that prompted these pleas, except that the psalmist was afflicted and needy (86:1b) and that the circumstances were distressing (86:7a)—his very life was being threatened (86:2a; also 86:14b).[9] (But an equally dire situation had occurred before and God had delivered him then [86:13b].)

The anxious poet describes himself as "a devout one [חָסִיד, chasid]" (86:2a), deserving the "lovingkindness [חֶסֶד, chesed]" (86:5b; also see 86:13a, 15b) of the one he confesses twice in this section as his deity with the second-person pronoun, "You [אַתָּה]" (86:2b, 5a).[10] Indeed, his "cry" lasts "all" the day (86:3b), but he is confident of God's grace to "all" who "cry" out to him (86:5b). Notice also that אֵלֶיךָ, 'eleka, is found thrice in three verses: "in You" (86:2b); and "to You" (86:3b, 4b). The pathos is palpable!

The psalmist's reasons for appealing to God, marked by the כִּי־clauses, occupy only part of 86:1, 2, 3, and 4, but in 86:5 the כִּי־clause takes over the whole verse, with its credal formula, alluding to Exod 34:6–9. This is the basis of the supplicant's plea.

Praiseworthiness Proclaimed; Praise Promised (86:8–10, 11–13)

The pleas turn to the praiseworthiness of God and praise is promised him in the central section of the psalm (Ps 86:8–13). God's praiseworthiness is first proclaimed (86:8–10), with a view to

---

9. The nebulous character of the agony lends the psalm an omnitemporal utility.

10. "For to you" also occurs twice, in 86:3b, 4b. Also see 86:10ab, 12a, 15a, 17c for "You [אַתָּה]" and "God"/"Yahweh" juxtaposed.

the eschaton when all peoples will glorify this deity who alone is worthy of worship. This, the psalmist knows, is the sure end of all things in the future, and that puts into perspective his present sufferings. He does not simply describe God but addresses "who Yhwh is over against other gods, the other masters that this servant might call on but does not: because Yhwh is not merely unique in the way that everyone is unique but is uniquely powerful in deeds," and able to deliver.[11] Why would the psalmist want to call upon any other deity? The center of the structure of 86:8 makes the contrast stark between other "gods" and the one true "Lord":

> אֵין־כָּמוֹךָ, 'en-kamoka
> "There is no one like you
> בָאֱלֹהִים, ba'elohim
> among the gods,
> אֲדֹנָי, 'adonay
> Lord,
> וְאֵין כְּמַעֲשֶׂיךָ, w'en kma'aseka
> and there is nothing like Your doings."

There is also a structural balance in 86:8–10 between the uniqueness of God's person and that of his doings:

86:8a	Uniqueness of God's person ("gods," אֱלֹהִים, 'elohim)	
86:8b	Uniqueness of God's "doings" (עשׂה, 'sh)	
86:9	**God's praiseworthiness** ("made," עשׂה)	
86:10a	Uniqueness of God's "doing" (עשׂה)	
86:10b	Uniqueness of God's person ("God," אֱלֹהִים)	

There is no other entity that one may call upon for help in times of distress. The unusually frequent—six—instances of אַתָּה, "You" (noted earlier), sprinkled through the psalm, underscores this even further, and even provides the "storying" of the whole psalm:[12]

86:2b	"*You* are my God"	Help anticipated—future
86:5a	"For *You*, Lord"	Creedal formula
86:10a	"For *You* are great"	God's uniqueness
86:10b	"*You* ... alone are God"	God's uniqueness
86:15a	"But *You* Lord"	Creedal formula
86:17c	"For *You*, Yahweh"	Help accomplished—past

Thus, it comes as no surprise that the psalmist promises praise to this unique deity (86:11–13). "If there were lots of gods, it might be reasonable to spread one's reverence—one's worship and prayers—around them. But if Yhwh is the only real God, as Yhwh's deeds [and essence] indicate, then the suppliant's heart cannot be divided in that way. Yhwh's singleness needs to

---

11. Goldingay, *Psalms*, 2:623.
12. From Brueggemann, *Message of the Psalms*, 62.

be matched by an undivided commitment of the person."[13] This incomparable God deserves uncompromising allegiance from his people, as they walk in God's way, taught and guided by him, in his will (86:11). The manifestation of such an engagement with God is the praise of his people (86:12) in return for what God has done in the past (86:13). Nations may "glorify *Your name*" (86:9c), but it will be God's people—those with undivided hearts and undiluted devotion who "fear *Your name*" (86:11c)—who will "glorify *Your name* forever," i.e., in the future (86:12b). It is those with "hearts" such as these (86:11c) who can give thanks to God with all their "hearts" (86:12a). Such an expression of thanksgiving assumes that God will act in this present distress to deliver the supplicant and his cohort just as he has done in the past. "Praise is not just given when God fixes our lives. Praise is also offered in the midst of petitions for help. To reinforce this point, the attributes of God are the ones that Israel has always depended on," through thick and thin.[14] Because "You are *great*" (86:10a) and "Your lovingkindness is *great*" towards his people (86:13a), praise belongs to this infinitely great God, the only one who can deliver his people from all their distresses.

Plea 2 (86:14–17)

The psalmist reverts to his plea at the end of the psalm: God's lovingkindness was great "toward me [עָלַי, *'alay*]" (86:13a), but right now enemies are rising "against me" [עָלָי] (86:14).

Surely the God who rescued "my soul" in the past (86:13b; that historical aid is explicitly acknowledged in 86:17c) can, and ought to, deliver him now, when enemies are seeking "my soul" (86:14b). The parallels between *Plea 1* (86:1–7) and *Plea 2* (86:14–17) were noted earlier. All that to say the danger is still present, with a degree of aggression that was not manifest earlier (86:14).

Once again, as in 86:5, the psalmist seeks recourse to the creedal formula of Exod 34:6 in Ps 86:15, this time explicitly naming God as "merciful and gracious, slow to anger and abundant in lovingkindness and truth." The one who had submitted "supplications [for grace] [תַּחֲנוּן, *tachanun*]" (86:6b) expects God, the "gracious [חַנּוּן, *channun*]" one (86:15a), to "be gracious [חָנֵּ, *chnn*]" and deliver him (86:16a; also see 86:3a). The God whom the psalmist had acknowledged as "good" (86:5a) is now asked to rescue him, a sign, demonstration, of "good" (86:17a).[15]

The self-attestation of "son of Your handmaid," and not just "Your servant" (86:16bc), indicates how obliged the divine master ought to be to this lowliest member of his family. "The relationship [of master to servant] is not a merely contractual one, like those in modern employment. It makes demands on the servant and takes away from the servant's freedom, but it also makes demands on the master and takes away from the master's freedom. It gives the servant something to appeal to."[16] This God is unique, and unique are also his "doings [מַעֲשֶׂה, *ma'aseh*]" (86:8b)—he is the one who "made [עשׂה]" all the nations (86:9a), the one "doing [עשׂה]" wonders (86:10a). Surely, it is incumbent upon this deity to "do [עשׂה]" good to his people (86:17a). And yes, one day in the future the nations will worship before God's "face" (noun; 86:9b), but the need of the present is that God "face" his distressed people

---

13. Goldingay, *Psalms*, 2:625.
14. deClaissé-Walford et al., *Book of Psalms*, 663.
15. Perhaps the "sign" includes the "wonders" characterizing God's doings (86:10a).
16. Goldingay, *Psalms*, 2:630.

(verb; 86:16a) and deliver them, just as he had succored them in the past (86:17c). Thus, this psalm also ends without resolution, but if the past is any guide, the future with such a unique deity, their Lord, is, indeed, rosy for his people, his servants!

Sermon Map

I. Uniqueness of God's Proprietorship
   Sovereign (86:3a, 4b, 5a, 8a, 9b, 12a, 15a)
   Servant (86:2b, 4a, 16b, 16c)
   Suffering (86:1, 2a, 3b, 4b–7, 14, 16–17b)
   Move-to-relevance: Our lack of confidence in distress

II. Uniqueness of God's Person and Performances
   What God has done in the past (86:8–10, 13, 15, 17c)
   What his people will do in the future (86:11–12)
   Move-to-relevance: Our trust in God

III. *Servants of the Sovereign, Suffer, but Securely!*
   Confidence in their Master in times of suffering

PSALM 87:1–7

Psalm of Reorientation

New Citizens in the City of God

THIS IS A REMARKABLE psalm, looking far ahead into the future, and describing Yahweh's relationship, not with Israel, but with Gentiles, and that in terms hitherto unseen. The focus is clearly on Zion, the city of God, mention of which is made in every verse.[1] Tate thinks the location of this psalm after Psalm 86 makes it an amplification of 86:9, where all nations are said to "come" and worship Yahweh and glorify his name. Presumably their "coming" is to Zion, as Psalm 87 is at pains to assert. "The psalm expresses the expectation that Zion will become the 'mother city' in a universal worship of Yahweh."[2] Thus, while quite exclusive—Zion is *the* capital and *the* center of worship—it is astonishingly inclusive—all species of nations come there to worship Yahweh. "It is simultaneously one of the most particularist and one of the most universalist of psalms. It enthuses about Zion more dramatically than any other psalm, yet this celebration focuses on the fact that Zion belongs not just to Israel but also to the world."[3]

Translation

87:1   That which He founded is in the holy mountains—
87:2   Yahweh is loving the gates of Zion
       more than all the abodes of Jacob.
87:3   Glorifying things are being spoken of you, city of God.
87:4   "I will mention Rahab and Babylon among the ones who acknowledge Me;
       behold, Philistia and Tyre with Cush:
       'This one was born there.'"

---

1. "That which He founded" (87:1); "Zion" (87:2a, 5a); "city of God" (87:3); "there" (87:4c, 6b); "her" (87:5b, 5c); "the exalted one" (87:5c); "you" (87:7b).

2. Tate, *Psalms 51–100*, 389. For similar sentiments, see Isa 2:2 (= Mic 4:1); Isa 19:23–25; 45:22–23; 56:6–7; Zech 2:10–11; 14:16–19; Mal 1:11; and, of course, Rev 14:1–5; 7:9. The notion of Zion as a "mother" (Isa 49:19–25; 54:1; 66:7–8) comports with the mentions of birth in this psalm (Ps 87:4c, 5b, 6b).

3. Goldingay, *Psalms*, 2:632.

87:5 And to Zion it will be said,
"This person and this person were born in her";
and He—He will establish her the exalted one.

87:6 Yahweh—He will record when He registers the peoples,
"This one was born there."

87:7 And those singing, those piping, alike [will say]:
"All my springs are in you."

Structure

Based on the actants with speaking parts, a chiastic structure is clearly visible for Psalm 87, centering upon the trifold *Birth Proclamations* announcing the citizenship of the various nations in the city of God, and organized by who is uttering the address/birth proclamation:

87:1–2	Introduction	
87:3	Address to Zion: "of you [בָּךְ, *bak*]"	By Psalmist
87:4	Birth proclamation 1: "there"	**By Yahweh**
87:5	Birth proclamation 2: "in her [בָּהּ, *bah*]"	By All
87:6	Birth proclamation 3: "there"	**By Yahweh**
87:7	Address to Zion: "in you [בָּךְ]"	By Peoples

Theological Focus

God's people rejoice in the grand plan of God to incorporate, by divine fiat, all nations of the world into his divine kingdom—centered in his capital, the fulcrum of his operations in the eschaton, Zion—an act that will also cause those new citizens to rejoice.

Commentary

Introduction (87:1–2)

Interestingly enough, יְסוּדָתוֹ, *ysudato*, "that which He founded" (or "His foundation"; 87:1) is feminine, though the noun יְסוֹד, *ysod*, is masculine elsewhere.[4] The feminine gender here likely

---

4. See Exod 29:12; Lev 4:7, 18, 25, 30, 34; Ezek 13:14; 30:4; etc. The plural "mountains" (87:1a) is likely a plural of majesty—a "honorific plural" (deClaissé-Walford et al., *Book of Psalms*, 664n4). Or "perhaps Zion stands among a much broader range of imaginary mountains belonging to Yhwh, which the actual mountains around Jerusalem symbolize . . . the holy mountains are the holy land as a whole, at the center of which Zion is founded" (Goldingay, *Psalms*, 2:634). Indeed, there are a number of plural nouns in Psalm 87:

points to the referent being Zion, the "daughter" of God (see 9:14).⁵ In any case, God lays claim to Zion, the city he founded. Not only does he own it, he loves what he owns—especially its gates, the means of access of the people of God to their deity. "God loves Jerusalem; indeed, Zion is His dear 'daughter.' But God has an even greater love for Zion's gates, because the gates allow people to come near to Him in holy worship."⁶ Clearly, it is the fellowship of his people that he loves, symbolized by the gates of the city. For, as the psalm makes clear later, it is through these beloved gates that the whole world will stream to worship God.

Address to Zion 1 (Psalmist: 87:3)

Of this city, "glorifying [or 'glorious'] things" are spoken (87:3; a participle from כבד, *kvd*, "glory"⁷), and that opens up the rest of the psalm that is entirely made up of quotations—those "glorifying" things spoken: by God (87:4), by one and all (87:5bc⁸), by God again (87:6b), and by worship celebrants (87:7b; see below). Needless to say, in the glorifying of the city, it is God, the founder, owner, and lover of the city, who is actually being glorified.⁹ As we shall discover, "the glorious things that are spoken about Zion have to do precisely with her becoming a multiracial city as the old barriers are broken down. Zion was the place God chose to found the city he loved where he would dwell with his people. In time Zion came to designate not simply a geographical location, but the community of the redeemed, the city of God"—the gathering of *all* the people of God from *all* spaces and *all* time.¹⁰

Birth Proclamation 1 (Yahweh: 87:4)

And then comes a birth proclamation from the mouth of God. The stunning development here is who exactly has birthright in Zion, the "city of God." The announcement God makes is, of all things, a roll call of Israel's enemies! "Rahab" indicates Egypt (Isa 30:7), a mortal foe of God's people; Babylon was synonymous with idolatry (Rev 17:1–6); the others are no better, with Cush (likely Sudan¹¹) being the farthest nation in the known world of the day. "The enumeration of the five names is not meant to be taken as exclusive. Rather, the whole earth is in view, since Zion is proclaimed as its midpoint ('navel'). The names that are mentioned mark the four points of the

---

"mountains" (87:1a), "gates" (87:2a), "abodes" (87:2b), "peoples" (87:6a), "those singing" and "those piping" (87:7a), and "springs" (87:7b). And every one of them is related to God and his worship!

5. Also see Isa 1:8; 10:32; 16:1; Jer 4:31; 6:2; etc. On the other hand, the nation of Israel is the "son" of God (Exod 4:22).

6. Allen, Ronald B., "Psalm 87," 135.

7. These are therefore utterances that glorify the city of God.

8. I see 87:5 as an axiomatic or proverbial statement commonly uttered by everyone.

9. The verb following the plural participle translated "glorifying things" is another participle, but it is singular: "Glorifying things *is* being spoken of you" (87:3). That reflects the unified singularity of the various utterances made by the various participants in this psalm: all that is said is God-related, God-directed, God-glorifying, with all humanity speaking with one voice.

10. Jones, "Multiracial City," 68. See also Gal 4:26; Eph 2:13–14, 19–21; Heb 12:22–23. Of note, in relation to the Labor & Delivery language, Ps 87:5 LXX has μήτηρ Σιων, *mētēr Siōn*, "Mother Zion."

11. The LXX has Αἰθιόπων, *Aithiopōn* = "burnt faces," i.e., the melanin-rich inhabitants of faraway African lands (yet another dermatological factoid in Scripture!).

compass: west (Egypt), east (Babylon), north (Philistia and Tyre) and south (Cush)."[12] Goldingay notes that there are no European peoples mentioned in Ps 87:4, but an African nation is: "The psalm offers a promise of an ethnically diverse church."[13] A grand vision!

And it is these variegated peoples, currently foes of his people, that God chooses to "mention" in his *Birth Proclamation 1* (87:4a).[14] And what exactly does he "mention"? "This one was born there," in Zion (87:4c). That is to say, by the power vested in him by virtue of his founding and owning and loving authority, God declares in a unilateral diktat that even these adversarial peoples of the world are citizens of his kingdom with all the rights and privileges appertaining thereunto! How or when this will happen is not the concern of the psalm which simply asserts the event's certainty.[15] "To the consternation of the Israelite immigration officials, 'the sovereign Lord himself is going to cook the documents and record that these aliens, let alone non-patrial passport holders, were born there,' declaring that this will actually add to the nation's security, not detract from it; 'and what aliens they are!'—mostly enemies and oppressors."[16] So now these once-nefarious characters are numbered with "the ones who acknowledge [from ידע, *yd'*] Me" (87:4a), i.e., they are among those with whom Yahweh has a special relationship.[17] The Psalter mentions the different activities undertaken by the nations in relation to Israel, mostly unsavory and insalubrious: making war (2:1–2; 44:11, 14; 46:6), being defeated by God (9:5, 15; 10:16; 33:10), and paying homage to Yahweh (22:27–28; 46:10; 47:8). But to be *born* in Zion, and thus become not a naturalized citizen but one by birth? Extraordinary! That there is no mention of any call to Gentiles to contribute anything to such a metamorphosis suggests a remarkable act of divine grace! "Such poetic vision should neither be diminished by prosaic theological fears of universal salvation nor pressed into the confines of dogma."[18] It is simply a vision of the divine kingdom.[19]

Birth Proclamation 2 (All: 87:5)

Psalm 87:4 (God's utterance) is essentially restated by the psalmist in 87:5ab; it will be widely known, acknowledged, and "said"[20] that these inimical foreigners are now part of the people of God, one with God's own people.

---

12. Zenger, "Psalm 87," 455. For the centrality of Zion in the world, see Ezek 38:12; 1 En. 26:1; Jub. 8:12; b. Sanh. 37A.

13. Goldingay, *Psalms*, 2:641.

14. "I will mention" (87:4a) translates אַזְכִּיר, *'azkir*, that may be understood as "I will cause to remember."

15. Likely in the eschaton.

16. Goldingay, *Psalms*, 2:637, citing Hill, *Prayer, Praise and Politics*, 83.

17. See Pss 9:10; 36:10; 79:6; 91:14.

18. Tate, *Psalms 51–100*, 390.

19. There is probably an allusion here to the political process found in Assyrian culture, wherein a king victorious in battle would, by unilateral declaration, construe his conquered subjects as his own citizens, "counting" them (*manû* in Assyrian; ספר, *sphr*, in Hebrew) as Assyrian. See Liverani, "Ideology of the Assyrian Empire." Also see "*manû* 6," Oppenheim and Reiner, *Assyrian Dictionary*, 224–25. The verb means "to consider a person, a region, or an object as belonging to a specific class, region, or destination." As an example of such a reckoning, the lexicon entry cited notes 4,000 men of the land of Hatti who were assimilated by Tigleth Pileser I: "I took and *considered* them as people of my own land."

20. As was noted earlier, this becomes a truism and a self-evident maxim, uttered by one and all.

87:4 (Yahweh)	87:5ab (All)
"I will mention"	"it will be said"
"Rahab and Babylon" "Philistia and Tyre with Cush" "this one"	"this person" "this person"
"the ones who acknowledge Me"	"Zion"
"was born there"	"were born in her"

With her universal citizenry, Zion will be established by God (the statement in 87:5c is emphatic, with a redundant pronoun) as "the exalted one [עֶלְיוֹן, 'elyon]" (87:5c). The epithet most often refers to God, the "Most High,"[21] but here it talks of the preeminent status of Zion, thus making 87:1 parallel to 87:5c:[22]

87:1	"He founded"	"holy mountains"
87:6c	"He—He will establish"	"exalted one"

Birth Proclamation 3 (Yahweh: 87:6)

It is by a divine recording of the births of the peoples that this citizenship of those who were one's foes became statutory, and that makes Yahweh the מַזְכִּיר, *mazkir*, the "secretary/registrar."[23] And God repeats himself in 87:6b (see 87:4b). All that to say, this is official! So the resulting high status of the city of God is the personal work of God himself, emphasized by the fronted mention of "Yahweh" in 87:6a, in addition to the third-person suffix, "He," with the verb "will record": "Yahweh—He will record . . . ." This parallels the equally emphatic "He—He will establish . . ." (87:5c; noted above). Yes, the records have been altered, legislation has been enacted, and codification is complete: there are now (or will be, one day) new citizens in the city of God!

Address to Zion 2 (Peoples: 87:7)

The outcome is celebration involving singers and pipers (87:7). It is very likely that it is the recently Zion-naturalized peoples who are doing the music making, rejoicing in their newly conferred citizenship (by birth, no less). That explains their exclamation that their "springs,"

---

21. See Pss 7:17; 9:2; 18:13; 21:7; 46:4; etc.

22. Goldingay, *Psalms*, 2:638. See also 1 Kgs 9:8 and 2 Chr 7:21 that label the temple as עֶלְיוֹן. Of course, all this actually points to the divine inhabitant of the city (and of the temple) who is—and who alone is—the Most High. It is only the close identification of place and building with deity that render the former pair "exalted."

23. Goldingay, *Psalms*, 2:639. See 2 Sam 8:16; 1 Chr 18:15 for "secretary." The root of מַזְכִּיר was already deployed in Ps 87:4a, "mention [זכר, *zkr*]."

i.e., the source of divine blessing,[24] are in "you," Zion.[25] Ultimately, of course, it is the God who founded Zion who is being praised for the incorporation of all peoples into his glorious kingdom. That is undoubtedly cause for jubilation!

And with that, the psalm comes full circle, from holy "mountains" in 87:1 to divine "springs" in 87:7. It is all God's founding and all God's doing, as he introduces the vast spread of humanity into his divine kingdom. Unfortunately, these currently non-believing nations are not attending to this psalm which, read and preached in this dispensation, is for the people of God, reminding and encouraging them of God's grand ecumenical and cosmopolitan plan for Zion and, indeed, for the world—even for their enemies. The church is "constitutionally inclined to forget that God's purpose is to make all nations its citizens and so becomes gloomy and closed in on itself. The psalm thus sets God's vision before it."[26] A grand vision, indeed.

Sermon Map

I. Capital

God's grand plan for Zion (87:1–3)

Move-to-relevance: Our failure to see God's long-term plans

II. Citizenship

God's unilateral choice of peoples for his kingdom (87:4–6)

Move-to-relevance: Our own choice exemplifying God's plan

III. Celebration

God's name exalted for his grand plan (87:7)

IV. *Celebrate Citizenship!*

Specifics on periodic celebratory worship for being part of the chosen

---

24. For "springs" as God's blessing, see Isa 12:3; 41:18; Joel 3:18; for the absence thereof, depicted as dried springs, see Hos 13:15.

25. Both "that which He founded" in 87:1 and "you" in 87:7b are feminine (also note the "her" in 87:5b, 5c [suffixed]), indicating Zion. Also, as mentioned earlier, the parallels, "of you [בָּךְ, *bak*]" in 87:3 and "in you [בָּךְ]" in 87:7b, point to Zion as the feminine referent in the latter.

26. Goldingay, *Psalms*, 2:641. Needless to say, this is not a universalist free ticket that God is offering; rather, this psalm asserts that people from "every tribe and tongue and people and nation" will come to God (by grace, through faith, in Christ) one day, making them one with the rest of God's people. However, though this clarification may be worth making briefly in a sermon, it is not the thrust of this psalm. Neither does this text eliminate nuances of difference between the eschatological futures for believing Israel and for believing Gentiles. But all are considered together here, and in the rest of the Psalter, and often elsewhere in the OT, as a future, singular "people of God."

PSALM 88:1–18

Psalm of Disorientation

Darkness and Desperation

PSALMS 88 AND 89 conclude Book III of the Psalter and are considered "the darkest place in the whole book of Psalms. Both are prayers for help, and both end without resolution."[1] Psalm 88 is the lament of an individual abandoned by God, but lacking the usual ingredients—foes, guilt, promise to praise, and declaration of trust. It is, instead, a monologue addressed to God, but which, to the very end, is totally terrifying, goes completely unanswered, and remains utterly hopeless. The psalm is mostly about God's actions against the psalmist: 88:5c, 5d, 7a, 7b, 8a, 8b, 14a, 14b, 15b, 16a, 16b, 17a, 17b, 18a. And the psalmist's goal seems simply to get God to hear him: 88:1, 2, 9bc, 13. A number of descriptive locations, all relating to death, point to the dire situation of the sufferer: "Sheol" (88:3b); "pit" (88:4a); "tomb" (88:5b, 11a); "lowest pit" (88:6a); "darkness" (88:6b, 18b); "depths" (88:6b; "Abaddon" (88:11b); "dark places" (88:12a); and "land of oblivion" (88:12b). There are also "the dead" and "the departed spirits" populating this psalm (88:10). But the nature of this unrelieved distress and agony is unspecified, promoting its utility by God's people in many circumstances.

Translation

88:1 Yahweh, the God of my deliverance,
   [by] day I have wailed, by night before You.
88:2 May it come to Your face—my prayer;
   incline Your ear to my lament.
88:3 For it has been sated with troubles—my soul,
   and my life to Sheol has arrived.
88:4 I am considered with those who go down to the pit;
   I have become like a [mighty] one without strength,

---

1. deClaissé-Walford et al., *Book of Psalms*, 668. Perhaps an indication of its importance in history, Psalm 88 also has the longest superscription of any psalm (untranslated here).

88:5 among the dead, adrift,
> like the slain lying in the tomb,
whom You have not remembered any more;
> and they—from Your hand they have been cut off.

88:6 You have put me in the lowest pit,
> in darkness, in the depths.

88:7 Upon me Your wrath has landed,
> and with all Your waves You have afflicted [me].

88:8 You have distanced those who know me from me;
> You have made me abominable to them;
> [I am] imprisoned and I cannot go out.

88:9 My eye, it has languished from affliction.
I have called to You, Yahweh, all day;
> I have spread out my palms to You.

88:10 Will You for the dead perform wonders?
> Will the departed spirits rise to give You thanks?

88:11 Will it be recounted in the tomb—Your lovingkindness,
> Your faithfulness in Abaddon?

88:12 Will it be made known in the dark places—Your wonders,
> and Your righteousness in the land of oblivion?

88:13 And I, to You, Yahweh—I have cried for help,
> and in the morning my prayer comes to confront You.

88:14 Why, Yahweh, do You reject my soul,
> [and] hide Your face from me?

88:15 Afflicted I [was] and dying from my youth;
> I have borne Your terrors; I am powerless.

88:16 It has passed over me—Your burning anger,
> Your horrors have destroyed me.

88:17 They have surrounded me like water all day;
> they have encompassed around me altogether.

88:18 You have distanced from me the one who loves me and my neighbor,
> those who know me ... darkness ...

Structure

Three stanzas are clearly discernible in Psalm 88, each with a petition and a plaint:[2]

>   *STANZA 1 (88:1–9a)*
>   **Petition 1 (88:1–2)**
>
>   Protagonists: "Yahweh" (first word; 88:1a)
>   Psalmist (subject in second colon; 88:1b)
>   *Vocal*: "wailed," "prayer," "lament" (88:1b, 2a, 2b)
>   *Physical*: "come to Your face," "incline Your ear" (88:2)
>   *Temporal*: "day," "night" (88:1b)
>
>   **Plaint 1 (88:3–9a)**
>
>   *STANZA 2 (88:9b–12)*
>   **Petition 2 (88:9bc)**
>
>   Protagonists: "Yahweh" (second word; 88:9b)
>   Psalmist (subject in first colon; 88:9b)
>   *Vocal*: "called" (88:9b)
>   *Physical*: "spread out my palms to You" (88:9c)
>   *Temporal*: "all day" (88:9b)
>
>   **Plaint 2 (88:10–12)**
>
>   *STANZA 3 (88:13–18)*
>   **Petition 3 (88:13)**
>
>   Protagonists: "Yahweh" (third word; 88:13a)
>   Psalmist (emphatic subject, "I"; 88:13a)
>   *Vocal*: "cried for help," "prayer"
>   *Physical*: "comes to confront You"
>   *Temporal*: "morning" (88:13b)
>
>   **Plaint 3 (88:14–18)**

The petitions contain similar elements (vocal, physical, and temporal), but one sees a progressive discrepancy between them, depicting a progressively worsening situation from *Stanza 1* to *Stanza 3*. The syntactical location of the protagonists, Yahweh and the psalmist, change from the first petition to the third, both in position and in emphasis. The mention of "Yahweh" goes from the first word of the first petition (88:1a), to the second word of the second petition (88:9b), to the third word of the third petition (88:13a), whereas the psalmist moves from being the subject of the second colon in the first petition (88:1b), to the subject of the first colon in the second petition (88:9b), to the emphatic subject, "I," of the first colon in the third petition (88:13a). It is as if the very structure of the psalm is weeping in sympathy with the supplicant, God gradually becoming distant, and the psalmist increasingly becoming desperate, as the situation deteriorates with each stanza.

---

2. Modified from Maré, "Facing the Deepest Darkness," 178–80.

Theological Focus

> In times of utter devastation and abject distress, when darkness overwhelms and deity seemingly abandons, God's people continue to look to him for deliverance, never relenting, but always tenacious, in their faith and in their prayer.

Commentary

Stanza 1 (88:1–9a)

The petition in this stanza takes up two verses, 88:1–2. After invoking Yahweh in the entirety of the first colon (88:1a), the second colon displays the psalmist's wailing—he is hemmed in by "day" on one side and "night" on the other (88:1b); the wailing just does not stop. And God seems to be distant, present only at either end of the verse (88:1) and textually separated from the psalmist (by "day" and "night").

> "Yahweh, the God of my deliverance,
> [by] day
> **I have wailed,**
> by night
> before You."

That he addresses Yahweh as the "God of my deliverance" (88:1a) indicates continuing faith in deity. Will that faith prove to be misplaced? While there are petition sections in each stanza, 88:2 contains the only explicit pleas in the psalm, that God would listen. The psalmist is "before You" (88:1b), but apparently his prayer has not come "to Your face" (88:2a). How is that possible? Has deity turned his face away? Later we discover that the psalmist assumes that that is indeed the case: God *has* hidden his "face" (88:13–14).

88:2aα	"May it come to *Your face*"
88:2aβ	"my prayer"
88:13b	"my prayer"
88:14	"Why … do You … hide *Your face*"

Then, in 88:3, we see a disconsolate wrapping of the psalmist's "soul" and "life" in the center, with "troubles" and "Sheol" on either side (see below).[3]

---

3. In the midst of his disaster, the psalmist hasn't abandoned his skillful rhetoric!

"It has been sated	Verb (third person)
with troubles—	Preposition + noun
my soul,	Noun + first-person suffix
and my life	Noun + first-person suffix
to Sheol	Preposition + noun
has arrived."	Verb (third person)

"One can ... picture the suppliant as good as dead, tottering at the gates of Sheol, awaiting the moment when breath finally leaves the body and it is time to enter Sheol."[4] Ironically, the sufferer is not "sated" with the goodness of God's house (65:4), but with the horrors of death. There is no room for joy: he is saturated with adversity.[5] Indeed, the desperate petitioner is cut free ("adrift": חָפְשִׁי, *chaphshi*, literally means "freed"; 88:5a), not to relief but to an ominous termination of life—i.e., released into the underworld (88:4–5)![6]

And all this, caused by God, according to the psalmist: five times (88:6, 7a, 7b, 8a, 8b) God is accused of putting the supplicant in this dreadful situation, near death, subject to divine wrath, and distanced from all. So much so, "my soul" sated with calamity (88:3a) is "my soul" rejected by God (88:14a). What could be worse?[7]

Stanza 2 (88:9b–12)

This stanza, too, commences with a petition (88:9bc); the similarities with the other petitions in the psalm were noted above. But this petition, unlike in other stanzas, is followed by a sequence of questions put to Yahweh, each a variation on the same theme: "The dead will not further your reputation, God!" The psalmist is hoping that at least this will motivate God into delivering him. So, while the dead are cut off from God's "hand" (88:5d), the psalmist continues to raise his "palms" to God (88:9c), an attempt to rejoin the severed upper extremities. The questions in 88:11 and 88:12 are structured in parallel:

88:11	**88:12**
"Will it be recounted	"Will it be made known
in [בְּ, *b*] the tomb—	in [בְּ] the dark places—
Your lovingkindness,	Your wonders,
Your faithfulness	and Your righteousness
in [בְּ] Abaddon?"	in [בְּ] the land of oblivion?"

---

4. Goldingay, *Psalms*, 2:648.
5. Tate, *Psalms 51–100*, 402.
6. "One" in 88:4b is גֶּבֶר, *gever*, likely with the connotation of "strong man," thus "[mighty] one," as in 127:5; 128:4.
7. The languishing of the eye (88:9a)—normally an organ indicating the life and vigor of a person—stands for the afflicted state of the sufferer. Notice the wordplay: "my eye" is עֵינִי, *'eni*, and "affliction" is עֳנִי, *'oni*: his eye is now his affliction—gone is his health!

After the verb as a question in each verse, we have in chiastic sequence a location with the preposition בְּ, two divine attributes (each with a masculine singular suffix), and another location with the preposition בְּ. The location in every case indicates the domain of the dead: "tomb," "Abaddon,"[8] "dark places," "land of oblivion." The parallelism furthers the sense of deathly despondence, especially since each of the four central locations is starkly juxtaposed to four divine attributes: "Your lovingkindness," "Your faithfulness," "Your wonders," "Your righteousness"—all of which God does not seem to be extending to the psalmist![9]

Stanza 3 (88:13–18)

The petition in the third stanza (88:13) now reaches a peak, with the emphatic "I [אֲנִי, 'ani]" fronting the line. Indeed, this time the petitioner's prayer "confronts" God (88:13b).[10] He had wailed to the God of "my deliverance [יְשׁוּעָתִי, yshu'ati]" in 88:1a; now "I have cried for help [שִׁוַּעְתִּי, shiwwa'ti]" in 88:13a. Notice that "in the tomb" in 88:11a is בַּקֶּבֶר, baqqever, and "in the morning" in 88:13b is בַבֹּקֶר, vabboqer, the wordplay suggesting that while he is expectantly praying in the daylight hours, it seems utterly bleak and dark and hopeless.

This is a prelude to another detailing of the psalmist's woes—spurned by God, crushed by his wrath, annihilated by his terrors.[11] And there follows a further interrogation of God in 88:14 (as in 88:10–12), this time with an accusatory "Why?" Outside of the petitions in each of the three stanzas, 88:14 has the only other instance of "Yahweh" in the psalm—clearly, the situation is tense.[12] Another wordplay with "afflicted [עָנִי, 'ani]" and "I [אֲנִי, 'ani]" (88:15a) further identifies the person of the psalmist with his wretched misery and utter woe. In a mixing of metaphors, the psalmist is besieged both by fire ("Your burning anger," 88:16a) and by flood ("Your horrors . . . have surrounded me like water," 88:16b–17a). "All day" he calls (88:9b), but "all day" he is drowning (88:17a; and burning, 88:16a) in the terrors from the hand of God—"You have . . ." (88:18a). There is no letup of the calamity that has befallen him. And he repeats the accusation that God had "distanced" him from loved ones (88:8a, 18), though with a significant expansion and intensification (in italics, below).

---

8. "Abaddon [אֲבַדּוֹן, 'avaddon]" is another label for Sheol, derived from אָבַד, 'avad, "to perish/die." Sheol and Abaddon are used in parallel in Prov 15:11.

9. These four attributes, invisible to the sufferer, are in stark contrast to "Your wrath" and "Your waves" in 88:7, and "Your burning anger" and "Your horrors" in 88:16, all of which are agonizingly and intensely experienced.

10. The verb קדם, qdm, can also mean "meet," but "confront" is a common connotation (see 17:13; 18:5, 18).

11. Modified from Tate, *Psalms 51–100*, 402.

12. And all four instances are in the vocative in this psalm.

88:8a
"You have distanced
those who know me
from me"

88:18
"You have distanced
from me
the one who loves me
and my neighbor,
those who know me"

It was bad enough to be alienated from acquaintances (88:8a), but now even from near and dear, kith and kin? Both deity and humanity have abandoned the psalmist to "darkness..." (88:18b).

And so the psalm ends, with its last word an elliptical utterance, but catastrophic in its anguish: "darkness." What began with the hope of "deliverance" (88:1a) has culminated in the hopelessness of "darkness." The supplicant is utterly ruined, devastated and disconsolate! Needless to add, darkness and devastation are not entirely rare in a life of human frailty, lived on this side of eternity. They often overwhelm and drown the suffering people of God, with death looming on every side.[13]

But there are brighter notes in this otherwise bleak lament, though more implied than explicit: the supplicant is *still* talking to God (the entire psalm), *still* relating to God (88:1–2, 9bc, 13), *still* desiring to praise him (88:10–12), and *still* recognizing God's attributes (88:11–12). In other words, despite his precarious situation, he never ceases to have faith, he never stops praying![14] Never. Ever.

Sermon Map

I. Distress and Death
   The psalmist's dire situation (88:3–5, 9a)
   Move-to-relevance: Our times of utter woe

II. Deity and Distance
   God's responsibility (88:6–8, 14–18)
   Move-to-relevance: The seeming distance of God in our lives

III. *Tenaciously Trust When Tormented!*
   Ceaseless prayer (88:1–2, 9b–13)
   Specifics on persistently praying in faith

---

13. If one wonders why this psalm (and others like this) are included in the Psalter, one must also ask: How else could such traumatic cataclysms and excruciating agonies, not at all rare in the broken lives lived by broken people in a broken world, be expressed with the same pathos, potency, and power as do these utterances of dirge and lament?

14. And "fortunately, the psalm does not have to be read alone. The reader knows that the very next psalm in the present Psalter, though a lament, opens with the words חסדי יהוה, *chsdy yhwh*, 'Yahweh's deeds of loyal-love' ['lovingkindness'] and the speaker declares a desire to sing on and on about the merciful deeds and faithfulness of Yahweh. Praise is not far away from Ps 88" (Tate, *Psalms 51–100*, 404).

PSALM 89:1–52

Psalm of Disorientation

Faith in God's Faithfulness in Distressing Times

THIS PSALM, WITH FIFTY-TWO verses, is the third-longest psalm in the book (after Psalms 119 and 78). As one commences reading, one might suspect that the darkness of Psalm 88 has now dissipated into light in Psalm 89, but unfortunately that is not the case. This composition, too, accuses of God of failing the supplicant. But it is unique in that it reverses the order of the standard scheme in such laments: praise and a related promise section precede a litany of protests and petition: God has abandoned his leader (and, thereby, his people). Like the preceding psalm, this one, too, ends without any resolution.

Translation

89:1 Of the lovingkindness of Yahweh I will sing forever;
 [from] generation to generation I will make known
 Your faithfulness with my mouth.
89:2 For I said, "Forever lovingkindness—it will be built up;
 the heavens—You will establish Your faithfulness in them."
89:3 [God:] "I have made a covenant with My chosen;
 I have sworn to David My servant:
89:4 'Unto forever I will establish your seed
 and I will build up your throne from generation to generation.'"
89:5 And the heavens will praise Your wonders, Yahweh;
 Your faithfulness also in the assembly of the holy ones.
89:6 For who in the skies can compare with Yahweh?
 [Who] is like Yahweh among the heavenly beings,
89:7 God, inspiring reverence in the great council of the holy ones,
 and awesome over all those who are surrounding Him?
89:8 Yahweh, God of Armies, who is like You, mighty Yah?
 And Your faithfulness surrounds You.

89:9 You rule the pride of the sea;
           when its waves rise, You—You calm them.
89:10 You—You crushed Rahab like one slain;
           with the arm of Your might You scattered Your enemies.
89:11 To You [belong] the heavens, even to You the earth;
           the world and what fills it, You—You have founded them.
89:12 North and south, You—You have created them;
           Tabor and Hermon: at Your name they cry for joy.
89:13 To You [belongs] an arm with strength;
           Your hand is mighty, Your right hand is exalted.
89:14 Righteousness and justice are the foundation of Your throne;
           lovingkindness and truth meet Your face.
89:15 Blessing [upon] the people who know the joyful shout.
           Yahweh, in the light of Your face they walk.
89:16 In Your name they jubilate all day,
           and by Your righteousness they are exalted.
89:17 For the adornment of their might is You,
           and by Your favor it is exalted—our horn.
89:18 For to Yahweh [belongs] our shield,
           and to the Holy One of Israel [belongs] our king.
89:19 Then You spoke in a vision to Your devout ones,
           and You said, "I granted help unto a strong one;
           I exalted a chosen one from the people.
89:20 I found David My servant;
           with My holy oil I anointed him,
89:21 with whom My hand will be established;
           My arm also will strengthen him.
89:22 The enemy will not extort him,
           and the son of wickedness will not afflict him.
89:23 And before his face I will pound his adversaries,
           and those who hate him I will strike.
89:24 And My faithfulness and My lovingkindness [will be] with him,
           and in My name his horn will be exalted.
89:25 And I will set his hand on the sea,
           and his right hand on the rivers.
89:26 He—He will call Me, 'my Father,
           You [are] my God, and the rock of my deliverance.'
89:27 I also—I shall make him [My] firstborn,
           the most high of the kings of the earth.

89:28 Forever I will keep for him My lovingkindness,
    and My covenant shall be [faithfully] secured for him.
89:29 And I will set his seed for always,
    and his throne like the days of heaven.
89:30 If his sons forsake My law
    and in My judgments they do not walk,
89:31 if My statutes they profane
    and My commandments they do not keep,
89:32 then I will punish with a staff their rebellion,
    and with blows their iniquity.
89:33 But My lovingkindness I will not invalidate from him,
    and I will not deal falsely in My faithfulness.
89:34 I will not profane My covenant,
    and what comes forth from My lips, I will not change.
89:35 Once I have sworn in My holiness;
    if to David I lie . . .
89:36 His seed forever will continue,
    and his throne like the sun before Me.
89:37 Like the moon it will be established forever,
    and the witness in the sky is faithful."
89:38 And You—You have rejected and You have refused,
    You have been enraged at Your anointed.
89:39 You have disavowed the covenant of Your servant;
    You have profaned his crown to the ground.
89:40 You have breached all his walls;
    You have set his strongholds to ruin.
89:41 All who pass by the way plunder him;
    he has become a reproach to his neighbors.
89:42 You have exalted the right hand of his adversaries;
    You have made all his enemies rejoice.
89:43 You also turn back the blade of his sword,
    and You have not made him stand in battle.
89:44 You have made his splendor to cease,
    and his throne to the ground You have cast.
89:45 You have shortened the days of his youth;
    You have clothed shame upon him.
89:46 Until when, Yahweh—will You hide eternally?
    Will Your wrath burn like fire?
89:47 Remember—I—what [is a] lifespan,
    for what emptiness have You created all humanity?

89:48 What person can stay alive and not see death?
    Can he liberate his soul from the hand of Sheol?
89:49 Where are Your former lovingkindnesses, Lord,
    [which] You swore to David in Your faithfulness?
89:50 Remember, Lord, the reproach of Your servants;
    I carry in my bosom all [the reproaches] of many peoples,
89:51 with which Your enemies have reproached, Yahweh,
    with which they have reproached the footsteps of Your anointed.
89:52 Blessed be Yahweh forever.
    Amen and amen.

Structure

The structure of Psalm 89 is fairly straightforward, with "lovingkindness," "faithfulness," and "David" mentioned in every section of the psalm:[1]

Praise (89:1–18)
Praise for Davidic regent (**89:1–4**)
Praise for deity's rule (**89:5–18**)
    "lovingkindness" (89:1a, 2a, 14b)
    "faithfulness" (89:1c, 2b, 5b, 8b)
    "David" (89:3b)

Promise (89:19–37)
Promise for Davidic regent (**89:19–37**)
    "lovingkindness" (89:24a, 28a, 33a; and "devout ones" in 89:19a)
    "faithfulness" (89:24a, 33b); and "secure/is faithful" (89:28b, 37b)
    "David" (89:20a, 35b)

Protest, Petition, and Postscript (89:38–52)
Protest for Davidic regent (**89:38–45**)
Petition for lovingkindness (**89:46–51**)
Postscript (**89:52**)
    "lovingkindness" (89:49a)
    "faithfulness" (89:49b)
    "David" (89:49b)

In sum, the argument is: "You established our king because you are the King [*praise*], and you promised our king ... [*promise*], but ... [*protest*], so would you ... [*petition*]?"

---

1. Elements of the figure are modified from Floyd, "Psalm LXXXIX," 447, 449.

Theological Focus

The proven faithfulness of an incomparable God, the conqueror of chaos and the ruler of all, is extended forever to his people through his king, imbuing them with confidence in his lovingkindness to them despite the direness of their circumstances and the brevity of their lives, and even though human failure may incur divine discipline.

Commentary

Praise (89:1–18)

Praise to the divine King for the Davidic regent commences the psalm. The parallels between 89:1–2 (psalmist's general praise to God for his faithfulness) and 89:3–4 (psalmist's specific praise to God, citing God's faithfulness to the Davidic king and his line) compel the reader to think, at least in this psalm, of the two rulers/dynasties, heavenly and earthly, being closely related: God manifests his "faithfulness" through establishing his leaders for his people:

	89:1–2	89:3–4
"forever"	89:1a, 2a	89:4a
"generation to generation"	89:1b	89:4bβ
"built up"	89:2a	89:4bα
"establish"	89:2b	89:4a

Divine "lovingkindness" is "built up" and divine "faithfulness" is "established" (89:2); in parallel the Davidic "throne" is "built up" and his "seed" is "established" (89:4):

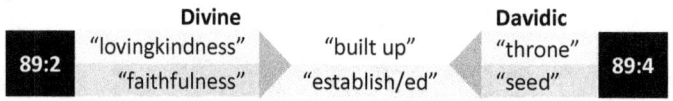

The pair of divine attributes are integrally linked to the pair of kingly elements. Also note the chiastic occurrence of words in 89:1–2aα and 89:2aβ–4 (below). The interweaving of the items is obvious: "forever" God's "lovingkindness" is "built up" (89:1–2a), but that morphs into how deity "forever establishes" and "builds up" (89:4) the Davidic line for his people (below).[2]

---

2. Also, the proclamation of divine faithfulness by the psalmist "generation to generation" (89:1c) becomes a building up of David's throne by God "generation to generation" (89:4b).

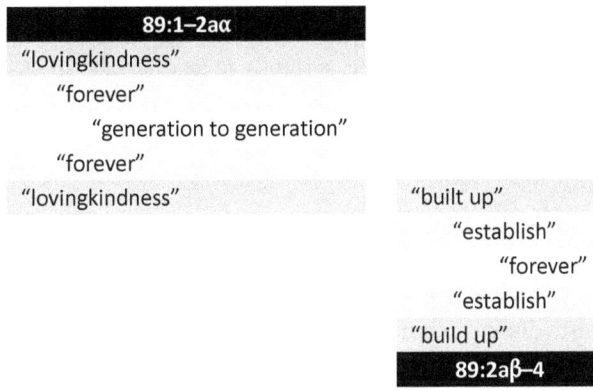

The psalmist is thereby asserting the certainty of God's lovingkindness (his grace) and the security of his faithfulness to his people in providing for them a ruler. Indeed, God's faithfulness is even established *in* the heavens (89:2b), almost as if it were visibly apparent in that realm.³ Surely the stability of the Davidic line should be as stable as the faithfulness of God in the cosmos! So the psalm begins with much confidence in God's building up and establishing the leaders of his people, a confidence grounded upon the stability of the cosmos ruled over by God (89:5–14; "rule" occurs in 89:9a).

This God, inspiring reverence even from members of the heavenly council ("holy ones," "heavenly beings," "great council," and "all those who are surrounding Him"; 89:5–7),⁴ is incomparable. He defeated chaos and created all things (89:8–13), and cares for his creation with "righteousness," "justice," "lovingkindness," and "truth" (89:14). In particular, these attributes signify deity's gracious benevolence towards his people who are rendered blessed and joyous (89:14–18). The dominance of the second person in 89:5–18, where deity's rule is praised,⁵ is striking, occurring thirty-two times.⁶ God is, without a doubt, ruling over all!

To that depiction of divine might, add his "righteousness," "justice," "lovingkindness," and "truth" (89:14), and you have a deity who is both powerful and providential, great and good. No wonder God's devotees rejoice in his care (89:15–18). It is in the divine Person ("Your name") that they exult; it is in God's righteousness that they themselves are exalted (89:16); it is deity and his power that is their might, and it is by divine favor that they have good fortune (89:17).⁷ The mention of the divine "throne" in 89:14a reflects the "throne" of David in 89:4b. There is a strong sense here that the earthly Davidic king is thus a

---

3. No doubt it is, as nature amply demonstrates: in absolute regularity the sun shines, heavenly bodies orbit, rains arrive, and seasons change. Indeed, "lovingkindness" and "faithfulness" occur seven times each in this psalm, a perfection of numbers! (They are paired six times: 89:1, 2, 24a, 33, 49, and in 89:28 where the word translated "secured" comes from the root אמן, *'mn*; "faithfulness" is אֱמוּנָה, *'emunah*, derived from the same root; hence the translation "[faithfully] secured.")

4. "Heavenly beings" in 89:6b is בְנֵי אֵלִים, *bne 'elim*, for which see on 29:1; 82:1.

5. I've chosen 89:5 as the beginning of the subsection on praise for Yahweh's rule: whereas 89:4 has Yahweh speaking in the first person, 89:5 has the psalmist speaking to Yahweh in the second person.

6. As pronominal suffixes (89:1b, 2bβ, 5a, 5b, 8a, 8bα, 10bα, 10bβ, 11aα, 11aβ, 12b, 13a, 13bα, 13bβ, 14a, 14b, 15b, 16a, 16b, 17b); as second-person verbs (89:2bα, 8bβ, 9bβ, 10aβ, 11bβ, 12aβ); and as the pronoun, "You" (89:9a, 9bα, 10aα, 11bα, 12aα, 17a).

7. "Horn" (89:17b) signifies success and strength. And the exaltation of God's people likely also refers to their honor, perhaps in the victory over their foes.

representative of the cosmic divine King: the two appear to be closely associated. In fact, the former belongs to the latter: "to the Holy One of Israel [belongs] our king" (89:18b). This God, who appoints leaders for his people, is rightly to be praised!

Promise (89:19–37)

The King of the cosmos established his representative, the king of his people, making some wide-ranging promises, to which the psalmist draws God's attention, actually citing deity himself. The *Promise* section (89:19–37) is entirely God's direct speech: "You spoke," and "You said" (89:19ab). These utterances of God deal with the Davidic monarchy: promises made to the king (89:21–28), promises made to the king's seed (89:29–33), and promises made to the king's line in perpetuity (89:34–37).

Striking, however, are the parallels between the description of Yahweh's rule (89:5–18) and that of Yahweh's promise to the ruler of his people: what pertains to Yahweh also pertains to his Davidic king. Yahweh is the powerful cosmic ruler (89:5–13; "to You [belong] the heavens, even to You the earth," 89:11a) and David is the powerful earthly one (89:22–27; "the most high of the kings of the earth," 89:27b). Yahweh's mighty extremities, including his "arm," sustain his divine regency (89:13a), and David's reign is also sustained by Yahweh's "arm" (89:21–23; "arm" in 89:21b; "hand" in 89:21a). Yahweh's arm has "strength [גְּבוּרָה, *gvurah*]" (89:13a), and David is the "strong one [גִּבּוֹר, *gibbor*]" (89:19b).

No wonder, then, that the Davidide conquers his foes (89:22–23), just as Yahweh does (89:10). Yahweh subdues the "sea" and the waters of chaos (89:9), and so does David (89:25; "sea" in 89:25a). Yahweh's "hand" is mighty and his "right hand" is exalted (89:13b); this same divine "hand" will also be with the king (89:21a). Indeed it is Yahweh who sets the king's "hand" on the "sea" and his "right hand" on the rivers, overcoming their chaos (89:25).[8] Yahweh's "throne" is *par excellence* (89:14a), and so is the Davidic king's "throne" (89:36; also see 89:4b, 29b). Yahweh's "lovingkindness" and "faithfulness" govern his own rule (89:1a, 1c, 2a, 2b, 5b, 8b, 14b), as well as rule of his king (89:24a). Yahweh is "exalted" (89:13b), and his earthly representative is also "exalted" (89:24b).

The parallels continue. It was the heavenly council that was awestruck by Yahweh (89:7); it is earthly rulers who are stunned by the Davidic king, "the most high of the kings of the earth" (89:27b; and that by the power of God, 89:22–23). Indeed, the similarities between divine and human kingship are so strong here that David is actually labeled עֶלְיוֹן, *'elyon* ("most high," 89:27b), a term usually reserved for Yahweh[9]—82:6 calls Yahweh עֶלְיוֹן, in the context of the heavenly council (the same group that is prominent in 89:6–7). All that to say, "the עליון [*'lywn*]-status of the king is the counterpart of that of Yahweh in the heavenly realm . . . . The cosmic ruling power of God is invested, in considerable measure at least, in the Davidic king."[10]

All this indicates that the dominion of God in creation, in the cosmos, is shared in many aspects with the dominion on earth of God's king. No one may compare with Yahweh (89:6), but David does, it seems! "It is now the Davidic throne that guarantees cosmic

---

8. The "sea" could be the Mediterranean, and the "rivers," the Euphrates and Tigris, but more likely they indicate the chaotic waters, as in 89:9. Of note, "hand" is יָד, *yad*; "right hand" is יָמִין, *yamin*.

9. See 7:17; 9:2; 18:13; 21:7; etc. Twenty-one of the twenty-two instances of the appellation in the Psalter refer to God; the exception is in 89:27, leading us to suspect there is more to the identity of this human ruler than is immediately apparent.

10. Tate, *Psalms 51–100*, 423.

stability, the continuation of the order established through primeval combat. In Psalm 89, . . . the bond between the exaltation of the deity and the imperial politics of his earthly seat is patent. David is YHWH's vicar on Earth."[11] It will be through this viceroy, the earthly king—and his "seed" that is associated with synonyms indicating a permanent reign for them (89:4a, 29a, 36a)—that the divine King will rule over the earth.[12] All these remarkable correspondences between the Davidic king and Yahweh renders it possible to see this human regent, David, as (or representing) Christ himself in Psalm 89, as also in Psalms 2 and 45 (mention is made of the מָשִׁיחַ, *mashiach*, in all three: 2:2; 45:7; 89:38, 51), not to mention the reference to Christ as the "firstborn" (89:27; Rom 8:29 employs πρωτότοκος, *prōtotokos*, borrowing from the LXX of Ps 89:27).[13]

Needless to say, this bountiful blessing upon God's king is effectively a blessing upon God's people: Yahweh's favor "exalts" the "horn" of his people (89:17; also see 89:16b), and it also "exalts" the king's "horn" (89:24b; also see 89:19c). Yahweh's "name" rejoices his people (89:16a), and his "name" empowers his king (89:24b).

But a note of negativity creeps into this *Promise* section, in 89:30–36: the moral failures of the kingly line of David. Punishment is meted out to them as a consequence, but even if *they* "profane" divine statutes and commandments (89:31a), *God* will not "profane" the covenant with David (89:34a). Even if *they* fail to "keep" God's laws (89:31b; see 89:30–31), *God* would "keep" his lovingkindness through his covenant (89:28a; also see 89:33). This is emphasized in the structure of 89:29–37:[14]

89:29	"seed for always"; "throne like the days of heaven"
89:31a	"they profane"
89:32	Seeds' "rebellion" "punished" Seeds' "iniquity" ["punished"]
89:33	God's lovingkindness "not invalidated" God's faithfulness "not dealt falsely"
89:34a	"I will not profane"
89:36–37	"seed forever"; "throne like the sun … like the moon … in the sky"

Chiastically structured verses (and parallelisms), contrasting the unfaithfulness of David's seed (89:30–32) and the faithfulness of David's God (89:33–34), add pathos to this divine declaration (see below).

---

11. Levenson, *Creation and the Persistence of Evil*, 22–23.

12. A connection between the heavens controlled by divine King and the throne of the earthly king is made explicit in 89:29: the latter's "throne" will be set by Yahweh "like the days of heaven."

13. Note: Since both Yahweh and his Davidic representative are labeled "K/king" in this psalm, to make the distinction between divine and human regent clear, I have chosen not to capitalize references (including pronouns) to the latter, even though this individual is likely to be the Messiah, the Lord Jesus Christ.

14. Modified from Clifford, "Psalm 89," 45–46. It is notable that God is labeled "Father" in 89:26 and the seed of David are called "sons" in 89:30, though they are "*his* sons," i.e., David's, not of the "Father." Nonetheless, at least indirectly, the castigation of these "sons" is parental discipline from the hand of God; such remediation does not revoke the filial relationship.

Unfaithfulness of David's Seed
89:30–32

"If his sons forsake
    My law
        and in My judgments
they do not walk,"

"if My statutes   they profane
and My commandments   they do not keep,
    then I will punish
with a staff   their rebellion,
and with blows   their iniquity."

Faithfulness of David's God
89:33–34

"But My lovingkindness
    I will not invalidate
        from him,
    and I will not deal falsely
in My faithfulness."

"I will not profane
    My covenant,
        and what comes forth from My lips,
I will not change."

Throughout the *Praise* and *Promise* sections of the psalm the word "forever" echoes: 89:1a, 2a, 4a, 28a, 36a, 37a (as well, "generation to generation," 89:1b, 4b, and "always," 89:29a). This, of course, is a rhetorical ploy, to induce Yahweh to reconsider his current inexpedient treatment of king, seed, and people (see below). After all, God himself had promised—in his own holiness, a self-swearing oath of great solemnity (89:35)—about the long-lasting nature of the Davidic reign![15] How could he change his mind now, protests the psalmist (89:38–45)?

If, as was suggested above, Christ is the ultimate referent of the Davidic king, who are the seed? Certainly, the failure of the seed depicted in 89:30–32 indicates that the king's line is human, composed of sinful people. But perhaps it is deliberate that the failure of the seed is not declared, at least in this psalm, to be commencing with David, a regent of no few historical shortcomings himself.[16] In this text, David appears sinless, blemishless. This again suggests the originary king in this psalm, the David-like figure, has an unusually special status. Also note that only with David is God explicitly said to have a parent-child relationship (89:26–27); David's seed are pointedly called "his [David's] sons" (89:30a), and "his/your [David's] seed" (89:4a, 29a, 36a), and not expressly God's. Thus the unique Father-son

---

15. By an elliptical utterance in 89:35b, the consequences of God's violation of his promise are left to the horrors of one's imagination! The sun and moon are commandeered as witnesses—"the witness in the sky" (89:37b)—to God's oath.

16. The "anointed" with whom God was "enraged" (89:38b) is evidently one of that king's descendants, not David himself, as the reference to "*former* lovingkindnesses . . . to David" indicates (89:49a).

relationship here might also be pointing to the Father-Son filiation between the First and Second Persons of the Godhead.

But what about David's sons/seed—who might they be, beyond the historical and particular understanding of them as Davidides? One notices that at the end of Psalm 89, the psalmist refers to his cohort as God's "servants" (89:50a). "The 'servants' of Yahweh seem to be a descriptive expression for loyal worshippers."[17] But the king, of the seed of David, was also called "anointed" and "servant" (89:38b, 39a). That makes for an intriguing correspondence between the three entities to whom "anointed" and "servant(s)" are applied: David, the "original" one of that species; David's seed;[18] and the people these kings rule over:[19]

89:3b, 20a	God's "servant"	**David**
89:20b	God's "anointed"	
89:38b	God's "anointed"	**Seed**
89:39a	God's "servant"	
89:50a	God's "servants"	**People**
89:51b	God's "anointed"	

It is not much of a stretch to say that if the David references in this psalm point to the ultimate referent Christ, the God-King, then his followers, his people, are his "servants" and his "anointed,"[20] who like their Master are suffering and being reproached (89:50–51). In other words, for preaching purposes, and in the larger context of the canon, the "seed" refers to the followers of this God-King, the Messiah's heirs (Rom 8:17; Gal 3:29; 4:7; Eph 3:6; Titus 3:7). Therefore it is fair to interpret the psalm as speaking of the Anointed and the anointed, i.e., Christ, God's King, and his followers, God's people, the ones he redeemed with his life.[21]

Protest, Petition, and Postscript (89:38–52)

In any case, all had seemed fine and dandy thus far in the psalm, but now things take a dramatic turn for the worse, an "extraordinary somersault" in Ps 89:38–50, commencing with the disjunctive and emphatic "and You—You . . ." (89:38a). Everything from 89:1–37 is, for the psalmist, impossible to reconcile with the (then current) situation of Yahweh's seeming negligence of his people and their king (described in this final section of the psalm). The ruler has been defeated and humiliated (89:41–43, 45b), his grandeur besmirched (89:44), and his

---

17. Tate, *Psalms 51–100*, 417. See Isa 56:6; 63:17; 65:8–9, 13–15; 66:14; Neh 1:6–7, 10–11; Job 42:7–8; etc.

18. As was noted, "Your anointed" and "Your servant" in 89:38–39 refer to the Davidic seed; 89:38 begins the third section of the psalm, *Protest, Petition, and Postscript*, dealing with the current deplorable situation of the psalmist with one of the Davidides ruling the nation, and for whom the poet makes protest and petition. It is worth noting again that the notation, "*former* lovingkindnesses . . . to David" (89:49), validates this reading. David, the original in the line, "anointed" and "servant" in 89:3b, 20b, is neither the "anointed" nor the "servant" in 89:38–39: here they refer to the current Davidic king, one of David's sinful seed. After all, the seed are lawbreakers; David is not said to have been one of those offenders, at least not in this psalm.

19. The double chiasm is a bonus!

20. Which Christians are because of the Holy Spirit indwelling them (see 2 Cor 1:21).

21. The correspondence between the regent and the ruled goes further: as the king and his "horn" are "exalted" (89:19c, 24b), so also are the people and their horn (89:16b, 17b).

youth decimated (89:45a). God's "I will not invalidate" and "I will not deal falsely" and "I will not profane" and "I will not change" and "I have sworn" in 89:33–35 now clash vigorously with the psalmist's "You have rejected" and "You have refused" and "You have been enraged" and "You have disavowed" and "You have profaned" and "You have breached ..." and "You have set ... to ruin," in 89:38–40. Indeed, the one who had said, "I will not profane" (89:34a) even if his people "profane" (89:31a), is himself charged now with "profaning" (89:39b). And it continues: the second person pointing an accusatory finger at the divine defaulter occurs eighteen times in multiple forms in 89:38–45![22]

Yahweh, who had "set" the king's right hand over the waters (89:25a), and "set" his seed forever (89:29a), was now "setting" that ruler's strongholds to ruin (89:40b). The "enemies" God had scattered (89:10b) and the "enemies" who would not be able to touch God's king (89:22a) have now become the "enemies" who are rejoicing (89:42b) and "enemies" who are reproaching (89:51a)—they are "*Your* enemies" (89:10b, 51a). Whereas all the instances of God's "lovingkindness" and "faithfulness" thus far were laudatory, here in 89:49 the psalmist alleges that these same attributes have vanished from the scene! After all the formal oath-making that God had talked about ("swear ... David," 89:3b, 35a), now it is the psalmist's turn to ask what had become of the lovingkindnesses and faithfulness that God had "sworn to David" (89:49b). The "covenant" he had made and secured with David, that deity promised not to profane (89:3α, 28b, 34a), that same "covenant," the psalmist alleges, God had disavowed (89:39a). How could this be?

Ironically, whereas God's "right hand" was "exalted" (89:13b)—and the king's "right hand" was once in control of the chaotic waters (89:25b), with the king as one "exalted" by God (89:19c)—now it is his enemies' "right hand" that is "exalted" (89:42a). Whereas God had promised to pound and strike the king's foes (89:23), now it is the king's walls and strongholds that have been breached and ruined (89:40). In fact, it appears, in the psalmist's reckoning, that God himself is the destroying saboteur (89:40), supporting and sustaining Israel's adversaries and thwarting the defenses of his own people under their God-appointed king (89:42–43). Once it was God's people that were "jubilating" (89:16a); now the foes "rejoice" (89:42b). Earlier, it was noted how often in this psalm "forever" and its synonyms occurred. Here for the last time is a similar word, "eternally" (89:46).[23] But this does not evoke the sense of everlasting bliss. On the contrary, it charges God with hiding "eternally." The perdurance of David's throne likened to the days of "heaven" (89:29b; and to the stability of heavenly denizens, 89:36b, 37a) is now reversed, with the royal seat cast to the "ground [אֶרֶץ, *'erets*, 'earth']" (89:44b), as also is the king's crown—profaned "to the ground [אֶרֶץ]" (89:39b). The contrast is pungent and plangent. The "forever" dynasty is gone, and "God is the cause of shattered dreams."[24]

The power and pathos of this protest is only heightened by the extensive sections of praise and promise that had gone on for the first thirty-seven verses of the psalm. But only in this last section does the reader come to recognize the purpose of that earlier encomium:

---

22. As the pronoun, "You" (89:38aα); as second-person verbs (89:38aβ, 38aγ, 38b, 39a, 39b, 40a, 40b, 42a, 42b, 43a, 43b, 44a, 44b, 45a, 45b); and as pronominal suffixes (39:38b, 39a).

23. "Forever" does occur later in 89:52a, but as part of the postscript to Book III of the Psalter.

24. deClaissé-Walford et al., *Book of Psalms*, 682. The Hebrew of 89:44a reads: "You have made to cease from his splendor." The translation adopted here reflects an emendation that sees the מ, *m*, in מִטְּהָרוֹ, *mittharo*, not functioning as a preposition, "from," but as a nominal prefix with a substantive of abstraction, טְהָר, *thar*, "splendor." So: "You have made his splendor to cease."

all of 89:1–37 was a prelude to the incisive protest of 89:38–45, where the psalmist is "going for the divine jugular," so to speak.[25]

It is not surprising, then, that a series of questions follows in 89:46a, 46b, 47b, 48a, 48b, 49, as the psalmist enters the petition section of the psalm (89:46–51) and contends with Yahweh on the basis of the brevity of human life and the inevitability of death, and humanity's incapacity to prevent that termination. Earlier the psalmist had raised questions of wonderment about God (89:6, 8); here, however, he can only ejaculate questions of disillusionment about God.[26] Praise of what God had "created," the delight of exquisite nature (89:12a), has now become the pain of God's "creation," the distress of ephemeral mortals (89:47b). "Yhwh created the world, and it is a place of splendor; Yhwh created humanity, and the whole thing seems pointless."[27] In essence, the psalmist is declaring: "God, you are disinterested in our welfare. Your abandonment of us is bad enough; add to that the brevity of our lives and everything seems futile. All that talk about 'forever' is cheap. Life is short and everyone will die. Lord, why do you add to our burdens?"

But, remarkably, other than "remember" in 89:47a, 50a, there is no explicit petition in this psalm (as was also the case in Psalm 88). No doubt, that is all that is necessary for God's people. If God would only pay attention to them, everything would be solved! The root of the word translated "reproach" occurs three times in 89:50–51. If the catastrophe of military defeat wasn't bad enough to prompt God into action, the contempt of the enemies should, the supplicant claims. And on that unresolved note, the psalm comes to an end.

The postscript, 89:52, concludes Book III of the Psalter, but there may be a connection with the foregoing composition. Yes, seemingly God has abandoned his people. But, no, we will never lose faith in him. Instead we will bless him . . . "forever." It gives no hint of God's response to the psalm, and how things were—or if they ever were—resolved. It simply declares, with an adverb frequently employed in this psalm, that God is blessed . . . *forever*! Yes, he is. No matter what! "Amen and Amen!"

Sermon Map

I. God's Faithfulness: Acclaimed
   Praise for God's rule, God's king, God's people's joy (89:1–18)
   Move-to-relevance: Our life of God's praise

II. God's Faithfulness: Asserted
   Promise regarding God's for the king and the seed (89:19–37)
   Move-to-relevance: Our life in God's promise

III. God's Faithfulness: Asked
   Petition for God's action to king and people (89:38–52)

IV. *Following Servants of a Faithful God and His Firstborn King!*
   Trusting despite circumstances because of a faithful God's promises

---

25. Goldingay, *Psalms*, 2:684.

26. The supplicant is so affected by the calamity that has befallen his king and his people he can only express himself "in an appropriately spluttering way" as the shattered structure of 89:47 depicts (Goldingay, *Psalms*, 2:688).

27. Goldingay, *Psalms*, 2:688.

PSALM 90:1–17

Psalm of Disorientation

Lovingkindness and Lifespan

PSALM 90 IS A prayer of the followers of Yahweh, his servants (90:13, 16).[1] In 90:13, the psalm repeats the question of 89:46, "until when? (or "how long?") and with the unremitting and unresolved agonies of the two preceding psalms haunting the reader's memory, this accusatory query "does not make an encouraging beginning to Book IV" of the Psalter.[2] The wrath of God and the mortality of humankind—the two are linked—appear to the be main threats to the *shalom* of God's people in this composition. Since life is short, if only God would relent of his rage . . .

Translation

90:1 Lord, a shelter You—You have been
      to us, generation after generation.
90:2 Before the mountains, [before] they were born,
      and [before] You delivered the earth and the world,
      even from forever unto forever, You [were] God.
90:3 You return mortals into crushed matter,
      and say, "Return, children of humanity."
90:4 For a thousand years in Your eyes
      are like a day—yesterday when it passes by—
      and [like] a watch in the night.

---

1. These are the faithful, the devout, those of the community of God: see Isa 56:6; 63:17; 65:8–9, 13–15; 66:14; Neh 1:6–7, 10–11; Job 42:7–8; etc. The attribution of this psalm to Moses in the superscription (untranslated here) may have arisen from that fact that only in Exod 32:12 and Ps 90:13b does a human address God with an imperative to "repent/have pity [הִנָּחֵם, *hinnachem*]" (or even "change mind") and to "turn [שׁוּב, *shuv*]." Also the unusual יְמוֹת, *ymot* ("days") and שְׁנוֹת, *shnot* ("years") are found together only in 90:15 and Deut 32:7; as well, פֹּעַל, *po'al* ("doing," in Ps 90:16a) is found in the Pentateuch only in Deut 32:4; 33:11 (see Tate, *Psalms 51–100*, 438).

2. Goldingay, *Psalms*, 3:23.

90:5   You have ended their lives, they sleep;
           in the morning they are like grass which sprouts up.
90:6   In the morning it flourishes and sprouts up;
           toward evening it withers and dries up.
90:7   For we have been finished by Your anger,
           and by Your wrath we have been terrified.
90:8   You have set our iniquities before You,
           what we have hidden, to the light of Your face.
90:9   For all our days have slipped away by Your fury;
           we have finished our years like a groan.
90:10 And the days of our years—in them are seventy years,
           and if in strength, eighty years;
           and their pride is [only] toil and harm;
           for it has gone by quickly and we fly away.
90:11 Who knows the power of Your anger,
           and, according to fear for You, Your fury?
90:12 Make us know accurately [how] to count our days,
           and we will bring to You a heart of wisdom.
90:13 Return [to us], Yahweh—until when?
           and have pity on Your servants.
90:14 Satisfy us in the morning with Your lovingkindness,
           and we will shout for joy and rejoice all our days.
90:15 Make us rejoice according to the days You have afflicted us,
           the years we have seen evil.
90:16 Let Your doing be seen by Your servants,
           and Your majesty unto their children.
90:17 And may it be that the favor of the Lord our God [is] upon us;
           and the work of our hands may You establish for us;
           and the work of our hands, may You establish.

Structure

The structure of the psalm outlines God's eternality, indignation, and return, at the same time contrasting each divine attribute/action with humanity's ephemerality, iniquity, and rejoicing, respectively. It begins and ends with descriptors of deity employing Hebrew words that are anagrams, as shown (90:1a, 17a; below[3]).

---

3. In fact, the first word is מָעוֹן, *ma'on*, and the second is a precise palindrome of the first, נֹעַם, *no'am*, involving both consonants and vowels.

90:1–6
Eternality of God
Ephemerality of Humankind

God: אֲדֹנָי מָעוֹן, *'adonay ma'on*
("Lord, a shelter," 90:1a)

90:7–12
Indignation of God
Iniquity of Humankind

90:13–17
Return of God
Rejoicing of Humankind

God: נֹעַם אֲדֹנָי, *no'am 'adonay*
("favor of the Lord," 90:17a)

Theological Focus

The ephemerality of humankind impels the people of an eternal God to seek his lovingkindness and motivate him to relent of his wrath against their sin, so that with a reprieve, they may celebrate his majestic work of grace in them, satiated with his lovingkindness and rejoicing in his favor.

Commentary

Eternality of God; Ephemerality of Humankind (90:1–6)

At the very outset, in 90:1–2, a contrast is struck between human time and divine time: God is a shelter forever, even before the existence of the cosmos, but humans experience this divine shelter in time, generation after generation:[4]

"Lord,
a shelter You [אַתָּה, *'attah*]—You have been to us,
generation after generation *[human time]*.
Before the mountains,
[before] they were born,
and [before] You delivered
the earth and the world,
and from forever unto forever *[divine time]*
You [אַתָּה] [were]
God."

---

4. Modified from Auffret, "Essai sur la structure littéraire du Psaume 90," 263.

Indeed, the whole section, 90:1–6, seems to be oscillating between human and divine time:

90:1	Human time: Ephemeral
90:2	*Divine time: Eternal*
90:3	Human time: Ephemeral
90:4	*Divine time: Eternal*
90:5–6	Human time: Ephemeral

This primes the reader for what is to follow: this eternal shelter of God appears to have been removed (90:7–12; see below). All of this seems to be a reminder to God that he, the eternal deity who "does not suffer from the transitory nature of humanity and of all earthly things," should take into consideration the ephemerality of humankind.[5] There is also an appeal to God's maternal nature. The implication is that he who was before the mountains were "born," and he who "delivered" the cosmos (90:2) needs to take compassionate heed of the "children of humanity" (literally "sons of Adam," 90:3b), "mortals" who are being returned to "crushed matter," almost bespeaking a violent transformation unto death (90:3a).[6] He who is from "forever *unto* [עַד, *'ad*] forever" is turning mortals "*into* [עַד] crushed matter" (90:2c, 3a). Humanity's long (and painful) stretches of lived time are but an instant for God (90:4) who ends the lives of mortals—mere grass that lasts for a day (90:5–6).[7] Thus the stage is set for the lament that follows.

Indignation of God; Iniquity of Humankind (90:7–12)

After referring to humanity in the third person in 90:1–6, the language shifts to a first-person plural narratival description in 90:7–12: the psalmist includes himself in the cohort of mortals and speaks on their behalf. While the first section (*Eternality of God; Ephemerality of Humankind*) stated the situation in general terms, this second one (*Indignation of God; Iniquity of Humankind*) moves to a specific plaint. The crux of the problem is clearly visible in the structuring of 90:7–9—the sins of humankind (below).

---

5. Tate, *Psalms 51–90*, 440.

6. There is already a hint in 90:4b that this ephemerality of humankind has its roots in the indignation of God: "pass by" is עבר, *'br* (90:4b), and "fury" is עֶבְרָה, *'evrah* (90:9a, 11b).

7. The structure of 90:5–6 is also chiastic in terms of the time stamps: "sleep" / "morning" // "morning" / "evening."

90:7	"we have been *finished*" "by Your anger"; "by Your wrath" "we have been terrified"
90:8	"our iniquities before You" "what we have hidden, to the light of Your face"
90:9	"our days have slipped away" "by Your fury" "we have *finished* our years"

Holy divine rage that "finishes" sinful mankind (90:7a, 9b) is pictured as enveloping a nucleus of human culpability and guilt—"a radioactive core which poisons all of life" (90:8).[8] Besides, the oscillation between the first person ("we" and "our") and the second person ("You" and "Your") in these verses depicts this agonizing pairing of God's anger to humankind's sin with poignancy and pathos. "Your anger" (90:7a, 11a), "Your wrath" (90:7b), and "Your fury" (90:9a, 11b) make divine indignation a fearsome experience.

But the psalmist makes no excuse for the iniquity of the people of God (that includes himself, of course). Rather the focus is once again on time: "days" (90:9a, 10a, 12a) and "years" (90:9b, 90:10a [×2], 10b). "Yes, we have sinned and yes, you are rightfully angry. But would you please shorten your wrath since our days are already few?" Yahweh's eternal time, they plead, needs to be more considerate of humankind's ephemeral time. Goldingay notes that in the OT, seventy years (90:10a) is usually designated for calamitous times, at least in the collective memory of God's people (Jer 25:11–12; Zech 1:12; and both these texts deal with divine indignation at human iniquity).[9] Thus the "eighty years" of Ps 90:10b only intensifies that conventional seven-decade meme of suffering (90:10a) by appending another decade to the anguish, the piling on of catastrophic circumstances in a life that is only "toil and harm" in the first place (90:10c).

The power of divine indignation is unfathomable: "who *knows* . . . ?" (90:11a).[10] But for the supplicants, the only need is for God to "make us *know*" how to count the days (90:12a), i.e., to comprehend the brief span of this mortal life.[11] That is particularly important because God's fury threatens to shorten those already abridged years. Thus the "wisdom" that the people of God want to bring to the table (90:12b) is practical knowledge about how to live in light of God's indignation, i.e., how to conduct oneself in a life that is short to begin with, and abbreviated further by the wrath of God. In effect, the plea of 90:12 is a promise to correct one's ways and be wise in matters of sin and holiness, so that any further punitive reduction of life may be precluded. Perhaps that response of committed faithfulness will turn the heart of God and move him not just to relent from his wrath, but to show favor to his people. That brings the psalmist to the final section of the psalm.

---

8. Tate, *Psalms 51–100*, 442.

9. Goldingay, *Psalms*, 3:30. Rather than eighty years, it is a century or more that counts as a long life (Isa 65:20; Sir 18:9).

10. The rhetorical question of 90:11 seeks to match the knowledge of God's wrath with an equally appropriate fear and awe that is due to him.

11. "Accurately" in 90:12 translates כֵּן, *ken* (as in Jdg 12:6; 1 Sam 23:17).

Return of God; Rejoicing of Humankind (90:13–17)

Whereas the imperative "make us to know" (90:12a) is a petition in itself, a more extensive set of imperatival requests follow in the final portion of the psalm. Thus 90:1–12 serves as a prelude to the final and critical petitions of 90:13–17. Earlier, it was God "returning" mortals into dust as he ordered humanity to "return" (90:3). Here in 90:13 it is the people of God imploring *him* to "return." Thankfully, "Your servants" still retain their status as the divine ruler's subjects, despite their iniquity (90:13b). "In effect, they have already acknowledged that they have not been behaving as obedient servants. Their boldness lies in the assumption that Yhwh must still be committed to treating them as servants," as the repetitions show:[12]

90:13b	"Your servants"	
90:14	"us," "we," "our"	
90:15	"us," "us," "we"	
90:16a	"Your servants"	

"Relationship with God can be a struggle, and God can seem absent and angry with individuals, communities, and even a whole people. It is a frightening place to stand. Yet this psalm affirms that stand they did, even in the midst of fear and struggle . . . The people have taken on the former role of Moses," as they appeal to God's pity and lovingkindness.[13] Let the end of the days of divine wrath come soon—"in the morning"—so that God's people may rejoice, they beseech (90:14a). In 90:5b, 6a, "morning" was the metaphorical start of the life of humans, not particularly an exciting prospect, for they soon perished in the "evening" (90:6b). All that morning would bring was anticipation of an oncoming expiration in few wee hours. But the "morning" in 90:14a is different: may the lovingkindness of a returning, relenting, and reprieving God, they implore, saturate "all our days." Before the mercy of God is granted, "all our days" only slip away in divine indignation (90:9a); after the extension of God's lovingkindness, it is rejoicing that lasts "all our days" (90:14b). And may these days of rejoicing, they plead, be commensurate with their days of affliction (90:15a), so that the "years" once filled with wailing (90:9b; those and "years" of affliction in 90:10a, 10b), may become "years" filled with celebrating (90:15b).

Thus a new morning has dawned, bringing with it an expectation of a surfeit of divine lovingkindness. And thereby, the "children" of humanity, destined to be returned to dust (90:3b), become "children" who glimpse God's work and God's splendor (90:16b). That is to witness the "doing" of a relenting God, to gaze upon his gracious "majesty" (90:16), as he, a holy God, absolves his servants, sinful humans, from his wrath.[14] Right now they "see" only evil (90:15b), but soon they hope to "see" the liberation of God (90:16a).

And then, recycling verbiage from its commencement, the psalm concludes, depicting the reversal of the status of the people of God with a linguistic reversal, a clever palindrome (text picturing truth): God who is a "shelter," מָעוֹן (90:1a), is now, more importantly, the God who grants "favor," נֹעַם (90:17a; see below).

---

12. Goldingay, *Psalms*, 3:32.

13. deClaissé-Walford et al., *Book of Psalms*, 696.

14. The ground for such absolution is not given in this psalm, except for divine lovingkindness (90:14a), but what more could one ask for than this grace of God?

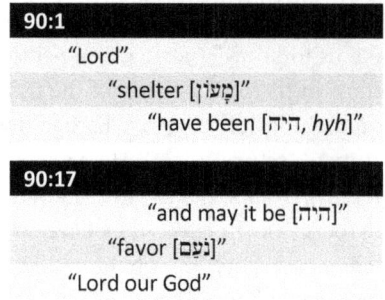

"The approval of the Lord . . . signals the end of the divine wrath and, concomitantly, an end to the perceived absence of God lamented in Ps 89."[15] The "days" of turmoil (90:9a, 10a, 12a) have been transformed into "days" of jubilation (90:14b, 15a). And may God thus secure his people in his favor and establish the work of their hands (90:17bc), that their lives may not be "solitary, poor, nasty, brutish, and short."[16] This gracious God is indeed "our help in ages past, and our hope for years to come."[17]

Sermon Map

I. Eternal God; Ephemeral Humans
    Eternality of God (90:1–2, 4)
    Ephemerality of Humans (90:3, 5–6)
    Move-to-relevance: The transience of our lives

II. Indignant God; Iniquitous Humans
    Iniquity of humans (90:8)
    Indignance of God (90:7, 9–11)
    Move-to-relevance: The sin in our lives

III. Relenting God; Rejoicing Humans
    Relenting of God (90:13)
    Rejoicing of humans (90:14–17)
    Move-to-relevance: The joy of our lives

IV. *Give in to the Grace of God!*
    Praying for the mercy of God and for experiencing his grace with joy

---

15. Tucker, "*Exitus, Reditus*," 152.
16. Hobbes, *Leviathan*, 97.
17. Isaac Watts, "O God, Our Help in Ages Past" (1719).

PSALM 91:1–16

Psalm of Orientation

Devout Delivered from Catastrophe

THERE IS NO DIRECT address to God anywhere in Psalm 91, only a *quotation* of a direct address to him (91:2). For the most part, the psalmist is addressing a fellow-believer in the second person, with God's voice heard towards the end of the psalm (91:14–16). There is no petition in this psalm either, rendering it a psalm of orientation, how things are in God's ideal world.[1]

Translation

91:1   The one who dwells in the shelter of the Most High,
      in the shadow of the Almighty he will remain.
91:2   I will say to Yahweh, "My refuge and my steadfastness,
      My God, I trust in Him."
91:3   For He it is who rescues you from the fowler's trap
      [and] from the ruinous plague.
91:4   With His pinion He gives cover to you,
      and under His wings you can seek refuge;
      a shield and a bulwark is His faithfulness.
91:5   You will not be in fear from the terror of night,
      from the arrow that flies by day,
91:6   from the plague that stalks in darkness,
      from the destruction that devastates at noontimes.
91:7   They may fall at your side, a thousand,
      and ten thousand at your right hand;
      to you it will not approach.

---

1. This ideal world of God is currently situated within the real world beset by evil, thus it is an "ideal real" world, as opposed to the "ideal ideal" world wherein evil is banished eternally and God's will is done forever (these designations are modified from Dworkin, *Sovereign Virtue*, 172–75.

91:8   You will, with your eyes, only gaze,
          and the requital of the wicked you will see,
91:9   for you—you have set Yahweh, my refuge,
          the Most High, as your dwelling place.
91:10 Evil will not happen to you,
          and affliction will not come near in your tent,
91:11 for His angels He will command for you,
          to keep you in all your ways.
91:12 Upon their hands they will bear you,
          lest you injure your foot on a stone.
91:13 Upon the lion and the snake you will tread,
          you will trample the young lion and the monster.
91:14 "For unto Me he has been devoted, and I will save him;
          I will secure him on high because he has known My name.
91:15 He will call upon Me, and I will answer him;
          with him I [will be] in distress;
          I will liberate him and I will honor him.
91:16 With length of days I will satisfy him,
          and I will let him see My deliverance."

Structure

This psalm's first two stanzas (91:1–8, 9–13) are parallel in structure and content and reflect an iteration and a subsequent reiteration of a prayer uttered in a time of distress. The third stanza of the psalm (91:14–16), a divine oracle, is the clincher, forming the basis of the psalmist's trust in God in times of persecution and plague.[2]

---

2. The structure is modified from Botha, "Psalm 91," 263–64; and Gaiser, "'It Shall Not Reach You,'" 194.

STANZA 1 (91:1–8)
  Profession of Faith (**91:1–2**)
      First person ("I"; "my")
      "Most High"; "Yahweh"; "my refuge"
  Protection from Danger 1 (**91:3–6**)
  Perishing of Enemies 1 (**91:7–8**)

STANZA 2 (91:9–13)
  Profession of Faith (**91:9**)
      First person ("my")
      "Yahweh"; "my refuge"; "Most High"
  Protection from Danger 2 (**91:10–12**)
  Perishing of Enemies 2 (**91:13**)

STANZA 3 (91:14–16)
  Piety of Servant (**91:14**)
  Preservation of God (**91:15–16**)

In sum, the psalmist ("I," "my"; 91:2, 9a) addresses another individual in the second person ("you," "your"; 91:1–13).[3] God then talks about this individual in the third person ("he," "him"; 91:14–16).[4] Perhaps this anonymous individual being addressed by the poet (in the second person) and being talked about by deity (in the third person) is the king or representative leader of God's people.[5]

Though the rhetorical situation appears be one in which that unknown individual (being addressed by the psalmist and about whom deity utters an oracle) is undergoing a wretched scourge of some sort, much of the language about foes and threats appears to be metaphorical (though the line between figure and reality is not easily discernible), rendering this psalm applicable in a myriad of afflictions and adversities suffered by the people of God, even spiritual warfare.

Theological Focus

Those devoted to God, making him their refuge in times of deathly distress from all manner of foes external, including demonic ones, are assured of God's reciprocation in his deliverance, his presence, his honor, and his reward, even as their enemies are decimated by divine agency.

---

3. Given the content of 91:1–13, it is also possible that, rather than the psalmist, the one uttering the words of 91:1–13 is the liturgist or priest, giving it the form of a benedictory address. (To keep things simple, I will refer to this first speaker in the psalm as the psalmist.)

4. Whom God is addressing (about this leader/king) is unclear; it could be the community of his people in general, perhaps in the same context of the cult where the liturgist/priest utters 91:1–13.

5. The masculine singular shows up in the psalmist's utterance in multiple verses: 91:3a, 4ab, 5a, 7, 8, 9a, 10, 11, 12, 13; and in God's utterance: 91:14, 15, 16.

Commentary

Stanza 1 (91:1–8)

The first stanza commences with a profession of faith in God, a declaration of confidence in the "Most High," "the Almighty"[6] (91:1), "Yahweh," and "God"—the supplicant's "refuge" and "steadfastness" (91:2). This piling on of appellations for deity emphasizes the intensity of the psalmist's faith (and hints at the direness of his straits). Resting "in [בְּ, *b*] the shelter of the Most High" (91:1a) and "in [בְּ] the shadow of the Almighty" (91:1b), the psalmist avers that his trust is "in [בְּ] Him," his God (92:2b).

Whatever may have been the travail of the one the psalmist is addressing, one thing is clear: God is utterly trustworthy and protects his people from danger (91:3–6).[7] The assonance of יַצִּילְךָ, *yatstsilka*, "He ... rescues you" (91:3a) and יָסֶךְ לָךְ, *yasek lak*, "He gives cover to you" (91:4a) underscores this truth. And the one who was "my refuge" (91:2a) is the one in whom the sufferer may "seek refuge" (91:4b). Whether it be "night" or "day," "darkness" or "noontime" (91:5–6)—*anytime*—there is no cause for fear.

The preposition מִן, *min*, is found eight times in the first stanza and only in that one: translated as "from" (91:3a, 3b, 5a, 5b, 6a, 6b) and "at" (91:7a, 7b). The instances translated "from" reveal a variety of threats—hunters, pestilences, militants. These may be literal, but the simultaneity of the attacks from multiple sources suggests a more symbolic reading, though they are all focused upon physical danger.

> At the same time there is a sinister quality about them which suggests that powers of a "fifth dimension" are involved. The realm of the occult, the realm of the superhuman and supramundane, lies close at hand. Lethal forces lurk along the ways of life and the abiding protection of the Almighty is essential for safety. Traps are ready to snap shut, arrows may fly suddenly, plagues stalk through dark nights and even rush forth to ravage at noonday.[8]

---

6. The only other instance of "Almighty" in the Psalter is in 68:15.
7. "Plague" in 91:3b, 6a translates דֶּבֶר, *dever*, as also in 41:8; 78:50.
8. Tate, *Psalms 51–100*, 458–59. Vreugdenhil describes the widely prevalent recognition, in both the ancient Near East and Israel, of the threatening presence of demons and the reality of their activities, and the historical use of Psalm 91 as a protection against these foes (*Psalm 91*, 33–119, 401). It is notable that both the LXX and Targum see 91:6b as referring to demons (δαιμόνιον, *daimonion*, and שֵׁד, *shyd*, respectively); the Targum also has "fiend," מזיק, *mzyq*, and "angel of death," מלאך מותא, *ml'k mwt'*, as the sources of terror in 91:5. Then there is Matt 4:6 that has Satan himself citing this psalm (Ps 91:11–12)! The possibility of sinister beings involved in these miseries inflicted on the sufferer may explain the presence of angels in 91:11–13. Many of the threats in 91:3–6, 13, recur in Scripture in the contexts of magic and sorcery: "fowler" (91:3; and Hos 9:8, and see 9:7–10 in the context of idolatry); "trap" (Ps 91:3; and Hos 5:1; see 4:11—5:7 in the context of idolatry); "ruinous" (Ps 91:3; and Isa 47:11; also see 47:9–12 in the context of sorcery; Ezek 7:26, and see 7:19–26 in the context of idolatry); "plague" (Ps 91:6; and Hos 13:14 in the context of death personified); "terror" and "night" (Ps 91:5; and Job 4:13–14, and see 4:12–16 in the context of apparitions; and Job 15:21 in the context of a "destroyer"; Job 22:10–11 has both "trap" and "terror"); "arrow" (Ps 91:5; and Ezek 39:3, and see 39:1–8 in the context of God's defeat of Gog and Magog); "destruction" (Ps 91:6; translated "sting" in Hos 13:14 in the context of death personified, as noted earlier; also in Isa 28:2, likely in the context of God's control of demonic agents); "devastates" (Ps 91:6; and Job 15:21 that uses the term for a "destroyer"; Ezek 32:12 in the context of God using "mighty ones" to punish Egypt); "tread" (Ps 91:13; and Deut 33:29 that deals with the destruction of "high places" of Canaanite worship); and "monster" (Ps 91:13; and Ezek 29:3; 32:2 in the context of likening evil individuals with that beast). The cognitive domains of many of these terms coincide with those of sorcery, magic, and witchcraft. Vreugdenhil concludes that "the terms, verbs and images deployed by the author—together with the mental images and associations evoked

In any case, the fate of foes (perishing of enemies, 91:7-8), whoever or whatever they may be, is assured, as manifested in the parallel *inclusio* structuring of 91:7ab and 91:8 with bookends of body parts and physiology ("side" and "right hand"; "eyes ... gaze" and "see") and a picture in the center of each of the defeated "wicked" falling in the thousands. But between 91:7ab and 91:8 is the "you," ostensibly the leader or king of God's people, unscathed and untouched by these assaults, protected from all the tumult around him—a literary depiction of life in God's care (91:7c):[9]

91:7ab	"They may fall at your *side*, a thousand, and ten thousand at your *right hand*."
91:7c	"to you it will not approach"
91:8	"You will, with your *eyes*, only *gaze*, and the requital of the wicked you will *see*."

Stanza 2 (91:9-13)

The second stanza continues the cycle of the first: a profession of faith in God (91:9), declaration of protection from danger (91:10-12) and a perishing of enemies (91:13). This reiteration of themes is reflected in that the negative particle, לֹא, *loʾ*, "not," is found only in the first two stanzas, in 91:5a, 7c and 91:10a, 10b, in assertions that evil will *not* touch the afflicted leader/king (the "you").[10]

The emphasis in this stanza is upon the active trust of the sufferer in God: "for you—you have set Yahweh ... as your dwelling place" (91:9). As was noted earlier, the preposition מִן, "from," is absent in Stanza 2, signifying a change in theme: there is nothing to be feared *from* any threat, not evil, not affliction (91:10). God and his angels are protecting the one in adversity (91:11-12). Even the mention of the vicious and treacherous beasts, "lion" and "snake," is only to pronounce victory over those trampled opponents (91:13). In fact, it is because one is borne "upon [עַל, *ʿal*]" the hands of God's angels (91:12a) that one can trample "upon [עַל]" leonine and reptilian fauna (91:13). Besides, it is the divine protection of the victim's "way [דֶּרֶךְ, *derek*]" (91:11b) that enables that one to "tread [דרך, *drk*]" upon dreaded adversaries (91:13a). This is no intrinsic power being exercised by a human to overpower adversaries, but rather a strength imbued by God himself that renders one triumphant.[11]

---

by those images—form the cumulative evidence that a demonological interpretation of Psalm 91, one in the context of witchcraft and magic, is justified" (*Psalm 91*, 407). Therefore, in application, spiritual warfare is a possibility that may be utilized.

9. From Auffret, *Voyez de vos yeux*, 284. Notice that 91:7c has אֵלֶיךָ לֹא, *ʾeleka loʾ* ("to you it will not ..."); and 91:10a has לֹא ... אֵלֶיךָ, *loʾ ... ʾeleka* ("[it] will not ... to you").

10. For the shift in tenor of *Stanza 3*, that lacks these negations, see below.

11. This was adumbrated in *Stanza 1*: all that the one in dire straits did was "gaze" and "see" as assailants were felled like ninepins (91:8).

Why God chooses to so aid the suffering one is revealed in *Stanza 3*.

Stanza 3 (91:14–16)

There is a remarkable change of tone and rhetoric as God begins to speak in *Stanza 3*. However, his utterance is *to* the psalmist/community *about* the leader/king who trusts in him—a divine testimony to his devotee, so to speak, and about this one's piety. No more negations (לֹא, "not"), and no more enemies "from" (מִן, *min*) which to be rescued. God has spoken[12] and in an oracle of approbation of the trust placed in deity by suffering humanity: "For unto Me he has been devoted" (91:14a). And the result of this trust is a cascade of first-person (divine) imperfects with third-person (human) suffixes asserting preservation by God: "I will save him," "I will secure him," "I will protect him," "I will answer him," "I will liberate him," "I will honor him," "I will satisfy him" with long life, and "I will let him see" divine deliverance (91:14–16), not to mention the verbless "with him I [will be]" in times of distress (91:15b). This is an incredible accumulation of God's promises—*seven* of them! For one terrified by missiles flying by "day" (91:5b), this is an astonishing turnaround—the delighted soul will now be the beneficiary of "length of *days*" (91:16a). The one who "saw" the fall of the wicked (91:8b) will now "see" God's rescue (91:16b).

It goes against the grain of the text to simply relegate the fulfillment of these promises to the hereafter: "In light of the Christian focus on eternal salvation, it is important to emphasize Yhwh's declaration that we do not experience such salvation only in the future and in heaven and in the inner person. Yhwh grants it now, on earth in the body."[13] It is also best to see these divine affirmations as dealing with corporate deliverance, with the individual specified, perhaps a leader or king, being the stand-in for the rest of the citizenry or congregation. "The psalm in its present context speaks of the protection and liberation of a captive people—God's work of justice, reversing the world's oppressive order—not of the random protection of one, selected capriciously."[14] God is faithful to care for his devout, even from supernatural threats.

Sermon Map

I. Profession of God (91:1–2, 9)

    Protection from danger, from humans and demons (91:3–6, 10–12)

    Perishing of enemies (91:7–8, 13)

    Move-to-relevance: God's deliverance of us

II. Piety of Servant (cause) (91:14)

    Preservation of God (effect) (91:15–16)

    Move-to-relevance: God's reciprocation of devotion to him

III. *Devote to Deity for Deliverance!*

    Specifics on developing devotion to God

---

12. Finally, "the long silence of Psalms 88, 89, and 90 is over. God speaks a word of deliverance to confirm all that has been said by the faithful one," the devout person, the psalmist who has spoken for all the people of God (deClaissé-Walford et al., *Book of Psalms*, 701).

13. Goldingay, *Psalms*, 3:49.

14. Gaiser, "'It Shall Not Reach You,'" 196.

PSALM 92:1–15
Psalm of Orientation

Righteous Flourish; Wicked Wither

PSALM 92 IS THE only poem in the Psalter that, in the MT, has a mention of the Sabbath (in its superscription).[1] Perhaps it is not coincidental that "Yahweh" also occurs seven times in this poem (in 92:1a, 4a, 5a, 8, 9a, 13a, 15a), the central instance being in the verbless 92:8, which itself is the central verse of the psalm, with seven verses before it and seven after.[2]

Translation

92:1   Good it is, to give thanks to Yahweh,
          and to make music to Your name, Most High,
92:2   to proclaim in the morning Your lovingkindness,
          and Your faithfulness in the nights,
92:3   with ten[-stringed instrument] and with harp,
          with playing on the lyre.
92:4   For You have made me glad, Yahweh, by Your doing;
          at the works of Your hands I will shout for joy.
92:5   How great are Your works, Yahweh;
          very deep are Your thoughts.
92:6   The senseless person has no knowledge,
          and a stupid one does not understand this:
92:7   When they flourished, the wicked—just like grass,
          even they blossomed, all those doing iniquity,
          [it was only] to be destroyed for always.

---

1. "For the day of Sabbath." (untranslated here). In their respective superscriptions, the LXX allots seven psalms for that day, including Psalm 92.
2. Tucker, "Ordered World," 362, notes that there are 52 words in the psalm before 92:8, and 52 words after.

92:8   And You [are] exalted for always, Yahweh.
92:9   For, behold, Your enemies, Yahweh—
          for, behold, Your enemies, they perish;
          they are scattered, all those doing iniquity.
92:10 And You exalt my horn like [that of] the wild ox;
          I have been soaked with fresh oil.
92:11 And my eye has gazed [triumphantly] upon my foes;
          of [the fate of] evildoers who rise against me, my ears hear.
92:12 The righteous like a palm tree will flourish,
          like a cedar in Lebanon he will grow high.
92:13 Planted in the house of Yahweh—
          in the courts of our God they will flourish.
92:14 They will still prosper in old age;
          healthy and fresh they will be,
92:15 to proclaim that Yahweh is upright—
          my rock, and there is no unrighteousness in Him.

Structure

In the structure shown below, 92:8 (*D*), a monocolon, forms the pivot of the psalm; this verse is directly preceded and followed by the only two tricola in the psalm, in 92:7 and 92:9. The exaltation of God at the psalm's center is the trigger for all the subsequent triumphs and flourishings of God's people.

A	*Praise of God:* his "lovingkindness" and "faithfulness" (**92:1–5**) ("Most High," 92:1b; "proclaim," 92:2a)	
	B	*Flourishing of the "wicked":* botanical similes (**92:6–7ab**) ("flourished," "just like grass," "blossomed," 92:7ab)
		C *Imminent destruction of the wicked* (**92:7c**) ("destroyed")
		D *Exaltation of God* (**92:8**) ("exalted")
		C' *Implemented destruction of the wicked* (**92:9–11**) ("perish," "scattered," 92:9ab)
	B'	*Flourishing of the "righteous":* botanical similes (**92:12–14**) ("flourish," "like a palm tree," "like a cedar," "grow high," 92:12)
A'	*Praise of God:* his "uprightness" and "no unrighteousness" (**92:15**) ("proclaim," "my rock")	

PSALM 92:1–15

Theological Focus

God is worthy of praise for his attributes and his actions rendering the righteous victorious over enemies and prospering them interminably, while the flourishing of the wicked is impermanent, only to end in self-destruction.

Commentary

Praise of God (92:1–5)

The psalm commences with the word "good," emphatic in its position at the head of the line: "*Good* it is" (92:1aα). It is the thanksgiving and music-making of Yahweh that is decreed "good" (92:1aβ–b). Whether it be "in the morning" or "in the nights"[3]—at every conceivable time—the lovingkindness and faithfulness of Yahweh, the Most High, is to be proclaimed (92:2). And this is to be done with lutes ("ten[-stringed instrument]"[4]), and harps, and lyres (92:3)—in every conceivable way.[5] Besides "Your lovingkindness" and "Your faithfulness" that need to be declared (92:2), there is also "Your doing," the works of "Your hands" (92:4), "Your works,"[6] and "Your thoughts" (92:5) that are worthy of acclamation. What exactly these performances of Yahweh were are not detailed, but likely include creation, redemption, and every other undertaking of Yahweh for the benefit and welfare of his people.

Flourishing of the "Wicked"; Imminent Destruction of the Wicked (92:6–7)

That the people of God rightly recognize God's "works" and "thoughts" for what they are— "great" and "very deep" (92:5)—is accentuated by the failure of the ignorant ("senseless person" and "stupid one"; 92:6) to acknowledge one critical aspect of deity's sovereign works and omniscient thoughts: the fact that the "flourishing" of the wicked and the "blossoming" of the iniquitous would be temporary ("just like grass," 92:7ab[7]) and would ultimately lead to their destruction (92:7c). The transience of their prospering likely reflects God's inscrutable timing for their decreed recompense: in any case, destruction is imminent, and they would be punished "for always" (92:7c). Short-lived would be their celebration, and long-lasting their dissolution.

---

3. The plural likely indicates the multiple watches of the night.
4. Literally, "with ten."
5. Calvin, of course, does not buy it. "Now that Christ has appeared and the Church has reached full age, [to engage in instrumental music] were only to bury the light of the Gospel, should we introduce the shadows of a departed dispensation" that was "terminated with the Gospel" (*Commentary on the Book of Psalms*, 3:495).
6. These "doings" and "work" likely indicate both God's acts of creation (8:3, 6; 19:1; 86:8; 102:25; 103:22; 104:24, 31; 139:14; 145:10) and acts of deliverance (44:1; 66:5; 74:12; 77:12; 95:9; 107:24). Of note, 92:4 is chiastic: "For You have made me glad, Yahweh, / by Your doing; // at the work of Your hands / I will shout for joy."
7. Botanical references show up again with regard to the righteous, in 92:12–13 (below).

Exaltation of God (92:8)

"For always" these wicked would be destroyed (92:7c) but, in contrast, "forever" would be the exaltation of Yahweh (92:8)—an infinitely broad span of time. "Very deep" were Yahweh's thoughts (92:5b), but "exalted" (מָרוֹם, *marom*, also meaning "high/elevated") is he—an infinitely broad span of distance. This exaltation turns the table on God's foes (and the foes of his people); the story itself takes a new turn at this glorious juncture, as detailed in the remaining verses of the psalm.

Implemented Destruction of the Wicked; Flourishing of the "Righteous" (92:9–14)

With the exaltation of God (92:8) comes the unqualified termination of the evildoers: "they perish" and "they are scattered" (92:9bc)—destruction implemented. Making 92:9 parallel to 92:7c is the presence in these verses of the only verbs of ruination in the psalm, all ending in ד, *d*: "destroy" (שׁמד, *shmd*; 92:7c), "perish" (אבד, *'vd*; 92:9b), and "scatter" (פרד, *prd*; 92:9c).[8] Strikingly, both the verbs in 92:9bc ("they perish" and "they are scattered") do not directly implicate divine agency: they take a passive sense and so it appears that the wicked cause their own downfall. Likewise, "be destroyed" in 92:7c is in the *niphal* "which makes the faithless the subject of the verb. They go through a process that has naturalness or inevitability built into it: you are faithless, you flourish, you pass away. Your destiny is in your hands, but you cannot evade the process working itself out."[9] The wicked thus essentially doom themselves, with a little help from God, of course. Yahweh's amazing "doing" (92:4a) led to jubilation; in contrast, the iniquitous "doing" of the wicked (92:7b, 9c) meets its appropriate recompense.

But the exaltation of Yahweh has drastically different consequences for the suffering supplicants of the psalm, the "righteous" (92:12a). In fact, because Yahweh is "exalted" (92:8), the people of God are, too: "And You *exalt* my horn" (92:10a), an event, potentially a military victory, that is marked by the celebratory anointing of oil (92:10b).[10] This triumph is underscored in 92:11, as the evildoers' demise is seen by the eyes and heard by the ears of God's people. That his people are fully on their deity's side is clear: "Your enemies" (92:9a, 9b) are "my foes," "evildoers who rise against me" (92:11).

In a dramatic reversal of images, the botanical description of the wicked in 92:7ab becomes a parallel botanical description of the righteous (below).

---

8. The only other verb in the composition ending in ד is נגד, *ngd*, "proclaim"; this, too, is found symmetrically in the first and last sections of the psalm, in 92:2a and 92:15a.

9. Goldingay, *Psalms*, 3:57. He puts it aptly: "They were being given plenty of rope, so that they could hang themselves."

10. The picture of the horn of the wild ox (92:10a) is symbolic of strength and power.

92:7ab
"flourished"
    "the wicked, just like grass"
"blossomed"
    "all those doing iniquity"

92:12
    "righteous like a palm tree"
"will flourish"
    "[righteous] like a cedar in Lebanon"
"will grow high"

"Unlike the grass [= wicked] that is multiple, the tree [= righteous] stands unique, alone. Unlike the grass that is transient, the tree endures, renews itself, produces fruit."[11] Reverting to the plural for God's people,[12] thus extending the implications far beyond those for the protagonists of the psalm, 92:13–14 continues the botanical allusions with the verbs "planted," "flourish," and "prosper" (as well as the adjective "fresh," 92:14b, as also in 92:10b). But these are not mere comparisons to plant specimens in these two verses: the similes of 92:12 ("like," כְּ, k; 92:12a, 12b) are transformed into the metaphors of 92:13–14 (without comparative particles in these verses). All of this contrasts the transient flourishing of the wicked with the permanent prospering of the righteous (even "in old age," 92:14a), and that in the very presence of God (in his "house" and in his "courts," 92:13).

Praise of God (92:15)

The psalm ends as it began, with the perennially blessed righteous ones "proclaiming" (92:2a, 15a) Yahweh's "uprightness" and the fact that there is "no unrighteousness" in him (92:15). And, corresponding to the appellation of "Most High" in 92:1b, God is labeled "my rock" in 92:15b. This God is worthy of praise!

---

11. Magonet, "Some Concentric Structures," 371. That is to say, perhaps, that while the whole company of evildoers is exterminated, not even a single devout God-fearer will suffer harm.

12. The oscillation between singulars and plurals is seen for both the wicked (singular in 92:6, but plural in 92:7) and the righteous (singular in 92:10–12, but plural in 92:13–14).

Sermon Map

I. Provisional Prospering of the Wicked (92:6–7b)
    Perishing of the Wicked (92:9–11)
    Move-to-relevance: God's triumph in his own time

II. Permanent Prospering of the Righteous (92:12, 14)
    Presence of God (92:13)
    Move-to-relevance: Long-term optimism in God

III. Proclamatory Praise for God (92:1–5, 15)

IV. *Prosper and Praise!*
    Specifics on developing long-term optimism in praise to God

PSALM 93:1–5

Psalm of Orientation

The God-King's Reign of Stability

WHILE PSALMS 2; 18; 20; 21; 45; 72; 101; 110; 132; and 144:1–11 are the ones usually reckoned as the "royal" psalms, this set of seven, Psalms 93; 95–99, also consider God as King.

Translation

93:1 Yahweh, He reigns; grandeur, He dons;
    He dons, Yahweh; [with] strength He girds Himself.
Indeed, established is the world,
    it will not be tottered.

93:2 Established is Your throne from of old;
    from eternity [are] You.

93:3 The rivers have lifted up, Yahweh—
    the rivers, their sound they have lifted up;
    the rivers lift up their crashing [waves].

93:4 More than the sounds of many waters,
    more majestic than the breakers of the sea,
    majestic on high [is] Yahweh.

93:5 Your [covenant] decrees have proven exceedingly reliable;
    holiness adorns Your house, Yahweh, for length of days.

Structure

The structure of the psalm interweaves Yahweh's *Rulership* (and aspects thereof) with the resulting state of the natural world (*Stabilized* and *Subjugated*) and, at the end, with the lives of his people (*Sanctified* by means of deity's decrees and divine demands):[1]

93:1ab	Rulership of Yahweh ("reign")
93:1cd	Stabilized world
93:2	Rulership of Yahweh ("throne")
93:3–4	Subjugated waters
93:5a	Rulership of Yahweh ("decrees")
93:5b	Sanctified worshipers

Theological Focus

God, the grand and majestic King, reigns from eternity past to eternity future, stabilizing the world by his creative activity, subjugating the chaotic waters of anti-God opposition by his strength, and sanctifying worshipers, the community and household of God, by his divine demands.

Commentary

Rulership of Yahweh; Stabilized World (93:1)

That Yahweh "reigns" is established at the forefront, with the emphatic placement of "Yahweh" before the verb (93:1aα): *Yahweh* is the one who rules, not any other god. This God-King dons grandeur and girds strength (93:1aβ–b). That is, he not only has the heft, gravitas, and resplendence of a regent, but girding himself with strength, he is also a mighty military commander.[2] The poetic structure of 93:1ab emphasizes the magnificent breadth of the kingship of Yahweh:[3]

"Yahweh,	He reigns; grandeur [with] strength	He dons; He dons, He girds Himself."	**Yahweh;**

The consequence of Yahweh's reigning is that the world is established without any disequilibrium—indeed, "world" is firmly hemmed in, in the text, on either side by "established"

---

1. In the psalm, there is an admixture of speaking *to* Yahweh (93:2, 3, 5) with speaking *of* Yahweh (93:1, 4).

2. However, as will be noted, the psalm has nothing explicit to say about this regent's martial activities.

3. Modified from Auffret, "Yahveh Regne," 102. Note also the repeats and assonance of לָבֵשׁ לָבֵשׁ, *lavesh lavesh* ("He dons; He dons," 93:1ab) and תֵּבֵל בַּל, *tevel bal* ("world, it will not," 93:1cd).

and "not be tottered" (93:1cd), a literary and textual depiction of its stability. That 93:1cd is a consequence of 93:1ab is suggested by the perfect verbs in the latter ("reigns," "dons" [×2], "girds"]) and the imperfect verbs in the former ("established," "be tottered"): what happened led to what is happening. Besides, "established is the world" (93:1c) is parallel to "established is Your throne" (93:2a): the former happens now because the latter happened "from of old." But how exactly the rulership of Yahweh produces stability in the world is not explained. In all likelihood, it is the creative activity of deity in the cosmos and his disestablishment of chaos (implied also in the subjugated waters, 93:3–4, below), manifestations of his already-existing regency, that are responsible for the ongoing equilibrium of the world. God has always been King (see 93:2), but after his creative enterprises, he is also enthroned over created and ordered matter. Later in the psalm, there are polemical allusions to the combat of contemporary gods in their primeval creation enterprise, but Yahweh, though girded for strength as if for battle, engages in no warfare at all in this text. He does not need to. He is the God-King, the uncontested, unchallenged, undisputed sovereign! He simply stabilizes the world.

Kingship of Yahweh; Subjugated Waters (93:2–4)

And thus we arrive at another affirmation of divine reign: God's throne is established "from of old," for he is "from eternity" (93:2).[4] And because he is King, the world remains stable. This God-King can be trusted to keep his creation intact, ordered, settled, and firm.

But just when we thought all was unassailable and unshakable, we find in 93:3–4 hostile voices being raised. And it is elements of water that are clamorous: the rivers and their "sound" (93:3b), and the "many waters" and their "sounds" (93:4a). These chaotic waters allude to Canaanite cosmogony and combat (the god Baal vs. the god of chaos, Yam [= "sea"]) and to the Babylonian creation myth, *Enuma Elish* (the god Marduk vs. Tiamat [the primordial sea]).[5] And so, in the context of God's creative activity mentioned in 93:1cd, the liquid antagonists of 93:3–4 are likely to be those chaotic waters that God had tamed at creation; they, not annihilated yet, are raising their heads again (93:3). Notably, 93:3ab has perfect verbs ("have lifted up," ×2), but 93:3c has an imperfect verb ("lift up"), the latter indicating a resurgent remnant from the past activity of chaos that is continuing on to the present day.[6] No doubt, those waters have demonic entities behind them and their disruptive behaviors.

Thus, though Yahweh is King and regnant, the danger of this mayhem of hydrological elements is a constant and ongoing threat to both God's reign and to God's people: anti-God agents are always active, and will continue to be so, until their final put-down in the eschaton. But unlike ancient fables with gods and unruly waters scrapping and skirmishing without a clear winner, there is no indication in Psalm 93 of any struggle at all between Yahweh and his antagonists. They are simply overcome and restrained, in the past and even in the present, as made abundantly clear in the textual structure of 93:3–4. The climactic staircase parallelisms in the tricolon of 93:3 ("rivers ... rivers ... rivers"; "lifted up ... lifted up ... lift up") attest to the fact that these waters are, indeed, raising their voices.[7] But the similar parallelism in the

---

4. The verse is chiastic: "established is Your throne / from of old; // from eternity / [are] You."
5. See Human, "Psalm 93," 160–61.
6. But 93:4 is verbless: it appears as though God does not have to do a thing to render these watery mutineers obtund.
7. One can almost feel the increasing surge of the waves in the parallelism, as the fury of chaos swells.

tricolon of 93:4 ("majestic . . . majestic"[8]) and the repeated comparative ("more . . . more . . . ") affirms that Yahweh's might and majesty exceed the contemptible squeals of these anarchic entities (93:4). Waters may raise ("lift up," 93:3a, 3b, 3c) their voices, but they are no match for Yahweh who is "more" (93:4a, 4b) "majestic" (93:4b, 4c) and who is on "high" (93:4c), elevated way above the lowly chorus of those cantankerous predators of God's creation.

Besides, one finds that there are five epithets for these forces of chaos: "rivers" (×3; 93:3), "waters" (93:4a), and "sea" (93:4b), and—as if countering the evil—five instances of "Yahweh" in the psalm (93:1a, 1b, 3a, 4c, 5b). The strength that Yahweh girds himself with (93:1b) renders him indomitable; no power can endanger his reign. Indeed, the regency of Yahweh is not determined by, and does not commence with, the defeat of his foes. Rather, this God-King reigns "from of old" and "from eternity" (93:2ab)—he has always been supreme over all things. In other words, "Yahweh is victor over the chaos, because he is [God-King]. He is not [God-King] because he has proven himself to be victor over chaos powers."[9] The ending of 93:4 is thus a fitting climax: "majestic on high [is] Yahweh." Yahweh is, and always has, the last word!

Yet the fact is that the victory of God is yet to be fully consummated, and threats of chaos remain (as implied in the imperfect verb of 93:3c); thus, our psalm permits no blithe and complacent understanding of a trouble-free, enemy-devoid world. At least not yet. Nonetheless, God's people can be confident that the God-King can handle even the most vociferous and ferocious of those of agents of malevolence.

Rulership of Yahweh; Sanctified Worshipers (93:5)

Not only is his reigning authority responsible for the stability of the world (93:1) and the subjugation of the waters (93:3–4), his government is characterized by divine decrees—his covenant law, his divine demands[10]—that have been "proven exceedingly reliable" (93:5a). And thus this majestic God-King of cosmos-stability and chaos-subjugation fame, "the transcendent God, whose eternal kingship is described in mythical terms in . . . [93:1–4], can be experienced in the concrete reality of the Torah and holiness of the temple" and, in the current dispensation, through Scripture and in the community of God's people, the "holy temple in the Lord" and the "dwelling of God in the Spirit" (Eph 2:21–22).[11] And this end, community sanctification—holiness adorning deity's abode (Ps 93:5b)—is accomplished by means of Yahweh's "decrees," his divine demand guiding the holy behavior of his faithful.[12] Indeed, 93:5 is implicitly asserting

---

8. Here, in 93:4b, the text literally reads: "majestic the breakers of the sea," which does not fit the sense of the rest of the verse. This syntactical difficulty is ameliorated if the final מ, *m*, of אַדִּירִים, *'addirim*, is moved to the next word, מִמִּשְׁבְּרֵי־יָם, *mimishbre-yam*, thus reading 93:4b as "more majestic than the breakers of the sea" (or "majestic more than . . ."). That would leave אַדִּירֵי, *'addire*, with a paragogic י, *y* (see Pardee, "Poetic Structure," 164).

9. Human, "Psalm 93," 162n73.

10. As in 19:8; 25:10; 78:5, 56; 99:7; 132:12.

11. Human, "Psalm 93," 165. As in 93:1 and 93:3, here in 93:5 also there is an alternation between a perfect verb (93:5a; "have proven": the long-standing and unimpeachable reliability of divine demand) and an imperfect one (93:5b; "adorns": the ongoing holiness that that divine demand inculcates and calls for in God's household and God's Kingdom).

12. Notions like this do not invalidate divine grace: the Christ-imaging holiness called for in all of Scripture is God-glorifying, Spirit-driven, merit-excluding, grace-accepting, and faith-exercising obedience, that pleases God, not self-glorifying, flesh-driven, merit-seeking, grace-denying, and faith-negating works that

that it is the decrees of this God-King that render his people sanctified and holy—fixed and firm, unchaotic and ordered, as stable as the natural world.

The reign of the God-King, Yahweh, thus extends from eternity past ("from of old," "from eternity," 93:2) to eternity future ("for length of days," 93:5b). And "this temporal description ['for length of days'] puts an exclamation mark behind the realization that Yahweh's kingship is durable and can be experienced as reality in history. Chaotic and destructive powers pose no threat to his kingship."[13] Instead, divine demands, the decrees of God, that produce holiness in the people of God (the "house" of God, 93:5b), create stability in the divine community. Holiness, therefore, *is* the stability God desires in his own house—produced by the sanctifying word of God in the lives of the people of God. Thus the psalm leaves the readers with the implication that just as the world was stabilized (and rambunctious waters subjugated), so too must the people of God be stabilized (and rebellious humans subdued): and that happens by means of Scripture (and through the gracious agency of its Author, the Holy Spirit).

Sermon Map

I. Stabilizing World
    God's reign of grandeur and strength from eternity past (93:1ab, 2)
    The stabilized world (93:1cd)
    Move-to-relevance: God's creative power

II. Subjugating Waters
    The subversive waters (93:3)
    The subjugated waters (93:4)
    Move-to-relevance: God's control over all other powers

III. Sanctifying Word
    The steadfast word (93:5a)
    The sanctifying word (93:5b)

IV. *Stabilized and Sanctified!*
    Stability of God's house is the sanctity of God's house

---

are nothing but legalism, and displeasing to God.

13. Human, "Psalm 93," 166.

PSALM 94:1–23

Psalm of Disorientation

God's Care for the Assaulted Weak

THOUGH PSALM 94 HAS pleas (94:1–2), and the supplicant is in obvious distress from oppression—making this a psalm of disorientation—the tenor of the composition exudes considerable confidence in the ways and workings of deity.

Translation

94:1 God of vengeance, Yahweh—
   God of vengeance, shine forth.
94:2 Lift yourself up, Judge of the earth,
   return recompense upon the proud.
94:3 Until when will the wicked, Yahweh—
   until when will the wicked exult?
94:4 They pour out [words], they talk with insolence;
   they speak boastfully, all doers of iniquity.
94:5 Your people, Yahweh, they crush,
   and Your inheritance they afflict.
94:6 The widow and the stranger they slay,
   and the orphans they murder.
94:7 And they say, "Yah does not see,
   and the God of Jacob does not pay attention."
94:8 Pay attention, senseless ones among the people;
   and the stupid, when will you understand?
94:9 Will not the One who planted the ear—does He not hear?
   Even the One who shaped the eye, does He not observe?
94:10 Will not the One who instructs the nations—does He not rebuke,
   the One who teaches humankind knowledge?

94:11 Yahweh, He knows the thoughts of humankind,
          that they are a breath.
94:12 Blessing [upon] the one whom You instruct, Yah,
          and whom You teach from Your law,
94:13 to grant rest to him from days of evil,
          until a hole is dug for the wicked.
94:14 For Yahweh will not abandon His people,
          and His inheritance He will not forsake.
94:15 For judgment will return unto righteousness,
          and all the upright in heart will follow it.
94:16 Who will rise up for me against evil ones?
          Who will stand firm for me against doers of iniquity?
94:17 Were Yahweh not a help to me,
          soon my soul would have abided in silence.
94:18 If I said, "My foot has tottered,"
          Your lovingkindness, Yahweh, supports me.
94:19 When my anxieties are in abundance within me,
          Your consolations delight my soul.
94:20 Can a throne of ruin ally with You—
          one that shapes trouble by statute?
94:21 They band together against the soul of the righteous,
          and the blood of the innocent they condemn.
94:22 But Yahweh has been to me a stronghold,
          and my God, the rock of my refuge.
94:23 He returns upon them their iniquity,
          and in their evil, He destroys them—
          He destroys them, Yahweh our God.

Structure

Two stanzas (or cycles) of *Pleas* for divine intervention and *Professions* of faith make up the structural core of the psalm. It opens with petition (*Plea 1*, 94:1–7), and goes to a declaration of faith in God's punishment of the wicked and preservation of the righteous (*Profession 1*, 94:8–15). There is then seemingly a return to petitioning in the second stanza (*Plea 2*, 94:16), voiced with a rhetorical question.[1] The subsequent declaration (*Profession 2*,

---

1. *Plea 2* (94:16) is not exactly a petition since there are no explicit imperatives directed to Yahweh; in the totality of the poem these are found only in 94:1–2. But *Plea 2* reuses "doers of iniquity" from 94:4 and the format of a question from 94:3, i.e., from *Plea 1*, rendering these pleas similar. Besides, both 94:3 and 94:16 have duplicated interrogative particles ("until when" and "who," respectively) and both these verses name foes twice ("wicked" ×2 in 94:3; "evil ones" and "doers of iniquity" in 94:16).

94:17–23) concludes the psalm. Each of the *Professions* deals with both the punishment of the wicked and the preservation of the righteous:[2]

> STANZA 1 *(94:1–15)*
> **Plea 1** (94:1–7)
> "doers of iniquity" (94:4b); question: "when" (×2; 94:3)
> **Profession 1 (94:8–15)**
>   "evil" (94:13a); "wicked" (רָשָׁע, *rashaʿ*; 94:13b)
>   "shape" (94:9b); "return" (94:15a)
>
> STANZA 2 *(94:16–23)*
> **Plea 2 (94:16)**
> "doers of iniquity" (94:16b); question: "who" (×2; 94:16)
> **Profession 2 (94:17–23)**
>   "evil" (94:23b); "condemn" (רשׁע, *rshʿ*; 94:21b)
>   "shape" (94:20b); "return" (94:23a)

Theological Focus

> In dangerous circumstances of oppression, particularly from inside forces of power wielded in wickedness and evil, the suffering people of God remain confident of their omniscient and loving God's knowledge of their distress and his care for his own and, with this understanding gathered from God's law, they rest in faith upon God their rock and their refuge, who will repay the doers of iniquity and vindicate the righteous.

Commentary

Stanza 1: Plea 1; Profession 1 (94:1–15)

Stanza 1—the first cycle, *Plea 1* and *Profession 1* (94:1–15)—is neatly constructed to focus upon the folly of ignorance (the assumption that God does not see or know the plight of his people) and its counterpart, the blessedness of being taught from divine law (see below).[3]

---

2. Modified from Girard, *Les Psaumes Redécouverts*, 544–46. The psalm also alternates between addressing Yahweh (94:1–7, 12–13, 18–20) and addressing others (94:8–11, 14–17, 21–23).

3. Modified from Auffret, "Essai sur la structure litteraire du Psaume 94," 63; and Auffret, "Qui se lèvera pour moi?," 137.

94:1–2	"judge" (94:2a); "return" (94:2b)
94:3–6	"until when" (עַד־מָתַי, 'ad-matî, ×2; 94:3); "wicked" (×2; 94:3)
	"Your people" (94:5a); "Your inheritance" (94:5b)
94:7–8	Yahweh does not *see or know*
	"senseless ones" / "the stupid" who do not "understand" (94:8)
94:9–12	Yahweh does *see and know*
	"blessing" on those who are "taught" (94:12)
94:13–14	"until" (עַד, 'ad; 94:13b); "wicked" (94:13b)
	"His people" (94:14a); "His inheritance" (94:14b)
94:15	"judgment"; "return"

The emotional impact of the plea is intensified by the staircase parallelisms in 94:1 ("God of vengeance, Yahweh—God of vengeance") and 94:3 ("until when will the wicked, Yahweh—until when will the wicked"). It laments the self-aggrandizing words (94:4, 7) and horrific deeds (94:5–6) of the wicked. The psalmist does not hold back his rhetorical punches: it is "Your people" and "Your inheritance," he insists to Yahweh, who are being oppressed (94:5). It might well be that these wicked ones are part of the divine community, since they seem to be capable of persecuting even the weak and disenfranchised within the congregation. In fact, these evil ones even talk about God as "Yah" (94:7a). They definitely wield power, as 94:20a implies, labeling them a "throne of ruin," symbolizing their destructive authority: "they are not just citizens, but people with the power to harm by statute and law."[4] Thus "the psalm is only a step away from suggesting that the people in power have forfeited their membership in this community."[5]

The egregious error of these powerful wicked is that they think Yahweh is oblivious and unable to see what is going on, or that he is uncaring and unwilling to see (94:7). Their words are thrown back at them: they who thought Yahweh was not "paying attention" (94:7b) are now held to account: *they* had better "pay attention," otherwise they remain "senseless" and "stupid" (94:8).[6] Earlier the supplicant had pled with God: until "when [מָתַי]" would these malefactors self-aggrandize? (94:3); now he admonishes those wicked directly: "when [מָתַי] will you understand?" (94:8b).

The logic is irrefutable: how can the one who created the ear and the eye not hear or know, as the evildoers assume? Yahweh, the Creator, the psalmist avers, is not oblivious (94:9). The oppressors are thereby put on notice: the omniscient deity, who instructs nations and teaches humankind knowledge, is surely cognizant of what is going on in his community (94:10). The section, 94:9–12, is itself constructed chiastically, to emphasize the exclusively divine sourcing of knowledge (below).[7]

---

4. deClaissé-Walford et al., *Book of Psalms*, 713 (italics removed).

5. Goldingay, *Psalms*, 3:78.

6. These foolish ones are likely to be the oppressors themselves, who vaunt themselves as untouchable as they go about their nefarious ways within the community.

7. From Girard, *Les Psaumes Redécouverts*, 554.

94:10abα	"instructs"; "teaches"
94:10bβ	"humankind"
94:10bγ	**"knowledge"**
94:11aα	**"knows"**
94:11aβ	"humankind"
94:12	"instruct"; "teach"

Yahweh, the one who teaches "knowledge" (94:10b), certainly "knows" that his subjugated and discriminated and assaulted people are feeble, frail, and mortal (94:11), widows, strangers, and orphans among them (94:6). And so the people of God can rest assured that Yahweh is concerned for his own, and that he will never abandon or forsake them (94:14).

At any rate, the one who has absorbed this datum of knowledge taught by Yahweh from his law—i.e., the one who comprehends divine omniscience and divine care for God's own—is blessed (94:12). That makes sense in the context of oppression, because this well-taught, sensible, and sage person acknowledges confidently that Yahweh will "grant rest to him" in these "days of evil" (94:13).

> Yhwh's teaching makes promises about how Yhwh will put things right. There are then two possible senses in which Yhwh gives people rest in the meantime. Even if the faithless do not actually fall yet, Yhwh provides interim respite from their attacks; they do not finally overwhelm Yhwh's people. And further, because Yhwh is going to put things right in due course, one can stay calm in times of trouble, stay calm from them (be distanced from them), knowing that Yhwh will bring them to an end.[8]

Judgment, the psalmist assures, will return to its God-ordained state and baseline of "righteousness" that the upright will experience, as they "follow" in its wake, reveling in their vindication (94:15). Once it was "*all* the doers of iniquity" who were flying high (94:4a), ranting and raving; soon it will be "*all* the upright in heart" who will have "righteousness" (i.e., vindication) on their side (94:15). Thus, the ones due punishment will receive their deserts; the ones due relief, their deliverance. So the righteous can enjoy "rest" even amidst the ongoing storm, "*until* a pit is dug for the wicked" (94:13) when evildoers are eliminated once for all, thus answering the earlier question of the psalmist: "*until* when" will the wicked thrive? (94:3a).[9] The "Judge of the earth" was asked to rise up (94:2a), and he is soon going to do so—"judgment" will return (94:15a)! The long and short of it is that the one who discerns this work of God in times of trouble remains unshakable—blessed is he (94:12a)!

The particular good fate of the blessed righteous is depicted chiastically, centering upon the indisputable and comforting fact that God never abandons or forsakes his own (94:13b–15; see below).[10]

---

8. Goldingay, *Psalms*, 3:81. Of course, the "rest" God provides may take numerous forms. Perhaps it will be relief from oppression. Perhaps it will be relief *amidst* oppression. The preacher will not be able to tell the flock the shape and size of these "rests," but one thing is sure: God *will* grant rest, one way or another.

9. Again, it is best that the people of God leave the timetable of his deliverance up to divine sovereignty, trusting in his solicitude for them at all times.

10. Auffret, "Qui se lèvera pour moi?," 140n29.

94:13b	"until [עַד] ... wicked"	
	"for"	
	"Yahweh will not [לֹא, *loʾ*] abandon"	
94:14		**"His people"**
		"His inheritance"
	"He will not [לֹא] forsake"	
	"for"	
94:15	"unto [עַד] righteousness"	

Stanza 2: Plea 2; Profession 2 (94:16–23)

The first occurrence of the first person is in this second cycle of plea and profession, in 94:16. The psalmist feels all alone, no one to arise to render him help. With two questions and the employment of "doers of iniquity" and "evil ones" in 94:16, this quasi-plea, *Plea 2*, becomes a restatement of *Plea 1*. However, the plaintive query quickly moves to a confident profession: Yahweh is a help to him (94:17); if it were not for deity and his aid, the psalmist would have been dwelling in silence, i.e., in the grave. The section, 94:16–23, is also neatly crafted, centering upon the delighted "soul" of the righteous:[11]

94:16a	"evil ones"; "who will rise up for me"
94:16b	"iniquity"; "who will stand firm"
94:17a	"Yahweh"; "to me"; "help"
94:17b	"soul"; "silenced"
94:19b	**"soul"; "delighted"**
94:21	"soul"; "condemned"
94:22a	"Yahweh"; "to me"; "stronghold"; "refuge"
94:23a	"iniquity"; "He returns upon them"
94:23bc	"evil": "He destroys them ... Yahweh our God"

"Evil ones" and "doers of iniquity" cause the psalmist to ask "who" will deliver him (×2; 94:16).[12] The end of the structural sequence answers the question emphatically: "He [God] returns upon them" their "iniquity" and "*Yahweh our God* destroys them" in their "evil" (94:23), an assertion made all the more poignant with the staircase parallelism in 94:23bc ("He destroys them—He destroys them").[13] Within the chiasm, at the center is the delighted "soul" (94:19b) reveling in "Your lovingkindness" that support and "Your consolations" that exhilarate (94:18b, 19b). Yes, his "anxieties are in abundance" (94:19a), as literally depicted

---

11. Modified from Girard, *Les Psaumes Redécouverts*, 557; and Auffret, "Essai sur la structure litteraire du Psalume 94," 57.

12. That they are represented by a "throne of ruin" suggests their governmental and systemic power, as was noted (94:20a); that they are the "wicked [רָשָׁע]" of 94:3a, 3b is evident in that they are the ones who "condemn [רשׁע]" the righteous (94:21b).

13. Thus the psalm ends as it began with staircase parallelisms bookending the composition (94:1, 3 and 94:23).

with the "soul" "silenced" and the "soul" "condemned" (94:17b, 21) on either side of the "soul" "delighted" (94:19b). But "Yahweh" has been "to me" a "help" (94:17a) and "Yahweh" has been "to me" a "stronghold" and a "rock of my refuge" (94:22). The "God of vengeance, Yahweh" (94:1a), who had been asked at the commencement of the psalm to "return . . . upon" the wicked recompense (94:2b), will, in fact, do so: "He returns upon them their iniquity" (94:23). Not only is this deliverance being anticipated by the supplicant, he considers it almost accomplished, as indicted by the *qal wav* consecutive in 94:22: . . . וַיְהִי יְהוָה, *wayhi yhwh* . . . , "and Yahweh *has been* . . ." Quite a profession of faith, indeed!

Sermon Map

I. Plea for Help
   The distress of God's people (94:1–3, 16)
   The arrogance of evildoers within the community (94:4–7, 20–21)
   Move-to-relevance: Situations of oppression from within community
II. Profession of Hope
   God's knowledge and support (94:8–11, 14–15, 16–19, 22–23)
   God's educational program for the distressed (94:12–13)
   Move-to-relevance: Learning about God's help in distress
III. *Ravaged but Restful!*
   Specifics on resting upon the faithful assurance of God's help

PSALM 95:1–11

Psalm of Orientation

Worship and Submission

PSALM 95 IS AN extended exhortation to worship God, with explanations as to why his people should do so. But the last section gives the psalm a twist: it touches on the critical issue of faithful obedience of God's people to the God whom they worship.

Translation

95:1	Come, let us shout for joy to Yahweh;	
	let us proclaim triumphantly to the rock of our deliverance.	
95:2	Let us approach His presence with thanksgiving;	
	with songs let us proclaim triumphantly to Him.	
95:3	For a great God is Yahweh,	
	and a great King above all gods,	
95:4	in whose hand are the depths of the earth,	
	and the peaks of the mountains are His,	
95:5	to whom is the sea, and He—He made it,	
	and the dry land His hands—they shaped it.	
95:6	Enter, let us worship and let us bow down;	
	let us kneel before Yahweh our Maker.	
95:7	For He is our God,	
	and we the people of His pasture and the sheep of His hand.	
	This day, if you listen to His voice,	
95:8	do not harden your hearts, as at Meribah,	
	as in the day of Massah in the wilderness,	
95:9	"where your fathers tested Me,	
	[where] they tried Me, though they had seen My deeds.	

95:10 Forty years I was loathing the generation,
> and I said [they are] a people who go astray in the heart of theirs;
> and they—they do not know My ways:

95:11 of whom I swore in My anger,
> 'If they enter into My rest . . .'"

Structure

Three rounds of exhortation and explanation structure this psalm, dealing respectively with the *Sounds, Stance,* and *Submission* of worship:[1]

> ***Sounds of Worship*** (95:1–5)
> *Exhortation:* Sounds of worship (**95:1–2**)
> "come" (95:1a); "presence [פָּנֶה, *paneh*]" (95:2a)
> *Explanation:* "King"; "Maker" (**95:3–5**)
> "for"; "God" (95:3a); "gods" (95:3b); "hand" (95:4a, 5b)
>
> ***Stance of Worship*** (95:6–7b)
> *Exhortation:* Stance of worship (**95:6**)
> "enter" (95:6a); "before [לִפְנֵי, *liphne*]" (95:6b)
> *Explanation:* Shepherd (**95:7ab**)
> "for"; "God" (95:7a); "hand" (95:7b)
>
> ***Submission of Worship*** (95:7c–11)
> *Exhortation:* Submission [of worship] (**95:7c–8**)
> *Explanation:* Discipliner (**95:9–11**): *Oracle of God*

The first two sections, making up 95:1–7b, deal with the sounds and stance of worship;[2] the last, 95:7c–11, with the submission of worship—faithful obedience in the lives of the worshipers. In 95:1–7b, the psalmist identifies himself with his people (first person plurals in the form of suffixes and a pronoun: 95:1a, 1b [×2], 2a, 2b, 6a [×2], 6b [×2], 7a, 7b); in 95:7c–8, the psalmist challenges them in the second person plural (verbs: 95:7c, 8a). In 95:9–11, the psalmist disappears; instead, God takes over, directly warning his people in an oracle. Worship is all well and good, the psalmist (and God) appears to be saying, but the question (implied entirely in the words of deity) is: "Will you submit worshipfully to me/God, to live in faithful obedience?"

---

1. Modified from Girard, *Les Psaumes Redécouverts*, 562.

2. The exhortation of the first section has an imperative ("come") followed by four cohortatives ("let us shout for joy," "let us proclaim triumphantly" [×2], and "let us approach"; 95:1–2); the exhortation of the second section likewise has an imperative ("enter") followed by three cohortatives ("let us worship," "let us bow down," and "let us kneel"; 95:6; also note the other similarities between these exhortations: see figure above). The exhortation of the last section is different, with a single jussive that is preceded by a conditional "if" ("if you listen to His voice, do not harden your hearts"; 95:7b–8a).

PSALM 95:1–11

Theological Focus

> God's people appropriately worship their deity with sounds of praise and stances of prostration, but if such undertakings are not accompanied by submission in piety—a life of faithful obedience—they run the risk of displeasing their God and dispossessing eternal rewards.

Commentary

Sounds of Worship; Stance of Worship (95:1–7b)

The first word of the psalm, "come," translates the imperative of הלך, *hlk*, "to walk," "meaning more like 'move it' or 'let's get going.'"[3] This motion is directed towards the "presence" of Yahweh (95:2a), literally to his "face" (פָּנֶה), emphasizing the reality of encountering him personally in worship. But the exhortation in 95:1-2 is actually about making noise—the *Sounds of Worship*.

> Both the noise and clamor of shouting and the beauty and order of melody contribute to Yhwh's praise. The repetition of reference to shouting ["let us proclaim triumphantly," 95:1b, 2b] underlines further that it is not enough for worship of Yhwh to be a heart attitude. One reason is that worship has to glorify Yhwh publicly. Heart worship cannot do this . . . Another reason is that we are physical beings, with voices. Heart praise is not praise by the whole person. In worship as in other aspects of life, we naturally express ourselves with cries and shouts. It is difficult to imagine how there can be praise without these.[4]

The explanation for this vocal acclamation in worship follows in 95:3-5: because he is "a great God" and "a great King" (95:3a, 3b) above every other conceivable power—a "vertical" view of deity ("*above* all gods," 95:3b) in a supernatural dimension. With "great" repeated in 95:3, there is no doubt that this is an impressive deity! Notice the Hebrew order of its words:

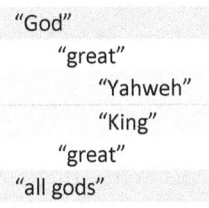

---

3. deClaissé-Walford et al., *Book of Psalms*, 716. After the first word, the rest of 95:1 is synonymously parallel: "let us shout for joy" and "let us proclaim triumphantly," to "Yahweh" and to "the rock of our deliverance," respectively. Following that, 95:2 is chiastic: "Let us approach his presence / with thanksgiving; // with songs / let us proclaim triumphantly to Him."

4. Goldingay, *Psalms*, 3:91. And later we will agree with the psalmist that it is also difficult to imagine how there can be praise without a proper *stance* and without a proper *submission*.

But there is also another sense in which one can ascribe greatness to God—in a natural dimension: he is the Creator of all things, from the depths of the earth to its peaks (another vertical span). Indeed 95:4 has the earth and the mountains ensconced at either end by God:

> "in whose [God's] hand
> are the depths of the earth,
> and the peaks of the mountains
> are His"

And we also have a "horizontal" aspect of God's greatness: both the seas and the dry land are of his making, the scope of divine creation extending horizontally everywhere (95:5).[5] A great God, indeed.

The psalm then cycles back to a second round of exhortation and explanation, the *Stance of Worship* (95:6–7b). And once again the "face" of God appears: "let us kneel before [לִפְנֵי, *liphne*, 'before the face of'] Yahweh" (95:6b). Thus, the people of God are again brought face-to-face with their deity in worship. The "enter" in 95:6a might well indicate access into the sanctuary (as in 96:8; 100:2). And the exhortation is specifically to "worship" (that has the sense of prostration), to "bow down" (that has the sense of genuflection), and to "kneel" (95:6)—all physical aspects: the *Stance of Worship*.

"Although 'come in' ['enter'] suggests horizontal movement, perhaps with irony the spelling out of the invitation involves vertical movement, and none of it upward . . . all three Hebrew words denote downward bodily movement"—"worship," "bow down," and "kneel."[6] Thus, after an exhortation of the *Sounds of Worship* in 95:1–5, we have here in 95:6–7b the *Stance of Worship*, the posture of God's people in the presence of their awesome deity. It is not enough to have an attitude of humility before God—that attitude should work itself out in the physicality of both sounds and stances of worship, audible and visible to the natural (and supernatural) world. The one to whom such a physical stance of homage is due is "Yahweh our *Maker*" (עשׂה, *'sh*; 95:6b). God's creative "making" (also from עשׂה) had been referred to in 95:5a; here the emphasis is on God as "*our* Maker"—the calling out of a people who would be his own (see 95:7ab).[7]

God is a big, unmanageable, cosmic, awesome, omnipotent deity. "Why, then, does God often seem so small in church? Maybe it has something to do with the fact that when we hear the words 'O come, let us worship and bow down, let us kneel before the LORD, our Maker!' no one either kneels or bows down," or raises shouts of acclamation.[8] Sadly true, in most churches! Both vocal proclamation by, and physical prostration of, worshipers are necessary, as this psalm makes clear, because—and here is the explanation (95:7ab)—this transcendent deity is "our God," and immanent as our Shepherd! In his pasture are his people, and in his hand, his sheep. When God who is utterly other comes near to his people, we *must* worship in soniferous verbalizing and self-abnegating veneration.

---

5. The verse, 95:5, is parallel in its structure: each line has object ("sea," "dry land"), deity ("He," "His hands"), and verb ("He made it," "they shaped it").

6. Goldingay, *Psalms*, 3:93.

7. For this specific sense of God "making [עשׂה]" or forming his chosen people, see 100:3, in addition to Deut 32:6, 15; Isa 44:2. Thus the sense is not creation, but redemption, calling out.

8. Byars, "Psalm 95," 77–78.

Submission of Worship (95:7c–11)

While sounds and stances of worship took up more than half the psalm, it is the attitude of faithful obedience that is dealt with in its remainder—and that in the words of God directly cited.

> One can imagine that the exhortation in ... [95:1–7b] might be easy to accept, even welcome. Yet with hindsight we may reckon that ... [95:1–7b] have set us up. Yes, people might be able to enthuse about showing some noisy enthusiasm ... But the enthusiasm concerns Yhwh's being king, and such liturgical submission to Yhwh as king presupposes that it is a liturgical expression of a submission in everyday life. The last section of the psalm implicitly raises questions about the reality of the praise and prostration in ... [95:1–7b]. It has taken it from shouting to prostration; now it takes the people on further.[9]

Indeed, it leads God's people to the key demand of God: listening to him/obeying him in faith, as the psalmist's preamble to God's oracle (95:9–11) makes clear: "listen to [or 'obey'] His voice" and "do not harden your hearts" (95:7c–8a).[10] And such obedience begins today—"this *day*" (95:7c)—even as the "*day* of Massah," the yesterday of the recalcitrant and non-listening ancient community of God's people, is brought to mind (95:8b).[11] The lack of faith in God demonstrated by those ancestors, particularly the doubting of God's presence with them (Exod 17:7), was what ignited divine ire. Their hardening of "hearts" (Ps 95:8a) is equated with "going astray in the *heart* of theirs" (95:10b):[12]

> "and I said
>   [they are] a people who go astray in the heart
>   of theirs [הֵם, *hem*];
>   and they [וְהֵם, *whem*]—
>   they do not know My ways:
>   of whom I swore in my anger ...."

The long and short of it, according to God himself, is that such unfaithful ones "do not know My ways" (95:10c), even though they had "seen My deeds" (95:9b)—likely the exodus, or perhaps more generally his gracious acts to them. God was mighty displeased then, and for a long time—forty years; even after that he was irate with them (as suggested by the *yiqtol* verb, translated "was loathing," 95:10a—an ongoing vexation). And he will still, "this day" (95:7c), be equally displeased with the current generation of his people for inheriting and displaying that same faithless non-listening/non-obedience.

And this faithlessness and failure to listen/obey would have serious consequences, spelled out in the enigmatic oath of 95:11b that emphasizes divine resolve to *not* permit the unfaithful ones to "enter" into his rest.[13] Paradoxically, the community of God was exhorted

---

9. Goldingay, *Psalms*, 3:94.

10. Both "listen" and "obey" translate the same verb, שָׁמַע, *shm'* (95:7c). For more on "faithful obedience," see my *Privilege the Text!*, 196–210.

11. That history is found in Exod 17:1–7; Num 20:13, 24; Deut 6:16; 9:22; 32:51; 33:8; it is also recounted in Pss 81:7; 106:32.

12. Figure from Auffret, "Essai sur la structure littéraire du Psaume 95," 59.

13. "The form of an oath in Hebrew often leaves the consequence [self-pronounced bane] of

to "enter" (95:6a), because they were the "people" of the divine pasture (95:7b). Now they are "people" who are wayward (95:10b) and they will *not* be allowed to "enter" (95:11b):

> "enter" (95:6a): *entrance prescribed*
> "people" of the divine pasture (95:7b)
>
> "people" who are wayward (95:10b)
> "[not] enter" (95:11b): *entrance proscribed*

"Rest" in 132:8, 14 refers to the location of God's dwelling, the temple. Goldingay concludes that the failure to "enter into My rest" (95:11b) is thus a refusal to allow this intractable people of God to worship their deity. The fact that in 95:6 they were exhorted to "enter" and worship might incline one in that direction.[14] But in the current dispensation, that cannot be the interpretive thrust. Instead, it is best to consider "rest" as the promise of future rewards in the eschaton, one's inheritances, that are in danger of being forfeited for living a faithless Christian life.[15] Such rewards are conditional upon holiness/sanctification, as even our psalm makes clear in the parallels between 95:7c–8a and 95:10–11:[16]

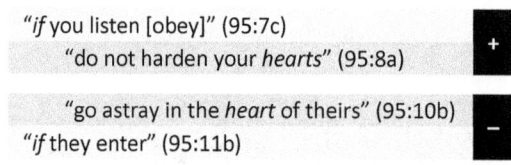

The listening/obeying (or not) determines the reception (or not) of rewards, the entry into the promised rest of God. The fact is that failure to obey in faith strongly displeases God.[17]

What a threatening way to conclude a psalm! "The effect of ending as it does is to put us readers on the spot."[18] That, of course, is the intention.[19] "Psalm 95 reminds us that worship of this God is serious business. This God is mighty and powerful, and our reverence is due our Great Creator. It also reminds us that worship and the way we live are related."[20] The *Sounds of Worship* and the *Stance of Worship* must be matched by *Submission of Worship*—in life and in our relationship to God, the King, the Maker, and the Shepherd.

---

nonfulfillment unstated in the manner of . . . [95:11b]; for the complete form, see, for example, 1 Sam 25:22. Of course, God could not swear in this way, by calling for divine sanction upon [his own] nonfulfillment; the literal logic of the oath is ignored when it appears on God's lips" (Goldingay, *Psalms*, 3:97).

14. See Goldingay, *Psalms*, 3:97, for his view.

15. As I see the author of Hebrews also asserting in Heb 4:1–11. Rather than justification, this refers to rewards for practical sanctification (empowered by God the Spirit), an obedience that is God-glorifying, Spirit-driven, merit-excluding, grace-accepting, and faith-exercising. See Kuruvilla, *Privilege the Text!*, 189–209, 252–68.

16. From Girard, *Les Psaumes Redécouverts*, 568.

17. But the obedience of faith does please God (Col 1:10).

18. Goldingay, *Psalms*, 3:98.

19. And the intention of every pericope of Scripture, I might add.

20. deClaissé-Walford et al., *Book of Psalms*, 717.

PSALM 95:1–11

Sermon Map

I. Sounds of Worship and Stance of Worship
   Sounds of praise (95:1–5)
   Stance of prostration (95:6–7b)
   Move-to-relevance: Our failure to recognize the greatness of God
II. Submission of Worship
   Submission in piety (faithful obedience) is essential (95:7c–8aα)
   Failure of such submission has consequences (95:8aβ–11)
   Move-to-relevance: The linkage of worship with life
III. *Praise and Prostration with Piety!*
   Specifics on faithful obedience as part of a worshipful lifestyle

PSALM 96:1–13

Psalm of Orientation

Community, Converts, and Creation
Worship the God-King

PSALM 96 IS A grand composition that calls for all creation to be praising Yahweh. A "new song" is certainly needed (96:1a) for this universal acclaim of deity.

Translation

96:1 Sing to Yahweh a new song;
      sing to Yahweh, all the earth.
96:2 Sing to Yahweh, bless His name;
      proclaim day to day His deliverance.
96:3 Recount among the nations His glory,
      among all the peoples His wonderful doings.
96:4 For great is Yahweh and exceedingly to be praised;
      He is the One who is to be feared above all the gods.
96:5 For all the gods of the peoples are worthless,
      but Yahweh—the heavens He made.
96:6 Splendor and majesty are before Him,
      strength and beauty are in His sanctuary.
96:7 Ascribe to Yahweh, families of the peoples—
      ascribe to Yahweh glory and strength.
96:8 Ascribe to Yahweh the glory of His name;
      bear an offering and come into His courts.
96:9 Worship Yahweh in [His] holy majesty;
      tremble before Him, all the earth.

96:10 Say among the nations, "Yahweh reigns;
         yes, the world is firmly established, it cannot be tottered;
         He judges the peoples with uprightness."
96:11 Let the heavens be joyful, and let the earth jubilate;
         let the sea roar, and all its fullness;
96:12   let the field exult, and all that is in it.
         Then all the trees of the forest will shout for joy
96:13   before Yahweh, for [He] comes—
         for [He] comes to judge the earth.
         He judges the world in righteousness,
         and the peoples in His faithfulness.

Structure

This psalm is another of the praise compositions with several exhortation-explanation cycles. But Psalm 96 gradually widens its scope: from praise of God by community (96:1–6), to praise of God by converts (foreigners who have, ostensibly, turned to Yahweh; 96:7–10), to praise of God by creation itself (96:11–13):[1]

	PRAISE of GOD	
96:1–3	Exhortation to Community	"peoples" (96:3b) "earth" (96:1b)
96:4–6	Explanation 1	"peoples" (96:5a) "heavens" (96:5b)
96:7–9	Exhortation to Converts	"peoples" (96:7a) "earth" (96:9b)
96:10	Explanation 2	"peoples' (96:10c) "world" (96:10b)
96:11–13aα	Exhortation to Creation	"heavens," "earth" (96:11a)
96:13aβ–d	Explanation 3	"peoples" (96:13d) "earth," "world" (96:13bc)

---

1. Modified from Girard, *Les Psaumes Redécouverts*, 585–86.

Theological Focus

New praise and worship is due to God from his community and his converts (who engage in missional activity to enlarge the body of those praising God), and from all of his creation, for the unprecedented doings of the great and glorious Creator and Deliverer, whose reign is stable, whose judgment is righteous, and whose coming is imminent.

Commentary

Exhortation to Community; Explanation 1 (96:1–6)

Perhaps the layout of the psalm explains why a "new song" is needed (96:1). After all, all humanity (God's community[2] and converts/nations/peoples) and all creation are going to be praising Yahweh: this is a new thing that is happening (though adumbrated in other texts and even in the Psalter)—and new things happening call for new songs to be sung.[3]

At any rate, the psalm commences with a staccato of six imperatives: "sing" (×3), "bless," "proclaim," and "recount"—all vocal undertakings. And these are to occur "among the nations" and "among all the peoples" (96:3): the entirety of human-occupied space is envisaged as being an arena for this announcement of praise. Besides, the proclamation occurs "day to day" (96:2b): the entire span of time is now viewed as occasion for praise. This is a venture that takes up all space and all time!

With a couple of "for" clauses (96:4a, 5a), the *Explanation 1* for the exhortation to praise is given: the greatness of Yahweh (and the wretchedness of all other gods). Yahweh is the Deliverer par excellence (96:2–3)—"His wonderful doings" (96:3b) is, here and elsewhere, linked to his saving actions.[4] Moreover, this deity is supreme "above all the gods [אֱלֹהִים, *ʾelohim*]" (96:4b), "for all the gods [אֱלֹהִים] of the peoples are worthless [אֱלִילִים, *ʾel-ilim*]" (96:5a): the wordplay makes that assertion all the more pungent. "Gods" they may be to some, but utterly contemptible they are.[5] The very structure of 96:4–5 emphasizes the contrast between the fear-worthy Yahweh and unworthy gods.

---

2. Though there is no explicit mention of Israel, "deliverance" (in 96:2b) and the exhortation to recount among the nations and peoples (96:3) suggest that the first section (96:1–6) is addressed to the community of God's people.

3. Or the new song may be this very psalm itself?

4. Psalms 9:1–6; 17:7; 77:14; 78:11–16; 98:1; 105:2; 106:7, 22; etc.

5. In fact, the LXX has δαιμόνια, *daimonia*, for the MT's אֱלִילִים, hinting at something far more sinister.

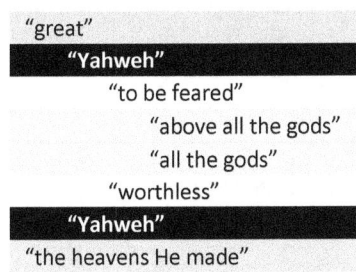

This "great" God is therefore enrobed with splendor and majesty, and his sanctuary is the embodiment of his strength and beauty—divine magnificence and grandeur beyond compare and beyond words (96:6)!

Exhortation to Converts; Explanation 2 (96:7–10)

The exhortation to worship is then directed to the families of the "peoples" (95:7a), the very "peoples" whose own gods were worthless (96:5a). The encouragement is for them to turn from these no-gods to *the* God, Yahweh, the one characterized by "glory and strength" and "holy majesty" (94:7b, 8a, 9a). Effectively, those praising humans have (or should be) converted to the true God. Whereas it was "sing" that was repeated thrice (96:1a, 1b, 2a), here it is a triplet of "ascribe" (96:7a, 7b, 8a).[6] What is to be ascribed to God is "glory" (96:7b, 8a). One wonders if this is a direct consequence of the people of God, his community, "recounting among the nations His *glory*" (96:3a), as well as of their singing the "new song" to Yahweh, proclaiming his deliverance (96:1–2). There is clearly an ongoing missional thrust directed to the converts as well, that they too, in turn, may "say among the nations" how great God is (96:10a). Of course, the fact that the nations are not hearing this song sung or this poem uttered suggests that the implied imperative is to these proclaimers of praise themselves (not to the hearers of their praise): may they keep ceaselessly ascribing to God glory and strength as they worship him.

At any rate, to the courts of their newly acknowledged God-King, the ruler of the cosmos (and its maker, 96:5b), come these converts bearing "offerings" as tribute (96:8b) as they worship "Yahweh in [His] holy majesty," for they—and everyone else: "all the earth" (96:9b)—can do naught but tremble "before Him" (מִפָּנָיו, *mipanayw*, i.e., "from before his face"; 96:9b). After all, Yahweh is the one who has splendor and majesty "before Him" (לְפָנָיו, *lphanayw*, i.e., "before His face"; 96:6a).

The *Explanation 2* for the preceding exhortation is formally set out in 96:10: This majestic, splendorous, and glorious deity before whom all tremble reigns with justice and uprightness (96:10a, 10c). And with this divine rule, nevermore will the earth totter (in injustice and unrighteousness, ostensibly; 96:10b)—i.e., God's reign will be absolutely stable, unlike human governances. This is what a Yahwistic regency will look like, soon and very soon! That will happen in its fullest sense only in the hereafter, under the aegis of the Messiah King, but God's people are already experiencing the fruits of divine rulership in the here-and-now.[7]

---

6. "Ascribe" in the sense of "give" or "attribute."

7. The imperfect verbs of 96:10bc could be read as indicating the future, "but this would leave the psalm,

Together the first two exhortation-explanation cycles (96:1–10) underscore the greatness of the God who is worthy of the worship of his community and the worship of his converts, the peoples/nations. The grandeur of the true God hems in the worthlessness of all the other gods:[8]

96:1	"all the earth" (96:1b)
96:2–3	"His name"; "glory"; "peoples" (96:2a, 3a, 3b)
96:4	"for"; "all the gods" (96:4a, 4b)
96:5–6	"for"; "all the gods" (96:5a)
96:7–8a	"glory" (×2); "His name"; "peoples" (96:7a, 7b, 8a)
96:8b–10	"all the earth" (96:9b)

Exhortation to Creation; Explanation 3 (96:11–13)

As the psalm enters its final round of exhortation-explanation, it is all of creation that is now called to worship God. Understandably then, the mention of "peoples," present in each of the exhortation and explanation sections of the psalm (96:3b, 5a, 7a, 10c, 13d; see figure above; also "nations" in 96:3a, 10a), is absent in the *Exhortation of Creation* in this third cycle (96:11–13aα). But the "face" of Yahweh shows up once more in this last phase of praise, as also in 96:6a, 9b: the denizens of the woods and forest will "shout for joy before [לִפְנֵי, *liphne*, i.e., 'before the face of'] Yahweh" (96:12b–13a).

The exhaustiveness of the elements of creation being involved in praise of this great God is depicted structurally:[9]

96:10	"world"; "peoples"
96:11a	"be joyful," "jubilate"; "earth"
96:11b	"all its fullness"
96:12a	"all that is in it"
96:12b–13b	"shout for joy"; "earth"
96:13cd	"world"; "peoples"

Indeed, if the "heavens" that Yahweh made (96:5b) are the "heavens" that are joyous (96:11), and creation is jubilant, then surely humankind, both veteran community and novice converts, ought be equally, if not more, joyous!

The *Explanation 3* section (96:13aβ–d) is like the preceding one (96:10), reflecting the "already, but not yet": "Yahweh ... comes" (96:13a)—his coming has commenced "already," though the consummation thereof is "not yet." Thus those verbs in 96:13bc display what will be characteristic of Yahweh and his regal judgment: He "comes to judge" and he "judges" with

---

its author, and its singers stranded between a past and a future neither of which they experience. The psalm's enthusiasm ... suggests they do not merely look back on what Yhwh once did and forward to what Yhwh will one day do. They know Yhwh is involved in the world in the present" (Goldingay, *Psalm*, 3:106). That "Yahweh reigns" (96:10a) indicates that God's work has begun in the present, but is yet to be consummated.

8. From Girard, *Les Psaumes Redécouverts*, 578.
9. From Girard, *Les Psaumes Redécouverts*, 579, 583.

righteousness and faithfulness. While it is true that he *will* come in the future and that he *will* judge then,[10] it is also appropriate to expect the outcome of his ongoing rule now, with a more concrete and comprehensive manifestation thereof happening in the future.

Goldingay's conclusion is apropos:

> There is no immediate way in which the nations themselves hear [this psalm]. So what is the point of Israel overhearing the psalm's exhortation to the nations? First, it adds to the magnitude of the praise that the psalm offers Yhwh. The God Israel worships is the only real God, so that all the nations ought to acknowledge this God. By implication, Israel itself ought also to do so, rather than being attracted by other peoples' gods. Conversely, this both heightens and reduces Israel's own significance. It heightens the significance of Yhwh's deliverance of Israel; this is also designed to speak to the nations. It reduces Israel's significance, because Yhwh is not satisfied with Israel's acknowledgment; Yhwh has an eye on the whole world. Perhaps it implies a missionary commission to Israel [as 96:3a, 10a enjoin].[11]

May the great God, above all the gods, be praised and glorified, by community, converts (who join community as a result of the latter's missional endeavors), and by all of creation, for the reign of this King, already on the throne, is soon going to be consummated!

Sermon Map

I. Praise of Community
   The greatness of God calls for praise by community (96:1–5)
   Praise involves mission (96:3)
   Move-to-relevance: Missions in praise, directed to unbelievers

II. Praise of Converts
   The reign of God calls for praise by converts (96:7–10)
   Praise involves further mission (96:10)
   Move-to-relevance: Missions in praise, directed worldwide

III. Praise of Creation
   The coming of God calls for praise from creation (96:11–13)
   Move-to-relevance: Recognition of the praise of creation

IV. *Praise and Promote!*
   Specifics on praise as a missional undertaking

---

10. With the reign of Christ established in the last days.
11. Goldingay, *Psalms*, 3:108.

PSALM 97:1–12

Psalm of Orientation

Joy in the God-King

PSALM 97 IS ANOTHER psalm about God's reign that continues the sequence of similarly themed psalms, Psalms 93 and 95–99.

Translation

97:1 Yahweh, He reigns, let the earth be glad;
  let many foreign shores rejoice.
97:2 Clouds and darkness surround Him;
  righteousness and justice are the foundation of His throne.
97:3 Fire, it goes before Him,
  and scorches His adversaries surrounding.
97:4 His lightnings lit up the world;
  the earth saw and trembled.
97:5 The mountains, they melted like wax from before Yahweh,
  from before the Lord of all the earth.
97:6 The heavens proclaimed His righteousness,
  and all the peoples saw His glory.
97:7 May they be ashamed, all those serving an image, those boasting in idols.
  Worship Him, all gods.
97:8 Zion heard and rejoiced,
  and the daughters of Judah are glad
  because of Your justice, Yahweh.
97:9 For You are Yahweh,
  Most High over all the earth,
  greatly elevated over all gods.

97:10 Those loving Yahweh, hate evil—
> the One who preserves the souls of His devout ones;
> from the hand of the wicked He rescues them.
97:11 Light is sown for the righteous one,
> and for the upright in heart, joy.
97:12 Rejoice, righteous ones, in Yahweh,
> and give thanks to His holy memory.

Structure

While this praise psalm does have exhortations (imperatives: 97:7b, 10a, 12a; jussives: 97:1a, 1b, 7a), the bulk of the composition is made up of a variety of expressions (or declarations) about the rulership of God, the reverence for God, and the rescue effected by God:[1]

97:1		Exhortation 1 to "earth" and "foreign shores": "be glad," "rejoice"
97:2–6		**Expression 1: *Rulership of God*** "righteousness" (97:2b, 6a); "lit [אוֹר, 'wr]" (97:4a)
97:7		Exhortation 2 to "those serving an image": "be ashamed," "worship"
97:8–9		**Expression 2: *Reverence for God*** "rejoice" (97:8a)
97:10a		Exhortation 3 to "those loving Yahweh": "hate evil"
97:10b–11		**Expression 3: *Rescue by God*** "light [אוֹר, 'or]"; "righteous" (97:11a)
97:12		Exhortation 4 to "righteous ones": "rejoice," "give thanks"

The central expression of reverence to God is the only direct address to Yahweh in this song (97:8–9), and this centerpiece is bookended on one side by "those serving an image, those boasting in idols" (97:7a), and on the other by "those loving Yahweh" (97:10ab).

Theological Focus

The rulership of the absolute and supreme sovereign, God, to whom all beings and all things submit, calls for reverence to him for his righteousness and justice, and results in rescue by him of his people from evil—all of which cause them to rejoice exceedingly.

---

1. Modified from Auffret, *Merveilles à nos yeux*, 65.

Commentary

Exhortation 1; Expression 1: Rulership of God (97:1–6)

The reign of God is, at the outset, the basis for the exhortations to the earth to be glad and to foreign shores to rejoice (97:1).[2] The expression of God's rulership (97:2–6) is almost a theophany with fire and lightning that surrounds deity's appearance (97:3–4a). The result of this incendiary presence of deity is that the earth trembles and the mountains melt at his presence (97:4b–5):[3]

97:2	"righteousness" (and "justice")
97:3	"before" (לְ + פָּנֶה, *l* + *paneh*)
	"world," "lit up"
97:4–5aα	"earth," "trembled"
	"mountains," "melted"
97: 5aβ–b	"before" (פָּנֶה + לְ) [×2]
97:6	"righteousness" (and "glory")

The structure of *Expression 1* (97:2–6) implies that it is the glory of God's righteousness that is blazing, which nothing, not even inanimate nature, can withstand. When the fire of his glory goes "before" him (97:3a), everything decomposes and disintegrates "before" Yahweh, the Lord of all the earth (×2; 97:5). Clouds and darkness "surround" God (97:2), but divine flames scorch his enemies who are "surrounding" God's people (97:3b). No foe will escape. So the entire *Exhortation 1* + *Expression 1* section (97:1–6) commences with the rejoicing of the "earth" (and foreign lands; 97:1) and concludes with the exclamations of the "heavens" (and all the peoples seeing divine glory; 97:6). No space is exempt; no person is exempt![4]

That "clouds and darkness" (97:2) accompany "fire" and "lightnings" (97:3a, 4a) is odd, but not unusual; 18:9–11 has darkness juxtaposed to all kinds of fiery manifestations of deity in 18:8, 12, 14, not to mention the incongruous mix of hailstones with coals of fire (18:12). All causing, as in our text, dramatic tectonic disturbances (18:7, 15; 97:4b–5a). While the descriptions certainly sound contradictory, it is no doubt because of an utter inability to describe in comprehensible language what is seen in the theophany. The boundaries of rhetoric are breached when God shows up. The God who begins to reign is making a stupendous appearance ("from before" whom everything falls apart; 97:5a, 5b): everyone will see him, everyone will rejoice![5]

---

2. "Foreign shores" indicate faraway places, even to the ends of the earth.

3. Figure below modified from Girard, *Les Psaumes Redécouverts*, 595.

4. The chiastic structure of 97:4b–6 depicts it well: "the earth *saw*" / "from before" // "from before" / "all the peoples *saw*."

5. In the next duet of *Exhortation 2* + *Expression 2* (97:7–9), there will be a distinction made between the reactions to this theophany by those faithful to God and by those who are not.

Exhortation 2; Expression 2: Reverence for God (97:7–9)

The second cycle, *Exhortation 2 + Expression 2*, is about reverence to God. There are some who revere him and others who do not. The latter are the subjects of the exhortation—"those serving an image, those boasting in idols" (97:7a): they are to "be ashamed" of their idolatrous undertakings. Even all those false gods—images and idols, and the nefarious entities behind them—"all gods" are urged to worship Yahweh (97:7b).[6] One notices the wordplay between "idols," אֱלִילִים, *'elilim*, and "gods," אֱלֹהִים, *'elohim* (97:7ab). The psalmist has carefully omitted any reference to Yahweh as אֱלֹהִים from this composition and so, in Psalm 97, the אֱלֹהִים are, without exception, equated to the אֱלִילִים—a remarkable put down!

The contrast between the responses of the those serving false gods and the responses of those serving the true God is sharp: Those in "Zion" and in the "daughters of Judah"[7]—unlike those image servers and idol worshipers—hear of Yahweh and rejoice in him because of his justice, the righteous rule of the God-King (97:8). "Justice" is one of the foundations of the divine throne (97:2b); it is therefore appropriate that God's people rejoice at his "justice" (97:8c). Whereas the song had commenced with an exhortation to the earth to be "glad" and for foreign lands to "rejoice" (97:1), it is the townships of Judah who are already "glad" and "rejoicing" (97:8ab)—the chiastic ordering of the verbs makes it poignant:

97:1a	"let the earth *be glad*"
97:1b	"let ... foreign shores *rejoice*"
97:8a	"Zion ... *rejoiced*"
97:8b	"daughters of Judah *are glad*"

The reason is obvious: this God-King, the awesomely glorious one, is "Most High" (עֶלְיוֹן, *'elyon*, from, עלה, *'lh*) and "greatly *elevated*" (נַעֲלֵיתָ, *na'aleta*, also from עלה, 97:9bc). Add to this assonance the preposition עַל, *'al*, "over," used twice, and you have a finely tuned composition!

97:9b
עַל־כָּל־הָאָרֶץ עֶלְיוֹן
'al-kal-ha'arets *'elyon*
"over all the earth" "Most High"

97:9c
עַל־כָּל־אֱלֹהִים נַעֲלֵיתָ
'al-kal-'elohim *na'aleta*
"over all gods" "elevated"

Both appellations designate a deity who is "*over all* the earth" and "*over all* gods," respectively. May the entire world respond as did Zion and Judah to this most supreme regent!

---

6. Later, in 97:9c, the reason is given: God is supreme over "all gods."

7. These "daughters" were the towns of Judah, as in 48:11 (also see Josh 15:45, 47; etc., for similar use of "daughters").

Exhortation 3; Expression 3: Rescue by God (97:10–11)

The next round, *Exhortation 3 + Expression 3*, focuses appropriately enough on the faithful ones of God. They, who love God, are urged to hate evil (97:10a). The expression (or the consequence) of faithful obedience to their regent is noted in 97:10b–11: they will experience rescue by God, deliverance accomplished by their King. So much so, they, who serve a God whose thunderbolts "light [אוֹר]" the world (97:4a), will themselves live in "light [אוֹר]," immersed in joy (97:11). This verse, 97:11, is chiastic, picturing "joy" and "light" surrounding the people of God who walk with him.

> "Light is sown
>   for the righteous one,
>   and for the upright in heart,
> joy."

Exhortation 4 (97:12)

The psalm ends with a final *Exhortation 4*: rejoice! How can the righteous ones, those who acknowledge the rulership of God, those who revere God, and those who have experienced the rescue of God—how can they do aught but rejoice, with hearts filled with gratitude at every thought and remembrance of this great King of theirs (97:12)? The potency of this exhortation is embedded in the structure of 97:11–12:

97:11a	"righteous one"
97:11b	"joy [שִׂמְחָה, *simchah*]"
97:12aα	"rejoice [שׂמח, *smch*]"
97:12aβ	"righteous ones"

In fact, "rejoice" occurs symmetrically in this psalm, in 97:1b, 8a, and 12a (see the psalm's structure). Those who express the rulership of God, reverence for God, and rescue by God, "those loving Yahweh," "His devout ones," "the righteous ones," and "the upright in heart" (97:10a, 10b, 11a, 11b) will—and should be—joyful, all their days. For the King, he cometh!

Sermon Map

I. Rulership of God
   An awesome theophany marks God's reign (97:1–4)
   Before his glorious appearance, nature and peoples submit (97:5–6)
   Move-to-relevance: Our recognition of God's incredible glory

II. Reverence for God
   God's just reign calls for reverence towards him (97:7)
   Such joyous reverence characterizes the people of God (97:8–9)
   Move-to-relevance: Our expectation of God's just reign

III. Rescue by God
   God's reign also means that his faithful are delivered (97:10–11)
   Move-to-relevance: Our need for God's rescue

IV. *Rejoice with Reverence for the Ruler Who Rescues!*
   Rejoice (97:12)!
   Specifics on corporate and individual rejoicing

PSALM 98:1–9

Psalm of Orientation

Joy of Creation in the Justice of the Creator

PSALM 98 IS CLEARLY a song of praise, with only a hint of oppression by enemies (in the "deliverance" Yahweh accomplished: 98:1c, 2a, 3d). There is no explicit mention of foes in the composition.

Translation

98:1   Sing to Yahweh a new song,
        for He has done wonders;
        His right hand and His holy arm have accomplished deliverance for Him.

98:2   Yahweh has made known His deliverance;
        before the eyes of the nations He has revealed His righteousness.

98:3   He has remembered His lovingkindness and His faithfulness
        to the house of Israel;
   all the ends of the earth
        have seen the deliverance of our God.

98:4   Shout triumphantly to Yahweh, all the earth;
        break forth and shout for joy and make music.

98:5   Make music to Yahweh with the lyre—
        with the lyre and the sound of musicmaking,

98:6   with trumpets and the sound of the horn—
        shout triumphantly before [the face of] the King, Yahweh.

98:7   Let the sea and its fullness roar,
        the world and those dwelling in it.

98:8   The rivers, let them clap the palm;
        the mountains, let them shout for joy

98:9   before Yahweh, for He is coming to judge the earth.
       He will judge the world with righteousness,
       and the peoples with uprightness.

Structure

This psalm also patterns itself with exhortations and explanations in two rounds, as shown below. The first round is addressed *To God's Community* ("our," 98:3d), the second *To God's Cosmos* ("all the earth," 98:4a[1]). Both groups are exhorted to praise Yahweh.

TO GOD'S COMMUNITY: PRAISE!

98:1a	**Exhortation 1** "sing"	[*brief*]
98:1b–3	**Explanation 1** "for" (98:1b) finite verbs: perfect *Yahweh's righteousness,* *lovingkindness, faithfulness*	[*extended*]

TO GOD'S COSMOS: PRAISE!

98:4–9aα	**Exhortation 2** "shout triumphantly" (98:4a, 6a) "break forth"; "shout for joy" (98:4b); "make music" (98:4b, 5a)	[*extended*]
98:9aβ–c	**Explanation 2** "for" (98:9a) finite verb: imperfect *Yahweh's righteousness,* *uprightness*	[*brief*]

One notices that the finite verbs in the explanation section of *To God's Community* are all perfects ("He has done," "have accomplished," "has made known," "He has revealed," "He has remembered," "have seen": 98:1b–3), while the lone such verb in the explanation section of *To God's Cosmos* is an imperfect ("He will judge"; 98:9b). What Yahweh *has done* for his people in the past, then, is paradigmatic for what he *will do/does* for the rest of humankind. He came to "deliver" (98:1c, 2a, 3d) and he is coming to "judge" (98:9). The one who manifested his "righteousness" in the past (98:2b) will manifest his "righteousness" again (98:9b).

That is to say, the kind of God he was to his community is the kind of God he is and will be to the world. Of course, considering it unlikely that the rest of the world would hear this psalm, it must be regarded as a strong reminder to God's community that his purposes are broad in scope, encompassing the whole cosmos of humanity. Perhaps it is also an encouragement that the praise of God's people is significant and important, in that it influences the

---

1. To be precise, the psalm exhorts only the earth, not the heavens or the rest of the universe; in that sense, "cosmos" is inaccurate, but I felt the urge to alliterate . . .

attitudes of "all the ends of earth" (98:3c) In this implied sense of mission, Psalm 98 is similar to Psalm 96, but in the former, it is specifically his deliverance that is exalted, whereas in the latter a polemic against false (or non-)gods predominates.

Theological Focus

The deliverance of a righteous deity experienced by God's community and praised by them before all the earth will become, on the day of the coming of this King and Judge, righteousness experienced by God's world for which they and all creation, animate and inanimate, will praise him.

Commentary

To God's Community: Praise! (98:1–3)

The community of God's people is exhorted to sing a "new song" to Yahweh because of his "wonders"—the "deliverance" (emphasized thrice: 98:1c, 2a, 3d) wrought by deity for his people, with his illimitable power symbolized by "His right hand" and "His holy arm" (98:1c)—supernatural and awe-inspiring.[2] And these deliverances of his, accomplished in his righteousness, have been made known to the world (98:2, 3cd), and his lovingkindness and faithfulness manifested "to the house of Israel" have been recognized by the cosmos (98:3b). All that to say, the entirety of the world has perceived the "deliverance of our God," his particular works of liberation on behalf of his community, that demonstrate his righteousness, lovingkindness, and faithfulness, (98:2–3). And these undertakings by deity for his own have impressed "all the ends of the earth" (98:3c).

To God's Cosmos: Praise! (98:4–9)

The previous section pointed out that the actions of God towards community were beheld by God's world (98:2b, 3d). The consequence of such a beholding was their own worship of Yahweh—the praise expressed by God's cosmos, in response to the wonders he performed for his faithful. That there is a cause (work of God's upper limb: God's actions before the cosmos) and effect (the response of the world's upper limbs: reactions of cosmos) is clear in the parallelisms (below).[3]

---

2. "Wonders" elsewhere in the Psalter are linked to God's actions of deliverance accomplished for his people: 9:1–6; 17:7; 77:14; 78:11–16; 96:3; 105:2; 106:7, 22; etc.

3. See Auffret, *Merveilles à nos yeux*, 74. As was noted earlier, Yahweh's "righteousness" unto the community (98:2b) is later directly experienced by the world (98:9b).

98:1c	"His *right hand* and His holy *arm*"	Actions of God
98:2b	"before the *eyes* of the nations"	
98:3c	"all the ends of the earth"	
98:4a	"all the earth"	Reactions of cosmos
98:6b	"before [the *face* of] the King, Yahweh"	
98:8a	"*palm*"	

It was God's powerful "arm" and "right hand" that accomplished deliverance for his people (98:1c); it will be the "palm[s]" of all creation that applaud this great God (98:8a). God's deliverance for his community was displayed "before" the world (98:2b)—i.e., לְעֵינֵי, *l'ene*, "before their eyes." And so the world will rejoice in praise "before [the face of] [לִפְנֵי, *liphne*]" Yahweh (98:6b) (the parallels here, too, are obvious). Because God's righteousness, lovingkindness, and faithfulness to his people (i.e., his work of deliverance) is witnessed by "all the ends of the earth" (98:3c), especially as the delivered people of God sing his praises, so "all the earth" will shout for joy in praise of Yahweh (98:4a). All that clamor and fanfare raised by God's world is strikingly depicted in 98:4-6, structured with staircase-like repetitions that give the entirety of the acclamation of God the sense of a resounding echo:[4]

98:4a	"shout triumphantly to … Yahweh"		
98:4b	"make music"		
98:5a	"make music"	"lyre"	
98:5b		"lyre"	"sound of musicmaking"
98:6a			"sound of the horn"
98:6b	"shout triumphantly before … Yahweh"		

In short, all of the cosmos, God's world—and not just humanity (98:1-3) or even God's community (98:4-6), but also inanimate nature (98:7-8)—is engaged (or will engage) in praise of this great God.

The *Explanation 2* for the extended exhortation of 98:4-9aα is quite brief: the God-King is coming as Judge and he will execute his judgment with "righteousness" and "uprightness" (98:9bc). Once again, a repetitive structure, almost a staircase parallelism, emphasizes the King's coming and the Judge's actions (98:9aβ-c):[5]

"for He is coming		
to judge	the earth.	
He will judge	the world	with righteousness,
	and the peoples	with uprightness."

---

4. From Girard, *Les Psaumes Redécouverts*, 607. The verse, 98:5, is itself structured chiastically: "make music" / "lyre" // "lyre" / "musicmaking."

5. From Auffret, *Merveilles à nos yeux*, 73.

> This hymn, celebrating God as Ruler and Judge, performs the Psalms' characteristic function of overturning our ordinary perceptions of the world ... The psalmist challenges us to see judgment, not as a matter for local or private celebration by the righteous and, correspondingly, dread for the wicked, but rather as the occasion of cosmic jubilation. Moreover, by invoking praise from the rivers and mountains, the song topples the complacent and dangerous modern view of the nonhuman world as passive, insensible—nothing more than the stage for human actors with their magisterial and often frenetic gestures. Thus the world is revealed for what it really is: in fact, not Nature at all but rather Creation, still exquisitely sensitive to the presence and will of its Maker, eager to the point of impatience for the full manifestation of God's will in human life, which is the final goal of judgment.[6]

All that to say, Yahweh's righteousness and uprightness in judging (and ruling) is good news for the whole world, for all of creation, for the entirety of the cosmos! The "righteousness" which God had revealed in his deliverance of the community (98:2b), is the "righteousness" going to be manifest in his judging of the cosmos and all peoples (98:9b).

All of humankind can learn this lesson from how God has dealt with his community. "While Yhwh has been irrevocably committed to Israel and to the Jewish people from the beginning of Israel's story, and they gain immeasurably from that, blessing Israel is not the extent of Yhwh's purpose. Yhwh's blessing of Israel has implications for the world. On the other hand, Yhwh never relates to the world independently of relating to Israel."[7] As with God's community in the past, so it will be with God's world in the present and in the future, thankfully!

Sermon Map

I. God's Work Praised: His Community
   Deliverance of a powerful, righteous, loving, faithful God (98:1, 3ab)
   Work of this God and his community's praise visible to all (96:2, 3cd)
   Move-to-relevance: Missional praise of God's deliverance

II. God's Work Praised: His World
   Deliverance in the form of judgment, righteous and upright (98:9)
   God's world, including all creation, praises him (98:4–8)
   Move-to-relevance: God's grand plan for the whole earth

III. *Praise God's Preservation; Promote God's Plan!*
   Specifics on praise as an undertaking furthering God's cosmic plan

---

6. Davis, "Psalm 98," 171. Indeed, "all creation groans ..." (Rom 8:22).
7. Goldingay, *Psalms*, 3:123–24.

PSALM 99:1–9

Psalm of Orientation

Exalting a Great, Just, Merciful God-King

PSALM 99 IS THE last in a series of songs dealing with Yahweh's Kingship (Psalms 93; 95–99).

Translation

99:1 Yahweh, He reigns—let the peoples tremble;
    He sits [enthroned] [above] the cherubim—let the earth quake.

99:2 Yahweh is great in Zion,
    and exalted is He above all the peoples.

99:3 Let them praise Your name, great and awesome;
    holy is He.

99:4 And the strength of the King, it loves justice;
    You—You have established uprightness;
    justice and righteousness in Jacob You—You have executed.

99:5 Exalt Yahweh our God,
    and worship at the stool of His feet;
    holy is He.

99:6 Moses and Aaron among His priests,
    and Samuel among those calling on His name—
    they were calling to Yahweh and He—He would answer them.

99:7 In the pillar of cloud He spoke to them;
    they kept His decrees
    and the statute He gave to them.

99:8 Yahweh our God, You—You answered them;
    a forgiving God You were to them,
    and One taking revenge upon their wantonness.

99:9 Exalt Yahweh our God
and worship at His holy mountain,
for holy is Yahweh our God.

Structure

As with several of the preceding psalms, Psalm 99 also follows a recurring pattern, but this one also has a chorus or refrain, that divides the poem into three sections; each chorus is intimately related to the word "exalt," occurring precisely two lines above each refrain, quite appropriate for a psalm that repeatedly exhorts praise of God (99:3a, 5a, 5b, 9a, 9b). Of note, the confessions also progressively increase in length as the song proceeds:[1]

GREATNESS OF THE HOLY GOD-KING
99:1aα	Confession 1	[2 words]
99:1aβ	Consequence 1	
99:1bα	Confession 2	[2 words]
99:1bβ	Consequence 2	
99:2	Confession 3	[8 words]
99:3a	Consequence 3	
99:3b	Chorus ["exalt," 99:2b]	

JUSTICE OF THE HOLY GOD-KING
99:4	Confession 4	[12 words]
99:5ab	Consequence 4	
99:5c	Chorus ["exalt," 99:5a]	

MERCY OF THE HOLY GOD-KING
99:6–8	Confession 5	[31 words]
99:9ab	Consequence 5	
99:9c	Chorus ["exalt," 99:9a]	

One can see a narratival movement in each of the sections: from the exodus in the first section (99:1–3); to the establishment of "Jacob," the nation, with land and with law, in the second section (99:4–5); to the mediators between God and his people, Moses, Aaron, and Samuel, standing in for the people (who fail to keep the law) in the third (99:6–9).[2] This creates the story arc upon which the psalm is built.

---

1. Modified from Auffret, *Merveilles à nos yeux*, 78; and Goldingay, *Psalms*, 3:128.
2. See Goldingay, *Psalms*, 3:127–30.

Theological Focus

The greatness of the holy God-King's awesomeness, the justice of the holy God-King's law, and the mercy of the holy God-King's dealings motivate his people to serve and to worship this exalted deity in humility.

Commentary

Greatness of the Holy God-King (99:1–3)

Three separate confessions and three consequential responses (in the jussive) make up the first section of the psalm, all focusing on the greatness of the holy God-King. The enthroned Yahweh is depicted above the cherubim (99:1b), with them serving as his transportation (18:10). Or it refers, perhaps, to the station of God above the cherubim in the tabernacle and the temple (1 Sam 4:4; 2 Sam 6:2; 2 Kgs 19:15). In any case, the responses of the peoples and the earth to this God-King's reign and enthronement (the first two confessions, Ps 99:1aα, 1bα) are trembling and quaking, respectively (the first two consequences, in jussives: 99:1aβ, 1bβ). The "trembling" of the peoples, in particular, is reminiscent of the response of pagan nations to Yahweh's victories over them in the exodus generation (Exod 15:15; Deut 2:25). The third confession (Ps 99:2) acknowledges the supremacy of this divine regent in Zion ("great," 99:2a), to which the consequent response is praise for this "great" one (also in a jussive: 99:3a). The chorus affirms, after the "exaltation" in 99:2b, "holy is He" (99:3b). This God-King is great, this God-King is holy—praise be to this God-King!

Justice of the Holy God-King (99:4–5)

While the previous section alluded to the exodus, this section suggests Yahweh's activity at Sinai and the establishment of the nation, Israel. It takes up more space in its confession (twelve words in Hebrew; 99:4) than in each of the ones before in the first section of the psalm (two, two, and eight words; 99:1aα, 1bα, 2, respectively). But tying in with the previous section is the shared root between "reign" (מלך, *mlk*; 99:1a) and "King" (מֶלֶךְ, *melek*; 99:4a). "Uprightness," "justice," and "righteousness" (99:4bc) were established in "Jacob" as God made his people a nation and settled them in a land with a constitution—the Law (on which more below). The emphasis on God's doings here is remarkable—twice the redundant pronoun, "You [אַתָּה, *'attah*]," does its reinforcing work: "You—You have established uprightness," i.e., Yahweh and no one else (99:4b). And "justice and righteousness in Jacob You—You have executed," i.e., Yahweh and no other entity (99:4c). "Yhwh is not just about kingship, loftiness, holiness, and authority but also about ['uprightness' and 'justice' and 'righteousness']. And Yhwh is not just about a presence in Zion but also about an activity establishing such uprightness and faithfulness in the community."[3] Of course, these attributes are established and enacted and expressed through divine legislation.

---

3. Goldingay, *Psalms*, 3:129.

Such a just King deserves "exaltation" and so the consequence of the confession is that his people worship "at the stool of his feet" (in imperatives: 99:5a, 5b), i.e., the exalted one is lifted high by his subjects bowing low![4] This God-King is just, this God-King is holy—praise the name of this God-King!

Mercy of the Holy God-King (99:6–9)

This third section is the most extensive of the three, its confession section utilizing thirty-one words in Hebrew (99:6–8). Obviously, we have arrived at a significant juncture in the psalm, where it asserts its import, the powerful impact the poet wanted his readers to experience. It is the mercy of the God-King that is prominent here, as deity deigns to interact with his people, by means of his mediators, Moses and Aaron and Samuel.[5] All three are characterized primarily by their being agents through whom this God-King's law was proclaimed and performed among his people. Besides, significant for this section is the fact that they interceded with Yahweh and Yahweh answered them—that is to say, God mercifully heard his people (via the mediators).[6] This was a merciful God-King, no doubt.

The legislation of this God-King, deity's instructions for life, was followed by these leaders for the most part (99:7b; and thus, by corporate solidarity, by God's people themselves). But divine mercy was particularly exhibited in deity's forgiveness of his people when this trio of eminent ones pled for grace when the people contravened his law (note the emphatic "You—You answered them," 99:8a), *and* when he disciplined him for their profligacies (99:8bc; referring, no doubt, to Moses [Num 20:2–13]). "The conjunction of forgiveness and punishment may seem abrupt, but it is amply illustrated in the accounts of the three great priest-prophet-intercessor leaders in Israel's primal traditions. The juxtaposition of the God who forgives and the God who punishes may reflect Exod 34:6–7, where Yahweh is said to be both one who forgives and keeps his loyal-love and the one who punishes sin."[7] Yes, God is merciful: he forgives; but he is also merciful in his chastening, for that, too, is a means to straighten out his wayward people—the remedial and restorative correction of his children by their heavenly Father.

Again the emphases, by way of seemingly redundant pronouns, are powerful. "They [the people, through their leaders] were calling to Yahweh and He [הוא, *hu'*]—He would answer them," i.e., Yahweh would, not any other god (Ps 99:6c). And "Yahweh our God, You [אתה]—You answered them," i.e., Yahweh and no one else (99:8a).

And with that the consequential response of God's people to this confession is exhorted: this is a God who is to be exalted in worship at "His holy mountain,"[8] the appropriate dwelling of a "holy" God (in imperatives: 99:9a, 9b). This God-King is merciful, this God-King is holy—praise be to him!

---

4. The root of the verb "worship," חוה, *chwh*, has the sense of bowing down in obeisance. Perhaps the ark was what served as a footstool for the deity dwelling "[above] the cherubim" (99:1b).

5. Moses technically was not a "priest" (99:6), though he did perform some roles of that office, as also did Samuel, who was a prophet but was never labeled a "priest."

6. Moses's intercession: Exodus 32–34; Aaron's: Num 16:44–48; Samuel's: 1 Sam 7:7–12; 12:6–25. The three of them are linked in 1 Sam 12:6; Moses and Samuel show up together in Jer 15:1.

7. Tate, *Psalms 51–100*, 530.

8. And thereby, the conclusion of this psalm is linked to its commencement that had "Zion" in 99:2a.

Thus, in the psalm, "Yahweh our God" has resounded *four* times (99:5a, 8a, 9a, 9c[9]), and the song has, in sum, pointed out this deity's greatness, justice, and mercy—attributes of a holy God-King.[10] May his name be praised!

Sermon Map

I. The God-King's Holy Greatness
   God's awesomeness that inspires praise (99:1–3)
   Move-to-relevance: Our acknowledgment of God's greatness

II. The God-King's Holy Goodness
   God's justice and righteousness that motivates praise (99:4–5)
   Move-to-relevance: Our recognition of God's goodness

III. The God-King's Holy Graciousness
   God's mercy in forgiveness and discipline that excites praise (99:6–9)
   Move-to-relevance: Our experience of God's graciousness

IV. *Praise God's Greatness, Goodness, Graciousness!*
   Specifics on praise for the kingly, holy attributes of God

---

9. The appellation occurs only seven more times in the Psalter: 20:7; 94:23; 105:7; 106:47; 113:5; 122:9; 123:2.

10. That all these attributes of God in this psalm appear to be qualified by his holiness should not come as a surprise: his is a holy greatness, a holy justice, a holy mercy (as well as a holy love, a holy grace, a holy might . . .).

PSALM 100:1–5

Psalm of Orientation

Serving the Shepherd with Praise and Submission

PSALM 100 REJOICES WITH the praise of Yahweh, the God, Creator, and Shepherd of his people and flock, and of his lovingkindness and faithfulness towards them, which are forever. It might be considered the doxology of the preceding seven psalms (Psalms 93–99), most of which acclaim Yahweh as the God-King.

Translation

100:1 Shout triumphantly to Yahweh, all the earth.
100:2   Serve Yahweh with rejoicing;
          come before Him with shouts of joy.
100:3 Know that Yahweh—He [is] God;
          He—He made us, and His we [are]:
          His people and the flock of His pasture.
100:4 Come into His gates with thanksgiving,
          [and into] His courts with praise;
          give thanks to Him, bless His name.
100:5 For good [is] Yahweh;
          forever is His lovingkindness,
          and unto generation after generation, His faithfulness.

Structure

This is yet another psalm with the pattern of exhortation and explanation forming its structure:[1]

> **Exhortation 1** to Praise (**100:1–2**)
> "shout triumphantly"; "serve"; "come ... with [בְּ, b]"
> "with" (×2)
>
>> **Explanation 1**: *God the Begetter* (**100:3**)
>> "... that [כִּי, kî] Yahweh"
>
> **Exhortation 2** to Praise (**100:4**)
> "give thanks"; "bless"; "come ... with [בְּ]"
> "with" (×2)
>
>> **Explanation 2**: *God the Benefactor* (**100:5**)
>> "for [כִּי] ... Yahweh"

Each of the four sections has three lines (thus four tricola make up the entirety of the psalm), giving the composition a sense of balance. Also, each of the four prepositional phrases that begin with בְּ, "with," has a different expression of worship: "with rejoicing" (100:2a), "with shouts of joy" (100:2b), "with thanksgiving" (100:4a), and "with praise" (100:4b).

Theological Focus

> Enthusiastic praise, that also assumes exultant submission, is due to God alone, the begetter of his people who cares for them, and the benefactor of his people who is good to them all the time, unto forever.

Commentary

Exhortation 1; Explanation 1: God the Begetter (100:1–3)

Though the psalm is addressed to the whole world at its outset, there is more of a focus upon the community of "His [God's] people" who are the "flock of His pasture" (100:3c). In addition, "serve" (עבד, *'bd*; 100:2a) involves a holistic submission of oneself to this God, the personal God of his people, Yahweh. Such subjection implies not only vocal affirmation ("shout triumphantly," 100:1a) and attitudes of the heart ("with rejoicing," 100:2a; with "shouts of joy," 100:2c), but also submissive service (see 18:43; 22:30; 72:11; 95:7–11[2]). "The verb ["serve"] implies that worship is done for God's sake and not for ours; servants serve their master, not themselves. And the fact that serving God mostly takes place outside worship also hints that there needs to be some coherence between what happens in worship and

---

1. From deClaissé-Walford et al., *Book of Psalms*, 735; and Girard, *Les Psaumes Redécouverts*, 617. This is also the only psalm in the Psalter with "thanksgiving" in its superscription (untranslated here).
2. Notice the characterization of the "servant" of God as one who keeps the divine word (119:117, 176).

what happens outside."³ In fact, as Mays notes, this holistic approach to God with shouts and service and rejoicing is quite political:

> These terms [of worship] ... belong to Israel's cultic vocabulary, and designate the kind of things which Israel (and other peoples of the culture area) were accustomed to do in the public cult. They would form processions before the gates of the sanctuary area, enter its precincts where the deity was believed to dwell or come, all the while lauding him with epithets and affirmations. But cult in Israel's cultural world was not a self-contained and self-defining sphere. All these actions had meaning because they were expressed in the forms by which a people recognized the one who wielded power over them.⁴

The exodus tradition makes it clear that "serving Yahweh" is in stark contrast to remaining as servants of the Pharaoh: Exod 3:12; 4:23; 7:16; 8:1; 10:26—all employ עבד, "serve," as in Ps 100:2a. As well, in Deuteronomy, the verb distinguishes the "service" of God's people to Yahweh from "service" to other gods: Deut 7:4; 8:19; 11:16; 12:2. Thus Psalm 100 is a response of God's people to the God-King, their Creator, their Shepherd, whom they acclaim, and to whom they are wholeheartedly and singlemindedly committed.

> The invitation is a summons to activity whose nature and intention is the formation of a congregation as the realm of Yahweh. It can be called worship because its focus is god; but its rubrics and movements and responses come from the political life of human society, because it is the recognition . . . of the locus of power . . . Therefore the assembly which the psalm convokes cannot lose its political dimension if it is to fulfill its intention.⁵

The explanation of, or the reason for, the exhortation comes in 100:3—God is the begetter. There is an imperative in that verse, "know," but that likely is a poetic introduction to an explanation that normally should have begun with "for" (as does 100:5). But both 100:3 and 100:5 have כִּי ("that" in 100:3a; "for" in 100:5a), and both are in verbless clauses.⁶

The imperative, "know" (100:3a), is not so much calling for cognition as much as recognition, making it, in effect, a creedal statement.⁷ It is because this Yahweh is God, the begetter who fathered, fashioned, and formed his people (100:3bα) into a divine community of believers,⁸ that he is to be acclaimed with shouts and service (100:1–2). The sequencing of the pronouns in 100:3, including both independent and suffixed ones, is enlightening (see below).⁹

---

3. Goldingay, *Psalms*, 3:135.
4. Mays, "Worship, World, and Power," 321.
5. Mays, "Worship, World, and Power," 322.
6. The "is" has been added in translation to both 100:3a and 100:5a for clarity. The translation of 100:3b follows the *qere* ("and His [וְלוֹ, *wlo*] we are") not the *kethiv* ("and not [וְלֹא, *wlo'*] we ourselves"), reflecting the parallelism between 100:3b and 100:3c, and the similar usage in 79:13; 95:5, 7.
7. One might also translate the verb as "acknowledge" or even "confess."
8. As opposed to God's creation of humankind in general. God's "making [עשׂה, *'sh*]" (100:3b) in the specific sense of forming his chosen people is also found in 95:6, in addition to Deut 32:6, 15; Isa 44:2 (also see Isa 43:1, 21, employing a different verb).
9. Modified from Auffret, "'Venez à ses portails!,'" 237.

100:3a	God: "He"		Independent
100:3bα	God: "He"		Independent
100:3bβ		People: "us"	Suffixed to verb
100:3bγ		God: "His"	Suffixed to preposition
100:3bδ		People: "we"	Independent
100:3cα	God: "His"		Suffixed to noun
100:3cβ	God: "His"		Suffixed to noun

Not only does the pattern bespeak a high level of poetic artistry, it also emphasizes God's absolute ownership of his people, who are textually and literarily surrounded, shielded, and supported by him.[10]

The redundant pronouns in 100:3ab emphasize Yahweh's exclusive Godship and Creatorship: "Yahweh—He [is] God," i.e., he alone, and no one else; and "He—He made us," i.e., he alone, and no other entity (100:3ab). Readers would do well to harken to this tone of power inherent in the divine regent; that authority of God undergirds this psalm's *Exhortation 1*, because "to praise is to reject alternative loyalties and false definitions of reality. Praise is relentlessly polemical."[11]

Exhortation; Explanation: God the Benefactor (100:4–5)

Once again, the exhortation is to thank and praise this great God (100:4). The explanation of, or the reason for, the exhortation is because God is the benefactor: He is "good," the one who shows "lovingkindness" and "faithfulness" to his people, across generations and even to "forever" (100:5).

Notable is the fact that much of Book IV of the Psalter (Psalms 90–106) is a response to God's apparent failure to be faithful to his people, especially to the Davidic line of kings. "The last word in Ps 100 (אמונתו [*'mwntw*]) affirms the enduring faithfulness of Yahweh (note the occurrence of אמונה [*'mwnh*] in ... [Ps 89:1, 2, 5, 8, 24, 33, and 49]—it is probably of no special significance, but it is interesting to note the sevenfold use of 'faithfulness' in Ps 89 and the sevenfold summons to praise Yahweh for his enduring 'faithfulness' in Ps 100)"—"shout triumphantly," "serve," "come," "know," "come," "give thanks," and "bless."[12] It is one thing to praise God because he is a powerful deity capable of enforcing the submission of one and all; it is entirely another to praise God because he is the lover of his people, faithful to them for all time, come what may! Yes, God is good, indeed!

---

10. The motif of shepherd, flock, and pasture are not a bucolic aside, but integrally monarchical, as in 78:70–72 (also employed generally of leaders, especially in prophetic literature; see Isa 44:28; Jer 23:1–4; Ezek 34:1–10; Zech 10:3; etc.). Of course, Yahweh as shepherd is a major theme in the Psalter: 23:1 (also linked to Yahweh's regency); 28:9; 74:1; 77:20; 78:52–53; 80:1; 95:7.

11. Brueggemann, "Psalm 100," 66.

12. Tate, *Psalms 51–100*, 536.

Sermon Map

I. God, the Begetter of His People
    The maker and the shepherd of his flock, his chosen (100:1–3)
    Move-to-relevance: Our recognition of God's uniqueness as our begetter

II. God, the Benefactor of His People
    The only one who is good, loving, and faithful, all the time (100:4–5)
    Move-to-relevance: Our recognition of God's constant goodness

III. *Bless the Begetter and the Benefactor!*
    Specifics on praise for ownership and faithful goodness of God

Bibliography

Allen, Leslie C. "Psalm 73: Pilgrimage from Doubt to Faith." *Bulletin for Biblical Research* 7 (1997) 1–9.
———. "The Value of Rhetorical Criticism in Psalm 69." *Journal of Biblical Literature* 105 (1986) 577–98.
Allen, Ronald B. "Psalm 87, a Song Rarely Sung." *Bibliotheca Sacra* 153 (1996) 131–40.
Alter, Robert. *The Book of Psalms*. New York: Norton, 2007.
Althann, Robert. "Psalm 58,10 in the Light of Ebla." *Biblica* 64 (1983) 122–24.
Anderson, Craig Evan. "The Politics of Psalmody: Psalm 60 and the Rise and Fall of Judean Independence." *Journal of Biblical Literature* 134 (2015) 313–32.
Attard, Stefano. "The Bride and Her Companions in Psalm 45: Making Sense out of an Allegory." *Biblica et Patristica Toruniensia* 10 (2017) 463–75.
Auffret, Pierre. "'A Mon Aide Hâte-toi!' Nouvelle Étude Structurelle du Psaume 70." *Old Testament Essays* 24 (2011) 284–89.
———. "'Alors je jouerai sans fin pour ton nom': Étude structurelle du Psaume 61." *Science et Esprit* 36 (1984) 169–77.
———. "Certes il y un Dieu Jugeant sur la Terre! Étude Structurelle du Psaume 58." *Journal of the Ancient Near Eastern Society* 29 (2002) 1–15.
———. "C'est Dieu qui juge: Étude structurelle du Psaume 75." *Zeitschrift für de alttestamentliche Wissenschaft* 109 (1997) 385–94.
———. "Dans la Ville de notre Dieu: Étude structurelle du Psaume 48." *Science et Esprit* 42 (1990) 305–24.
———. "Essai sur la structure littéraire du Psaume 90." *Biblica* 61 (1980) 262–76.
———. "Essai sur la structure littéraire du Psaume 94." *Biblische Notizen* 24 (1984) 44–72.
———. "Essai sur la structure littéraire du Psaume 95." *Biblische Notizen* 22 (1983) 47–69.
———. "Et moi sans cesse avec toi—Étude structurelle du Psaume 73." *Scandinavian Journal of Theology* 9 (1995) 241–76.
———. "Fais luire ta face et nous serons sauvés: Nouvelle étude structurelle du Psaume 80." *Old Testament Essays* 19 (2006) 1052–63.
———. "'Il est Monté, Dieu': Étude structurelle du Psaume 47." *Science et Esprit* 52 (1990) 61–75.
———. "La droite du très-haut: Étude structurelle du Psaume 77." *Scandinavian Journal of Theology* 6 (1992) 92–122.
———. "La Ville de Dieu: Étude Structurelle du Psaume 46." *Science et Esprit* 41 (1989) 323–41.
———. "'Les oreilles, tu me (les) as ouvertes': Étude structurelle du Psaume 40 (et du Ps 70)." *Nouvelle Revue Théologique* 109 (1987) 220–45.
———. *Merveilles à nos yeux: Étude structurelle de vingt psaumes dont celui de 1Ch 16,8–36*. Beihefte zur Zeitschrift für die alttestamentliche Wissenschaft 235. Berlin: de Gruyter, 1995.
———. "Note sur la structure littéraire du Psaume LVII." *Semitica* 27 (1977) 59–73.
———. "Qu'elles sont aimables, tes demeures! Étude structurelle du psaume 84." *Biblische Zeitschrift* 38 (1994) 29–43
———. *Que seulement de tes yeux tu regardes . . . Étude structurelle de treize psaumes*. Beihefte zur Zeitschrift für die alttestamentliche Wissenschaft 330. Berlin: de Gruyter, 2003.
———. "Qu'ils Sachent Que Toi, Ton Nom Est YHWH! Étude structurelle du Psaume 83." *Science et Esprit* 46 (1993) 41–59.
———. "Qui se lèvera pour moi? Étude structurelle du psaume 94." *Rivista Biblica* 46 (1998) 129–56.

———. "'Venez à ses portails!' Étude structurelle du psaume 100." *Zeitschrift für de alttestamentliche Wissenschaft* 119 (2007) 236–40.

———. *Voyez de vos yeux: Étude structurelle de vingt psaumes, dont le psaume 119*. Vetus Testamentum Supplement 48. Leiden: Brill, 1993.

———. "Yahveh Regne: Étude Structurelle du Psaume 93." *Zeitschrift für de alttestamentliche Wissenschaft* 103 (1991) 101–109.

Ausloos, Hans. "Psalm 45, Messianism and the Septuagint." In *The Septuagint and Messianism,* edited by Michael A. Knibb, 239–51. Leuven: Uitgeverij Peeters, 2006.

Barbiero, Gianni. "The Risks of a Fragmented Reading of the Psalms: Psalm 72 as a Case in Point." *Zeitschrift für de alttestamentliche Wissenschaft* 120 (2008) 67–91.

Barré, Michael L. "A Proposal on the Crux of Psalm LXIV 9a." *Vetus Testamentum* 46 (1996) 115–19.

Benedetto, Robert. "Psalm 84." *Interpretation* 51 (1997) 57–61.

Beuken, W. A. M. "Psalm XLVII: Structure and Drama." In *Remembering All the Way . . . : A Collection of Old Testament Studies Published on the Occasion of the Fortieth Anniversary of the Oudtestamentisch Wergezelschap in Nederland,* edited by Bertil Albrektson and Ornan Rotem, 38–54. Leiden: Brill, 1981.

Bosma, Carl J. "Discerning the Voices in the Psalms: A Discussion of Two Problems in Psalmic Interpretation." *Calvin Theological Journal* 43 (2008) 183–212.

Botha, Phil J. "Psalm 53 in Canonical Perspective." *Old Testament Essays* 26 (2013) 583–606.

———. "Psalm 54: The Power of Positive Patterning." *Skrif en Kerk* 21 (2000) 507–16.

———. "Psalm 62: Prayer, Accusation, Declaration of Innocence, Self-Motivation, Sermon, or All of These?" *Acta Theologica* 38 (2018) 32–48.

———. "Psalm 67 in Its Literary and Ideological Context." *Old Testament Essays* 17 (2004) 365–79.

———. "Psalm 91 and Its Wisdom Connections." *Old Testament Essays* 25 (2012) 260–76.

———. "The Textual Strategy and Social Background of Psalm 64 as Keys to Its Interpretation." *Journal for Semitics* 11 (2002) 64–82.

Bracke, John M. "*šûb šebût*: A Reappraisal." *Zeitschrift für de alttestamentliche Wissenschaft* 97 (1985) 233–44.

Braude, William G., trans. *The Midrash on the Psalms*. Yale Judaica Series 13. New Haven, CT: Yale University Press, 1959.

Brueggemann, Walter. *The Message of the Psalms: A Theological Commentary*. Augsburg Old Testament Studies. Minneapolis: Augsburg, 1984.

———. "Psalm 100." *Interpretation* 39 (1985) 65–69.

———. "Pushing Past into Present." *Christian Century* 109 (1992) 741.

Brueggemann, Walter, and William H. Bellinger, Jr. *Psalms*. New Cambridge Bible Commentary. New York: Cambridge University Press, 2014.

Byars, Ronald P. "Psalm 95." *Interpretation* 56 (2002) 77–79.

Calvin, John. *Commentary on the Book of Psalms*. 5 vols. Translated by James Anderson. Grand Rapids: Eerdmans, 1949.

Cassian, John. *Conferences*. In *The Nicene and Post-Nicene Fathers, Series 2*, edited by Philip Schaff and Henry Wace, 11:291–545. New York: Christian Literature, 1979.

Cheung, Simon Chi-Chung. "'Forget Your People and Your Father's House': The Core Theological Message of Psalm 45 and Its Canonical Position in the Hebrew Psalter." *Bulletin for Biblical Research* 26 (2016) 325–40.

Clifford, Richard J. "In Zion and David a New Beginning: An Interpretation of Psalm 78." In *Traditions in Transformation: Turning Points in Biblical Faith,* edited by Baruch Halpern and Jon D. Levenson, 121–41. Winona Lake, IN: Eisenbrauns, 1981.

———. "Psalm 89: A Lament over the Davidic Ruler's Continued Failure." *Harvard Theological Review* 73 (1980) 35–48.

———. "What Does the Psalmist Ask for in Psalms 39:5 and 90:12?" *Journal of Biblical Literature* 119 (2000) 59–66.

Cohen, Samuel I. "Psalm 47: Numerical and Geometerical Devices Used to Emphasize the Author's Message." *Jewish Bible Quarterly* 23 (1995) 258–64.

Costacurta, Bruna. "L'aggressione contro Dio: Studio del Salmo 83." *Biblica* 64 (1983) 518–41.

Craigie, Peter C., and Marvin E. Tate. *Psalms 1–50*. Word Biblical Commentary 19. 2nd ed. New York: Thomas Nelson, 2004.

Cunha, Wilson de Angelo. "Creation, Kingship, and the Defeat of Evil: A Reflection on Psalm 74." *Revista de Cultura Teológica* 28 (2020) 127–45.

Dahood, Mitchell J. *Psalms II: 51–100*. Anchor Bible Commentary 17. Garden City, NY: Doubleday, 1968.

Davis, Ellen F. "Psalm 98." *Interpretation* 46 (1992) 171–75.

deClaissé-Walford, Nancy, et al. *The Book of Psalms*. New International Commentary on the Old Testament. Grand Rapids: Eerdmans, 2014.

Dickson, C. R. "The Hebrew Terminology for the Poor in Psalm 82." *HTS/Theological Studies* 51 (1995) 1029–45.

Dworkin, Ronald. *Sovereign Virtue: The Theory and Practice of Equality*. Cambridge, MA: Harvard University Press, 2000.

Edwards, Jonathan. *Dissertation II: The Nature of True Virtue*. In *Ethical Writings*. WJE Online Vol. 8, edited by Paul Ramsey, 539–627. http://edwards.yale.edu/archive?path=aHRocDovL2Vkd2FyZHMueWFsZS5lZHUvY2dpLWJpbi9uZXdaGlsby9nZXRvYmplY3QucGw/Yy43OjYud2plbw==.

Eldhose, Alias Kolakunnail. "Trinitarian Interpretation in Light of the Identity of YHWH as the Triune God." PhD diss., Dallas Theological Seminary, 2017.

Estes, Daniel J. "Psalm 84: The Pulse of Worship." *Criswell Theological Review* new series 17 (2020) 35–48.

———. "Spirit and the Psalmist in Psalm 51." In *Presence, Power, and Promise: The Role of the Spirit of God in the Old Testament*, edited by David G. Firth and Paul D. Wegner, 122–34. Downers Grove, IL: InterVarsity, 2011.

Floyd, Michael H. "Psalm LXXXIX: A Prophetic Complaint about the Fulfillment of an Oracle." *Vetus Testamentum* 42.4 (1992) 442–57.

Freedman, H., and Maurice Simon, trans. *The Midrash Rabbah: Numbers, Deuteronomy*. London: Soncino, 1977.

Gaiser, Frederick J. "The David of Psalm 51: Reading Psalm 51 in Light of Psalm 50." *Word and World* 23 (2003) 382–94.

———. "'It Shall Not Reach You': Talisman or Vocation? Reading Psalm 91 in Time of War." *Word and World* 25 (2005) 191–202.

———. "'I Will Tell You What God Has Done for Me' (Psalm 66:16): A Place for 'Testimony' in Lutheran Worship?" *Word and World* 26 (2006) 138–48.

Girard, Marc. *Les Psaumes: Analyse Structurelle et Interprétation (1–50)*. Recherches Nouvelle Série 2. Montreal: Éditions Bellarmin, 1984.

———. *Les Psaumes Redécouverts: De la Structure au Sens: 51–100*. Montreal: Bellarmin, 1984.

Goldingay, John. "Psalm 51:16a (English 51:14a)." *Catholic Bible Quarterly* 40 (1978) 388–90.

———. *Psalms: Volume 2: Psalms 42–89*. Baker Commentary on the Old Testament. Grand Rapids: Baker, 2007.

———. *Psalms: Volume 3: Psalms 90–150*. Baker Commentary on the Old Testament. Grand Rapids: Baker, 2008.

Gordon, Cyrus H. "The Wine-Dark Sea." *Journal of Near Eastern Studies* 37 (1978) 51–52.

Greene, Nathaniel E. "Creation, Destruction, and a Psalmist's Plea: Rethinking the Poetic Structure of Psalm 74." *Journal of Biblical Literature* 136 (2017) 85–101.

Grønbæk, Jakob H. "Baal's Battle with Yam—A Canaanite Creation Fight." *Journal for the Study of the Old Testament* 33 (1985) 27–44.

Handy, Lowell K. "Sounds, Words and Meanings in Psalm 82." *Journal for the Study of the Old Testament* 47 (1990) 51–66.

Harman, Allan M. "The Syntax and Interpretation of Psalm 45:7." In *The Law and the Prophets: Old Testament Studies Prepared in Honor of Oswald Thompson Allis*, edited by John H. Skilton et al., 337–47. Nutley, NJ: Presbyterian and Reformed, 1974.

Heim, Knut M. "The Perfect King of Psalm 72: An 'Intertextual' Inquiry." In *The Lord's Anointed: Interpretation of Old Testament Messianic Texts*, edited by Philip E. Satterthwaite et al., 223–48. Grand Rapids: Baker, 1995.

Heiser, Michael S. "Monotheism, Polytheism, Monolatry, or Henotheism." *Bulletin for Biblical Research* 18 (2008) 1–30.

Hill, Edmund. *Prayer, Praise and Politics; Reflections on 32 Psalms*. London: Sheed and Ward, 1973.

Ho, Shirley S. "Leviticus 26 in Psalm 79: The Defilement of the Sacred, Nations and Lament." *Jian Dao* 44 (2015) 1–24.

Hobbes, Thomas. *Leviathan*. Oxford: Clarendon, 1965.
Human, Dirk J. "Psalm 93: Yahweh Robed in Majesty and Mightier Than the Great Waters." In *Psalms and Mythology*, Library of Hebrew Bible/Old Testament Studies 462, edited by Dirk J. Human, 147–69. New York: T. & T. Clark, 2007.
Jacobson, Karl N. "Dualing (Read: Dueling) *Psalmos*." *Word and World* 40 (2020) 290–99.
Jacobson, Rolf A. "Psalm 46: Translation, Structure, and Theology." *Word and World* 40 (2020) 308–20.
Jensen, Joseph E. "Psalm 75: Its Poetic Context and Structure." *Catholic Bible Quarterly* 63 (2001) 416–29.
Jerome. *The Homilies of Saint Jerome 1 (1–59 On the Psalms)*. The Fathers of the Church 48. Translated by Marie Liguori Ewald, 79–89. Washington, DC: The Catholic University of America Press, 1964.
Jerome, Obiorah Mary. *"How Lovely Is Your Dwelling Place": The Desire for God's House in Psalm 84*. Dissertationen Theologische Reihe 87. St. Ottilien, Germany: EOS Verlag Erzabtei, 2004.
Jones, David Clyde. "The Multiracial City." *Presbyterion* 21 (1995) 67–72.
Kelly, Sidney. "Psalm 46: A Study in Imagery." *Journal of Biblical Literature* 89 (1970) 305–12.
Kim, Yeol, and H. F. van Rooy. "Reading Psalm 78 Multidimensionally: The Textual Dimension." *Scriptura* 74 (2000) 285–98.
Klein, Anja. "From the 'Right Spirit' to the 'Spirit of Truth': Observations on Psalm 51 and 1QS." In *The Dynamics of Language and Exegesis at Qumran*, edited by Devorah Dimant and Reinhard G. Kratz, 171–91. Tübingen: Mohr Siebeck, 2009.
Knohl, Israel. "Psalm 68: Structure, Composition and Geography." *Journal of Hebrew Scriptures* 12 (2012) 1–21.
Kselman, John S., and Michael L. Barré. "Psalm 55: Problems and Proposals." *Catholic Bible Quarterly* 60 (1998) 440–62.
Kugler, Gili. "Not Moses, but David: Theology and Politics in Psalm 78." *Scandinavian Journal of the Old Testament* 73 (2020) 126–36.
Kuruvilla, Abraham. *Genesis: A Theological Commentary for Preachers*. Eugene, OR: Resource Publications, 2017.
———. *Privilege the Text! A Theological Hermeneutic for Preaching*. Chicago: Moody, 2013.
LePeau, John Philip. "Psalm 68: An Exegetical and Theological Study." PhD diss., University of Iowa, 1981.
Levenson, Jon D. *Creation and the Persistence of Evil: The Jewish Drama of Divine Omnipotence*. Princeton: Princeton University Press, 1994.
Liverani, Mario. "The Ideology of the Assyrian Empire." In *Power and Propaganda: A Symposium on Ancient Empires*, edited by Mogens Trolle Larsen, 312–17. Copenhagen: Akademisk Forlag, 1979.
Magonet, Jonathan. "Some Concentric Structures in the Psalms." *Heythrop Journal* 23 (1982) 365–76.
Maré, Leonard P. "Facing the Deepest Darkness of Despair and Abandonment: Psalm 88 and the Life of Faith." *Old Testament Essays* 27 (2014) 177–88.
Marlowe, W. Creighton. "'Spirit of Your Holiness' (רוּחַ קָדְשֶׁךָ) in Psalm 51:13." *Trinity Journal* 19ns (1998) 29–49.
Martin, Lee Roy. "Chiastic Structure of Psalm 106." *Old Testament Essays* 31 (2018) 506–21.
———. "An Embedded Chiasm in the Narrative Structure of Psalm 105." *Journal of Semitics* 28 (2019) 1–14.
———. "Longing for God: Psalm 63 and Pentecostal Spirituality." *Journal of Pentecostal Theology* 22 (2013) 54–76.
Mays, James L. "Worship, World, and Power: An Interpretation of Psalm 100." *Interpretation* 23 (1969) 315–30.
McFayden, John E. "The Messages of the Psalms: Psalm 46." *The Biblical World* 27 (1906) 99–103.
Michael, Graham J. L. "The Works of God's Salvation: The Rhetorical Use of Creation Imagery in Psalm 74." *Southeastern Theological Review* 10 (2019) 5–29.
Middleton, J. Richard. "A Psalm Against David? A Canonical Reading of Psalm 51 as a Critique of David's Inadequate Repentance in 2 Samuel 12." In *Explorations in Interdisciplinary Reading: Theological, Exegetical, and Reception-Historical Perspectives*, edited by Robbie F. Castleman et al., 26–45. Eugene, OR: Pickwick, 2017.
Muilenburg, James. "Psalm 47." *Journal of Biblical Literature* 63 (1944) 235–56.
Murphy, Roland E. *A Study of Psalm 72 (71)*. Catholic University of America Studies in Sacred Theology 2. Washington, DC: The Catholic University of America Press, 1948.
Ninck, Carl Wilhelm. *Auf biblischen Pfaden*. Hamburg: Verlag der Expedition des Deutschen Kinderfreundes, 1892.

BIBLIOGRAPHY

Oppenheim, A. Leo, and Erica Reiner, eds. *The Assyrian Dictionary of the Oriental Institute of the University of Chicago: Volume 10: M Part I*. Chicago: The Oriental Institute, 1977.
Palmer, Martin. "The Cardinal Points in Psalm 48." *Biblica* 46 (1965) 357–58.
Pardee, Dennis. "The Poetic Structure of Psalm 93." *Studi Epigrafici e Linguistici* 5 (1988) 163–70.
Postell, Seth D. "A Literary, Compositional, and Intertextual Analysis of Psalm 45." *Bibliotheca Sacra* 176 (2019) 146–63.
Potgieter, J. Henk. "The Profile of the Rich Antagonist and the Pious Protagonist in Psalm 52." *HTS/Theological Studies* 69 (2013) 1–7.
Pritchard, James B., ed. *Ancient Near Eastern Texts Relating to the New Testament*. Princeton: Princeton University Press, 1969.
Raabe, Paul R. *Psalm Structures: A Study of Psalms with Refrains*. Journal for the Study of the Old Testament Supplement Series 104. Sheffield: Sheffield Academic, 1990.
Ross, Allen P. *A Commentary on the Psalms: Volume 2 (42–89)*. Grand Rapids: Kregel, 2013.
Scacewater, Todd A. "The Divine Builder: Psalm 68 in Jewish and Pauline Tradition." PhD diss., Westminster Theological Seminary, 2017.
Seneca. *Tragedies, Volume I: Hercules. Trojan Women. Phoenician Women. Medea. Phaedra.* Edited and translated by John G. Fitch. Loeb Classical Library 62. Cambridge, MA: Harvard University Press, 2018.
Smith, Mark S. "God and Zion: Form and Meaning in Psalm 48." *Studi Epigrafici e Linguistici* 6 (1989) 67–77.
Spero, Shubert. "The Menorah Psalm." *Jewish Bible Quarterly* 37 (2009) 11–16.
Spurgeon, C. H. *The Treasury of David, Volume 2: Psalms 27–57*. London: Marshall Brothers, 1880.
———. *The Treasury of David: Volume 3: Psalms 58–87*. London: Marshall Brothers, 1880.
Starbuck, Scott R. A. *Court Oracles in the Psalms: The So-Called Royal Psalms in Their Ancient Near Eastern Context*. Society of Biblical Literature Dissertation Series 172. Atlanta: SBL, 1999.
Sylva, Dennis. "Procreation Discourse in Psalms 74 and 77: Struggling with *Chaoskämpfe*." *Religion and Theology* 18 (2011) 244–67.
Talstra, Eep, and Carl J. Bosma. "Psalm 67: Blessing, Harvest and History: A Proposal for Exegetical Methodology." *Calvin Theological Journal* 36 (2001) 290–313.
Tate, Marvin E. *Psalms 51–100*. Word Biblical Commentary 20. Dallas: Word, 1990.
Tsumura, David Toshio. "The Literary Structure of Psalm 46, 2–8." *Annual of the Japanese Biblical Institute* 6 (1980) 29–55.
Tucker, W. Dennis, Jr. "*Exitus, Reditus*, and Moral Formation in Psalm 90." In *Diachronic and Synchronic: Reading the Psalms in Real Time: Proceedings of the Baylor Symposium on the Book of Psalms*, edited by Joel S. Burnett et al., 143–54. London: T. & T. Clark, 2007.
———. "The Ordered World of Psalm 92." *Old Testament Essays* 32 (2019) 358–77.
VanGemeren, Willem A. *Psalms*. Expositor's Bible Commentary 5. Rev. ed. Grand Rapids: Zondervan, 2008.
van Wolde, Ellen. "A Prayer for Purification: Psalm 51:12–14, a Pure Heart and the Verb ברא." *Vetus Testamentum* 70 (2020) 340–60.
Vincent, Mark Anthony. "From Sinai to Jerusalem: A Study of the Hebrew Text of Psalm 68." PhD diss., Durham University, 2001.
Vreugdenhil, Gerrit C. *Psalm 91 and Demonic Menace*. Oudtestamentische Studiën 77. Leiden: Brill, 2020.
Wallace, Howard N. "*Jubilate Deo omnis terra*: God and Earth in Psalm 65." In *The Earth Story in the Psalms and the Prophets*, edited by Norman C. Habel, 51–64. Sheffield: Sheffield Academic, 2001.
Weber, Beat. "'They Saw You, the Waters—They Trembled' (Psalm 77:17b) The Function of Mytho-poietic Language in the Context of Psalm 77." In *Psalms and Mythology*, edited by Dirk J. Human, 104–25. London: T. & T. Clark, 2007.
Wendland, Ernst R. "Aspects of the Structure, Style, and Transmission of Psalm 73." *The Bible Translator* 50 (1999) 135–49.
———. *Studies in the Psalms—Supplement*. Version 3.5, 2018. https://www.academia.edu/34291980/STUDIES_IN_THE_PSALMS_Supplement_version_3_5.
Zenger, Erich. "Psalm 87: A Case for Ideological Criticism." In *Reading from Right to Left: Essays on the Hebrew Bible in Honour of David J. A. Clines*, edited by Cheryl J. Exum and H. G. M. Williamson, 450–60. London: Sheffield Academic, 2003.

Index of Authors

Allen, Leslie C., 156, 157, 181
Allen, Ronald B., 273
Alter, Robert, 254
Althann, Robert, 84
Anderson, Craig Evan, 95
Attard, Stefano, 3
Auffret, Pierre, 12, 14, 15, 19, 26, 72, 78, 84, 100, 117, 118, 124, 142, 163, 182, 198, 207, 209, 219, 233, 249, 250, 257, 298, 307, 316, 322, 324, 325, 331, 341, 348, 349, 352, 358
Ausloos, Hans, 3, 5

Barbiero, Gianni, 176
Barré, Michael L., 65, 68, 117
Bellinger, William H., Jr., 74, 100, 112, 209
Benedetto, Robert, 254
Beuken, W. A. M., 18, 20
Bosma, Carl J., 133, 164
Botha, Phil J., 56, 60, 107, 114, 136, 304
Bracke, John M., 57, 260
Braude, William G., 174
Brueggemann, Walter, 74, 100, 112, 209, 268, 359
Bunyan, John, 255
Byars, Ronald P., 330

Calvin, John, 45, 311
Cassian, John, 163
Cheung, Simon Chi-Cheung, 2, 8
Clifford, Richard J., 212, 219, 221, 291
Cohen, Samuel I., 19
Costacurta, Bruna, 247
Craigie, Peter C., 11, 15, 19, 24, 27, 29, 33, 34
Cunha, Wilson de Angelo, 192

Dahood, Mitchell J., 137, 182
Davis, Ellen F., 350
deClaissé-Walford, Nancy, et al., 27, 49, 56, 58, 63, 68, 73, 78, 85, 88, 92, 96, 109, 112, 120, 129, 133, 142, 149, 154, 156, 161, 167, 182, 187, 193, 198, 199, 217, 228, 239, 240, 242, 249, 261, 269, 272, 277, 294, 301, 307, 323, 329, 332, 357
Dickson, C. R., 242
Dworkin, Ronald, 303

Edwards, Jonathan, 6
Eldhose, Alias Kolakunnail, 176
Estes, Daniel J., 46, 255

Floyd, Michael H., 287
Freedman, H., 174

Gaiser, Frederick J., 43, 128, 304, 307
Girard, Marc, 31, 38, 192, 221, 322, 323, 325, 328, 332, 335, 338, 342, 349, 357
Goldingay, John, 18, 24, 25, 27, 32, 37, 38, 44, 45, 46, 47, 52, 54, 56, 58, 59, 61, 62, 65, 68, 73, 77, 79, 90, 97, 106, 109, 111, 118, 125, 134, 135, 146, 154, 155, 156, 161, 166, 170, 183, 191, 193, 197, 202, 208, 209, 212, 218, 220, 226, 227, 232, 237, 238, 244, 246, 248, 249, 257, 259, 261, 264, 266, 268, 269, 271, 272, 274, 275, 276, 281, 295, 296, 300, 301, 307, 312, 323, 324, 329, 330, 331, 332, 338, 339, 350, 352, 353, 358
Gordon, Cyrus H., 25
Greene, Nathaniel E., 192
Grønbæk, Jakob H., 191

Handy, Lowell K., 241
Harman, Allan M., 2
Heim, Knut M., 172
Heiser, Michael S., 240
Hill, Edmund, 274
Ho, Shirley S., 227
Hobbes, Thomas, 302
Human, Dirk J., 317, 318, 319

Jacobson, Karl N., 54, 159
Jacobson, Rolf A., 11

INDEX OF AUTHORS

Jensen, Joseph E., 198, 199
Jerome, 212
Jerome, Obiorah Mary, 254
Jones, David Clyde, 273

Kelly, Sidney, 13, 15
Kim, Y., 217
Klein, Anja, 46
Knohl, Israel, 140
Kselman, John S., 65, 68
Kugler, Gili, 212
Kuruvilla, Abraham, 192, 331, 332

LePeau, John Philip, 144
Levenson, Jon D., 291
Liverani, Mario, 274

Magonet, Jonathan, 313
Maré, Leonard P., 279
Marlowe, W. Creighton, 46
Martin, Lee Roy, 110
Mays, James L., 358
McFayden, John E., 14
Michael, Graham J. L., 192
Middleton, J. Richard, 41
Muilenburg, James, 20
Murphy, Roland E., 173

Ninck, Carl Wilhelm, 14

Oppenheim, A. Leo, 274

Palmer, Martin, 24
Pardee, Dennis, 318
Postell, Seth D., 2, 3
Potgeiter, J. Henk, 51
Pritchard, James B., 24, 25, 85, 140, 145, 191

Raabe, Paul R., 31
Reiner, Erica, 274
Rooy, H. F., 217
Ross, Allen P., 61, 142, 254

Scacewater, Todd A., 141
Seneca, 82
Simon, Maurice, 174
Simon, Paul, 182
Smith, Mark S., 23
Spero, Shubert, 133
Spurgeon, C. H., 52, 116
Starbuck, Scott R. A., 1
Sylva, Dennis, 190

Talstra, Eep, 133
Tate, Marvin E., 60, 72, 85, 101, 102, 112, 114, 116, 117, 128, 141, 144, 154, 164, 174, 176, 181, 193, 197, 202, 207, 208, 222, 227, 233, 238, 245, 256, 257, 265, 271, 274, 281, 282, 283, 290, 293, 296, 299, 300, 306, 354, 359
Tsumura, David Toshio, 12
Tucker, W. Dennis, Jr., 302, 309

van Wolde, Ellen, 45, 48
VanGemeren, Willem A., 46
Vincent, Mark Anthony, 142, 146, 147
Vreugdenhil, Gerrit C., 306, 307

Wallace, Howard N., 124
Watts, Isaac, 302
Weber, Beat, 210
Wendland, Ernst R., 43, 181

Zenger, Erich, 274

Index of Scripture and Apocrypha

OLD TESTAMENT

Genesis

1–11	192n12
1:1–2	14, 192n12
1:2	192n12
1:5	192n12
1:9	192n12
1:10	192n12
1:14–16	192n12
1:21	192n12
1:26	240n2
2:7–8	192n12
2:9	192n12
2:10–14	13n10
2:10	192n12
2:13	192n12
2:19	192n12
3:22	240n2, 243n10
5:24	34, 184n12
6:11	56n4
6:12	56n4
7:4	220
7:11	192n12
8:2	192n12
8:7	192n12
8:14	192n12
8:22	192n12
8:27	44n11
11:7	240n2
12:3	135, 173n5
17:4–5	20
17:4	20
18:18	20, 173n5
19:15	84n11
19:24	220
22:18	20, 173n5, 176n18
26:4	173n5, 176n18
28:14	173n5
49:8	2n5
49:10	2n5, 173n5
49:11	2n5
49:12	2n5
49:22	232n5

Exodus

3:7	208n4
3:9	208n4
3:12	358
4:23	358
6:6	142n7
6:7	142n7
7:4	142n7
7:5	142n7
7:16	358
8:1	358
9:23	220
10:26	358
12:17	142n7
12:22	45n8
12:41	142n7
12:42	142n7
12:51	142n7
13:21–22	38n4
14:27	14
15	144, 209n15
15:1–18	221n15
15:1–12	221n15
15:2	142n7
15:3	142n7
15:7	221n15
15:8	209n15, 221n15
15:11–16	209n15
15:11	209n15, 240n2
15:13–18	221n15
15:13	209n15, 221n15
15:14	209n15
15:15	353
15:16	209n15, 221n15

Exodus (continued)

15:17–18	19n5
15:17	19n4, 221n15, 221n18
15:20–21	142n7
17:1–7	331n11
17:7	238n6, 331
18:13	242n6
19:4	78n2
19:16	7n22
19:18–19	38n4
19:21	243n11
20:14–16	39
25:20	78n2
29:12	272n4
32–34	354n6
32:12	296n1
32:28	243n11
33:13	47n19
34:5–7	61
34:6–9	267
34:6–7	354
34:6	47n19, 269
34:7	47n19
37:9	78n2

Leviticus

4:7	272n4
4:18	272n4
4:25	272n4
4:30	272n4
4:34	272n4
14:51	45n8
21:23	183n9
25:19	135n12
26	227
26:4	135
26:14–46	227
26:18	227
26:20	135
26:21	227
26:22	227
26:24	227
26:28	227
26:29	227
26:31	227
26:32	227
26:33	227
26:34	227
26:35	227
26:40	227
26:42	227
26:43	227

Numbers

6	134
6:24–26	134
6:25	134
10:35b	142
16:44–48	354n6
18:12	239n11
19:18	45n8
20:2–13	354
20:13–14	238n6
20:13	331n11
20:24	331n11
24:18	101n6
26:53	97n6
26:55	97n6
26:56	97n6
35:5	97n6

Deuteronomy

2:5	101n6
2:9	101n6
2:12	101n6
2:25	353
3:20	101n6
4:19	240n2
4:20	142n7
4:21	412n7
4:38	142n7
5:2–3	129n7
5:6	142n7
5:15	142n7
5:18–20	39
6:12	142n7
6:16	331n11
6:20–22	129n7
7:4	358
8:19	358
9:22	331n11
10:17	240n2
11:16	358
11:17	135n12
11:24	23
12:2	358
12:5	196n1
12:11	196n1
17:2–3	240n2
26:5–9	129n7
26:7	208n4
31:17	136
31:18	136
32:4	296n1
32:6	330n7, 358n8

32:7	296n1	10:24	176n16
32:8–9	19n4, 240n2, 244n13	12:6–25	354n6
32:11	78n2	12:6	354n6
32:13–14	239n11	15:22–23	157n21
32:14	144	17:55	113n11
32:15	330n7, 358n8	23:17	300n11
32:20	136	23:19	23
32:22	135n12, 136	23:24	23
32:51	331n11	25:22	332n13
33:2–3	240n2	26:19	19n4
33:2	38n4, 140n3		
33:8	238n6, 331n11		
33:11	156n16, 296n1		

2 Samuel

6:2	78n2, 353
7:12–13	2
7:16	2
8:16	275n23
11–12	41n1
12:7	7n20
13:5	156n15
13:7	155n15
13:10	155n15
14:16	19n4
15:10	19n5
15:21	113n11
16:16	176n16
20:19	19n4
21:3	19n4
22	159n1

33:22	144
33:26	140n3
33:29	306n8

Joshua

1:15	101n6
6:3	27n12
6:11	27n12
8:25	243n11
9:24	19n7
10:2	19n7
12:6	101n6
12:7	101n6
15:45	343n7
15:47	343n7
17:7	23
22:22	37n2

1 Kings

1:25	176n16
1:34	176n16
1:39	19n5, 176n16
2:45	2
6:23–28	78n2
8:6–7	78n2
9:5	2
9:8	275n22
9:28	7n21
22:19–23	240n2, 242n6

Judges

4–5	249
4:5	242n6
5	144
6–8	249
8:10	243n11
9:48	144
11:35	61n7
12:6	243n11, 300n11
20:44	243n11
20:46	243n11

2 Kings

2:3	34, 184n12
2:5	34, 184n12
2:9	34, 184n12
2:10	184n12
9:13	19n5
10	34
11:12	176n16
13:23	45n9
17:20	45n9

Ruth

4:2	242n6

1 Samuel

4:4	78n2, 353
7:7–12	354n6
10:1	7n20

2 Kings (continued)

19:15	78n2, 353
24:2	226n2
24:20	45n9

1 Chronicles

15:16	198n10
16:25	240n2
17:12	2
17:14	2
18:15	275n23
22:10	2
25:5	198n10
29:11	6n17
29:13	6n17
29:23	2

2 Chronicles

7:21	275n22
9:8	2

Ezra

3:12	198n10
9:6	198n10

Nehemiah

1:6–7	293n17, 296n1
1:10–11	293n17, 296n1
9:6	240n2

Job

1:6–12	240n2
2:1–6	240n2
4:12–16	306n8
4:13–14	306n8
12:23	135n10
15:21	306n8
18:20	23
22:10–11	306n8
22:24	7n21
28:16	7n21
33:14	103n2
38:7	240n2
38:8–11	14n14
40:5	103n2
40:15—41:34	146n28
40:16	155n16
42:7–8	293n17, 296n1
42:10	57n9

Psalms

(Also see within the appropriate psalms for references to verses of those chapters.)

1:1a	177n22
1:12–13	79n7
2	171n1, 291, 315
2:1–2	274
2:2	256n14, 291
2:11	175n14
3:3	256n15
3:5	79
4:6	134n6
4:8	79
5:8	135n10
6	41
7:17	75n13, 275n21, 290n9
8:3	311n6
8:6	311n6
9:1–6	336n4, 348n2
9:2	275n21, 290n9
9:5	274
9:7	2
9:10	274n17
9:14	2n8, 273
9:15	274
10:9	202n4
10:16	2, 274
11:7	1
13:1	106n5, 134n7, 155n14
13:2	106n5
14	54, 54n1, 159n1
14:2a	54n1
14:4b	54n1
14:5–7	54n1
14:6	54n1
14:7	57, 260
14:7b	54n1
16:9	79n12
16:10	34n11
17:7	209n12, 336n4, 348n2
17:8	78n2
17:13	282n10
18	159n1, 171n1, 315
18:2	256n15
18:5	34n11, 282n10
18:7	342
18:8	243n9, 342
18:9–11	342
18:10	353
18:12	342
18:13	275n21, 290n9
18:14	342
18:15	342

18:16–18	14n14	36:5	208n10
18:16	34n11, 184n12	36:7	78n2
18:18	282n10	36:10	274n17
18:30	256n15	38	41
18:35	209n12	38:16	198n9
18:43	357	39:2	198n9
18:46–47	79n7	40	159, 159n2
18:50	256n14	40:1–12	159n2
19:1	311n6	40:1a	159n2
19:8	318n10	40:1c	159n2
20	171n1, 315	40:2b	159n2
20:6	209n12, 256n14	40:3	159n2
20:7	355n9	40:3a	159n2
21	171n1, 315	40:3c	159n2
21:7	275n21, 290n9	40:4b	159n2
22:12	144	40:5a	159n2
22:24	155n13	40:5f	159n2
22:25	75n13	40:6	159n2
22:27–28	274	40:7	198n9
22:30	357	40:7b	159n2
23:1	359n10	40:8a	159n2
23:2	135, 135n10	40:9–10	159n2
25:5	262	40:9a	159n2
25:10	78n4, 262, 318n10	40:9c	159n2
25:16	155n13	40:10	78n4, 198n9, 262
26:3	78n4, 262	40:10a	159n2
27:2	117n10	40:10d	159n2
27:9	134n7, 155n14	40:11	78n4, 262
27:11	135n10	40:11a	159n2
28	171n1	40:11b	159n2
28:7	256n15	40:11c	159n2
28:9	142n7, 359n10	40:12b	159n2
29:1	240n2, 243, 289n4	40:12c	159n2
30:1	79n7	40:12d	159n2
30:3	34n11	40:13–17	159
30:5	33n10	41:4	198n9
30:6	198n9	42–44	3
30:7	155n14	42–43	252n1
30:12	79n12	43:3	135n10, 262
31:2	167n8	43:4	2
31:3	135n10	43:13–17	161
31:5	262	44:1	311n6
31:14	198n9	44:3	209n12
31:16	134n6	44:4a	1
31:22	198n9	44:8	2, 2n5
32	41	44:9	3
32:5	198n9	44:10	3
33:5	1, 208n10	44:11	274
33:6	14n14	44:13	203n9
33:10	274	44:14–16	3
33:12	142n7	44:14	274
33:20	256n15	44:19	3
34:3–4	79n7	44:20	61n6
34:18	47n23	44:23a	1

Psalms (continued)

44:24	3, 134n7, 155n14
44:26	3
45	171n1, 291, 315
45:7	291
46–49	3
46:1	3
46:4–5	3
46:4	22, 275n21
46:6	274
46:7	3
46:9–10	79n7
46:10	2, 274
46:11	3
47:1	3
47:2	2
47:6–9	3
47:6	2
47:8	2, 274
47:9	256n14
48	10n1
48:1–14	3
48:2	2, 8n25
48:8	2
48:10	1
48:11	343n7
49:15	184n12
49:17	184n12
50:2	8n25
50:2a	8n25
50:2b	8n25
50:7–15	157n21
50:14	75n13
51–72	177n23
51	49
51:9	134n7
51:13	49
51:18–19	157n21
52	54
53	159n1
53:6	260
54:6–7	75n13
55	73, 149n1
55:22	73
56	76
56:1a	76
56:2a	76
56:4	76
56:10–11	76
57	159n1
57:1	78n2
57:3	78n4
57:10	787n4, 208n10
58:1–2	240n2
59	63, 149n1
60	159n1
61:2–3	79n7
61:2	135n10
61:4	78n2
61:7	78n4
61:8	75n13
62	109
62:12	109
63:8	209n12
65	126
65:4	281
65:7	14n14
65:13	126
66:5	311n6
66:13–15	75n13
66:20	132n1
67:4	1
68:15	306n6
68:23	85n12
69	63, 161n4
69:6–7	161n4
69:6d	161n4
69:9	161n4
69:13	78n4
69:14a	161n4
69:17	134n7
69:19–20	161n4
69:29a	161n4
69:30–31	75n13
69:32a	161n4
69:33a	161n4
69:36b	161n4
72	159, 315
72:11	357
73–83	35n1
73:8	72n1
73:15	198n9
73:23	209n12
73:24	135n10
74	195, 196, 197
74:1	359n10
74:1a	196
74:1b	196
74:2	142n7
74:3–9	196
74:9c	197
74:10–11	197
74:10	197
74:12	311n6
74:13–14	146n28
74:18–23	197
74:22–23	196

74:23	197	89	277, 302, 308n12, 359
75:5	72n1	89:1	359
76	10n1	89:2	198n9, 359
76:2	22	89:4	2
77	229n1	89:5	359
77:12	311n6	89:6–8	240n2
77:14	336n4, 348n2	89:6	243
77:17	14n14	89:8	359
77:20	135, 135n10, 229n1, 359n10	89:10–11	146n28
		89:12	24, 125n12
78	229n1, 284	89:13	79n7
78:5	318n10	89:14	78n4
78:11–16	348n2, 336n4	89:17	197n7
78:14	135n10	89:18	256n14
78:25	182n4	89:20	7n20
78:29	182n4	89:24	197n7, 359
78:40	142n7	89:25–29	173n5
78:43	164n1	89:29	2
78:46	135n12	89:33	359
78:52–53	359n10	89:36–37	2, 173n5
78:53	135n10	89:46	155n14, 296
78:56	318n10	89:49	359
78:70–72	359n10	90–106	17
78:71–72	229n1	90	308n12
78:72	135, 135n10	90:14	33n10
79–80	237n3	91:1	144n13
79	63, 149n1, 229, 231, 232, 234n8, 239	91:3	78
		91:4	78n2
79:1	19n4	91:14	274n17
79:4	203n9	92:10	197n7
79:5a	229, 232	93–99	356
79:6–9	232	93	340, 351
79:6	274n17	93:2	2
79:13	229, 358n6	93:3–4	129
80	239	93:3	14n14
80:1	8n25, 38n4, 78n2, 359n10	94:1	8n25, 38n4
80:3	134n6	94:18	198n9
80:7	134n6, 331n11	94:23	355n9
80:19	134n6	95–99	315, 340, 351
81:9	61n6	95:3	240n2
82:1	289n4	95:5	358n6
82:6	198n9	95:6	358n8
84	10n1	95:7–11	357
84:9	20n8	95:7	358n6, 359n10
85:1	57	95:8–9	238n6
85:10	78n4	95:9	311n6
85:12	135	95:9b	238n6
86	177n23, 271	96	18n1
86:8	240n2, 311n6	96:3	348n2
86:9	271	96:4–5	240n2
86:15	78n4	96:6	1
87	10n1	96:8	330
88	284, 295, 308n12	96:11–12	125n12
88:14	134n7, 155n14	97:4b–5a	342

Psalms (*continued*)

97:7	175n14, 240n2
97:8	27n11
97:9	240n2
98:1	336n4
98:7–8	125n12
99:1	78n2
99:4	1
99:7	318n10
100	18n1
100:2	175n14, 330
100:3	330n7
101	171n1, 315
102	41
102:2	134n7, 155n14
102:22	175n14
102:25	311n6
103:22	311n6
104:1	1
104:5–9	14n14
104:21–22	202n4
104:24	311n6
104:29	134n7, 155n14
104:31	311n6
105:2	336n4, 348n2
105:5	164n1
105:7	355n9
105:11	19n4
105:27	164n1
106:7	336n4, 348n2
106:14	142n7
106:22	336n4, 348n2
106:32	331n11
106:36	175n14
106:39	185n13
106:47	355n9
107:3	23
107:4	142n7
107:21–22	38
107:22	75n13
107:24	311n6
108	159n1
108:1–5	79n8
108:4	78n4
108:5–6	79n7
108:7–13	95n1
108:9	97n4
109	63, 149n1
110	171n1, 315
111:3	1
112:9	197n7
113:5	355n9
114:1–2	19n5
115:1	78n4
116:11	198n9
116:14–18	75n13
117:2	78n4
118:7	61n7
118:15–16	79n7
119	212, 284
119:57	198n9
119:117	357n2
119:132	155n13
119:135	134n6
119:176	357n2
122	10n1
122:5	242n6
122:9	355n9
123:2	355n9
126:1	57, 260
126:4	57, 260
127:5	281n6
128:4	281n6
130	41
130:3	44n7
132	171n1, 315
132:8	332
132:11–12	2
132:12	318n10
132:14	332
132:15	182n4
132:17	197n7
134:1	175n14
135:9	164n1
137	63, 149n1
138–145	177n23
138:2	78n4
138:4–6	79n7
139:10	135n10
139:14	311n6
139:24	135n10
140:6	198n9
141:7	84n11
142:5	198n9
143	41
143:2	44n7
143:7	134n7
143:10	135n10
144	171n1, 315
145:5	1
145:10	311n6
145:13	2
148:2	240n2
148:14	197n7

Proverbs

8:22–31	14n14
15:11	282n8
20:8	242n6
21:6	103n2
24:16	117n10
24:17	117n10
30:15	103n2
30:18	103n2
30:21	103n2
30:29	103n2
31:30	103n2

Isaiah

1:8	273n5
1:10–17	157n21
1:23–24	82n2
2:2–4	173n5
2:2	271n2
2:13	144
3:8	117n10
5:1–7	233, 232n5
5:23	82n2
6:1–7	240n2
6:1	242n6
8:15	117n10
9:5–7	2n6
9:6	1n2, 61
9:7	173n5
10:1–4	82n2
10:21	1n2
10:32	273n5
11:1–5	173n5
12:3	276n24
13:12	7n21
14:13	240n2
16:1	273n5
16:5	242n6
17:12–14	14n14
19:1	140n3
19:23–25	271n2
22:4	2n8
24:18	243n9
24:21	240n2, 243n9
27:1	146n28
27:2–6	232n5
28:2	306n8
28:5	242n6
30:7	273
31:3	117n10
32:1	173n5
32:16–18	173n5
33:17	6n17
37:16	78n2
41:18	276n24
43:1	358n8
43:21	358n8
44:2	330n7, 358n8
44:28	359n10
45:1	156n16
45:14	173n5
45:22–23	271n2
47:9–12	306n8
47:11	306n8
49:8	155n12
49:19–25	271n2
50:1	3n10
51:17	198n11
51:22	198n11
54:1	271n2
54:5	3n10
54:6–7	3n10, 271n2
56:6	293n17, 296n1
58:5	155n12
59:15–20	14n14
60:1–12	173n5
61:3	7n20
62:3	7n22
62:11	2n8
63:3–6	85n12
63:10	46n13
63:11	46n13
63:14	46n13
63:17	293n17, 296n1
65:8–9	293n17, 296n1
65:13–15	293n17, 296n1
65:20	300n9
66:1–6	157n21
66:7–8	271n2
66:14	293n17, 296n1

Jeremiah

2:1–2	3n10
2:20	185n13
2:21	232n5
3:1–2	3n10
3:1	185n13
3:3	185n13
3:6	3n10, 185n13
3:8	3n10, 185n13
3:17	173n5
4:2	176n18
4:11	2n8
4:31	273n5
5:22	14n14

Jeremiah (continued)

5:26–29	82n2
6:2	273n5
7:15	45n9
8:2	240n2
12:10	232n5
15:1	354n6
23:1–4	359n10
23:5–6	173n5
23:18	240n2
23:22	240n2
25:11–12	300
25:15–17	198n11
25:38	202n4
31:32	3n10
33:15–16	173n5
46:6	117n10
46:12	117n10
46:16	117n10
46:24	2n8
49:12	198n11
50:32	117n10
51:39	198n11
51:51	183n9
52:3	45n9

Lamentations

2:2	2n8
4:21	2n8

Ezekiel

3:17–19	47n18
7:19–26	306n8
7:26	306n8
13:14	272n4
15:1–8	232n5
16	3n10
16:10	3n10
16:13–15	3n10
16:13	3n10
16:14	3n10, 8n25
16:15–34	3n10
16:25	3n10
16:53	57n9
19:10–14	232n5
23:31–35	198n11
28:14	240n2
29:3	306n8
29:7	156n16
30:4	272n4
32:2	306n8
32:12	306n8
33:7–9	47n18
34:1–10	359n10
34:25–27	173n5
34:27	135n12
35:10	226n2
35:15	226n2
36:5	226n2
36:25	46n15
36:26	46n15
38:12	274n12
39:1–8	306n8
39:3	306n8
39:18	144
48:10	23
48:16	23
48:17	23

Daniel

4:13	240n2
4:17	240n2
4:23	240n2
7:13–14	2n6
10:13–21	240n2, 243n11
11:19	117n10
12:1	240n2, 243n11

Hosea

1:2	3n10
2:2	3n10
2:16–20	3n10
4:11—5:7	306n8
5:1	306n8
9:7–10	306n8
9:8	306n8
10:1	232n5
13:14	306n8

Joel

2:20	23
3:18	276n24

Amos

3:4	202n4
4:1	144
6:8	19n4

Jonah

2:3	129
2:9	38

Micah

3:11	82n2
4:1–3	173n5
4:1	271n2

Nahum

1:4	14n14
2:2	19n4

Habakkuk

2:16	198n11
3:8	14n14

Haggai

1:10	135n12

Zechariah

1:12	300
2:10–11	271n2
8:12	135, 173n5
9:9	2n8
9:10	173n5
9:16–17	8n25
10:3	359n10
14:5	240n2
14:16–19	271n2

Malachi

1:11	271n2
3:1–6	2n6

NEW TESTAMENT

Matthew

4:6	306n8

Romans

8:17	7n22, 293
8:22	350n6
8:29	262, 291

2 Corinthians

1:21	293n20

Galatians

3:29	293
4:7	293
4:26	273n10

Ephesians

2:13–14	273n10
2:21–22	318
3:6	293

Colossians

1:10	332n17

Titus

3:7	293

Hebrews

1:8–9	1
4:1–11	332n15
12:22–23	273n10

Revelation

Rev 1:6	7n22
Rev 5:10	7n22
Rev 7:9	271n2
Rev 14:1–5	271n2
Rev 14:20	85n12
Rev 17:1–6	273

INDEX OF SCRIPTURE AND APOCRYPHA

APOCRYPHA

1 Enoch

10:9	240n2
12:2	240n2
12:4	240n2
14:3	240n2
15:2–3	240n2
20:1–7	240n2
26:1	274n12

Jubilees

15:31–32	240n2
35:17	240n2
8:12	274n12

Sirach

17:17	240n2
18:9	300n9

www.ingramcontent.com/pod-product-compliance
Lightning Source LLC
Chambersburg PA
CBHW060453300426
44113CB00016B/2579